Shojo Beat

Short-Tempered Melancholic *and Other Stories*

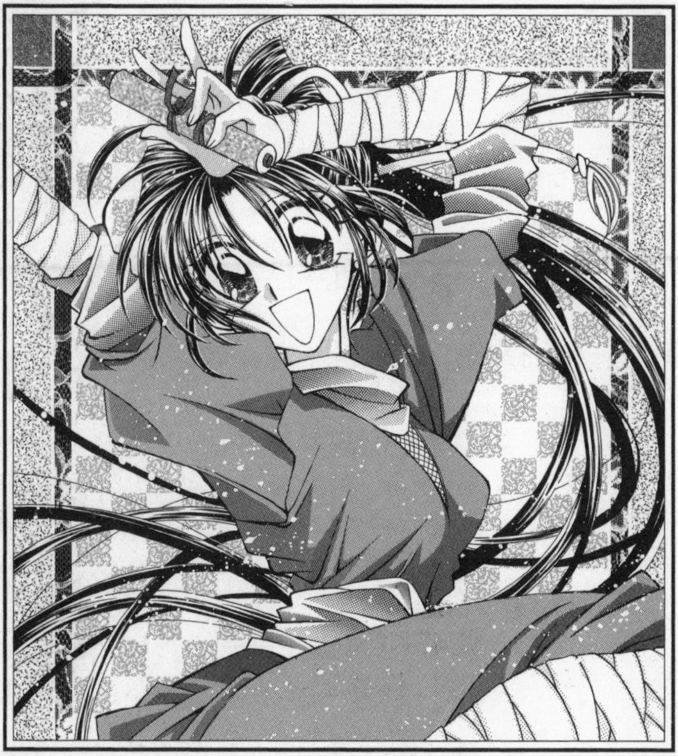

Story & Art by

Arina Tanemura

Contents

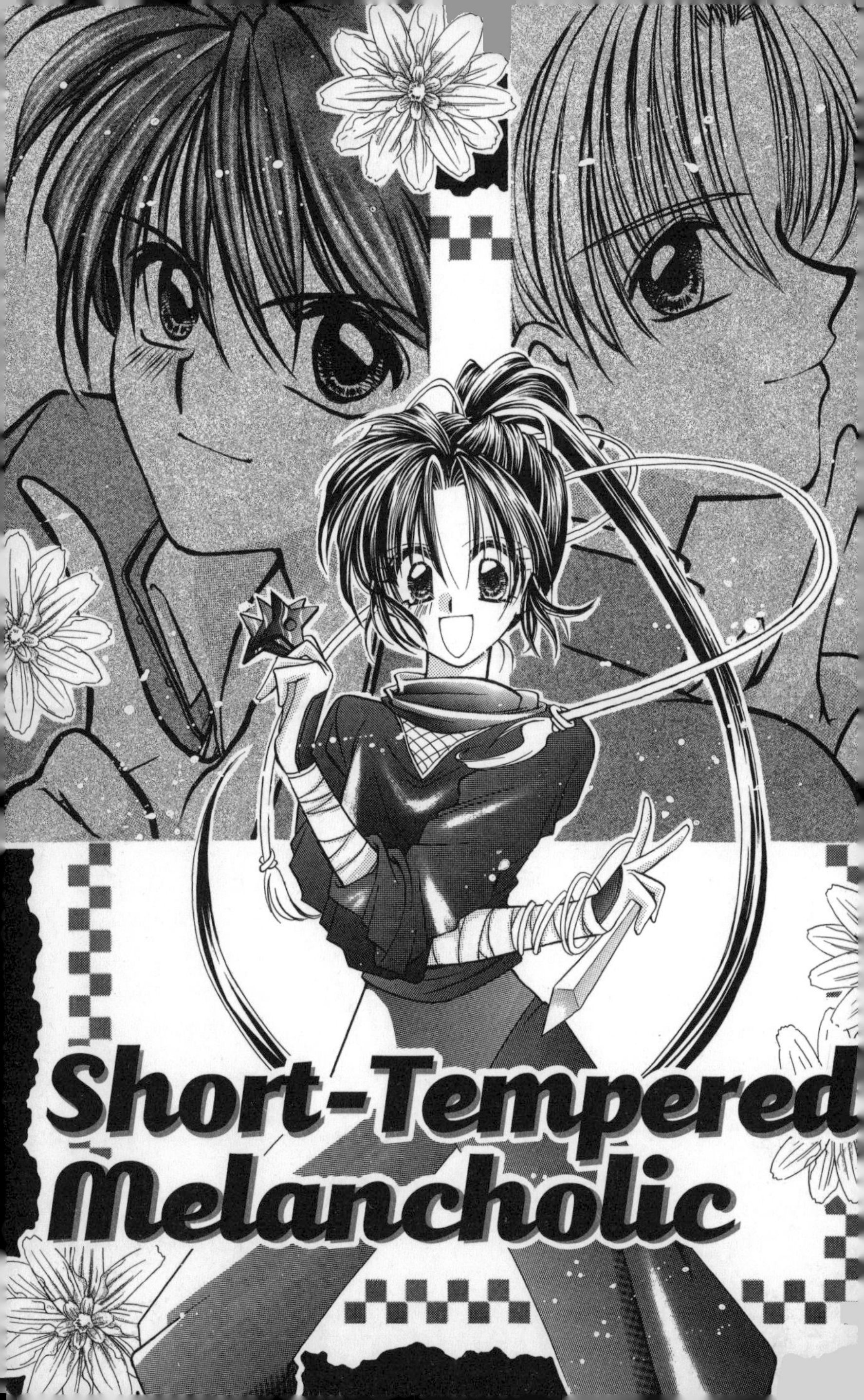
Short-Tempered Melancholic

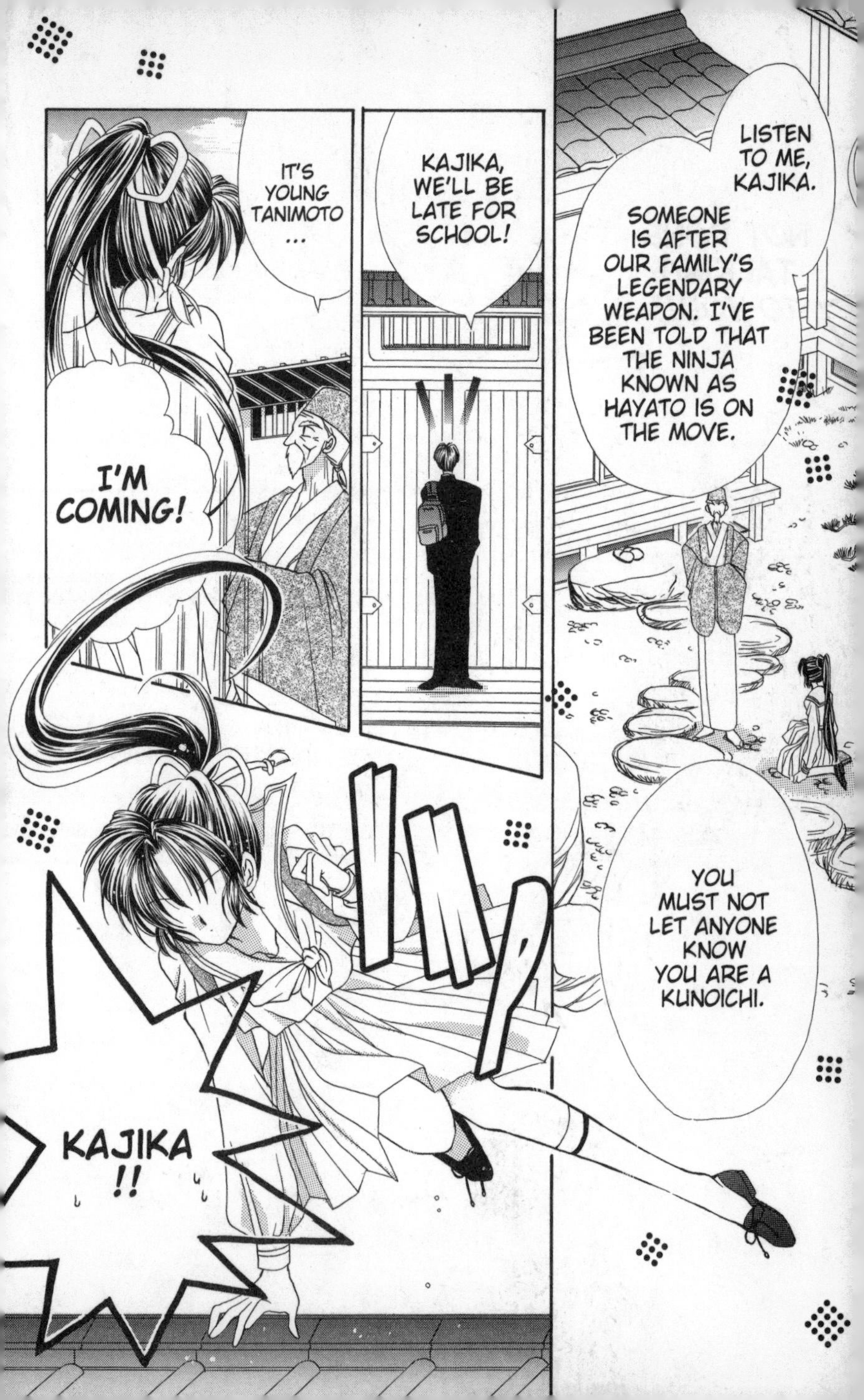
LISTEN TO ME, KAJIKA.
SOMEONE IS AFTER OUR FAMILY'S LEGENDARY WEAPON. I'VE BEEN TOLD THAT THE NINJA KNOWN AS HAYATO IS ON THE MOVE.
YOU MUST NOT LET ANYONE KNOW YOU ARE A KUNOICHI.
KAJIKA, WE'LL BE LATE FOR SCHOOL!
IT'S YOUNG TANIMOTO ...
I'M COMING!
KAJIKA !!

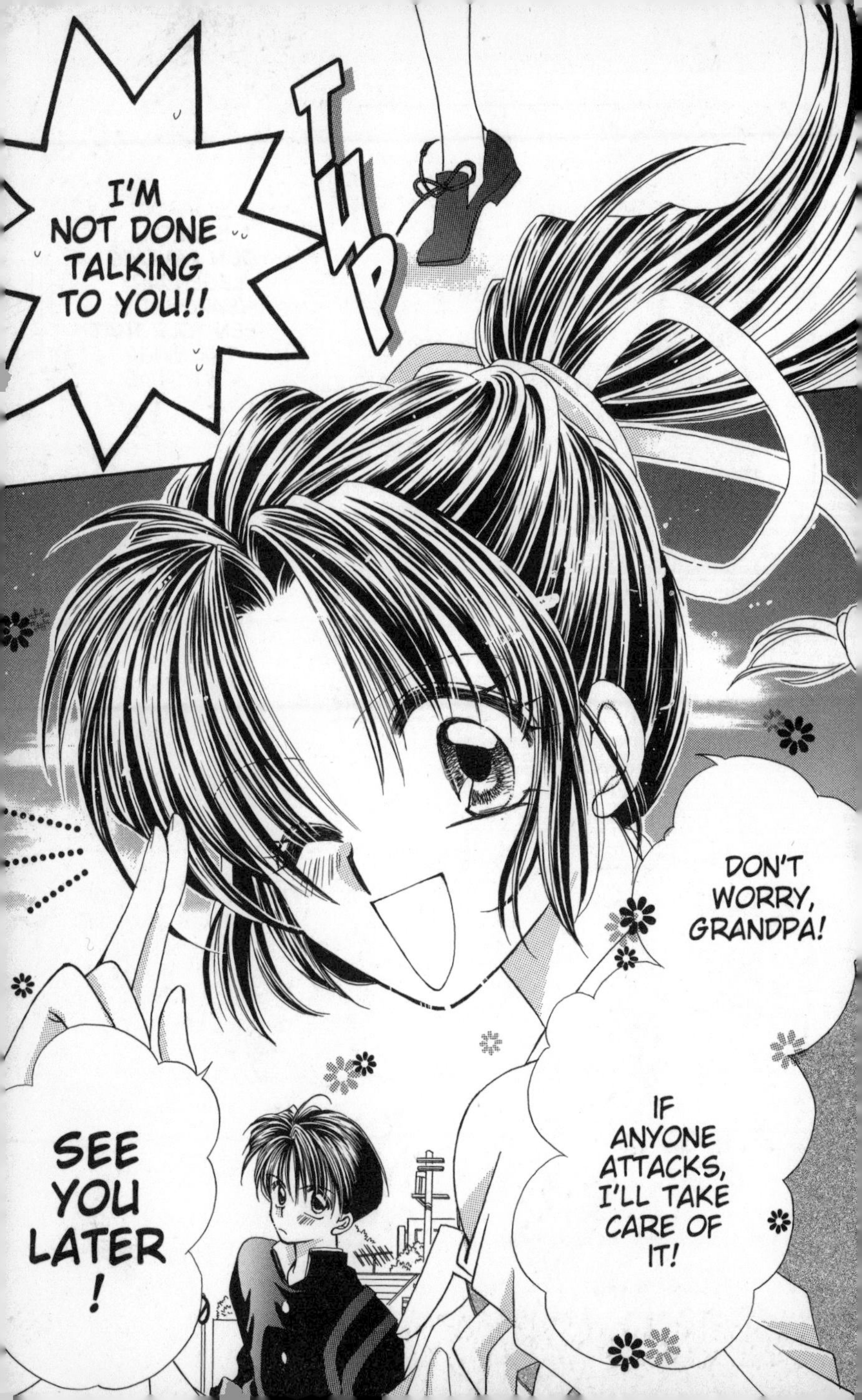
THUP
I'M NOT DONE TALKING TO YOU!!
DON'T WORRY, GRANDPA!
IF ANYONE ATTACKS, I'LL TAKE CARE OF IT!
SEE YOU LATER!

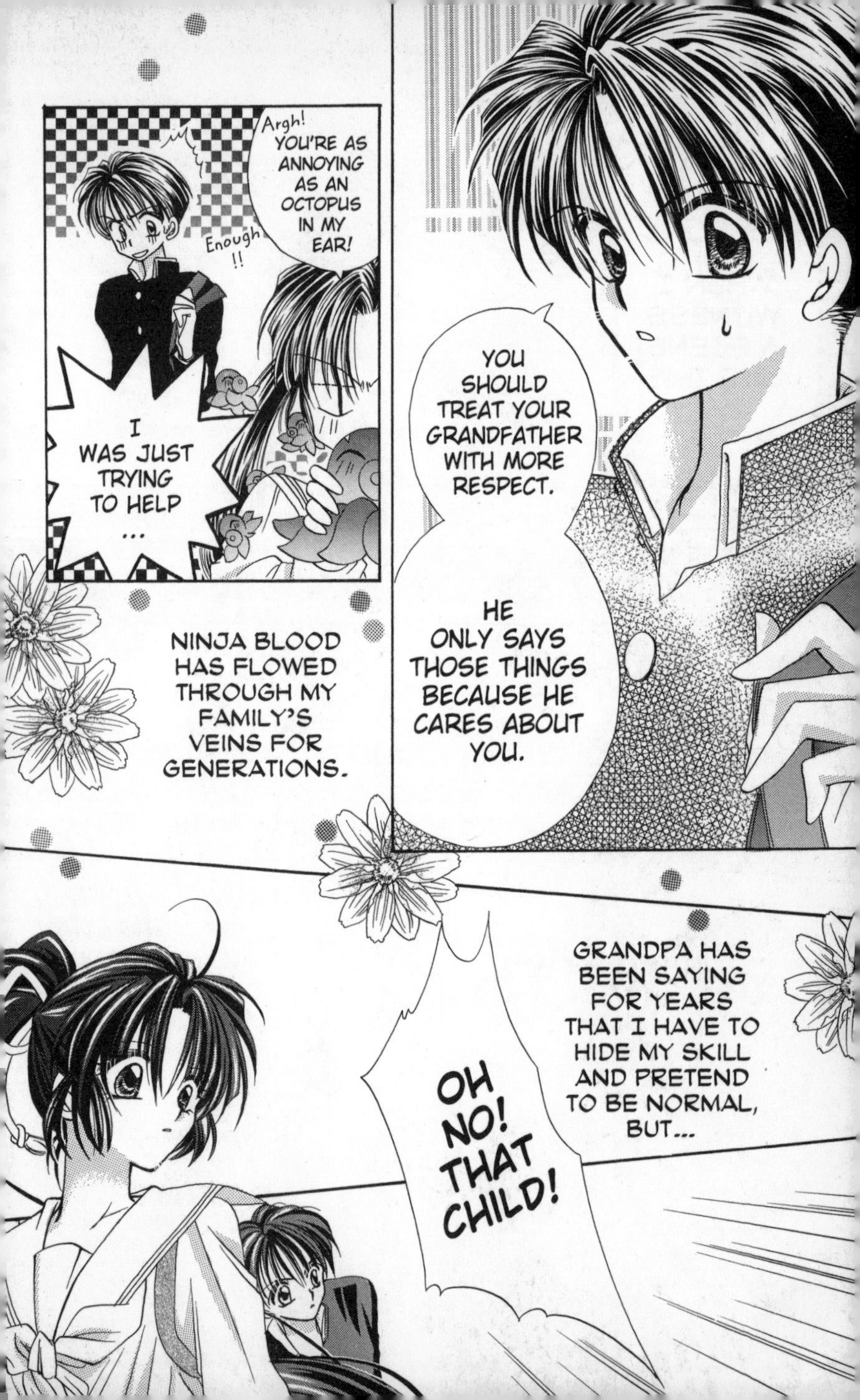
YOU SHOULD TREAT YOUR GRANDFATHER WITH MORE RESPECT.
HE ONLY SAYS THOSE THINGS BECAUSE HE CARES ABOUT YOU.
Argh! YOU'RE AS ANNOYING AS AN OCTOPUS IN MY EAR!
Enough!!
I WAS JUST TRYING TO HELP...
NINJA BLOOD HAS FLOWED THROUGH MY FAMILY'S VEINS FOR GENERATIONS.
GRANDPA HAS BEEN SAYING FOR YEARS THAT I HAVE TO HIDE MY SKILL AND PRETEND TO BE NORMAL, BUT...
OH NO! THAT CHILD!

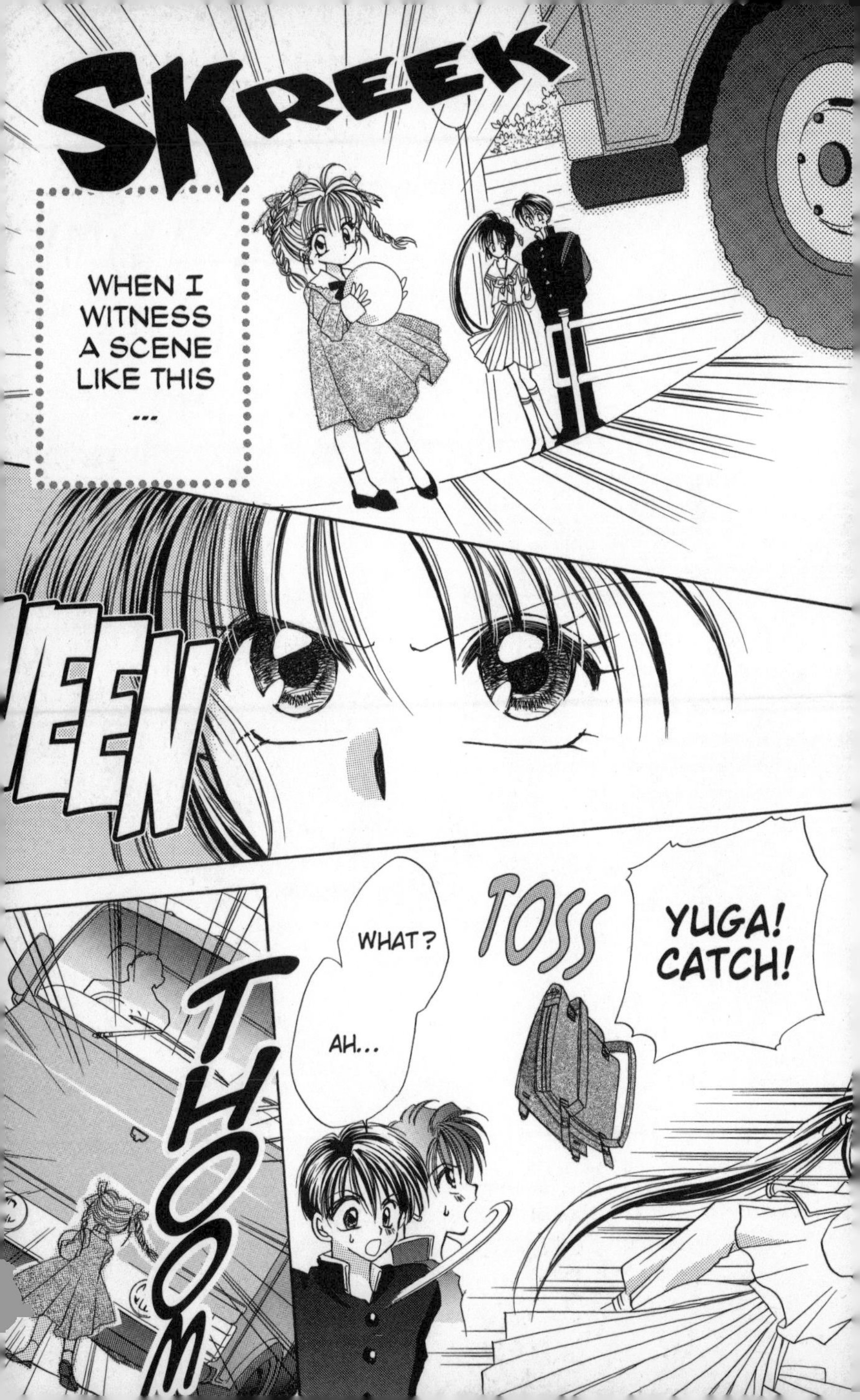
SKREEK
WHEN I WITNESS A SCENE LIKE THIS ...
EEN
YUGA! CATCH!
TOSS
WHAT?
AH...
THOOM

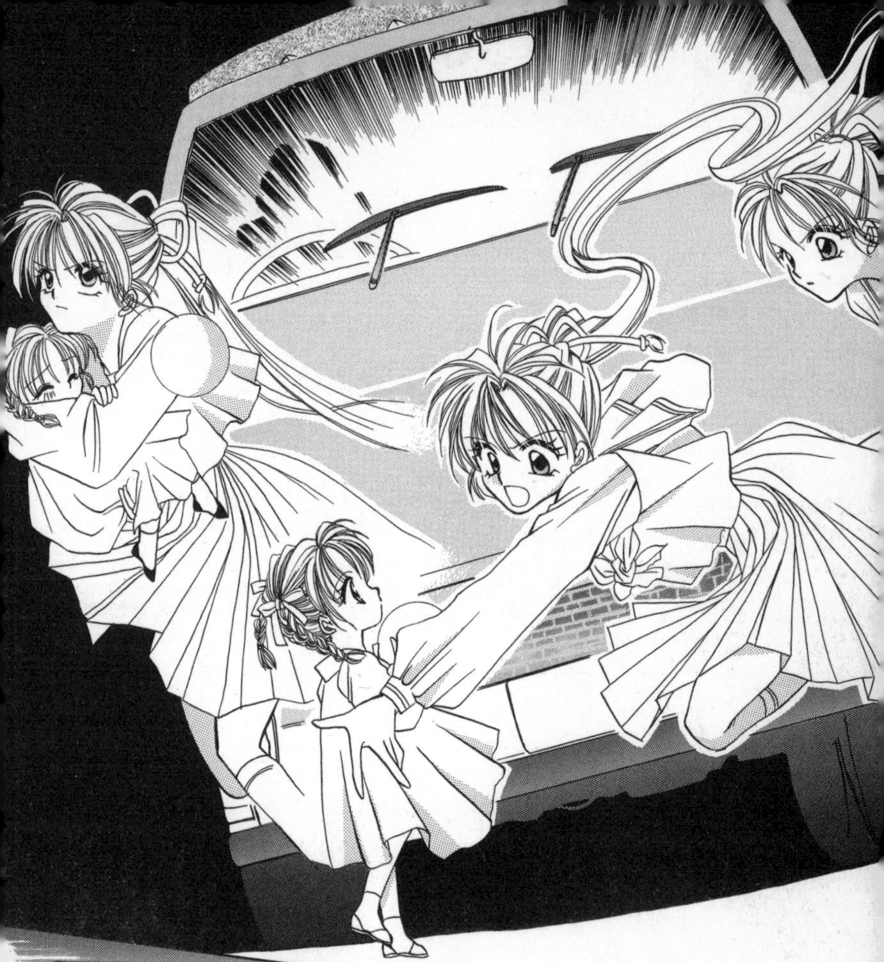

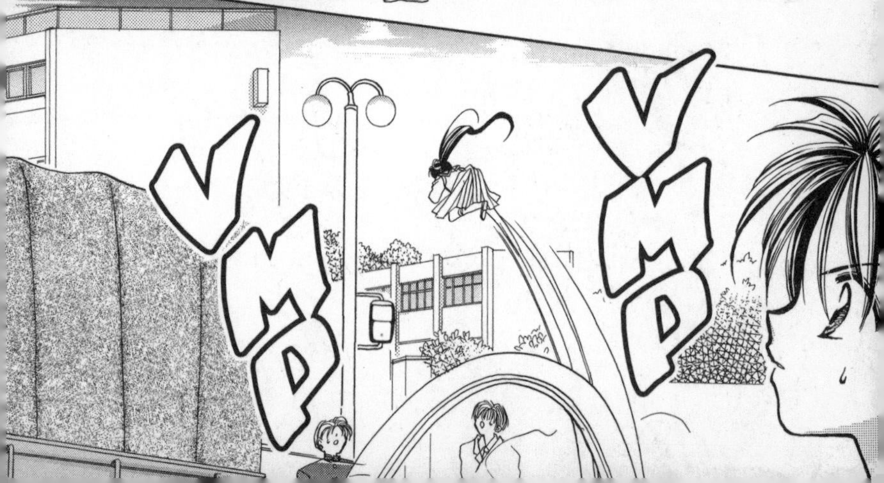
VMP
VMP

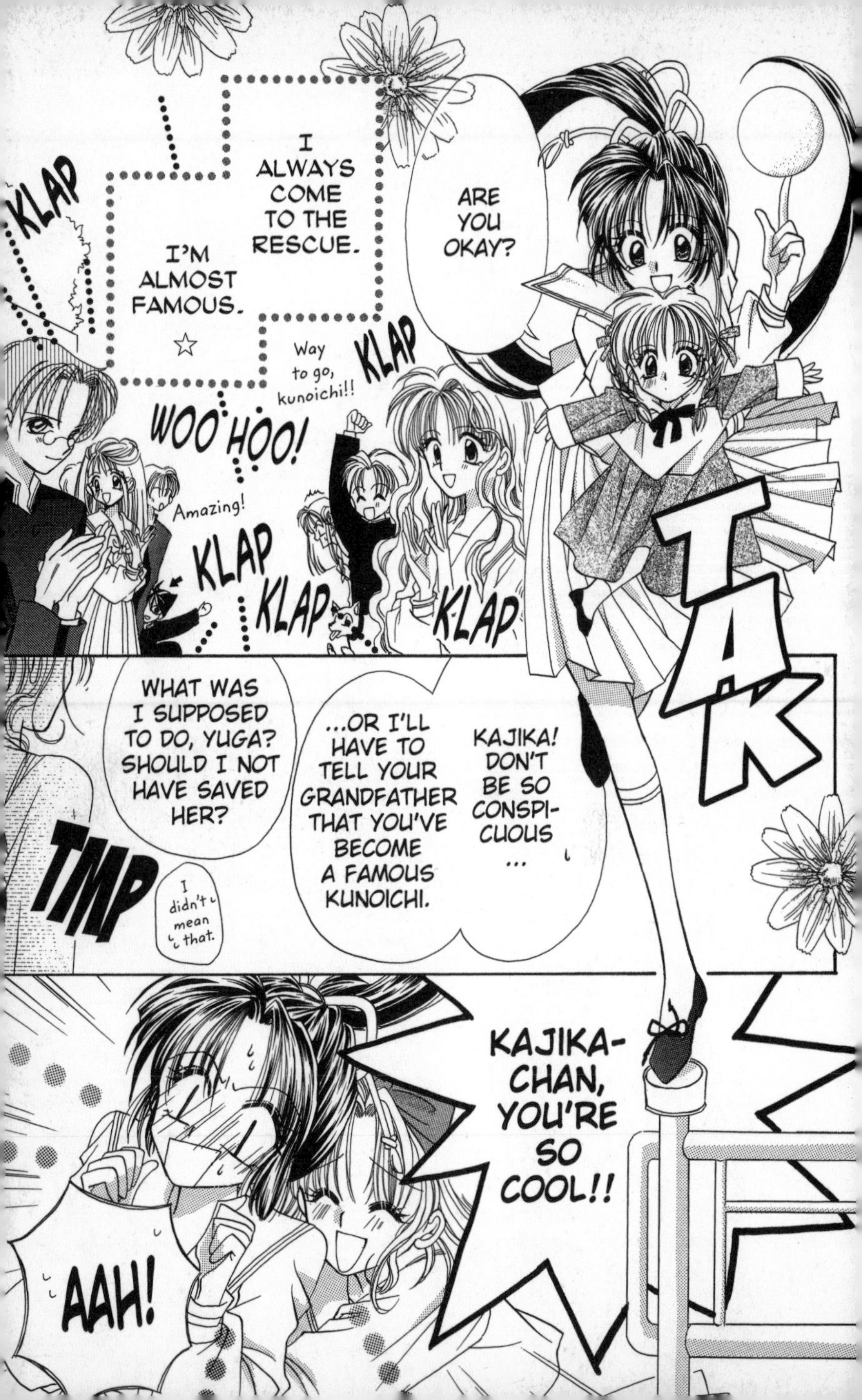
ARE YOU OKAY?
I ALWAYS COME TO THE RESCUE.
I'M ALMOST FAMOUS. ☆
TAK
KLAP
KLAP
Way to go, kunoichi!!
WOO HOO!
Amazing!
KLAP
KLAP
K-LAP
KAJIKA! DON'T BE SO CONSPICUOUS...
...OR I'LL HAVE TO TELL YOUR GRANDFATHER THAT YOU'VE BECOME A FAMOUS KUNOICHI.
WHAT WAS I SUPPOSED TO DO, YUGA? SHOULD I NOT HAVE SAVED HER?
I didn't mean that.
TMP
KAJIKA-CHAN, YOU'RE SO COOL!!
AAH!

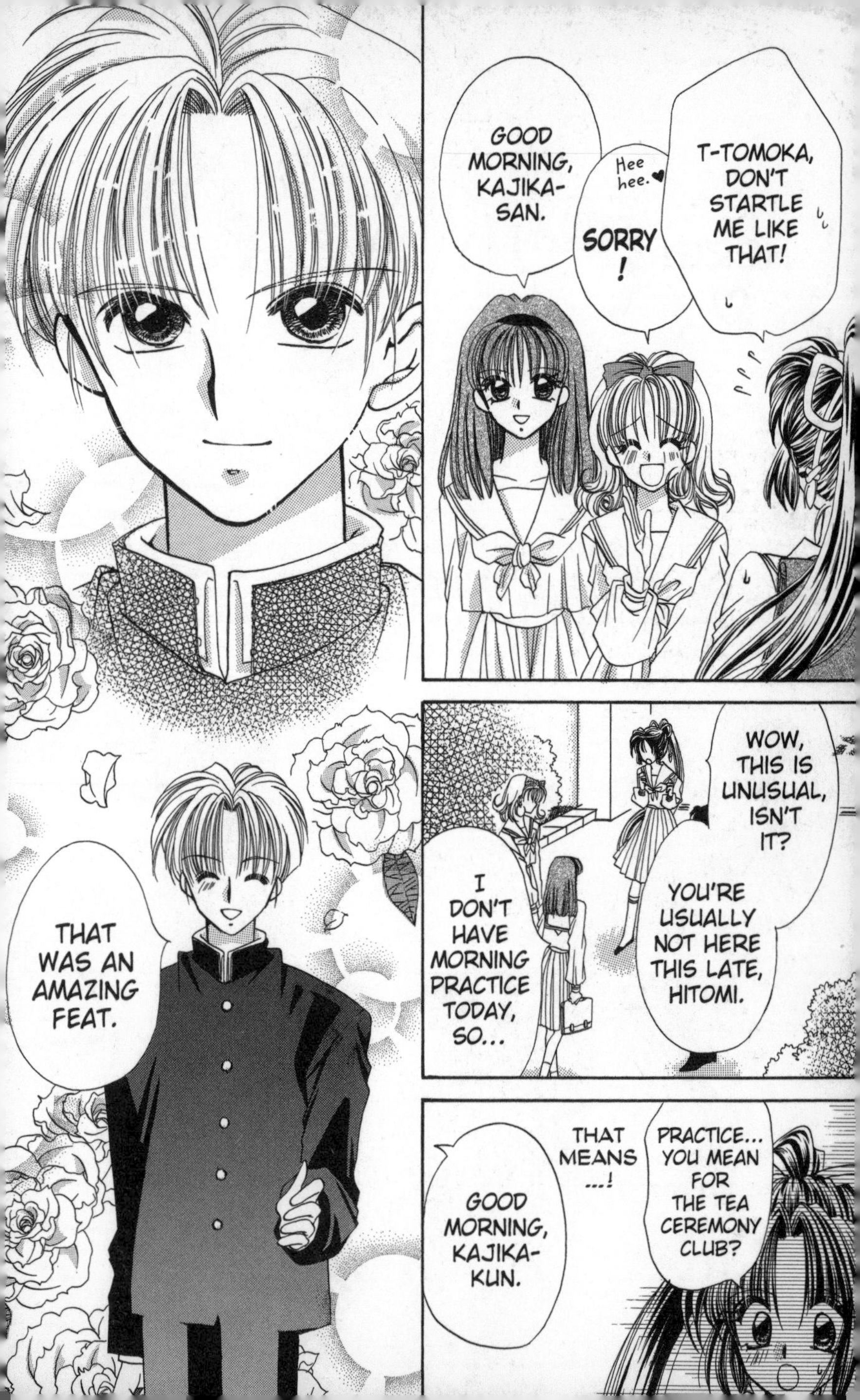

T-TOMOKA, DON'T STARTLE ME LIKE THAT!
Hee hee.♥
SORRY!
GOOD MORNING, KAJIKA-SAN.
WOW, THIS IS UNUSUAL, ISN'T IT?
YOU'RE USUALLY NOT HERE THIS LATE, HITOMI.
I DON'T HAVE MORNING PRACTICE TODAY, SO...
PRACTICE... YOU MEAN FOR THE TEA CEREMONY CLUB?
THAT MEANS ...!
GOOD MORNING, KAJIKA-KUN.
THAT WAS AN AMAZING FEAT.

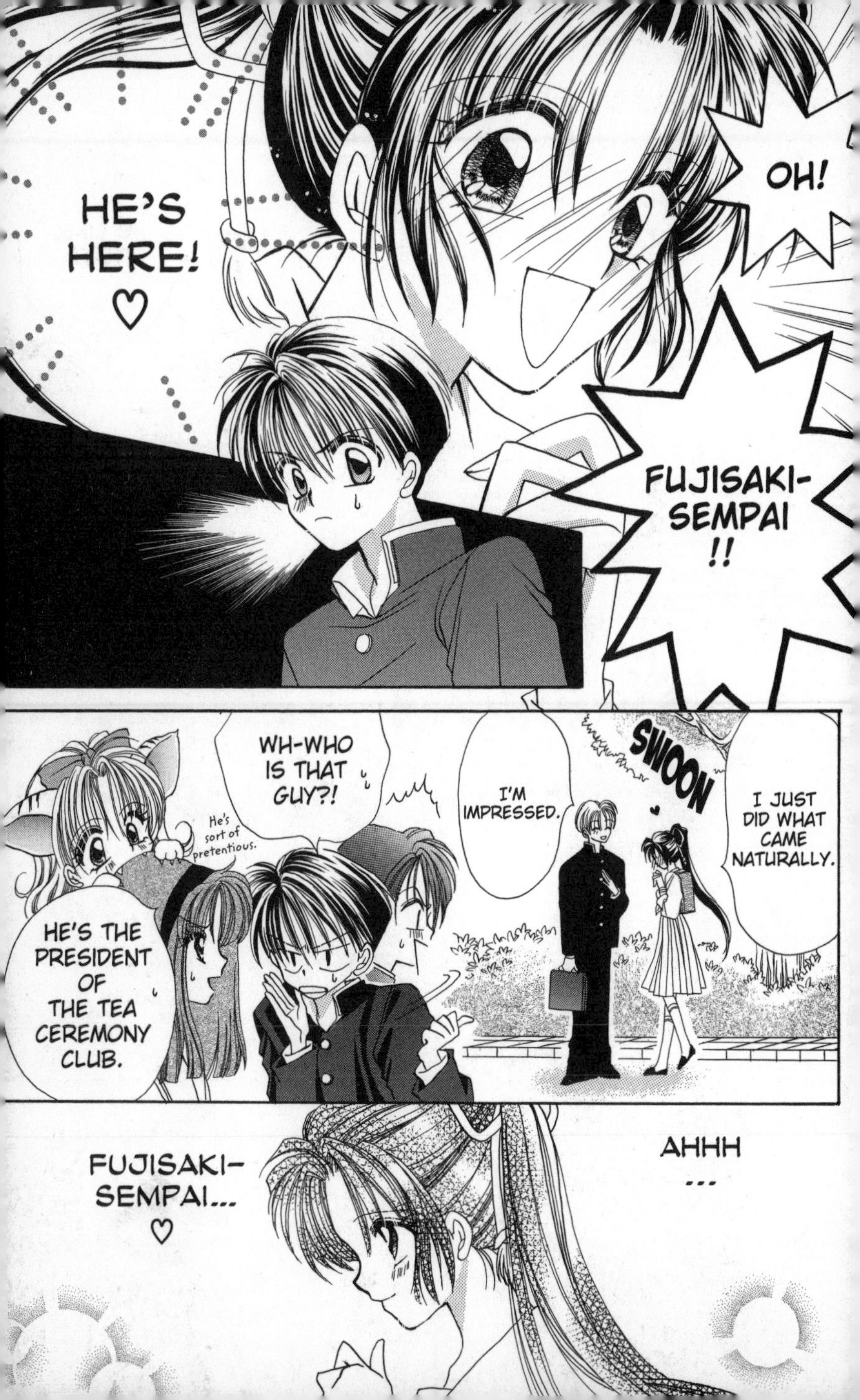
OH!
HE'S HERE! ♡
FUJISAKI-SEMPAI!!
I JUST DID WHAT CAME NATURALLY.
SWOON
I'M IMPRESSED.
WH-WHO IS THAT GUY?!
He's sort of pretentious.
HE'S THE PRESIDENT OF THE TEA CEREMONY CLUB.
AHHH...
FUJISAKI-SEMPAI... ♡

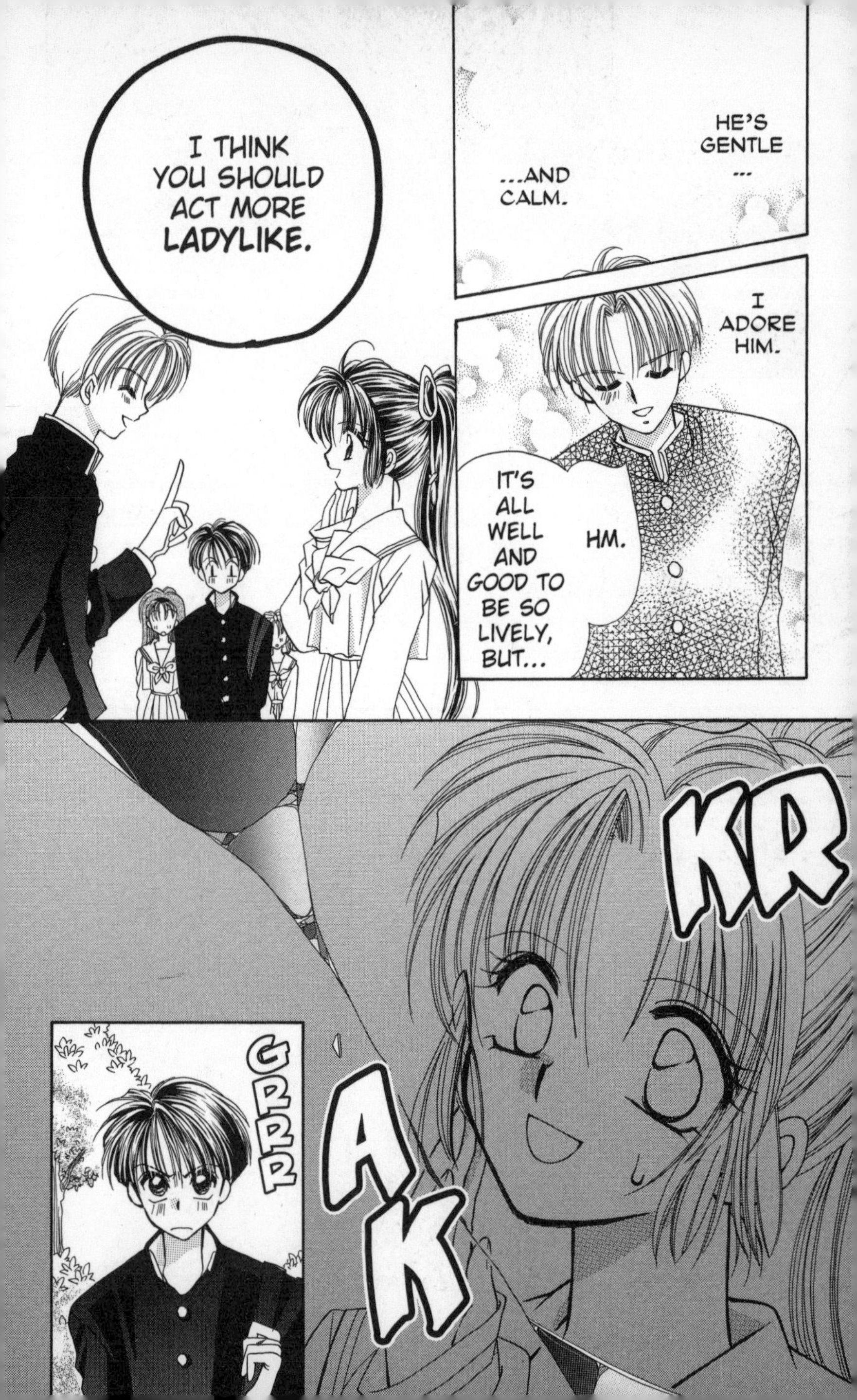
HE'S GENTLE ...
...AND CALM.
I ADORE HIM.
HM.
IT'S ALL WELL AND GOOD TO BE SO LIVELY, BUT...
I THINK YOU SHOULD ACT MORE LADYLIKE.
KRAK
GRRR

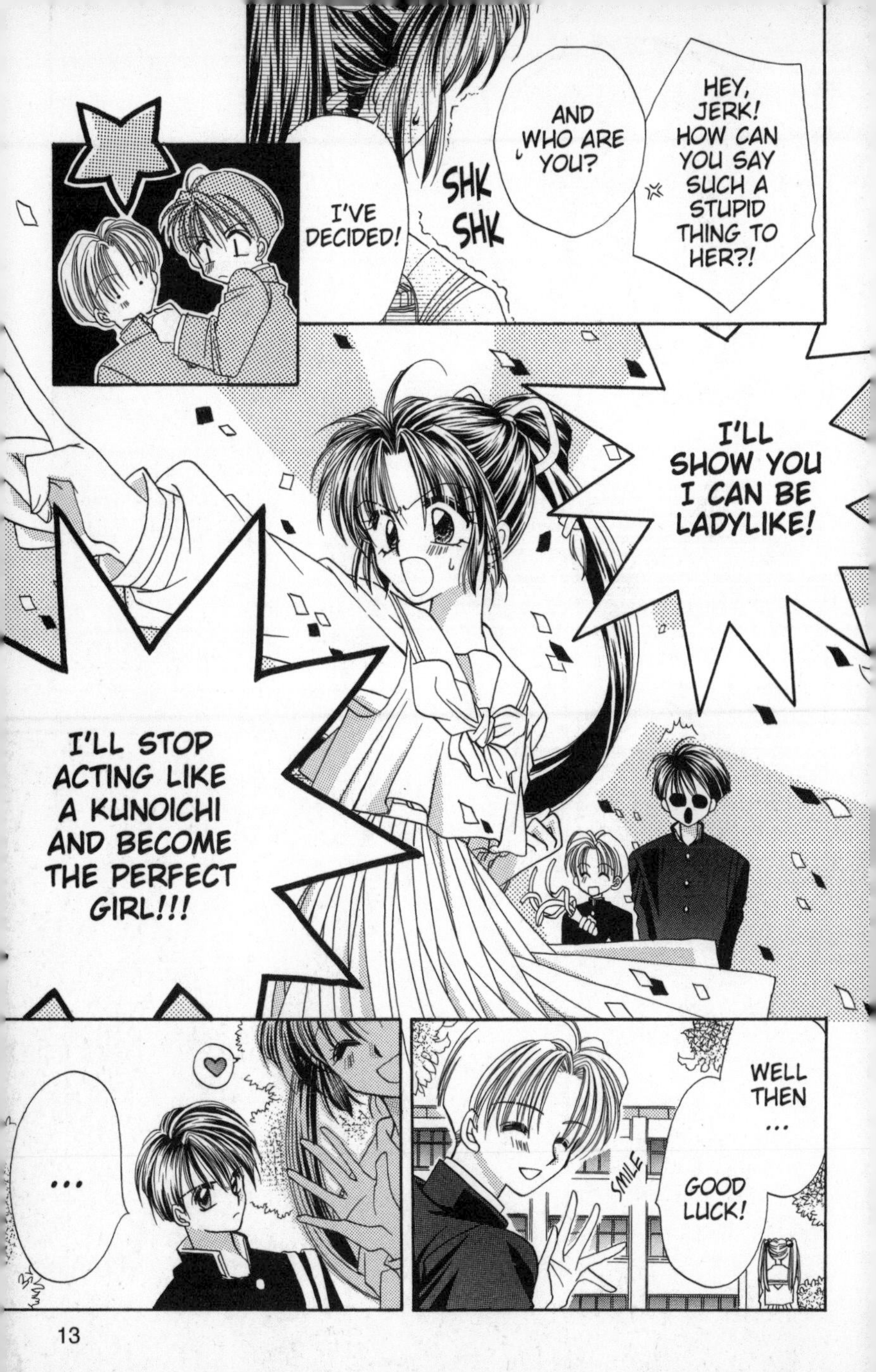
HEY, JERK! HOW CAN YOU SAY SUCH A STUPID THING TO HER?!
AND WHO ARE YOU?
SHK SHK
I'VE DECIDED!
I'LL SHOW YOU I CAN BE LADYLIKE!
I'LL STOP ACTING LIKE A KUNOICHI AND BECOME THE PERFECT GIRL!!!
WELL THEN ...
GOOD LUCK!
SMILE
...

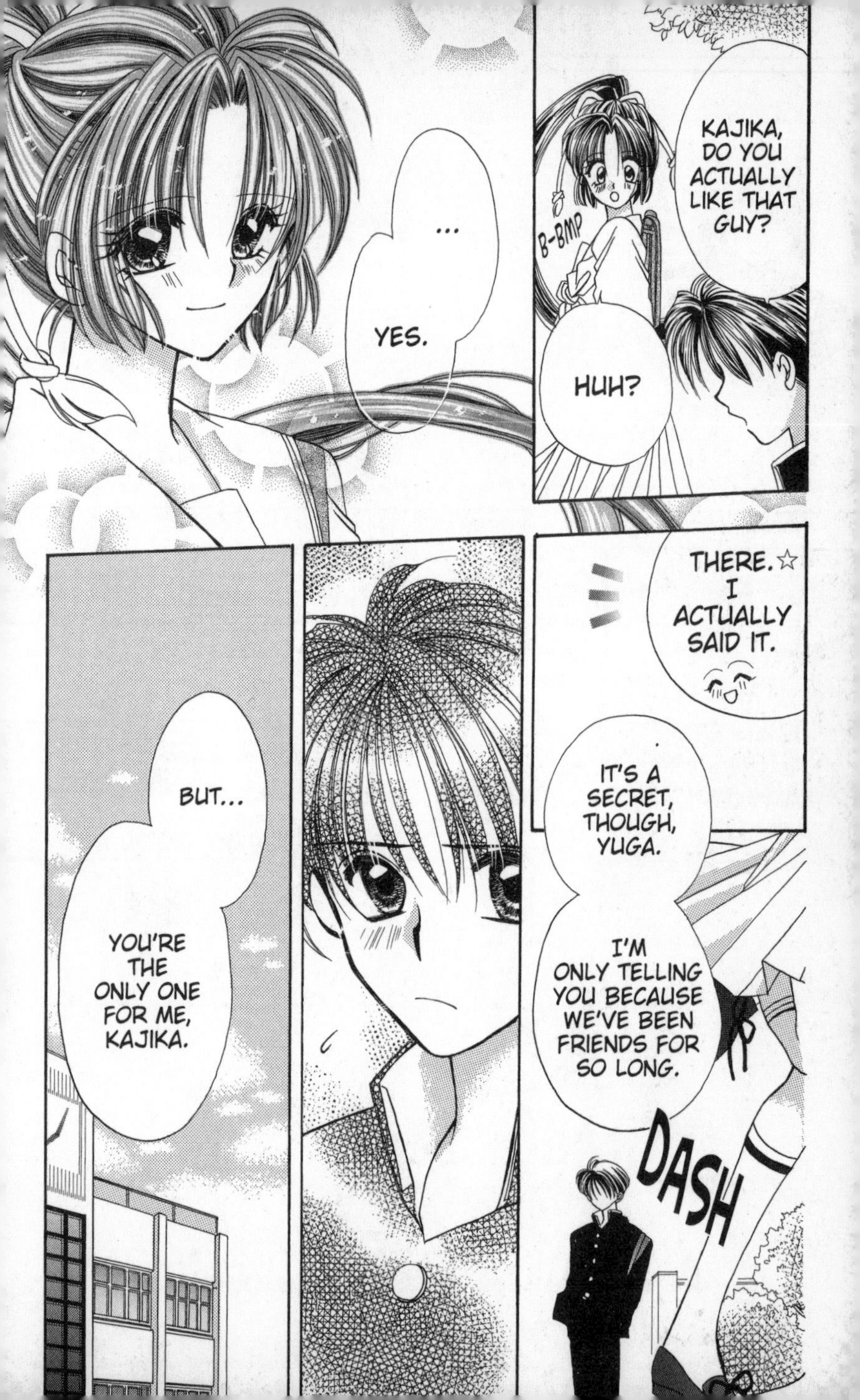
KAJIKA, DO YOU ACTUALLY LIKE THAT GUY?
B-BMP
HUH?
...
YES.
THERE. ☆ I ACTUALLY SAID IT.
IT'S A SECRET, THOUGH, YUGA.
I'M ONLY TELLING YOU BECAUSE WE'VE BEEN FRIENDS FOR SO LONG.
DASH
BUT...
YOU'RE THE ONLY ONE FOR ME, KAJIKA.

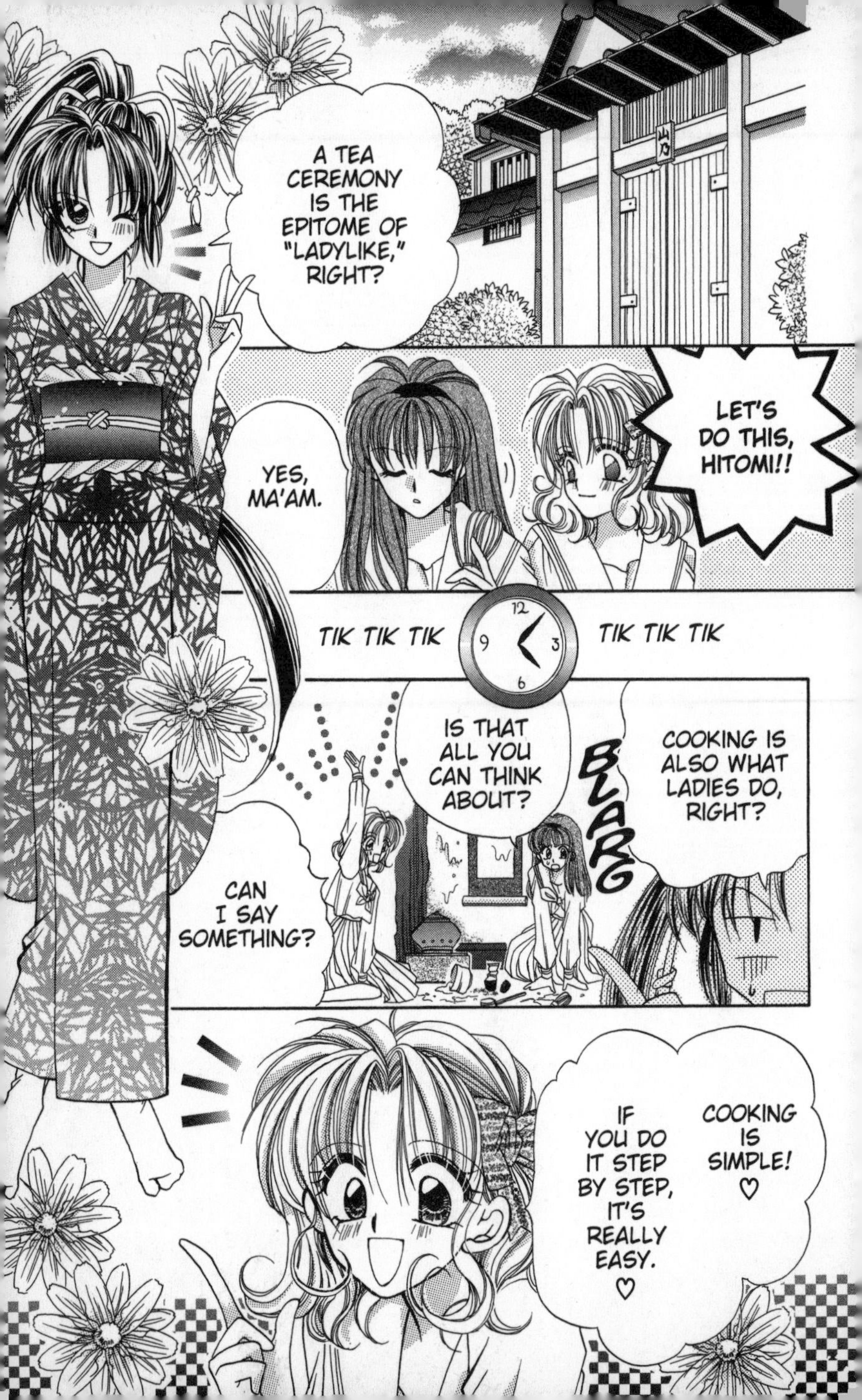
A TEA CEREMONY IS THE EPITOME OF "LADYLIKE," RIGHT?
LET'S DO THIS, HITOMI!!
YES, MA'AM.
TIK TIK TIK
TIK TIK TIK
COOKING IS ALSO WHAT LADIES DO, RIGHT?
BLARG
IS THAT ALL YOU CAN THINK ABOUT?
CAN I SAY SOMETHING?
COOKING IS SIMPLE! ♡
IF YOU DO IT STEP BY STEP, IT'S REALLY EASY. ♡

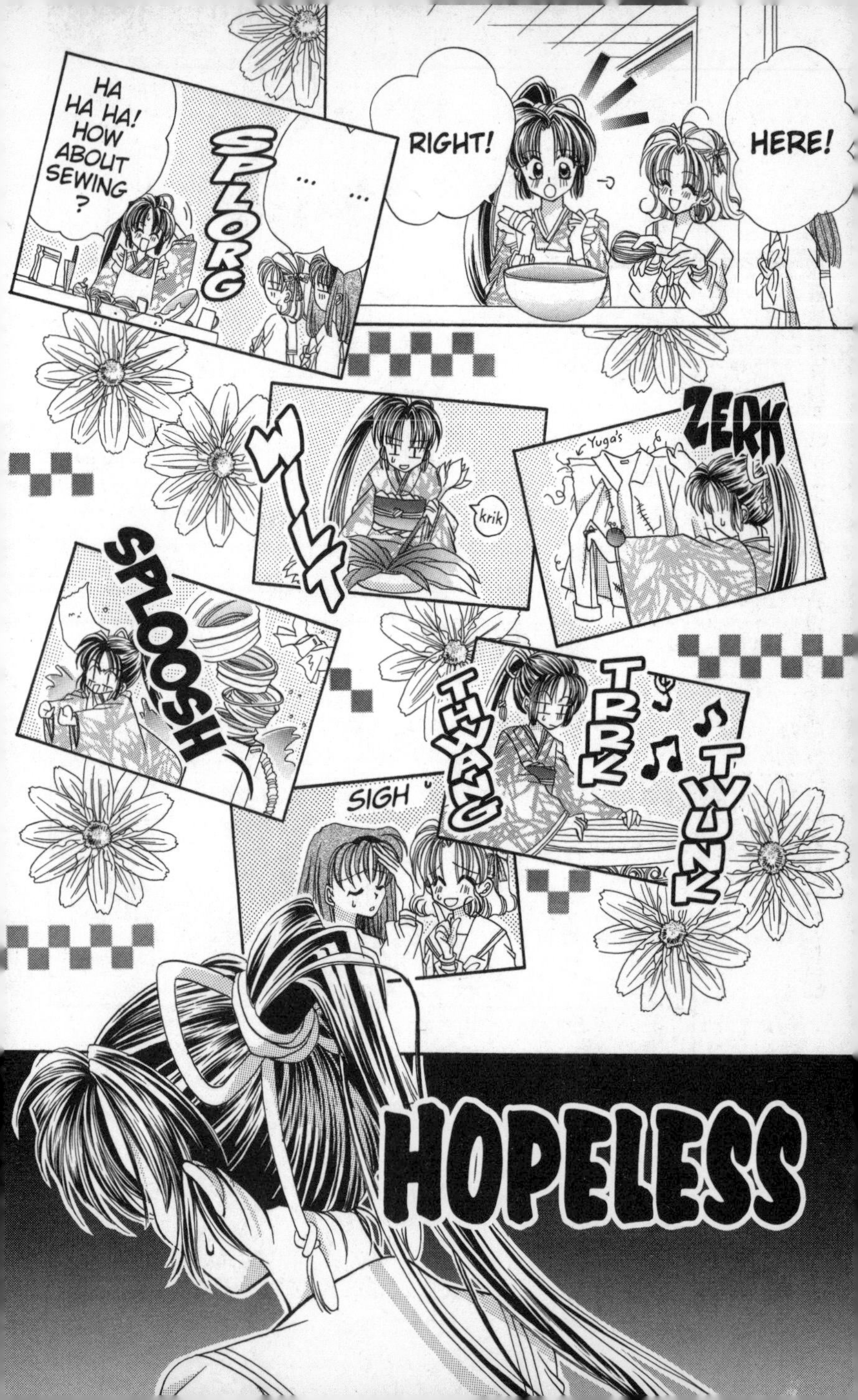
HERE!
RIGHT!
... ...
SPLORG
HA HA HA! HOW ABOUT SEWING?
ZERK
Yuga's
WILT
krik
TRK
TWUNK
THWANG
SPLOOSH
SIGH
HOPELESS

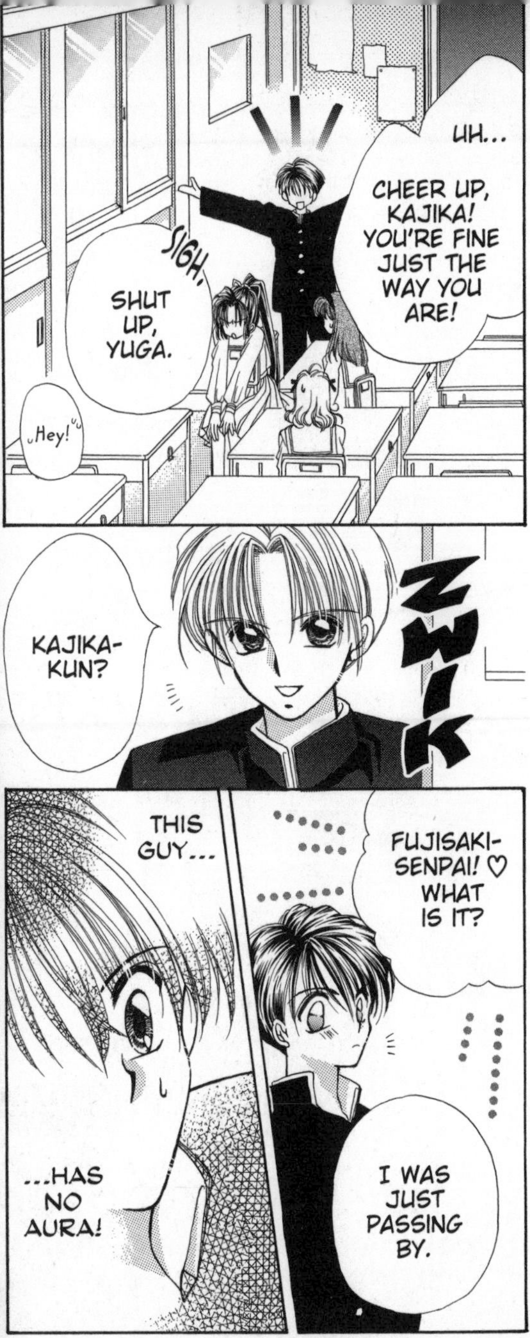
UH...
CHEER UP, KAJIKA! YOU'RE FINE JUST THE WAY YOU ARE!
SIGH
SHUT UP, YUGA.
Hey!
ZWIK
KAJIKA-KUN?
FUJISAKI-SENPAI! ♡ WHAT IS IT?
......
......
......
I WAS JUST PASSING BY.
THIS GUY...
...HAS NO AURA!

SPECIAL GUEST

IT'S MAICCHI ASATSUKI!

WE'VE BEEN HANGING OUT TOGETHER FOR TWO YEARS, MORE OR LESS. WE'RE SO CLOSE WE'VE ADOPTED EACH OTHER AS SISTERS, YAY!! THANKS FOR BEING MY GUEST! LET'S HAVE A LOT MORE LAUGHS TOGETHER IN THE FUTURE!!

ARINA-HAN, THANKS FOR BEING HAPPY THAT I'M YOUR GUEST! I'M VERY HAPPY! KAJIKA-CHAN·KARIN-CHAN·MINORI-CHAN·MANA-CHAN—THEY'RE ALL SO CUTE! I'M SORRY THAT ALL WE SEEM TO DO IN AICHI IS LAUGH UNTIL LATE AT NIGHT! PLEASE KEEP FIGHTING THE GOOD FIGHT AS "GAG MACHINE ARINA"!!

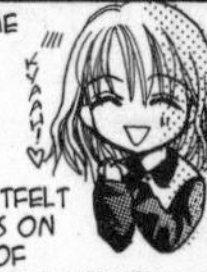
KYAAH!

HELLO. ♡ MY NAME IS MAI ASATSUKI, AND I JUST MADE MY DEBUT IN FEBRUARY OF THIS YEAR. ARINA NE-YAN, MY HEARTFELT CONGRATULATIONS ON THE PUBLICATION OF *SHORT-TEMPERED MELANCHOLIC.*

Is it really okay for me to be in this auspicious place?

YOUR DEBUT STORY, "SECOND LOVE" IS REPRINTED IN THIS BOOK, RIGHT? ♡ I REALLY LOVED YOUR DEBUT, AND I EVEN WROTE A FAN LETTER.

WHEN I FIRST STARTED SENDING SUBMISSIONS, I WAS STUDYING IN MANGA SCHOOL, AND I EVEN GOT PUBLISHED. ↖ WON THE AWARD FOR EFFORT TWO TIMES! AT THE TIME, NE-YAN WAS 16. I WAS 13. IT'S BEEN THREE YEARS SINCE THEN.

CURRENTLY I'M HELPING OUT AS A BACKGROUND ASSISTANT ON *KAMIKAZE KAITO JEANNE.* I'M LEARNING A LOT! I TRAVEL FROM KANAGAWA PREFECTURE TO AICHI.

NE-YAN IS EXACTLY AS SHE SEEMS IN THE MANGA. SHE'S AN EXCELLENT, FUN, AND A HARD WORKER. I OWE SO MUCH TO HER!! AND WHEN I WATCH NE-YAN'S BACK AS SHE IS WORKING...

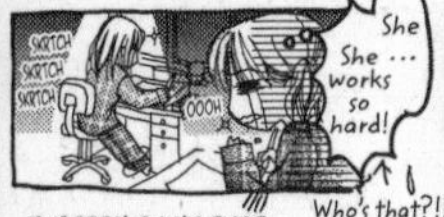
SKRTCH
SKRTCH
SKRTCH
OOOH
She
She... works so hard!

I OFTEN THINK THAT. *Who's that?!! Don't cry...*

ANYWAY, IT'S A REAL HONOR TO APPEAR IN A COMIC THAT CONTAINS SOME OF MY FAVORITE STORIES! NE-YAN, THANK YOU SO MUCH FOR THESE WONDERFUL STORIES.

MAI ASATSUKI

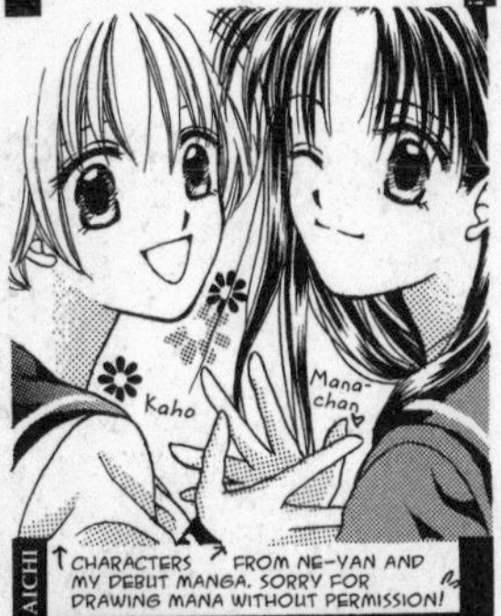
Kaho
Mana-chan

↑ CHARACTERS FROM NE-YAN AND MY DEBUT MANGA. SORRY FOR DRAWING MANA WITHOUT PERMISSION!

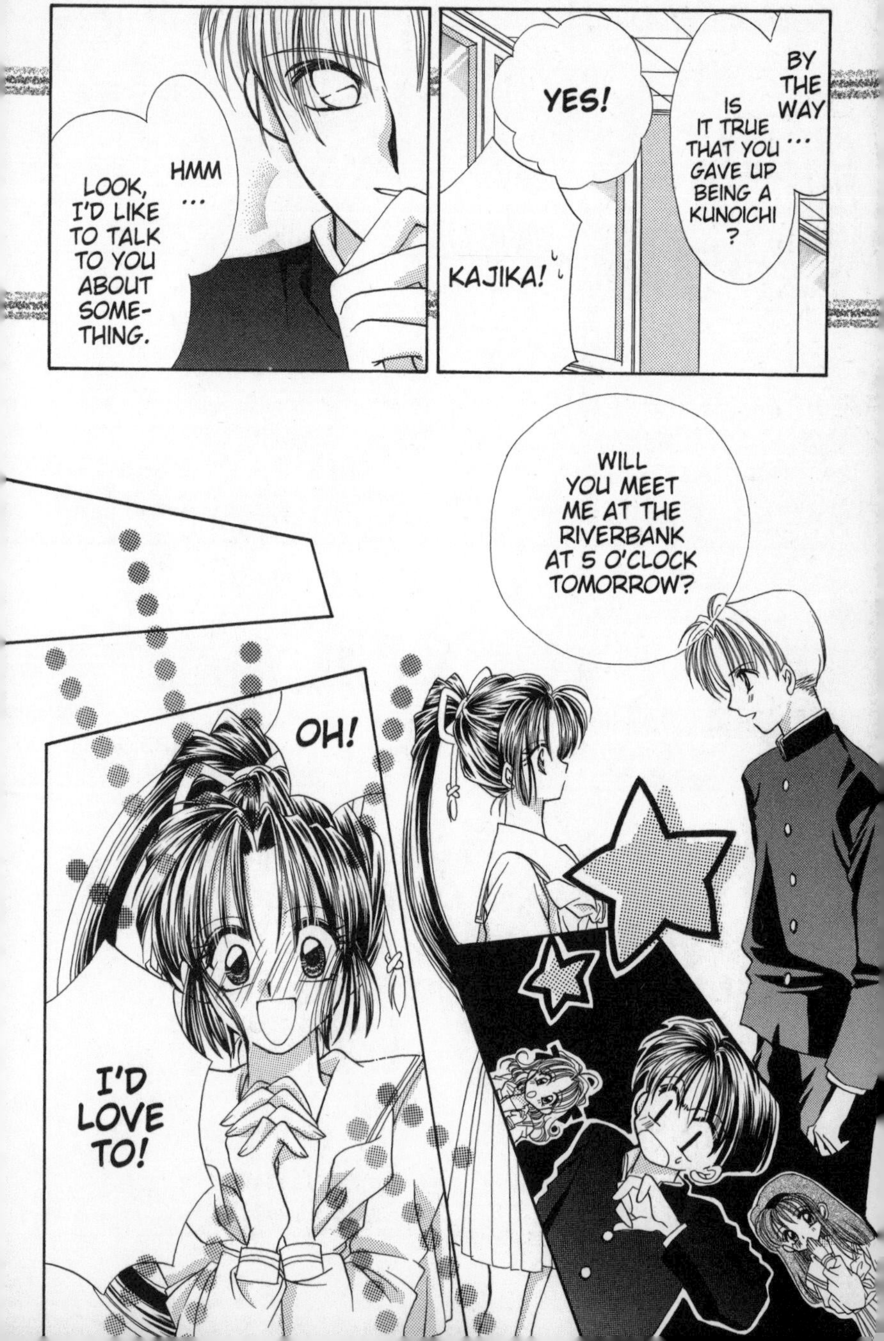
BY THE WAY...
IS IT TRUE THAT YOU GAVE UP BEING A KUNOICHI?
YES!
KAJIKA!
HMM...
LOOK, I'D LIKE TO TALK TO YOU ABOUT SOMETHING.
WILL YOU MEET ME AT THE RIVERBANK AT 5 O'CLOCK TOMORROW?
OH!
I'D LOVE TO!

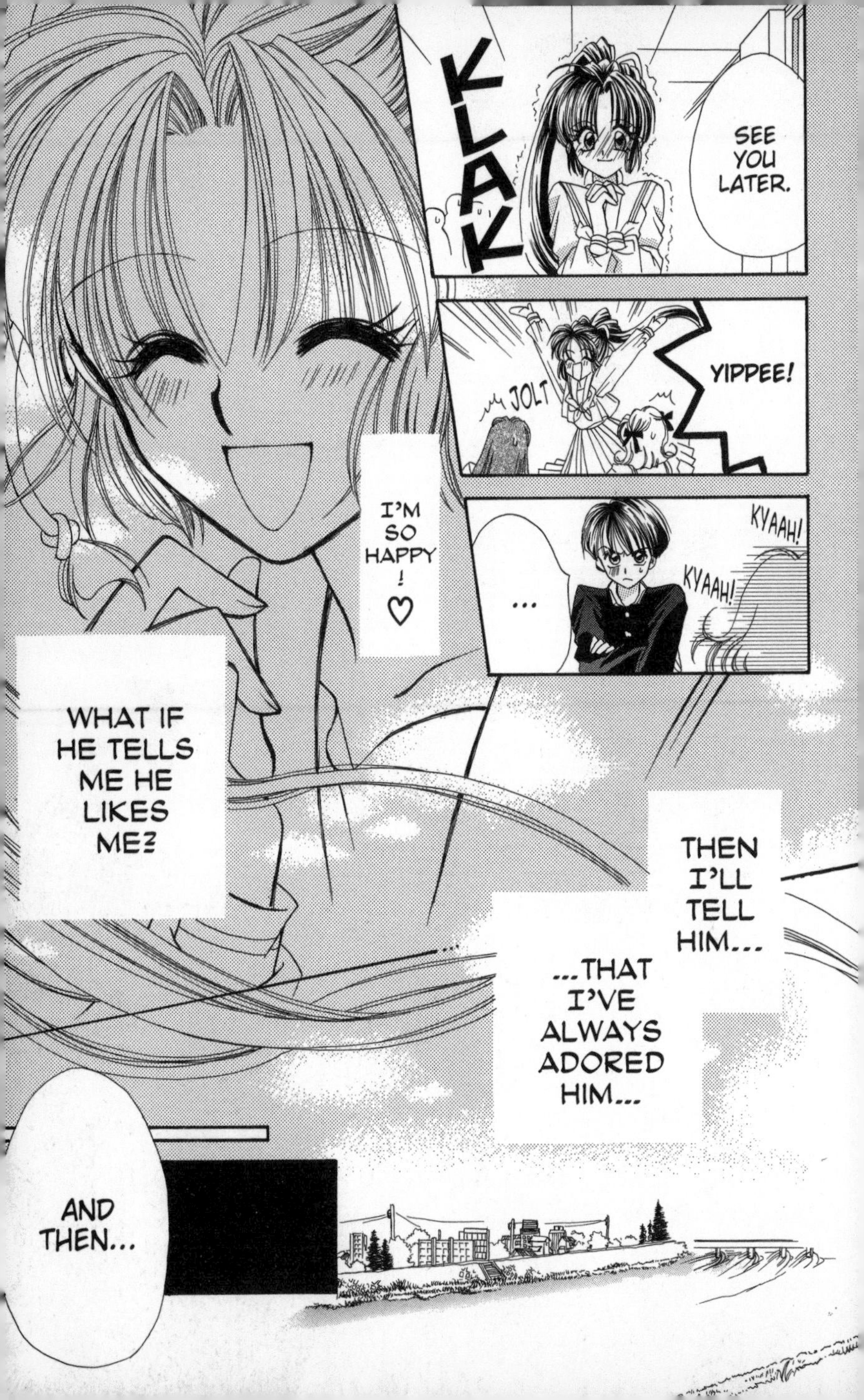
SEE YOU LATER.
KLAK
YIPPEE!
JOLT
KYAAH!
KYAAH!
...
I'M SO HAPPY! ♡
WHAT IF HE TELLS ME HE LIKES ME?
THEN I'LL TELL HIM...
...THAT I'VE ALWAYS ADORED HIM...
AND THEN...

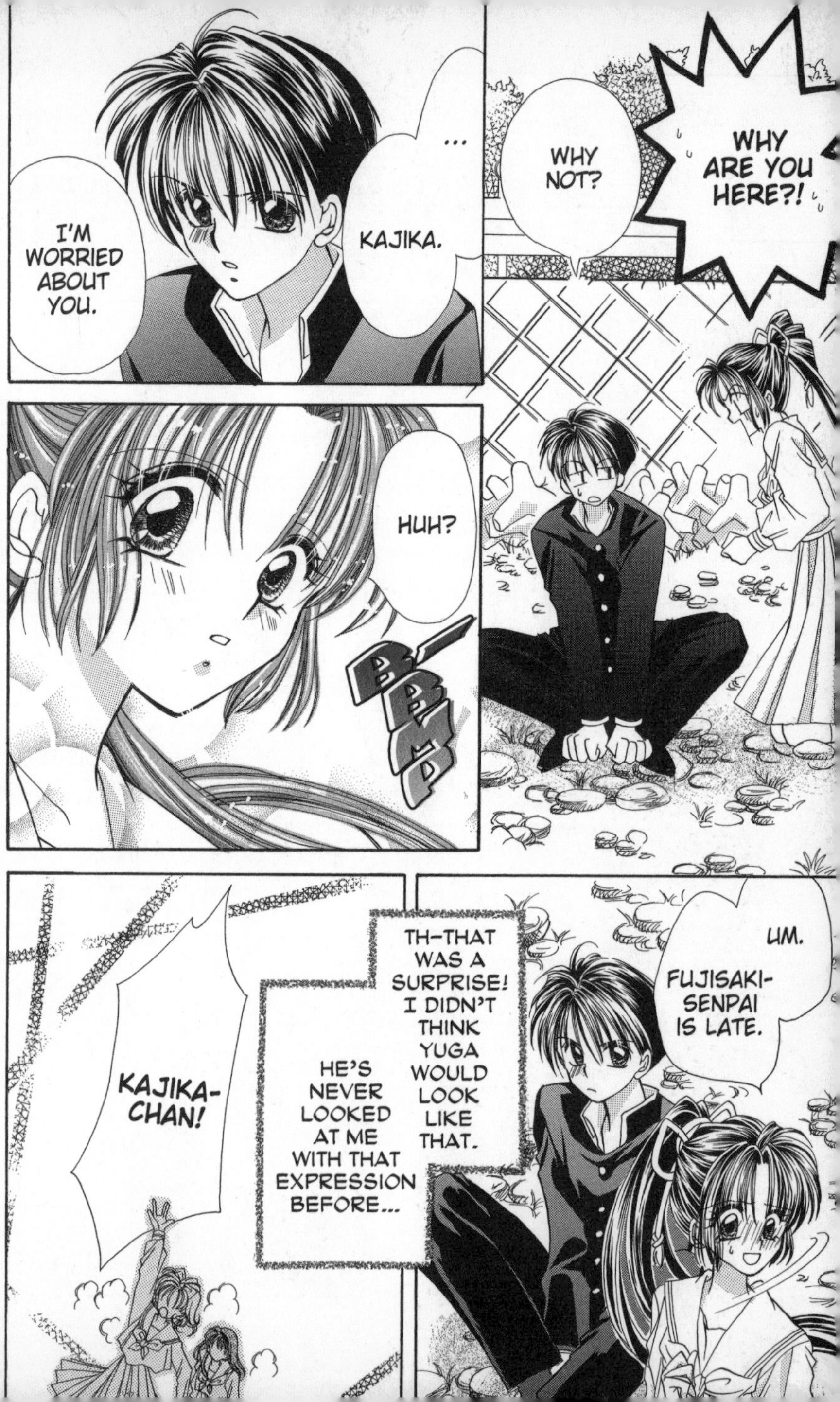
WHY ARE YOU HERE?!
WHY NOT?
...
KAJIKA.
I'M WORRIED ABOUT YOU.
HUH?
BBMP
UM.
FUJISAKI-SENPAI IS LATE.
TH-THAT WAS A SURPRISE! I DIDN'T THINK YUGA WOULD LOOK LIKE THAT.
HE'S NEVER LOOKED AT ME WITH THAT EXPRESSION BEFORE...
KAJIKA-CHAN!

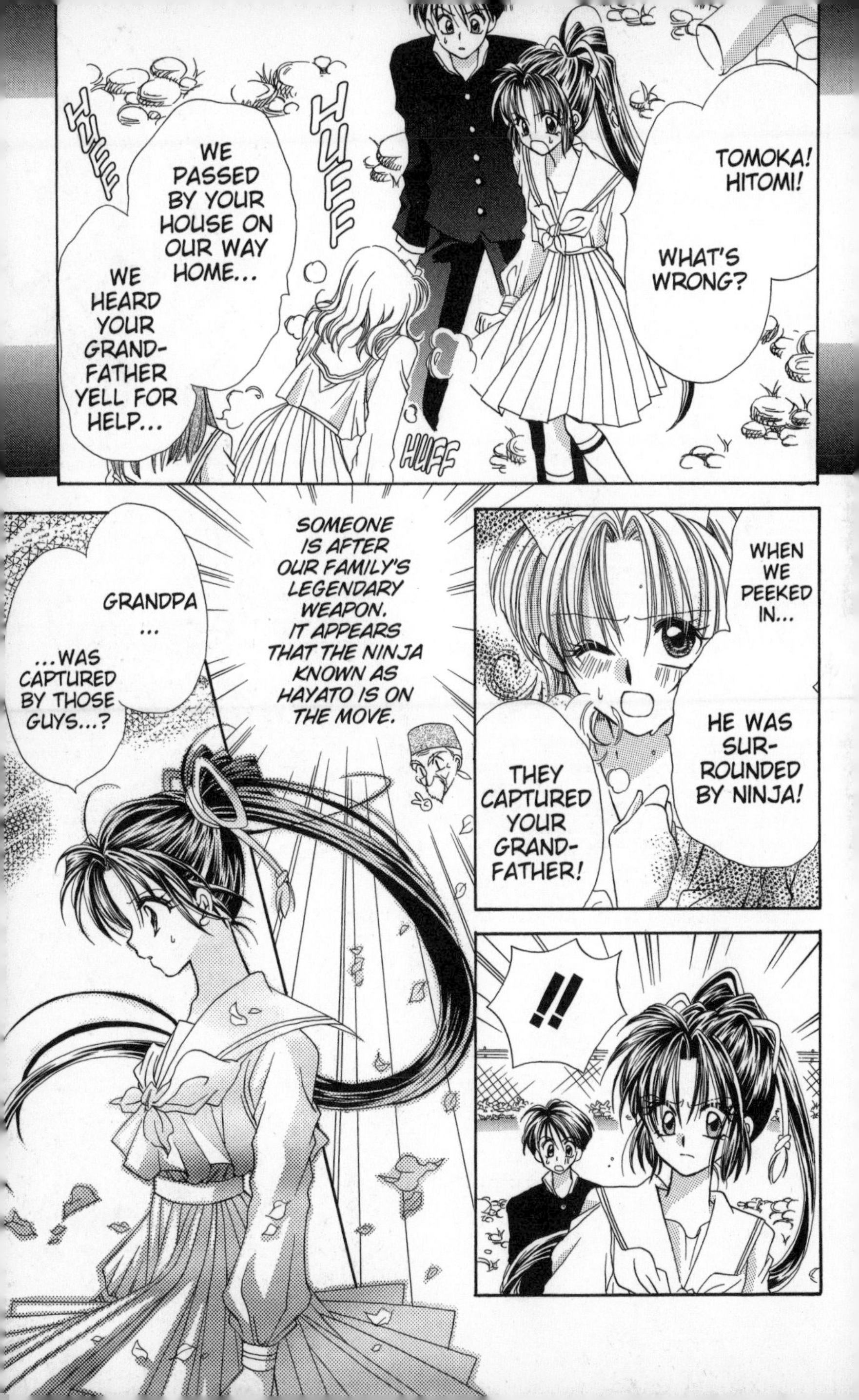
TOMOKA! HITOMI!
WHAT'S WRONG?
HUFF
HUFF
WE PASSED BY YOUR HOUSE ON OUR WAY HOME...
WE HEARD YOUR GRAND-FATHER YELL FOR HELP...
HUFF
WHEN WE PEEKED IN...
HE WAS SUR-ROUNDED BY NINJA!
THEY CAPTURED YOUR GRAND-FATHER!
!!
SOMEONE IS AFTER OUR FAMILY'S LEGENDARY WEAPON. IT APPEARS THAT THE NINJA KNOWN AS HAYATO IS ON THE MOVE.
GRANDPA...
...WAS CAPTURED BY THOSE GUYS...?

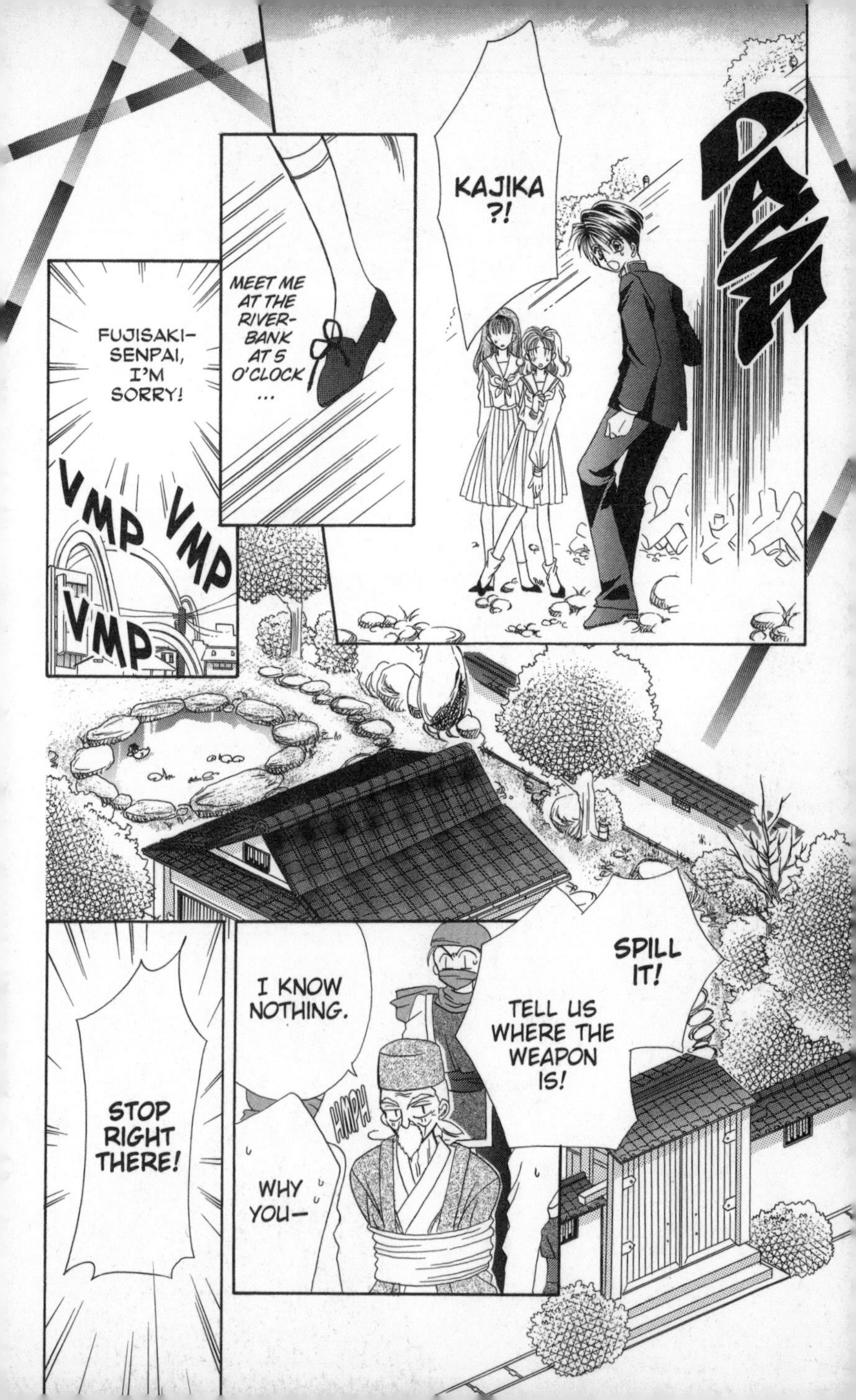
DASH
KAJIKA ?!
MEET ME AT THE RIVER-BANK AT 5 O'CLOCK ...
FUJISAKI-SENPAI, I'M SORRY!
VMP VMP VMP
SPILL IT!
TELL US WHERE THE WEAPON IS!
I KNOW NOTHING.
HMPH
WHY YOU—
STOP RIGHT THERE!

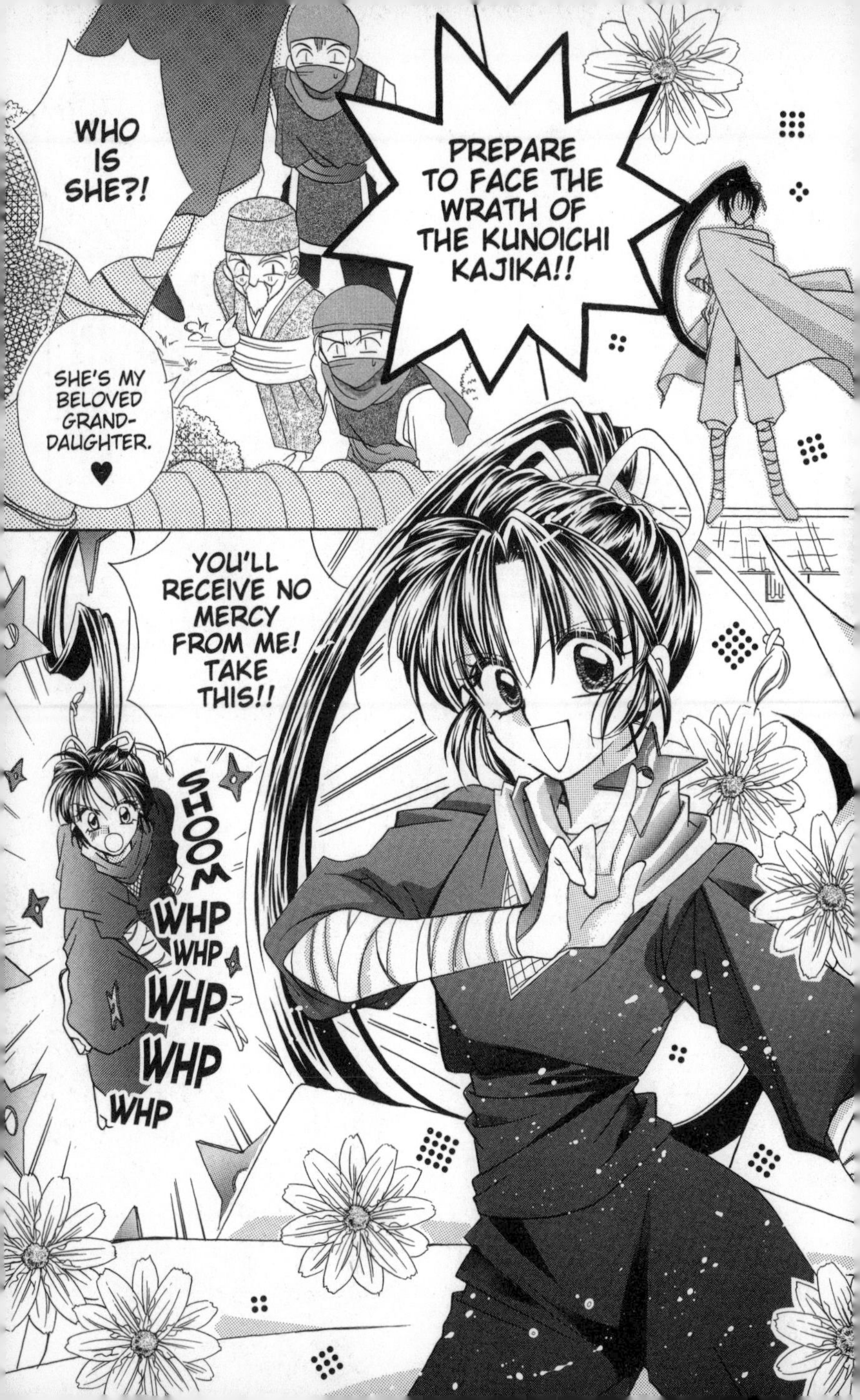
PREPARE TO FACE THE WRATH OF THE KUNOICHI KAJIKA!!
WHO IS SHE?!
SHE'S MY BELOVED GRAND-DAUGHTER. ♥
YOU'LL RECEIVE NO MERCY FROM ME! TAKE THIS!!
SHOOM
WHP
WHP
WHP
WHP
WHP

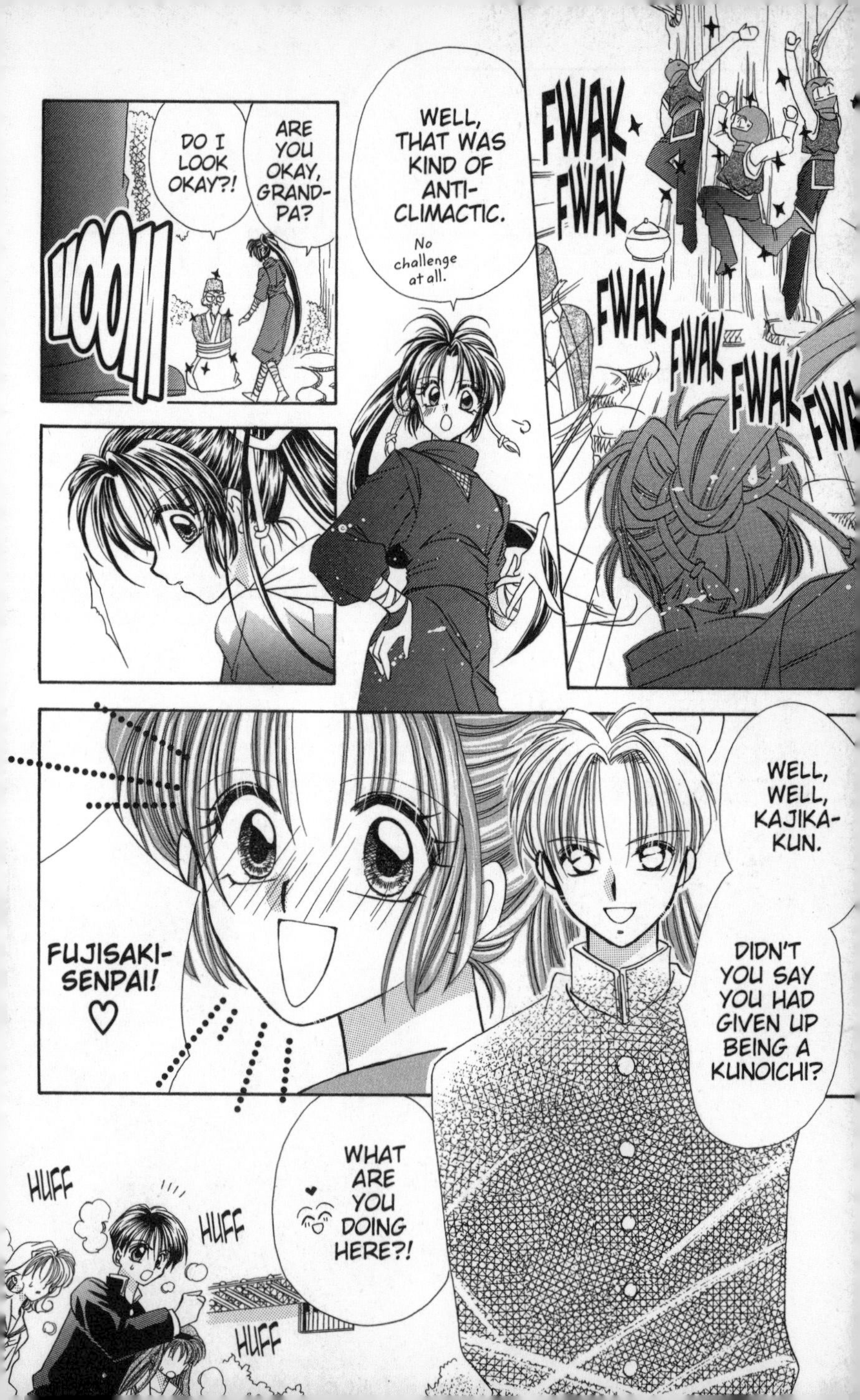
FWAK
FWAK
FWAK
FWAK
FWAK
FWA
WELL, THAT WAS KIND OF ANTI-CLIMACTIC.
No challenge at all.
ARE YOU OKAY, GRANDPA?
DO I LOOK OKAY?!
VOOM
WELL, WELL, KAJIKA-KUN.
DIDN'T YOU SAY YOU HAD GIVEN UP BEING A KUNOICHI?
FUJISAKI-SENPAI! ♡
WHAT ARE YOU DOING HERE?!
HUFF
HUFF
HUFF

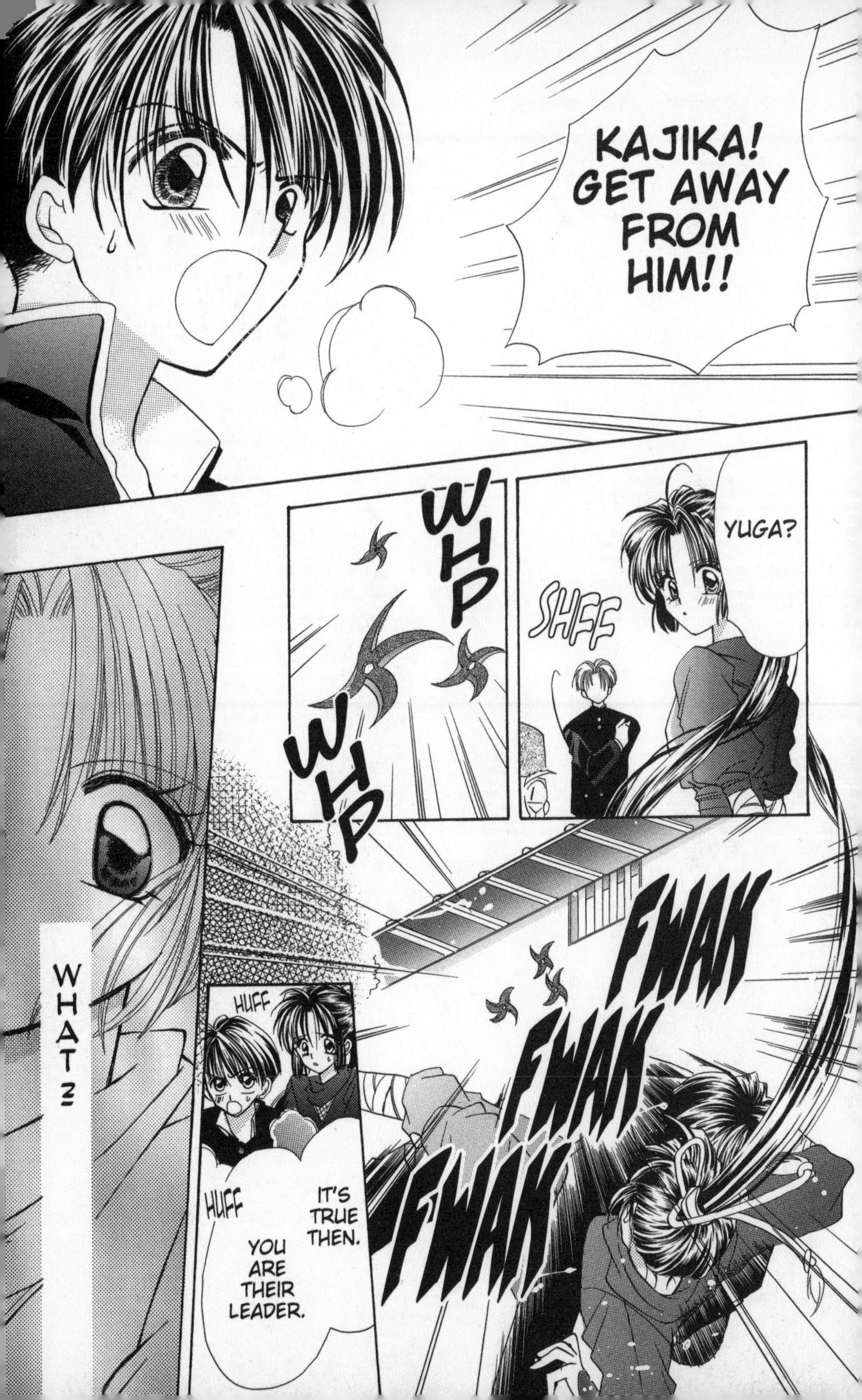
KAJIKA! GET AWAY FROM HIM!!
YUGA?
SHFF
WHP
WHP
FWAK
FWAK
FWAK
HUFF
HUFF
IT'S TRUE THEN.
YOU ARE THEIR LEADER.
WHAT?

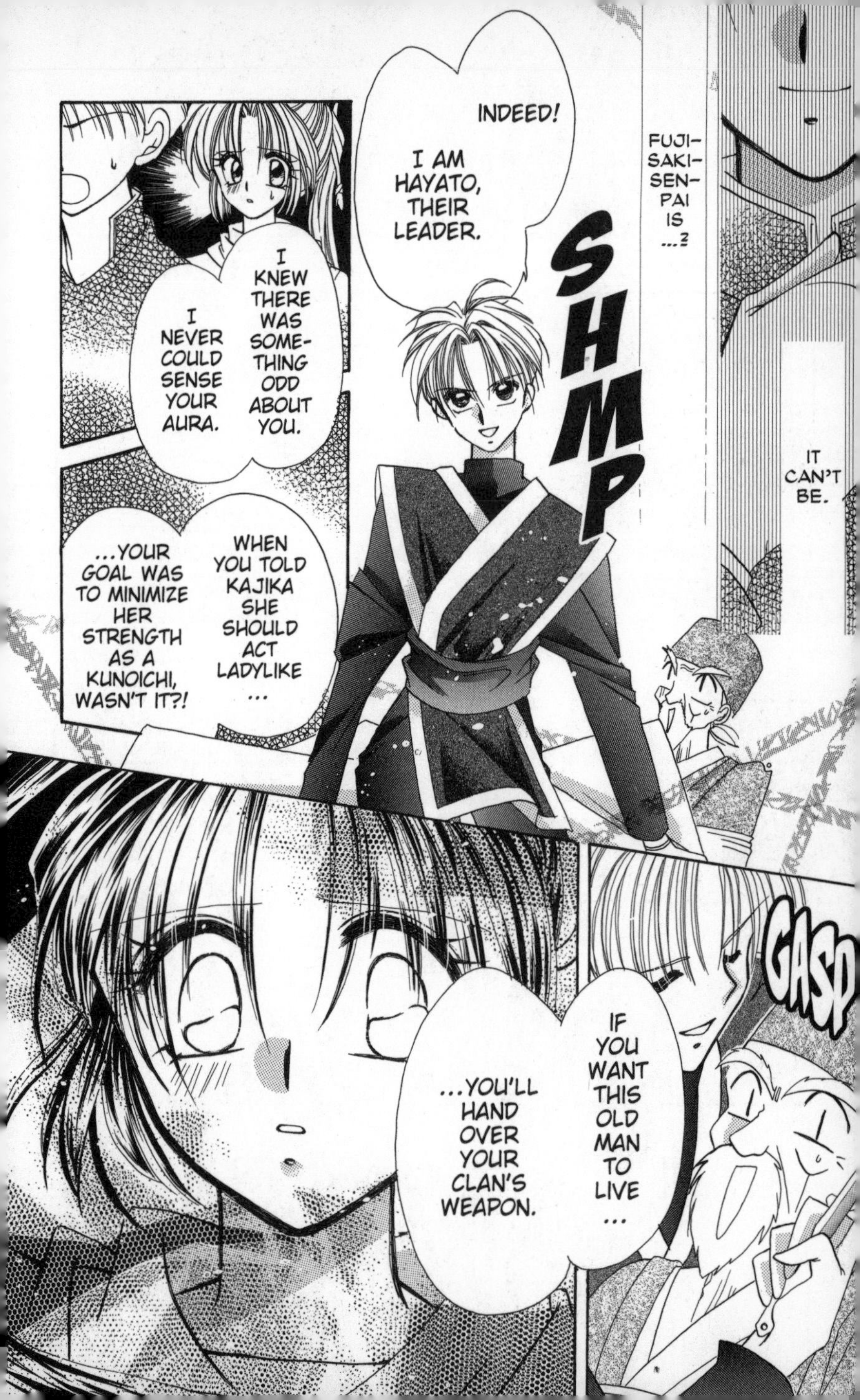

FUJISAKI-SENPAI IS ...?
IT CAN'T BE.
INDEED!
I AM HAYATO, THEIR LEADER.
SHMP
I KNEW THERE WAS SOMETHING ODD ABOUT YOU.
I NEVER COULD SENSE YOUR AURA.
WHEN YOU TOLD KAJIKA SHE SHOULD ACT LADYLIKE...
...YOUR GOAL WAS TO MINIMIZE HER STRENGTH AS A KUNOICHI, WASN'T IT?!
GASP
IF YOU WANT THIS OLD MAN TO LIVE...
...YOU'LL HAND OVER YOUR CLAN'S WEAPON.

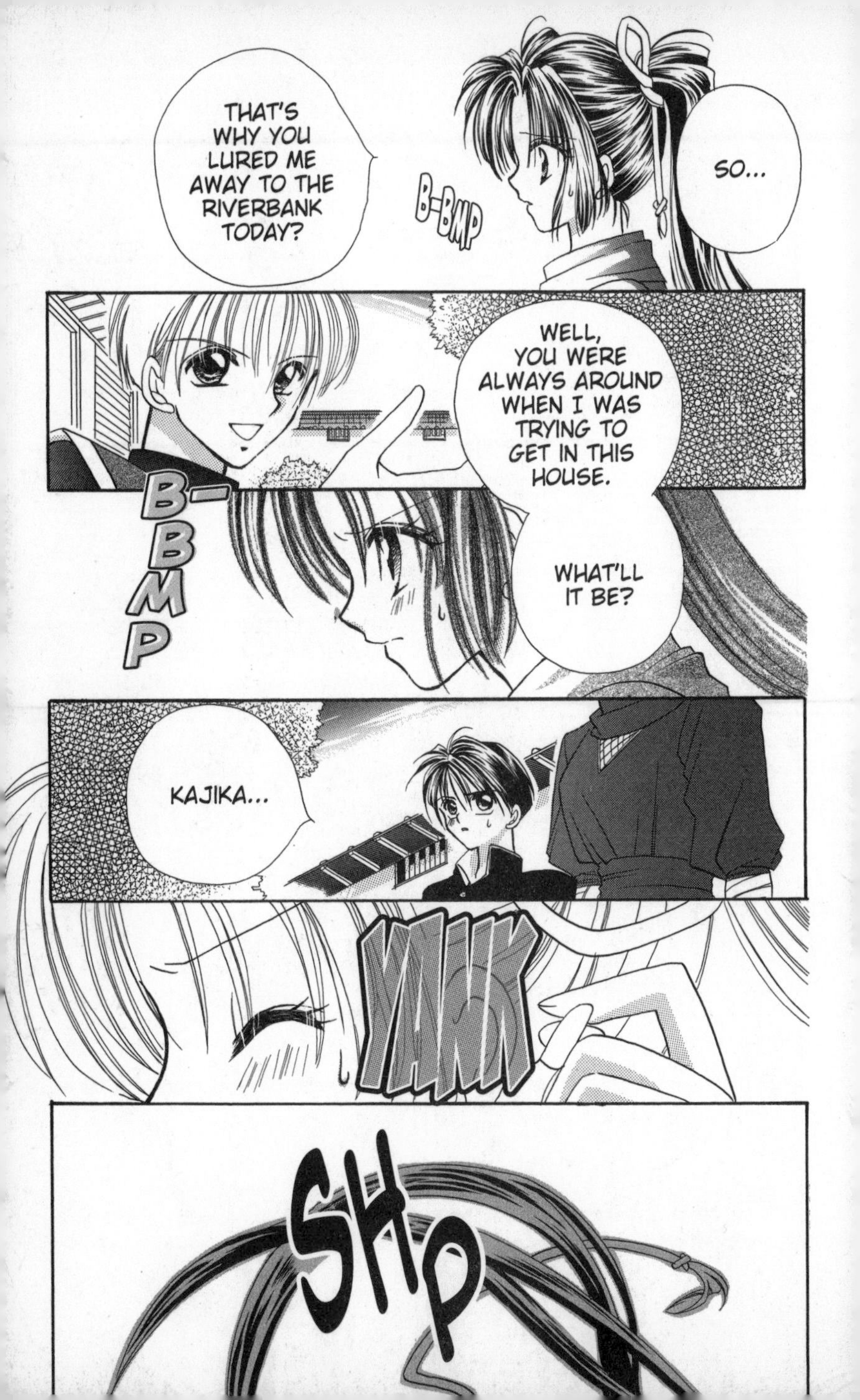
SO...
B-BMP
THAT'S WHY YOU LURED ME AWAY TO THE RIVERBANK TODAY?
WELL, YOU WERE ALWAYS AROUND WHEN I WAS TRYING TO GET IN THIS HOUSE.
WHAT'LL IT BE?
B-BMP
KAJIKA...
YANK
SHP

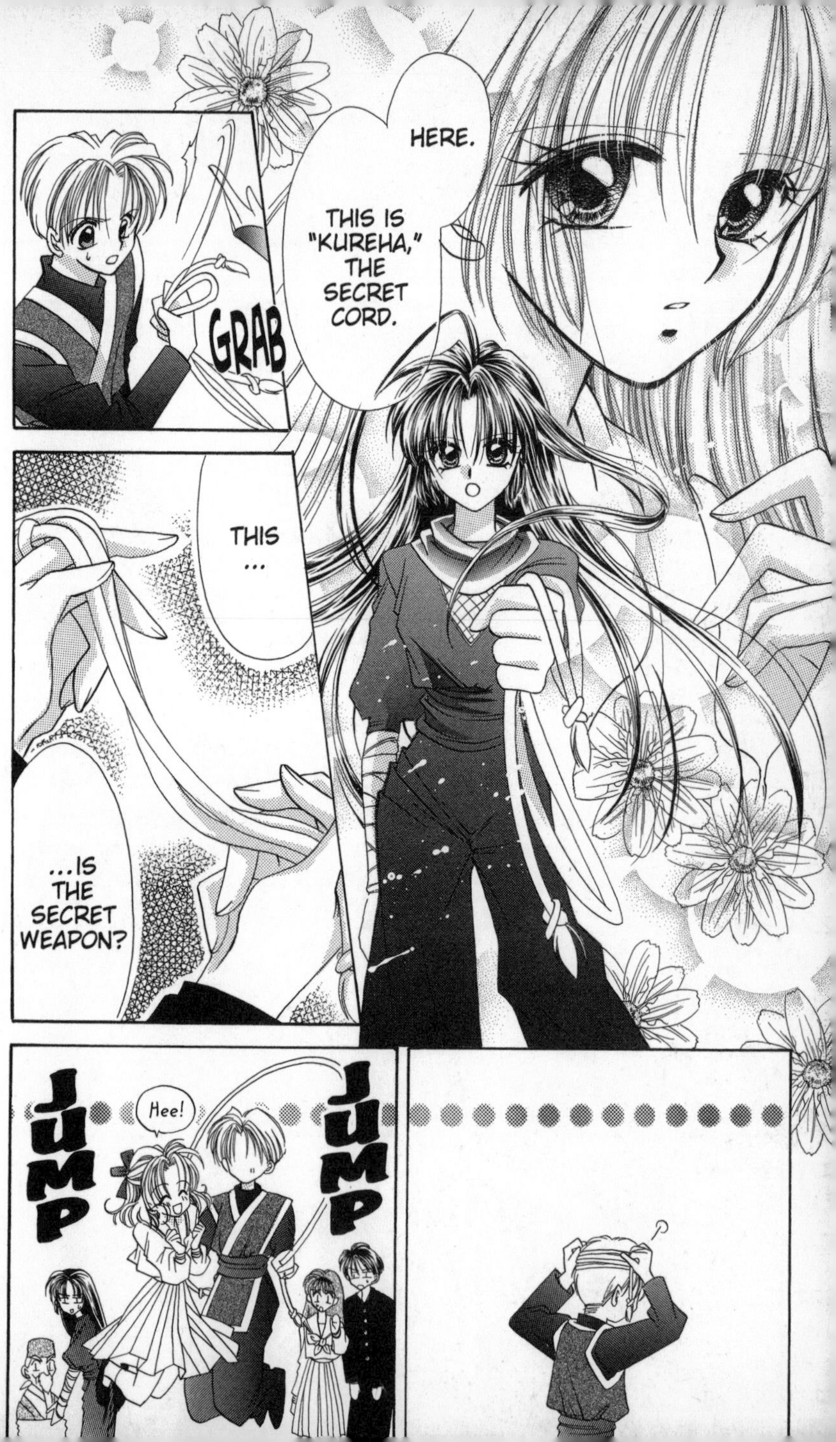
HERE.
THIS IS "KUREHA," THE SECRET CORD.
GRAB
THIS ...
...IS THE SECRET WEAPON?
JUMP
Hee!
JUMP

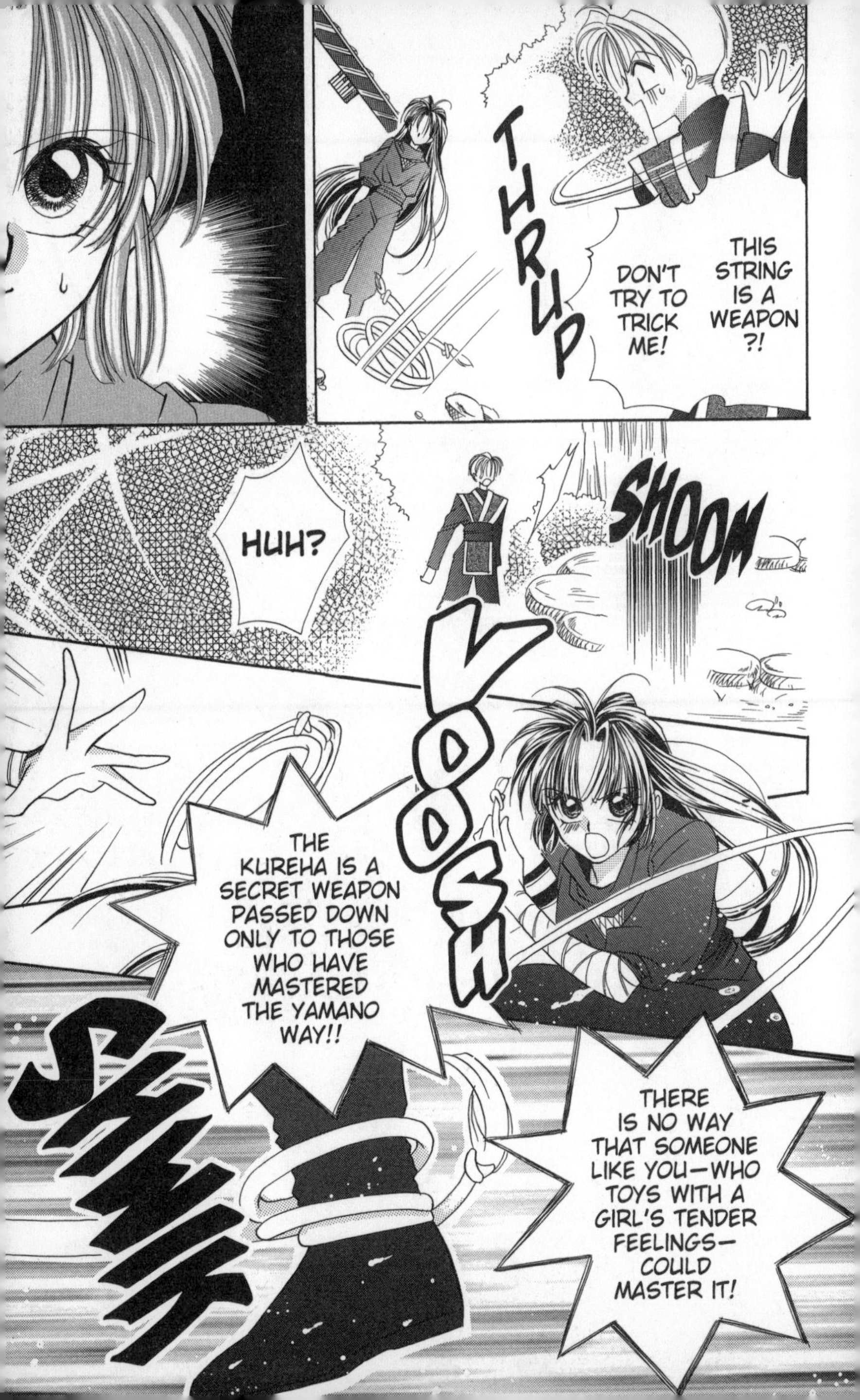
THIS STRING IS A WEAPON ?!
DON'T TRY TO TRICK ME!
THRUP
SHOOM
HUH?
VOOSH
THE KUREHA IS A SECRET WEAPON PASSED DOWN ONLY TO THOSE WHO HAVE MASTERED THE YAMANO WAY!!
THERE IS NO WAY THAT SOMEONE LIKE YOU—WHO TOYS WITH A GIRL'S TENDER FEELINGS—COULD MASTER IT!

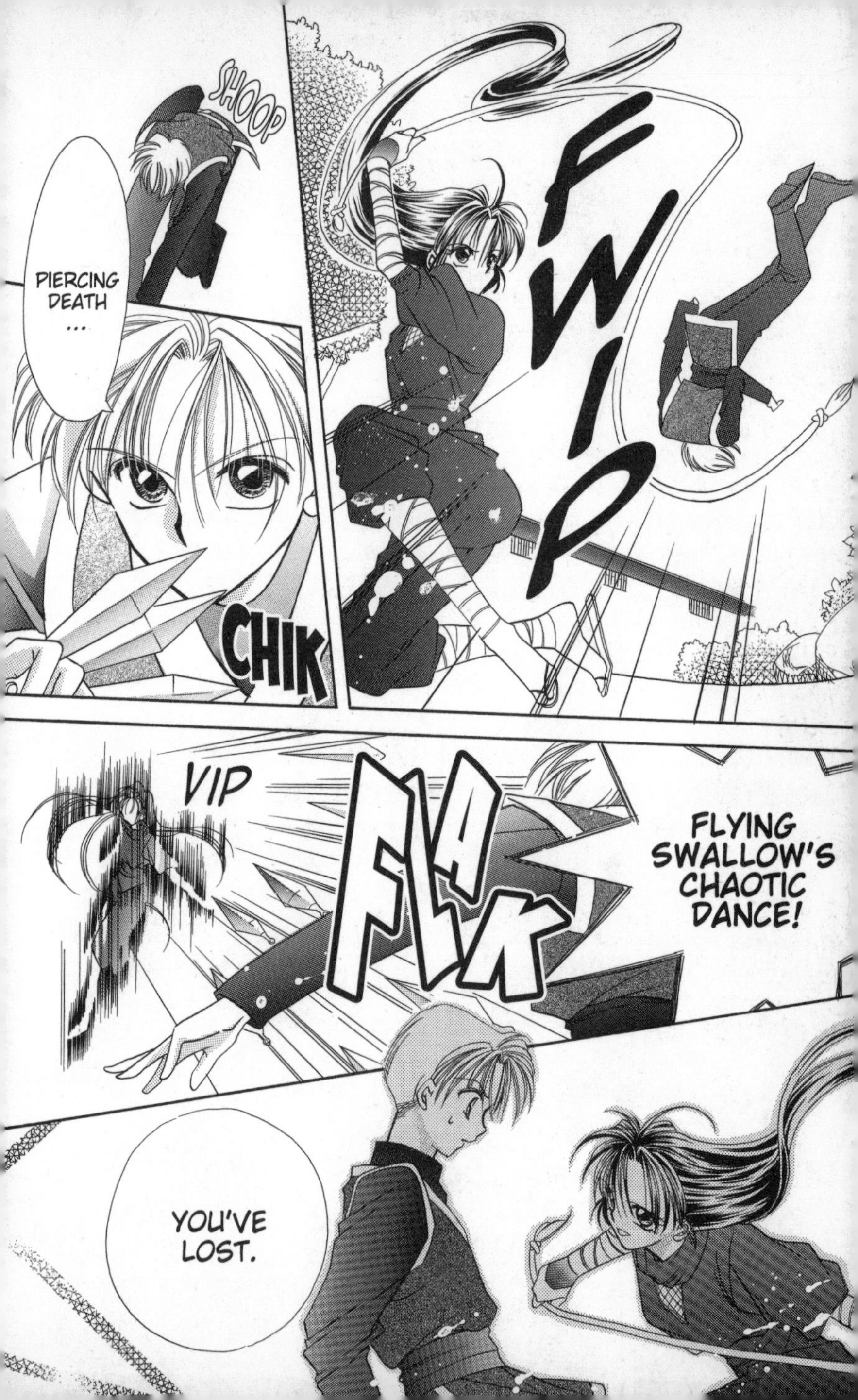
FWIP
SHOOP
PIERCING DEATH ...
CHIK
FLYING SWALLOW'S CHAOTIC DANCE!
FLAK
VIP
YOU'VE LOST.

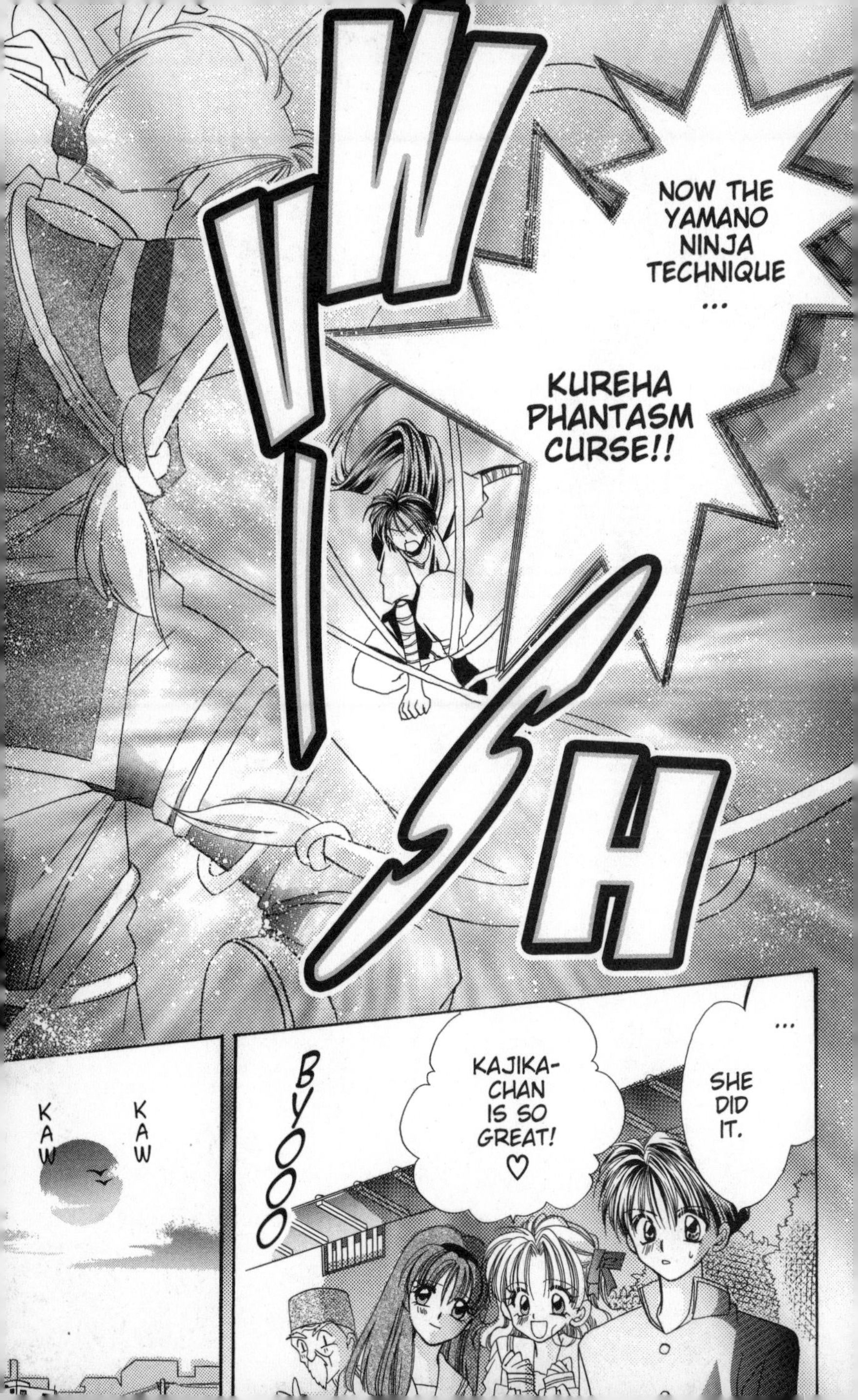
NOW THE YAMANO NINJA TECHNIQUE ...
KUREHA PHANTASM CURSE!!
VWISH
... SHE DID IT.
KAJIKA-CHAN IS SO GREAT! ♡
BYOOOO
KAW KAW

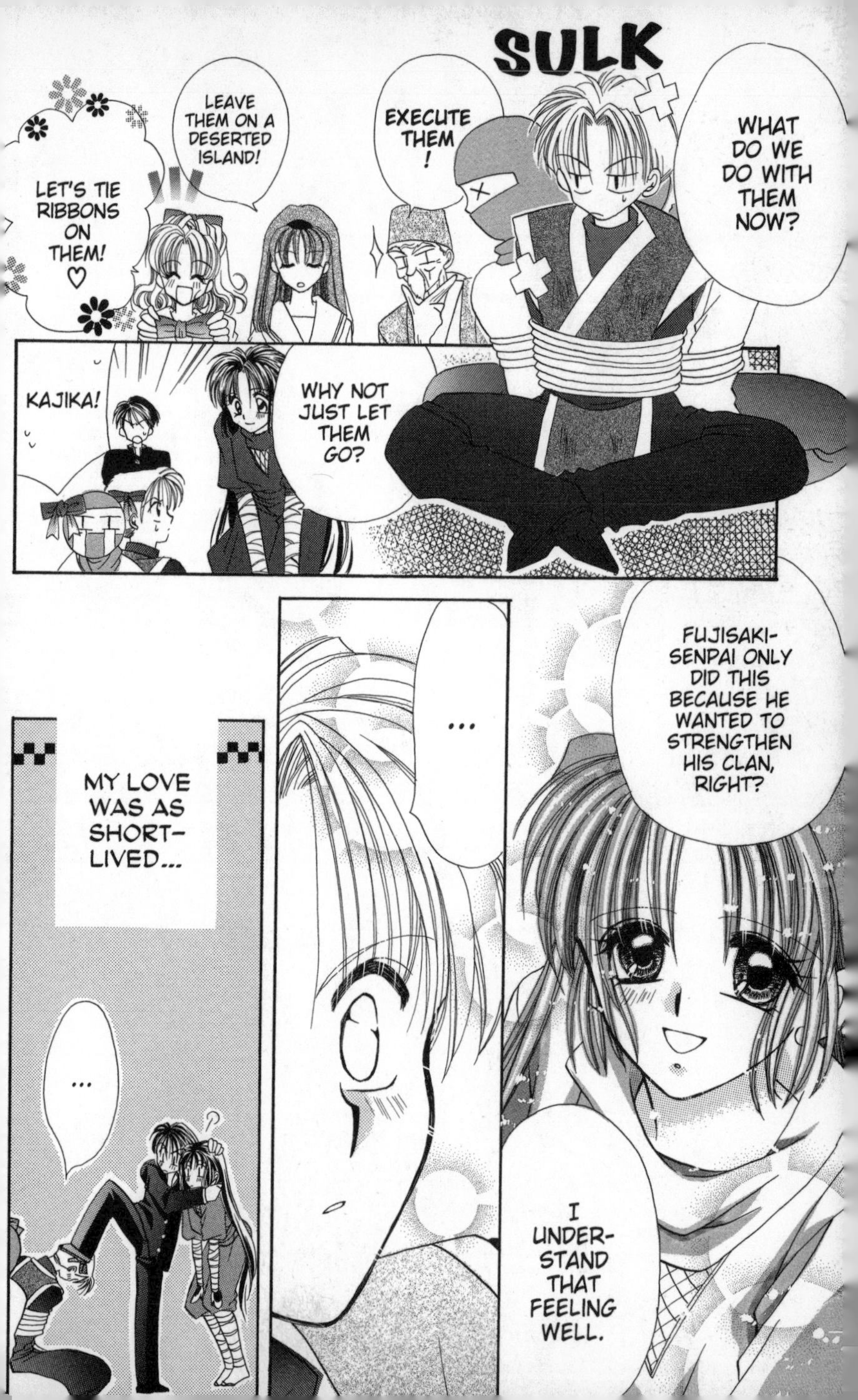
SULK
WHAT DO WE DO WITH THEM NOW?
EXECUTE THEM!
LEAVE THEM ON A DESERTED ISLAND!
LET'S TIE RIBBONS ON THEM! ♡
WHY NOT JUST LET THEM GO?
KAJIKA!
FUJISAKI-SENPAI ONLY DID THIS BECAUSE HE WANTED TO STRENGTHEN HIS CLAN, RIGHT?
I UNDER-STAND THAT FEELING WELL.
...
MY LOVE WAS AS SHORT-LIVED...
...

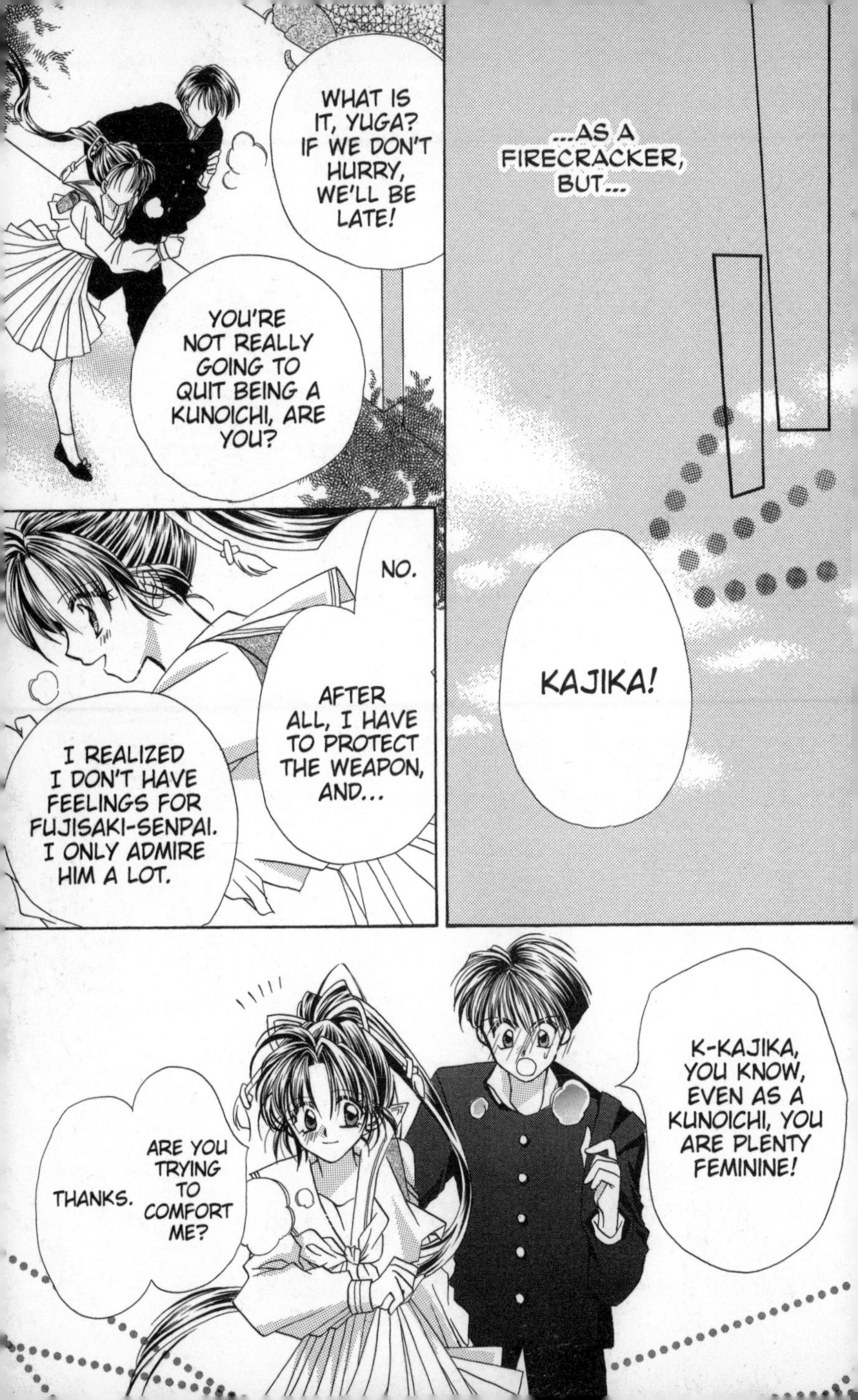
...AS A FIRECRACKER, BUT...
KAJIKA!
WHAT IS IT, YUGA? IF WE DON'T HURRY, WE'LL BE LATE!
YOU'RE NOT REALLY GOING TO QUIT BEING A KUNOICHI, ARE YOU?
NO.
AFTER ALL, I HAVE TO PROTECT THE WEAPON, AND...
I REALIZED I DON'T HAVE FEELINGS FOR FUJISAKI-SENPAI. I ONLY ADMIRE HIM A LOT.
K-KAJIKA, YOU KNOW, EVEN AS A KUNOICHI, YOU ARE PLENTY FEMININE!
ARE YOU TRYING TO COMFORT ME?
THANKS.

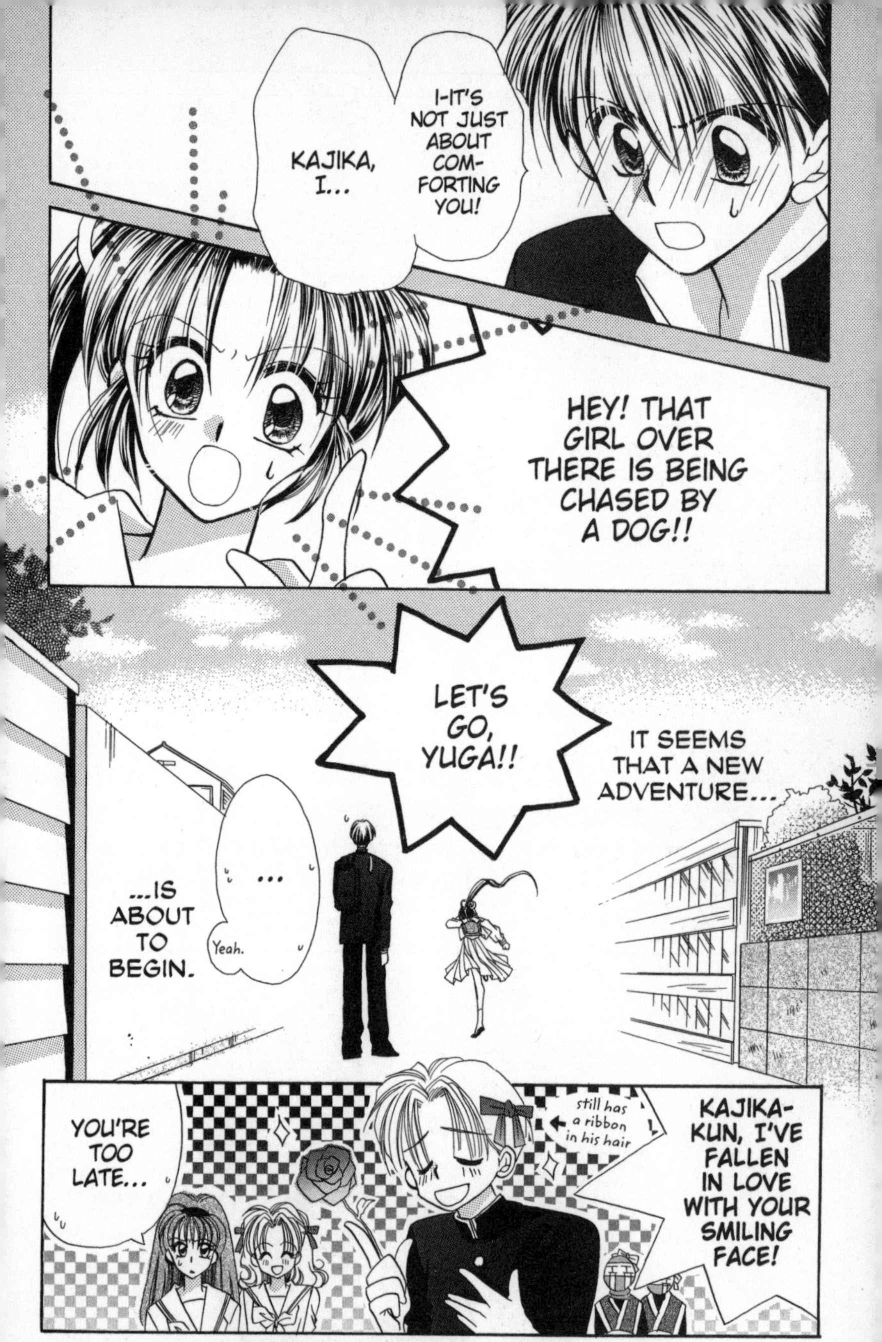
KAJIKA, I...
I-IT'S NOT JUST ABOUT COM-FORTING YOU!
HEY! THAT GIRL OVER THERE IS BEING CHASED BY A DOG!!
IT SEEMS THAT A NEW ADVENTURE...
LET'S GO, YUGA!!
...
Yeah.
...IS ABOUT TO BEGIN.
KAJIKA-KUN, I'VE FALLEN IN LOVE WITH YOUR SMILING FACE!
still has a ribbon in his hair
YOU'RE TOO LATE...

SHORT-TEMPERED MELANCHOLIC/END

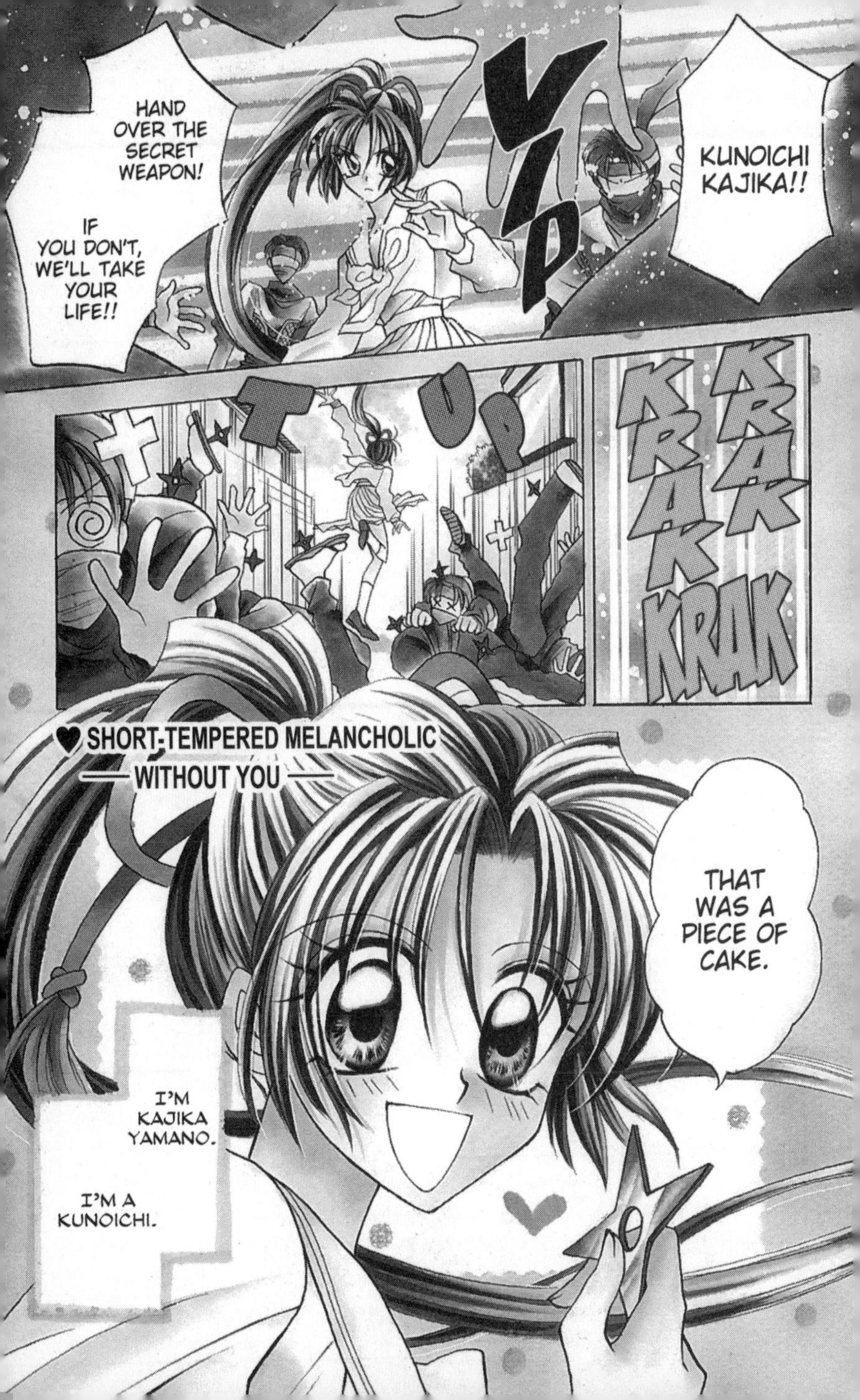
KUNOICHI KAJIKA!!
VIP
HAND OVER THE SECRET WEAPON!
IF YOU DON'T, WE'LL TAKE YOUR LIFE!!
KRAK KRAK KRAK
♥ SHORT-TEMPERED MELANCHOLIC
—WITHOUT YOU—
THAT WAS A PIECE OF CAKE.
I'M KAJIKA YAMANO.
I'M A KUNOICHI.

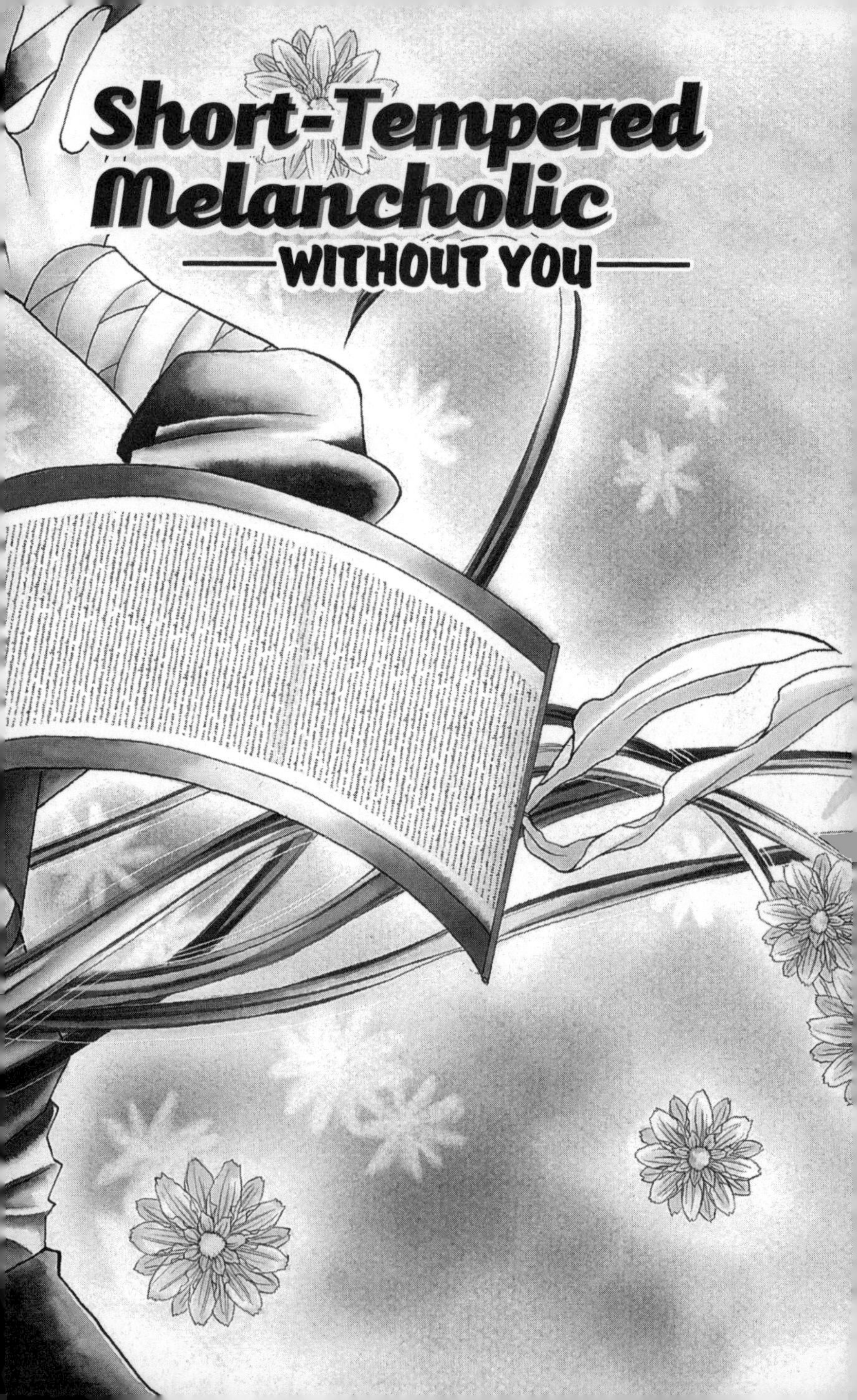
Short-Tempered Melancholic
—WITHOUT YOU—

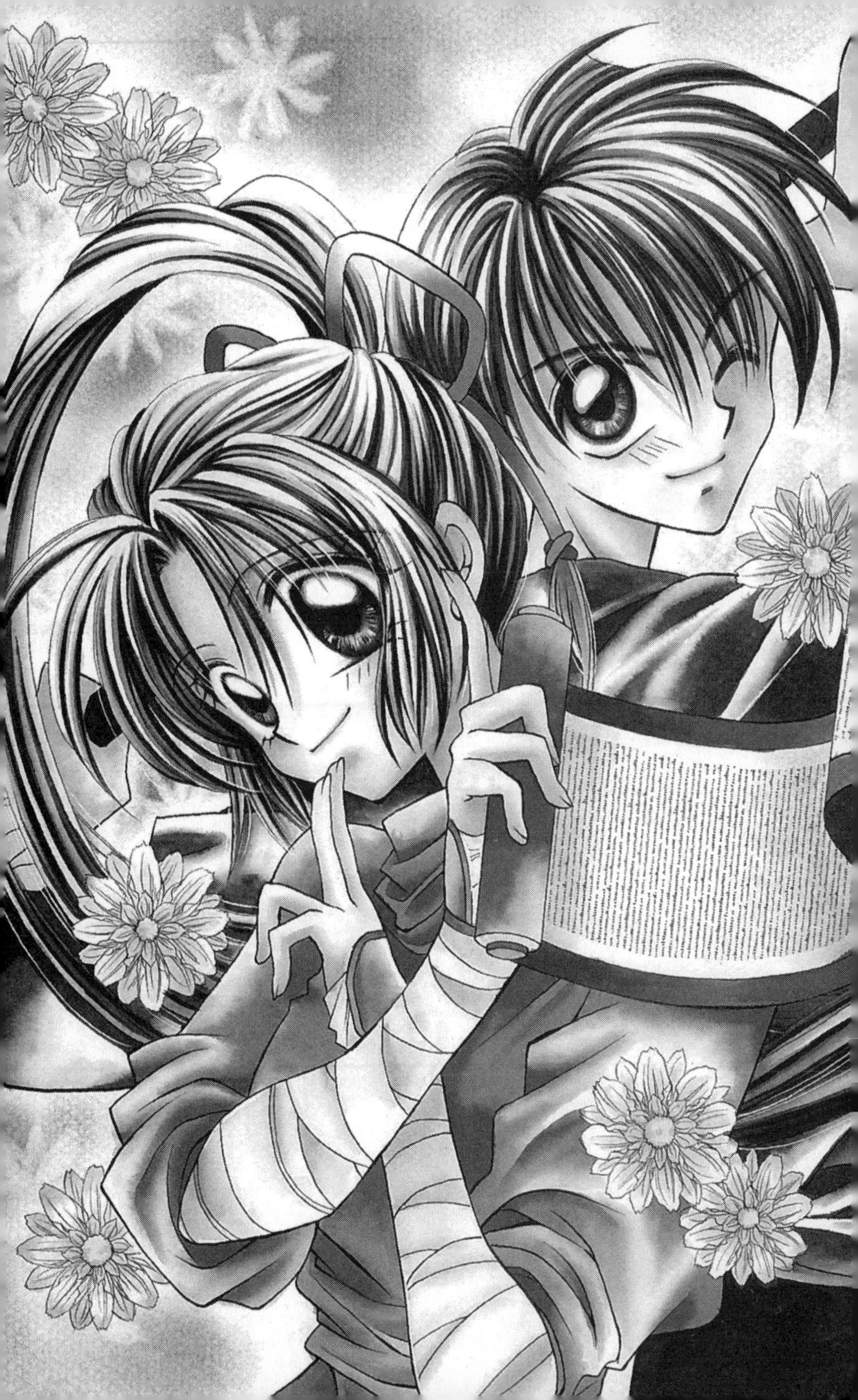

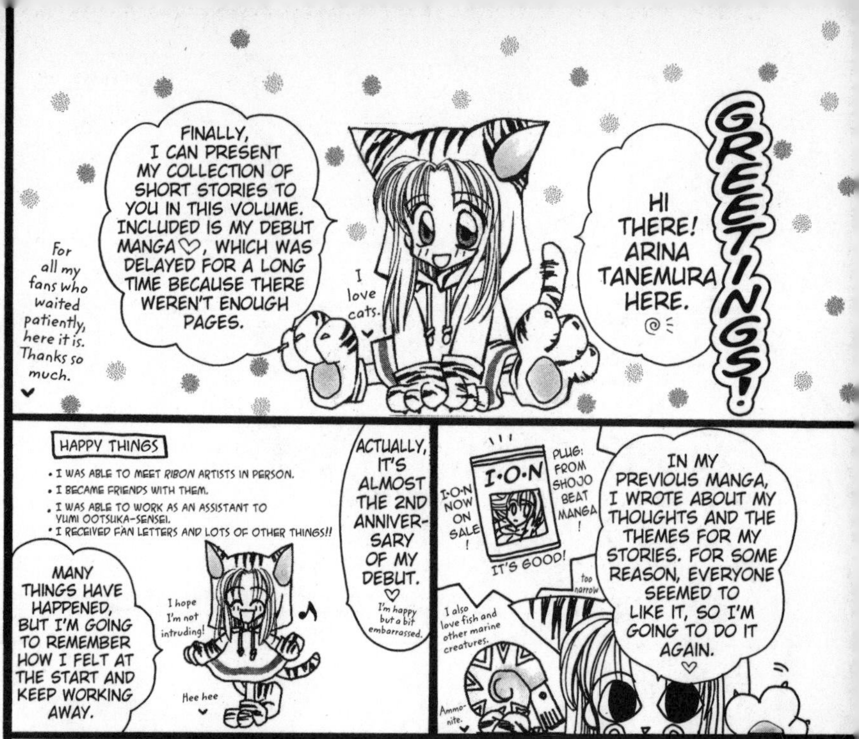
GREETINGS!
HI THERE! ARINA TANEMURA HERE.
I love cats.
FINALLY, I CAN PRESENT MY COLLECTION OF SHORT STORIES TO YOU IN THIS VOLUME. INCLUDED IS MY DEBUT MANGA♡, WHICH WAS DELAYED FOR A LONG TIME BECAUSE THERE WEREN'T ENOUGH PAGES.
For all my fans who waited patiently, here it is. Thanks so much.
IN MY PREVIOUS MANGA, I WROTE ABOUT MY THOUGHTS AND THE THEMES FOR MY STORIES. FOR SOME REASON, EVERYONE SEEMED TO LIKE IT, SO I'M GOING TO DO IT AGAIN.
PLUG: FROM SHOJO BEAT MANGA!
I·O·N
I·O·N NOW ON SALE!
IT'S GOOD!
too narrow
I also love fish and other marine creatures.
Ammonite.
ACTUALLY, IT'S ALMOST THE 2ND ANNIVERSARY OF MY DEBUT.
I'm happy but a bit embarrassed.
HAPPY THINGS
• I WAS ABLE TO MEET RIBON ARTISTS IN PERSON.
• I BECAME FRIENDS WITH THEM.
• I WAS ABLE TO WORK AS AN ASSISTANT TO YUMI OOTSUKA-SENSEI.
• I RECEIVED FAN LETTERS AND LOTS OF OTHER THINGS!!
MANY THINGS HAVE HAPPENED, BUT I'M GOING TO REMEMBER HOW I FELT AT THE START AND KEEP WORKING AWAY.
I hope I'm not intruding!
Hee hee

SHORT-TEMPERED MELANCHOLIC

THE TITLE IS FROM ONE OF MY FAVORITE SONGS BY FAIRCHILD. KAJIKA IS SUPPOSED TO BE SHORT-TEMPERED. HER MELANCHOLY RESULTS WHEN SHE IS UNABLE TO BE AS DOCILE AS SHE WOULD LIKE AND "EXPLODES" INSTEAD.

THIS IS THE TITLE STORY. IT WAS THE THIRD STORY AFTER MY DEBUT. I REMEMBER BEING REALLY NERVOUS WHILE WRITING IT BECAUSE IT WAS SUPPOSED TO RUN IN THE MAIN MAGAZINE. ALTHOUGH I'M THE TYPE WHO USUALLY WRITES WITH A PLOT IN MIND, THIS STORY WAS WRITTEN BASED ON A CHARACTER SUGGESTED BY MY EDITOR, O-SAN. (MAYBE THAT'S WHY AN EDITOR WHO NEVER PRAISES MANGAKA–OR MAYBE JUST ME–COMPLIMENTED ME ON THE CHARACTER. ❤) ANYWAY, I TRIED TO MAKE THE LEAD FEMALE CHARACTER AS COOL AS I COULD. THAT'S WHY I MADE HER A KUNOICHI. ❤ I WANTED TO TRY WRITING AN ACTION STORY (ALTHOUGH IT DIDN'T TURN OUT THAT WAY). BUT, MAYBE BECAUSE I WAS NEW TO IT, THE *NAME* TOOK SUCH A LONG TIME TO DO. IT WAS REALLY A MESS. ONE PAGE THAT WAS DISCARDED HAD A KISSING SCENE BETWEEN KAJIKA-CHAN AND YUGA-KUN. HEE HEE! ❤ KAJIKA-CHAN AND YUGA-KUN WERE REALLY POPULAR WITH THE READERS, WHICH MADE ME REALLY HAPPY. THE FEMALE CHARACTER IS USUALLY SOMEHOW LESS POPULAR THAN HER MALE PARTNER IN MY MANGA. HOWEVER, FOR THIS MANGA THERE WERE MORE KAJIKA FANS. I DIDN'T REALLY HAVE A THEME FOR THE STORY, BUT I WANTED TO WRITE ABOUT A GIRL WHO THINKS SHE NEEDS TO ACT MORE LIKE A GIRL BUT CAN'T. I THINK WORRYING ABOUT THAT AND FALLING FOR THE WRONG PERSON IS ACTING EXACTLY LIKE A GIRL ////. OF ALL THE HEROINES IN THIS BOOK, KAJIKA-CHAN IS THE MOST LIKE A GIRL. AND YUGA-KUN IS DEFINITELY AWARE OF THAT. ❤

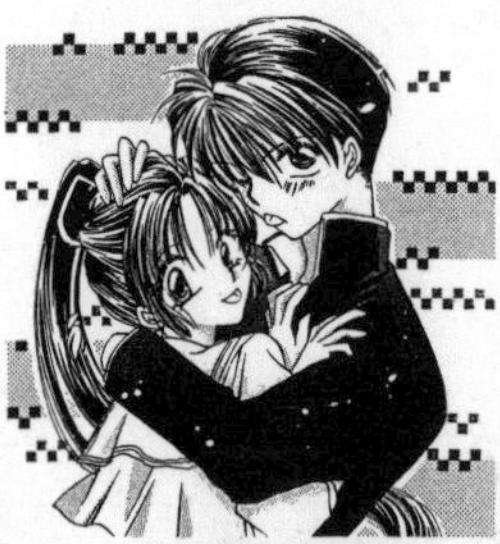

THE THEME SONG FOR "SHORT-TEMPERED MELANCHOLIC" IS "SOBAKASU" BY JUDY AND MARY. ❤

THE BONUS STORY WAS WRITTEN ON A SCHEDULE SO TIGHT THAT IT'S A MIRACLE IT EVER GOT FINISHED. IT WAS DUE RIGHT AFTER I FINISHED THE FIRST CHAPTER OF AN ONGOING SERIES, AND IT WAS REALLY TOUGH. (ON TOP OF THAT, THE DEADLINE FOR CHAPTER 2 OF THE SERIES WAS ONLY HALF A MONTH AFTER THE DEADLINE FOR THIS STORY.) ↑ IN ONE AND A HALF MONTHS, I DID 90 PAGES... IT JUST ABOUT KILLED ME. (TO MAKE MATTERS WORSE, I HAD TO DO A BUNCH OF ILLUSTRATIONS.) IT FELT LIKE I WAS JUST KNOCKING THEM OUT. THEY WEREN'T VERY GOOD–I DID 30 OF THEM... BUT I DID LIKE THE LAST ONE. I LIKED THE CHAPTER TITLE PAGE TOO. IT WAS MY FIRST STAND-ALONE STORY, AND THE ILLUSTRATION STRAYED FROM THE ACTUAL THEME OF THE STORY. → "IT IS OFTEN SAID THAT NINJA MUST SUPPRESS THEIR FEELINGS, BUT WOULDN'T THAT MEAN THEY HAVE TO GIVE UP ON FALLING IN LOVE?" THAT THOUGHT WAS THE STARTING POINT FOR MY MANGA. GRANDPA ANSWERED THAT QUESTION FOR ME. (LAUGH) ← I'M SAYING WHAT I LIKE AGAIN. PLEASE LISTEN TO IT WHILE READING THE MANGA. ❤

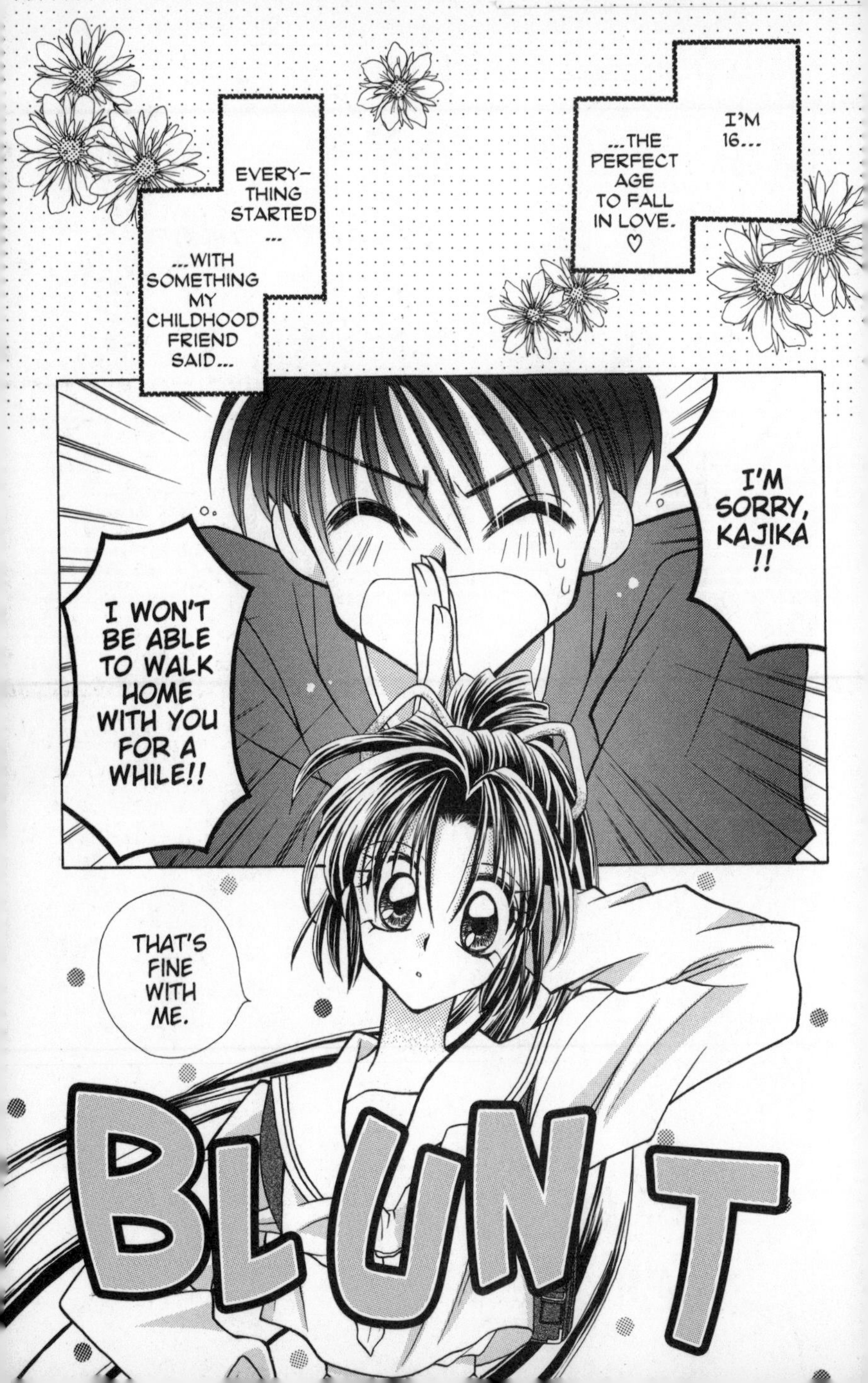
I'M 16...
...THE PERFECT AGE TO FALL IN LOVE. ♡
EVERYTHING STARTED...
...WITH SOMETHING MY CHILDHOOD FRIEND SAID...
I'M SORRY, KAJIKA!!
I WON'T BE ABLE TO WALK HOME WITH YOU FOR A WHILE!!
THAT'S FINE WITH ME.
BLUNT

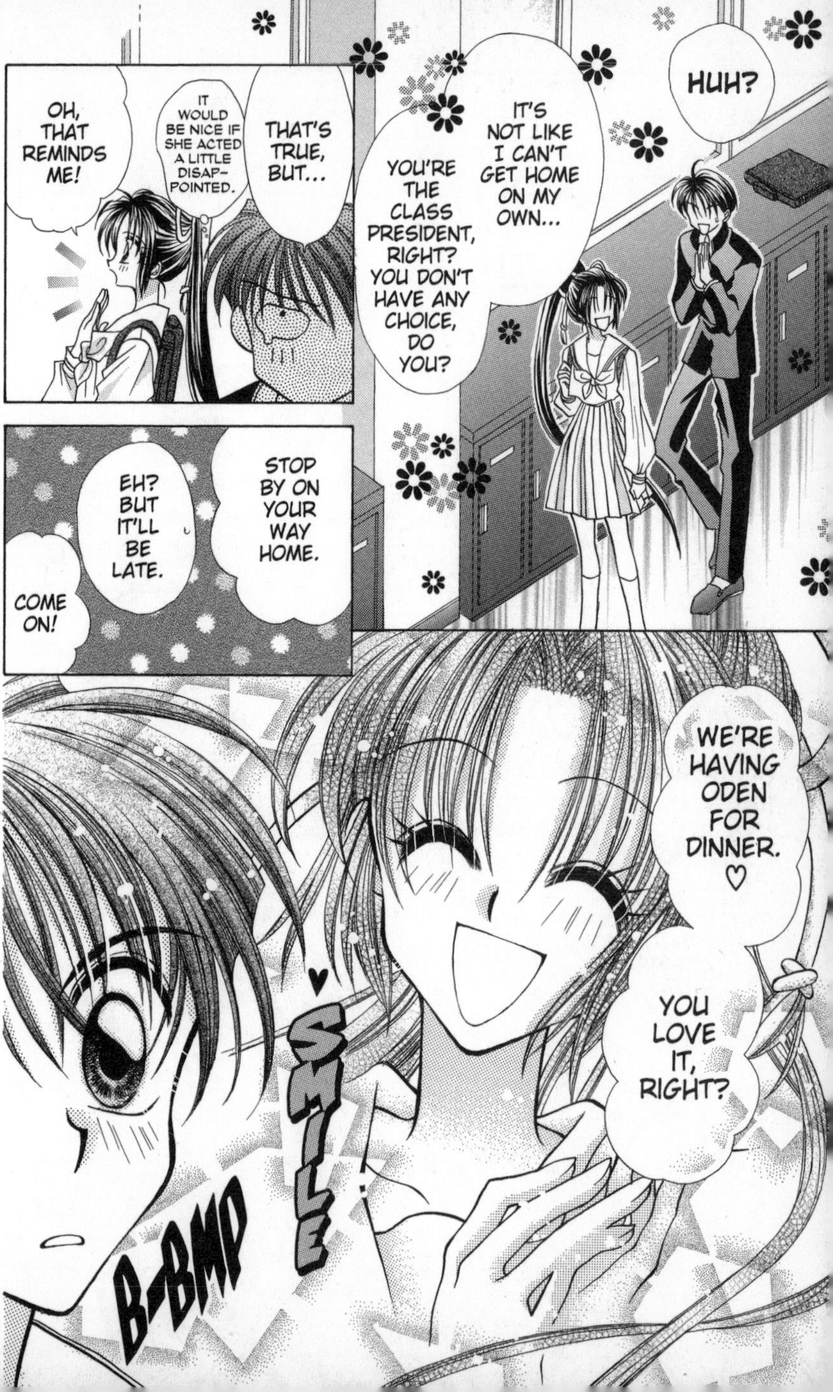
HUH?
IT'S NOT LIKE I CAN'T GET HOME ON MY OWN...
YOU'RE THE CLASS PRESIDENT, RIGHT? YOU DON'T HAVE ANY CHOICE, DO YOU?
THAT'S TRUE, BUT...
IT WOULD BE NICE IF SHE ACTED A LITTLE DISAP-POINTED.
OH, THAT REMINDS ME!
STOP BY ON YOUR WAY HOME.
EH? BUT IT'LL BE LATE.
COME ON!
WE'RE HAVING ODEN FOR DINNER. ♡
YOU LOVE IT, RIGHT?
♥ SMILE
B-BMP

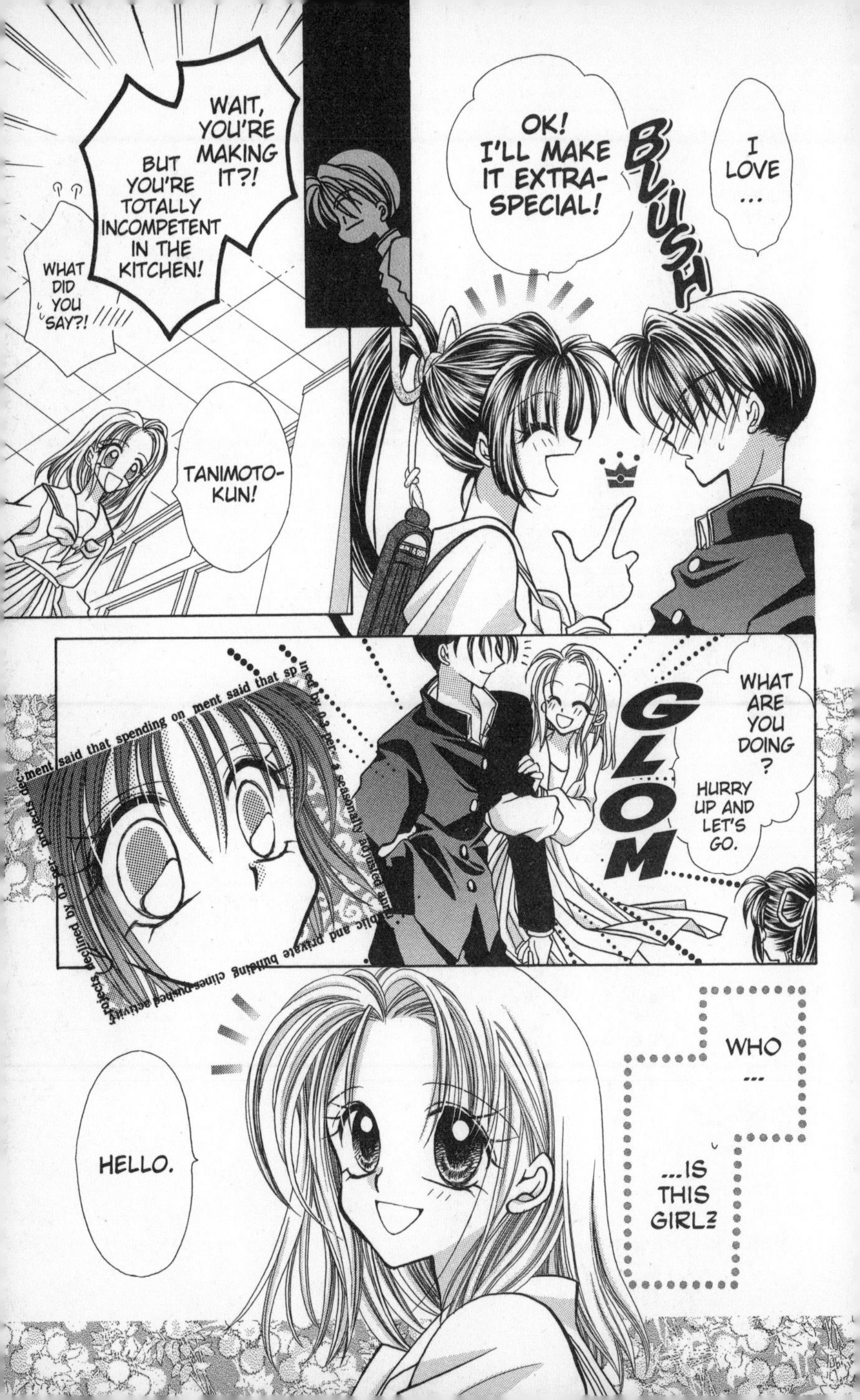
I LOVE ...
BLUSH
OK! I'LL MAKE IT EXTRA-SPECIAL!
WAIT, YOU'RE MAKING IT?!
BUT YOU'RE TOTALLY INCOMPETENT IN THE KITCHEN!
WHAT DID YOU SAY?!
TANIMOTO-KUN!
WHAT ARE YOU DOING?
HURRY UP AND LET'S GO.
GLOM
WHO ...
...IS THIS GIRL?
HELLO.

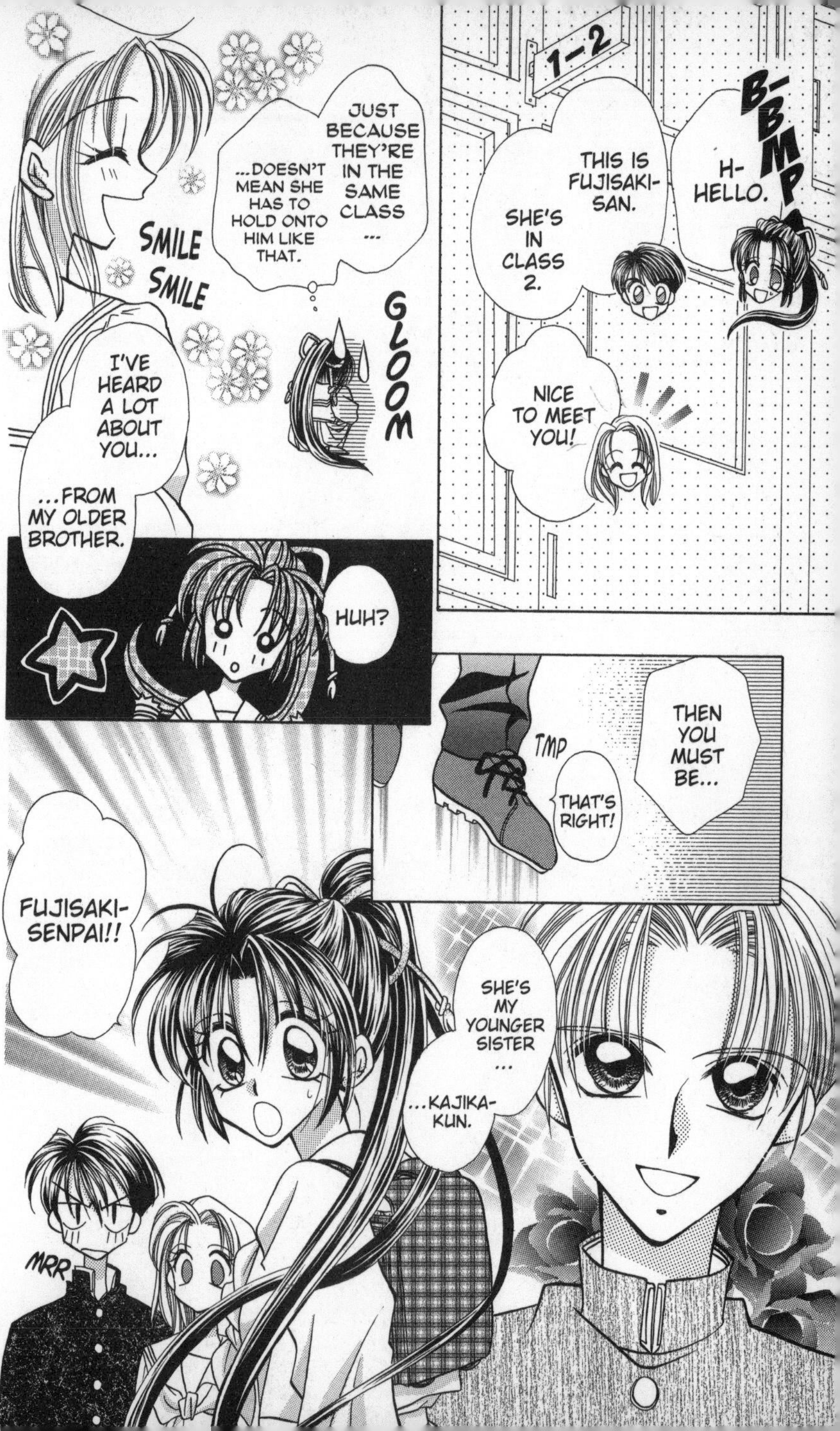
1-2
B-BMP
H-HELLO.
THIS IS FUJISAKI-SAN.
SHE'S IN CLASS 2.
NICE TO MEET YOU!
JUST BECAUSE THEY'RE IN THE SAME CLASS ...
...DOESN'T MEAN SHE HAS TO HOLD ONTO HIM LIKE THAT.
SMILE
SMILE
GLOOM
I'VE HEARD A LOT ABOUT YOU...
...FROM MY OLDER BROTHER.
HUH?
THEN YOU MUST BE...
TMP
THAT'S RIGHT!
FUJISAKI-SENPAI!!
SHE'S MY YOUNGER SISTER ...
...KAJIKA-KUN.
MRR

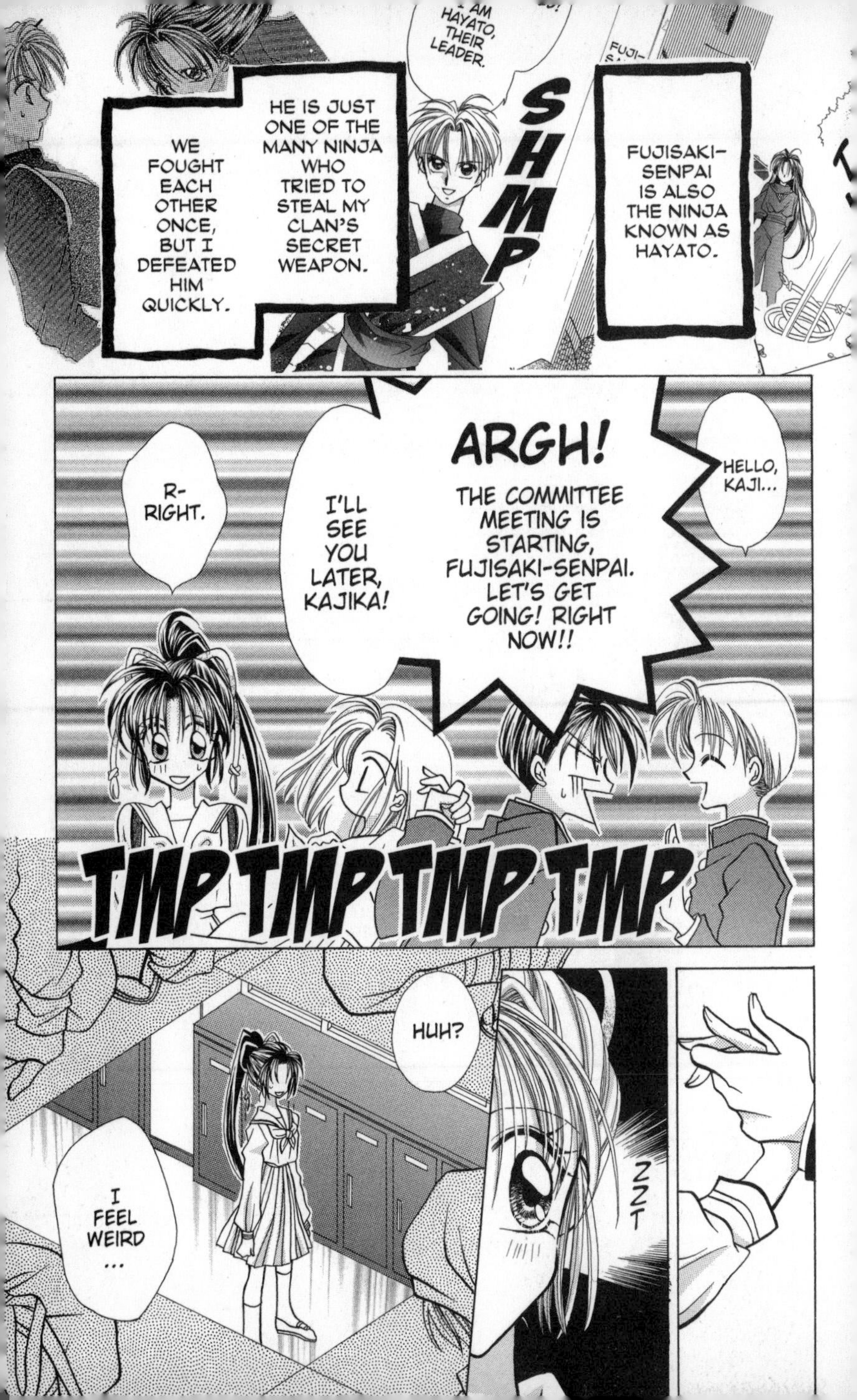
FUJISAKI-SENPAI IS ALSO THE NINJA KNOWN AS HAYATO.
I AM HAYATO, THEIR LEADER.
SHMP
HE IS JUST ONE OF THE MANY NINJA WHO TRIED TO STEAL MY CLAN'S SECRET WEAPON.
WE FOUGHT EACH OTHER ONCE, BUT I DEFEATED HIM QUICKLY.
HELLO, KAJI...
ARGH!
THE COMMITTEE MEETING IS STARTING, FUJISAKI-SENPAI. LET'S GET GOING! RIGHT NOW!!
I'LL SEE YOU LATER, KAJIKA!
R-RIGHT.
TMP TMP TMP TMP
ZZT
HUH?
I FEEL WEIRD...

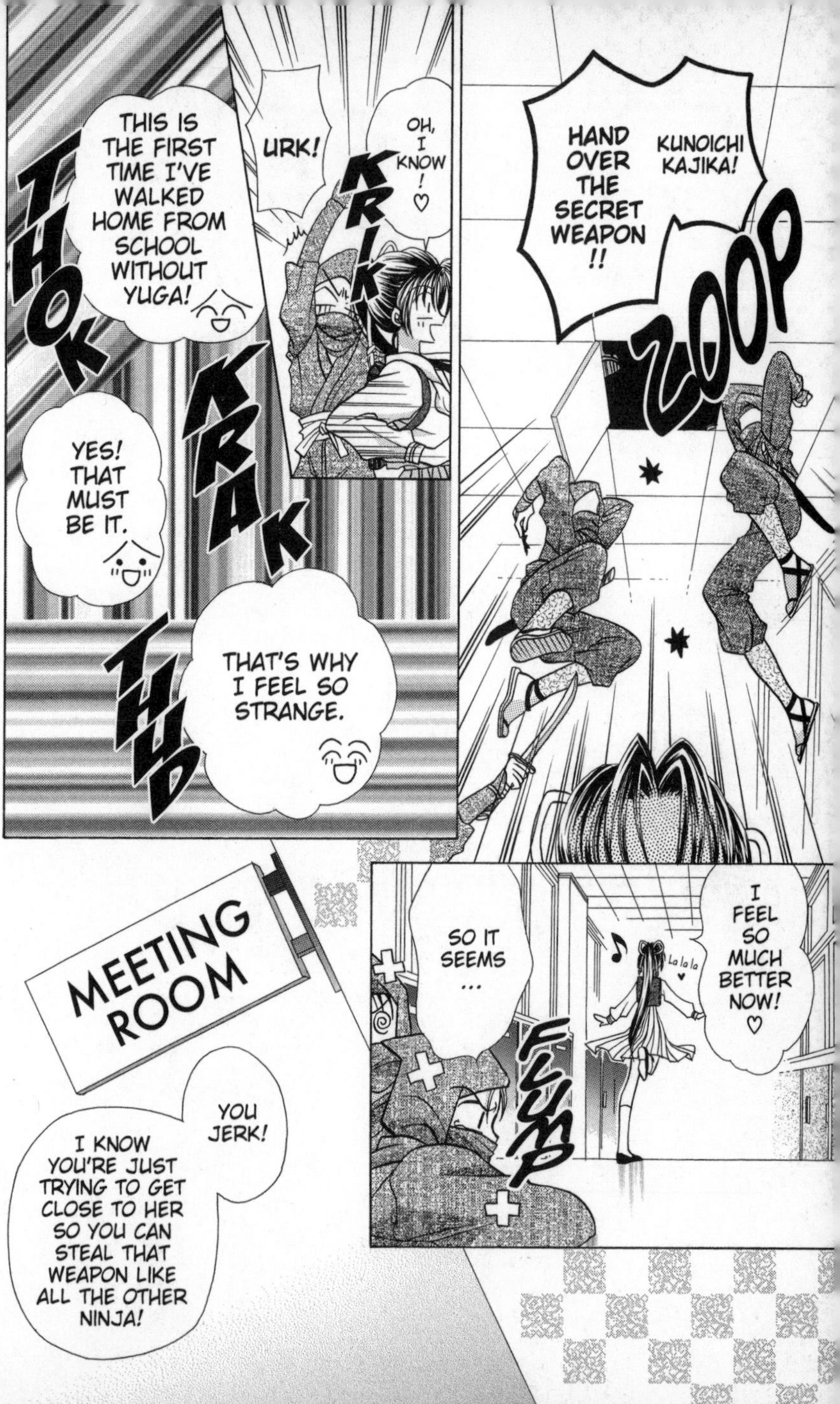
KUNOICHI KAJIKA!
HAND OVER THE SECRET WEAPON!!
ZOOP
OH, I KNOW! ♡
KRIK
URK!
THIS IS THE FIRST TIME I'VE WALKED HOME FROM SCHOOL WITHOUT YUGA!
THOK
YES! THAT MUST BE IT.
KRAK
THAT'S WHY I FEEL SO STRANGE.
THUD
I FEEL SO MUCH BETTER NOW! ♡
La la la ♥
SO IT SEEMS ...
FLUMP
MEETING ROOM
YOU JERK!
I KNOW YOU'RE JUST TRYING TO GET CLOSE TO HER SO YOU CAN STEAL THAT WEAPON LIKE ALL THE OTHER NINJA!

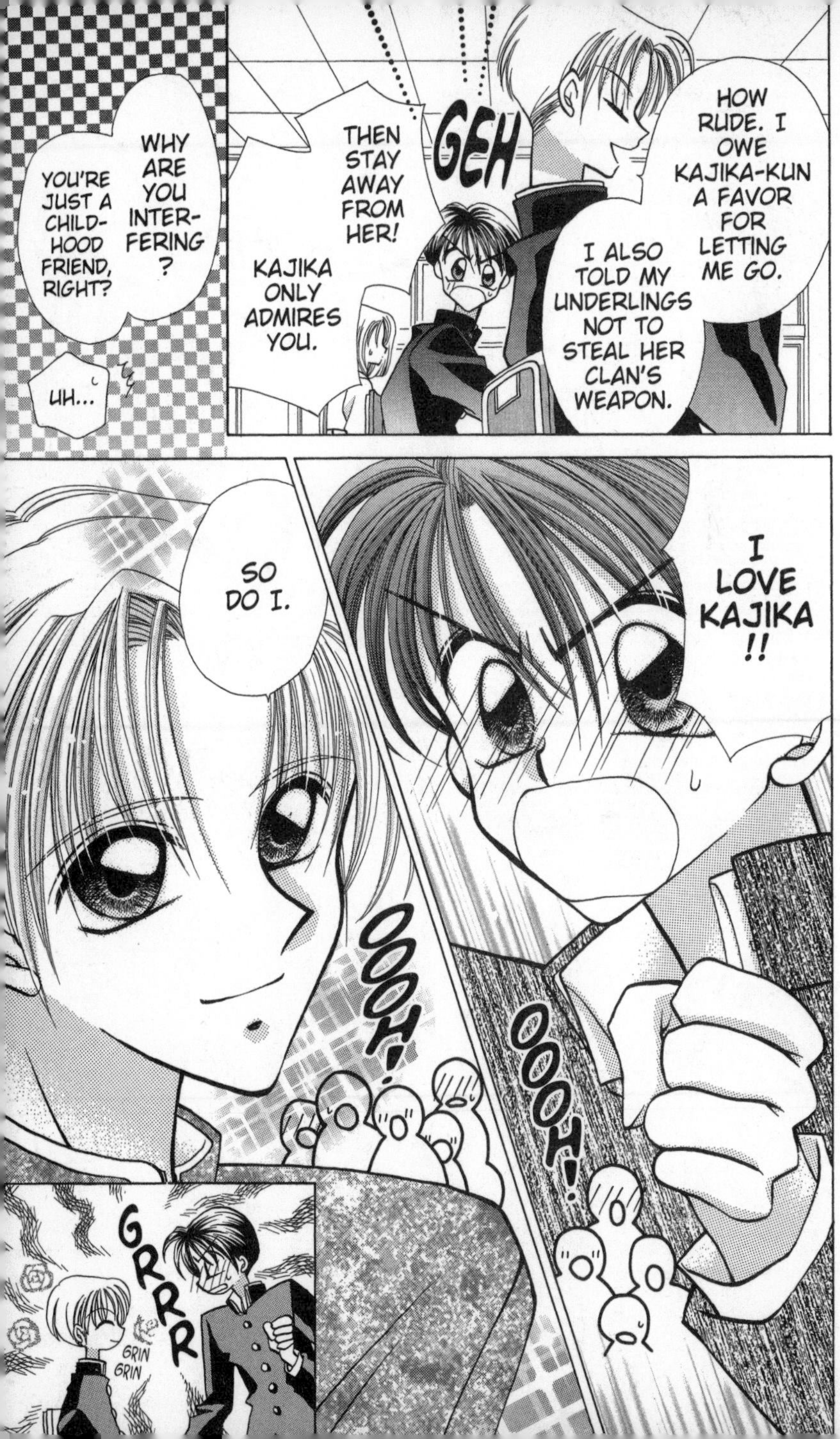
HOW RUDE. I OWE KAJIKA-KUN A FAVOR FOR LETTING ME GO.
I ALSO TOLD MY UNDERLINGS NOT TO STEAL HER CLAN'S WEAPON.
GEH
THEN STAY AWAY FROM HER!
KAJIKA ONLY ADMIRES YOU.
WHY ARE YOU INTERFERING?
YOU'RE JUST A CHILDHOOD FRIEND, RIGHT?
UH...
I LOVE KAJIKA!!
SO DO I.
OOOH!
OOOH!
GRRR
GRIN GRIN

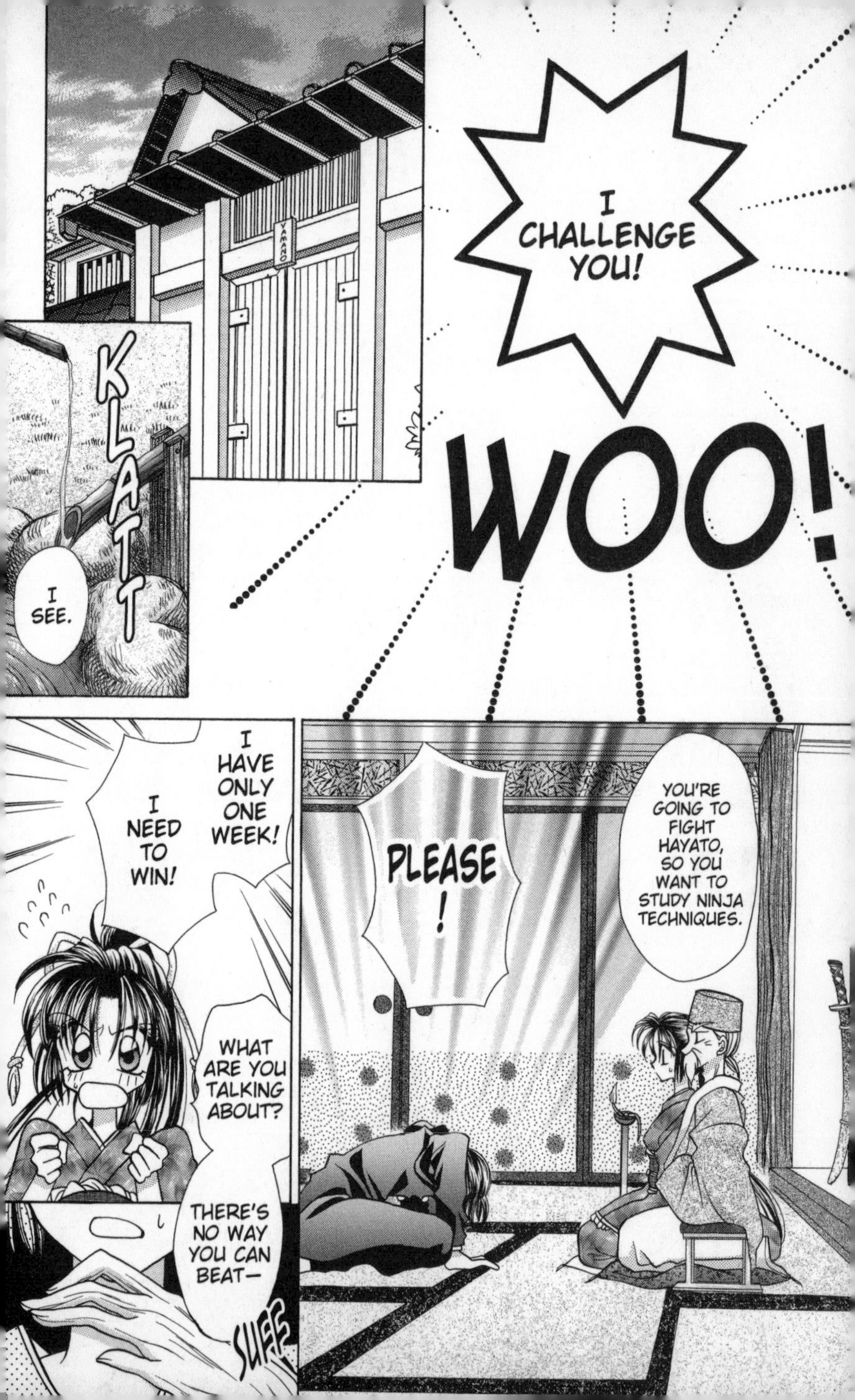
I CHALLENGE YOU!
WOO!
YAMANO
KLATT
I SEE.
YOU'RE GOING TO FIGHT HAYATO, SO YOU WANT TO STUDY NINJA TECHNIQUES.
PLEASE!
I HAVE ONLY ONE WEEK!
I NEED TO WIN!
WHAT ARE YOU TALKING ABOUT?
THERE'S NO WAY YOU CAN BEAT—
SUFF

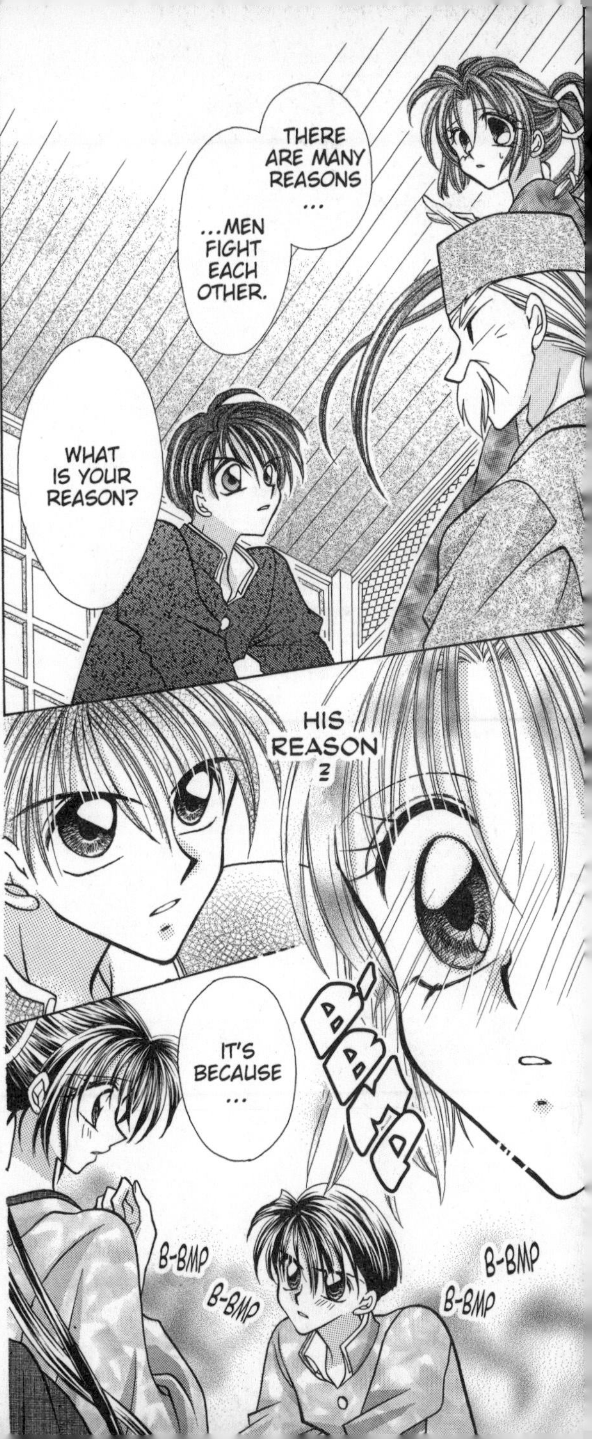
THERE ARE MANY REASONS ...
...MEN FIGHT EACH OTHER.
WHAT IS YOUR REASON?
HIS REASON?
IT'S BECAUSE ...
B-BMP
B-BMP
B-BMP
B-BMP

GOOD REVIEW?!

THE SERIAL
ARINA TANEMURA'S PENCHI DE SHAKIN ☆

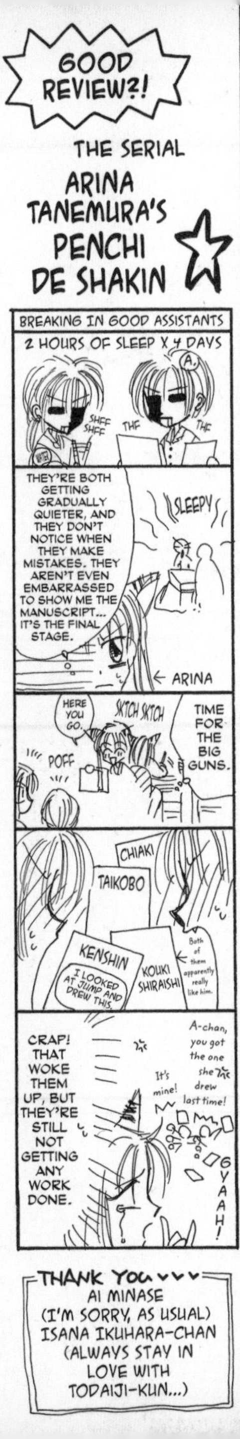
BREAKING IN GOOD ASSISTANTS
2 HOURS OF SLEEP X 4 DAYS
A.
SHFF SHFF
THF THF
THEY'RE BOTH GETTING GRADUALLY QUIETER, AND THEY DON'T NOTICE WHEN THEY MAKE MISTAKES. THEY AREN'T EVEN EMBARRASSED TO SHOW ME THE MANUSCRIPT... IT'S THE FINAL STAGE.
SLEEPY
← ARINA
HERE YOU GO.
SKTCH SKTCH
TIME FOR THE BIG GUNS.
POFF
CHIAKI
TAIKOBO
KENSHIN
I LOOKED AT JUMP AND DREW THIS.
KOUKI SHIRAISHI
Both of them apparently really like him.
CRAP! THAT WOKE THEM UP, BUT THEY'RE STILL NOT GETTING ANY WORK DONE.
A-chan, you got the one she drew last time!
It's mine!
GYAAAH!

THANK YOU ♥♥♥
AI MINASE
(I'M SORRY, AS USUAL)
ISANA IKUHARA-CHAN
(ALWAYS STAY IN LOVE WITH TODAIJI-KUN...)

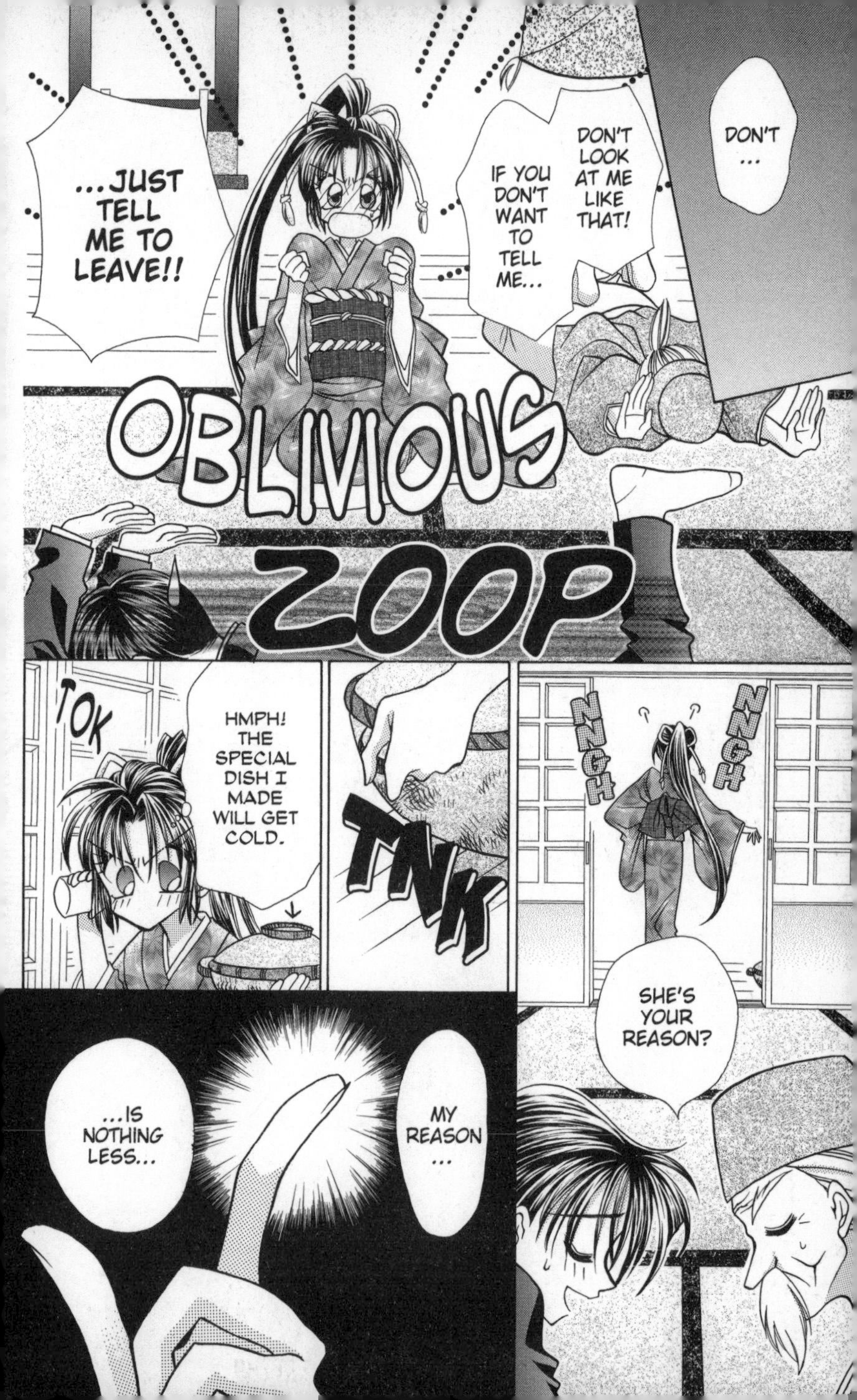
DON'T ...
DON'T LOOK AT ME LIKE THAT!
IF YOU DON'T WANT TO TELL ME...
...JUST TELL ME TO LEAVE!!
OBLIVIOUS
ZOOP
NNGH
NNGH
TNK
TOK
HMPH! THE SPECIAL DISH I MADE WILL GET COLD.
SHE'S YOUR REASON?
MY REASON ...
...IS NOTHING LESS...

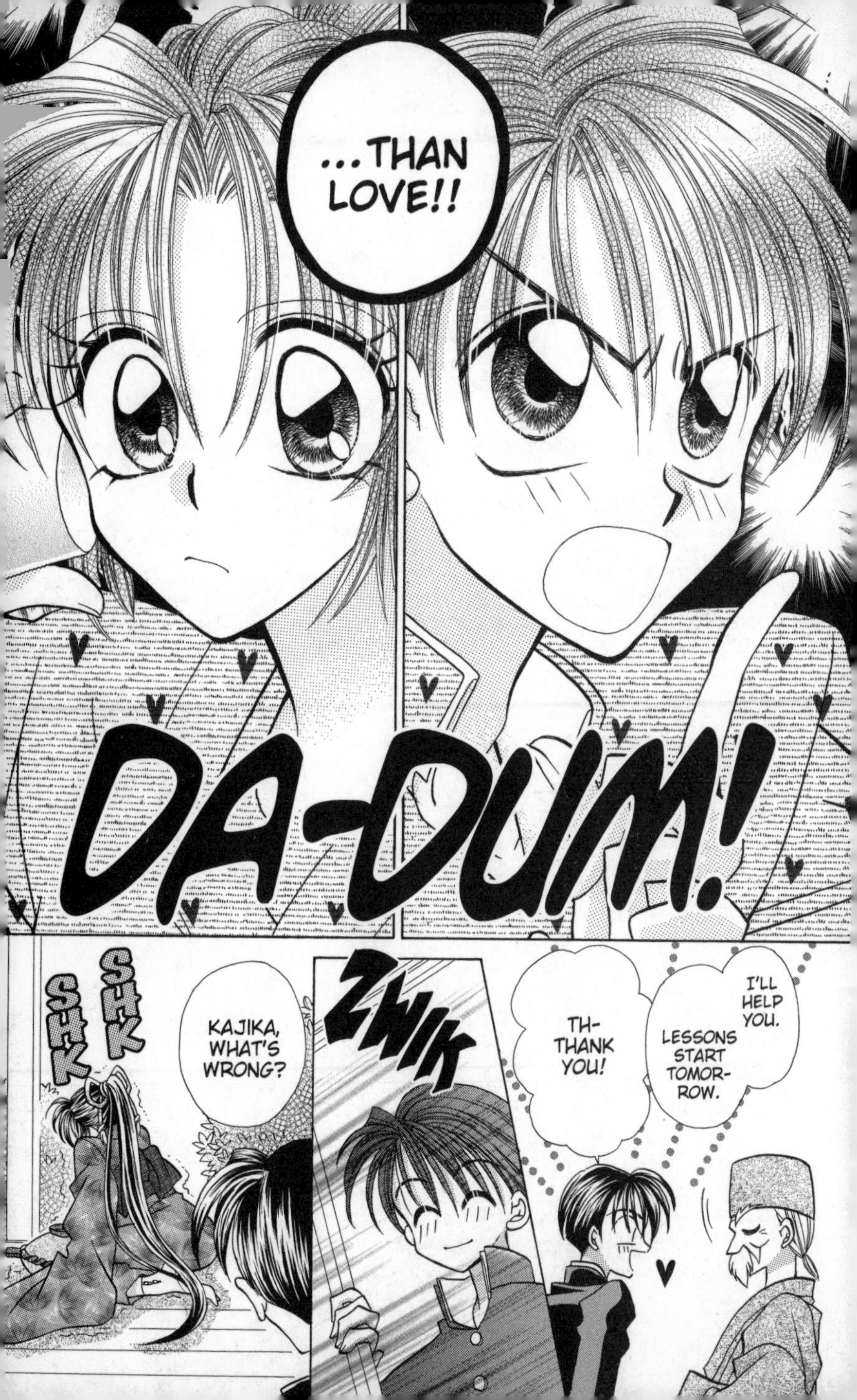
...THAN LOVE!!
DA-DUM!
I'LL HELP YOU.
LESSONS START TOMORROW.
TH-THANK YOU!
ZWIK
KAJIKA, WHAT'S WRONG?
SHK SHK

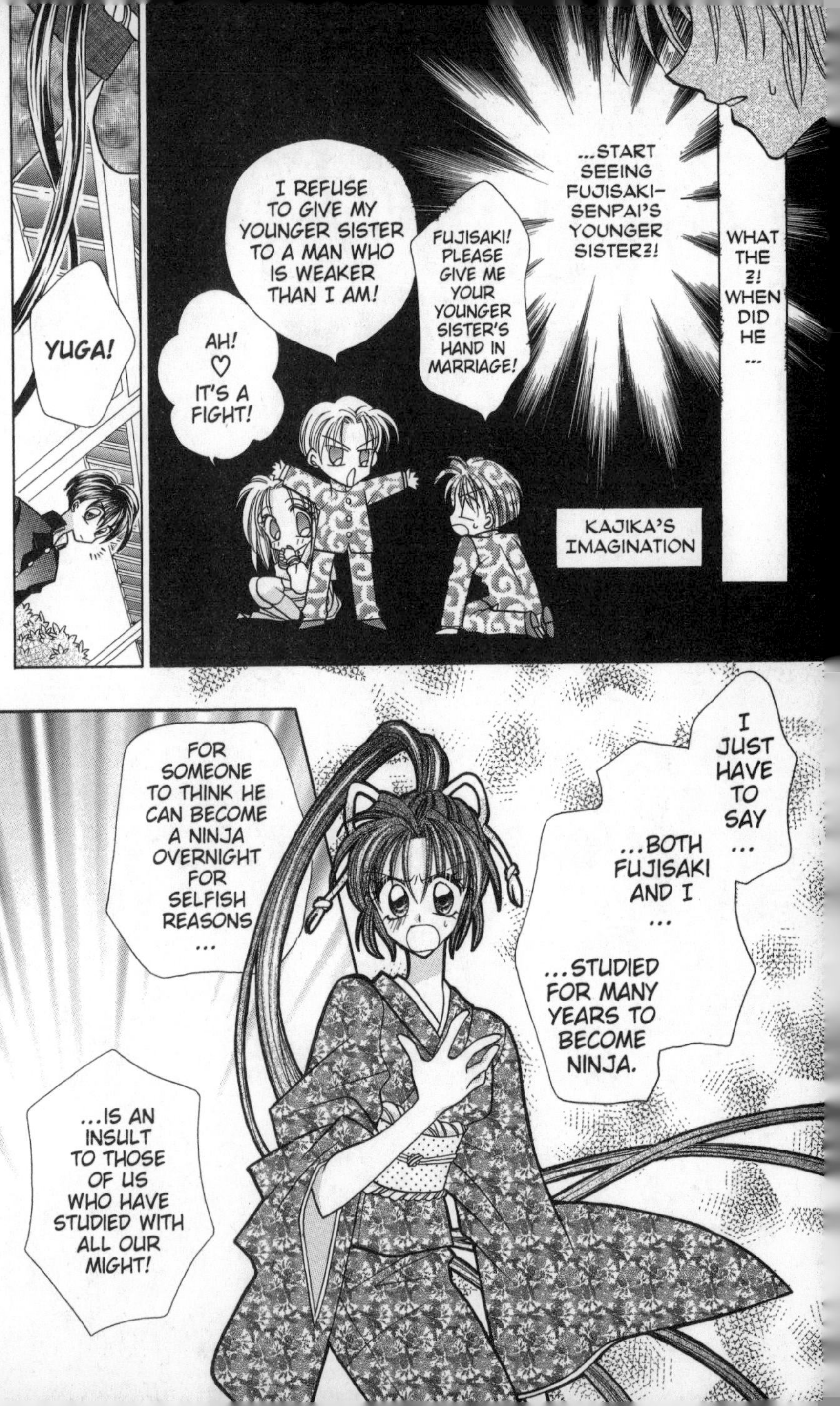
WHAT THE ?! WHEN DID HE ...
...START SEEING FUJISAKI-SENPAI'S YOUNGER SISTER?!
FUJISAKI! PLEASE GIVE ME YOUR YOUNGER SISTER'S HAND IN MARRIAGE!
I REFUSE TO GIVE MY YOUNGER SISTER TO A MAN WHO IS WEAKER THAN I AM!
AH! ♡ IT'S A FIGHT!
KAJIKA'S IMAGINATION
YUGA!
I JUST HAVE TO SAY ...
...BOTH FUJISAKI AND I ...
...STUDIED FOR MANY YEARS TO BECOME NINJA.
FOR SOMEONE TO THINK HE CAN BECOME A NINJA OVERNIGHT FOR SELFISH REASONS ...
...IS AN INSULT TO THOSE OF US WHO HAVE STUDIED WITH ALL OUR MIGHT!

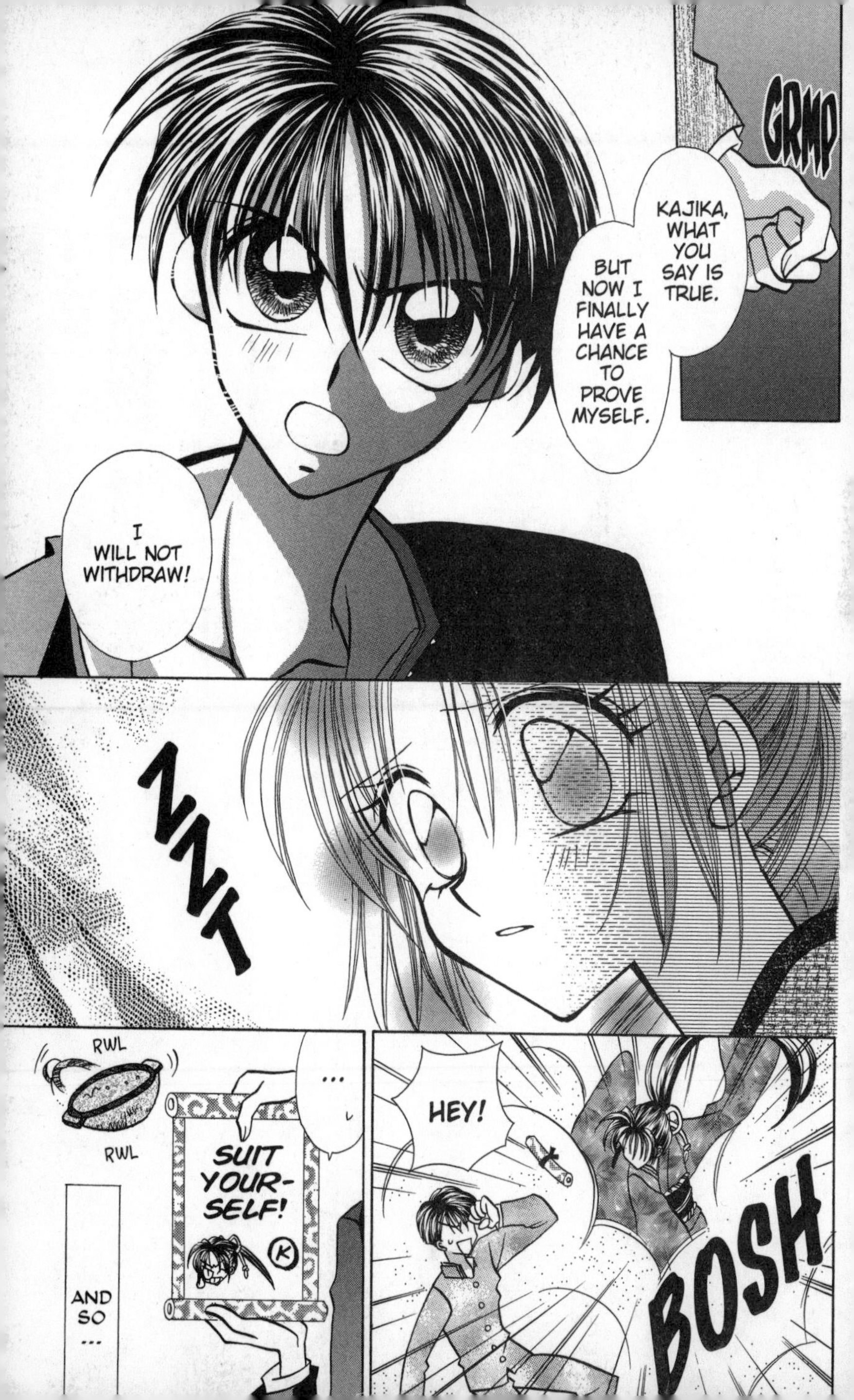
GRMP
KAJIKA, WHAT YOU SAY IS TRUE.
BUT NOW I FINALLY HAVE A CHANCE TO PROVE MYSELF.
I WILL NOT WITHDRAW!
NNNT
HEY!
BOSH
...
RWL
RWL
SUIT YOUR-SELF!
K
AND SO ...

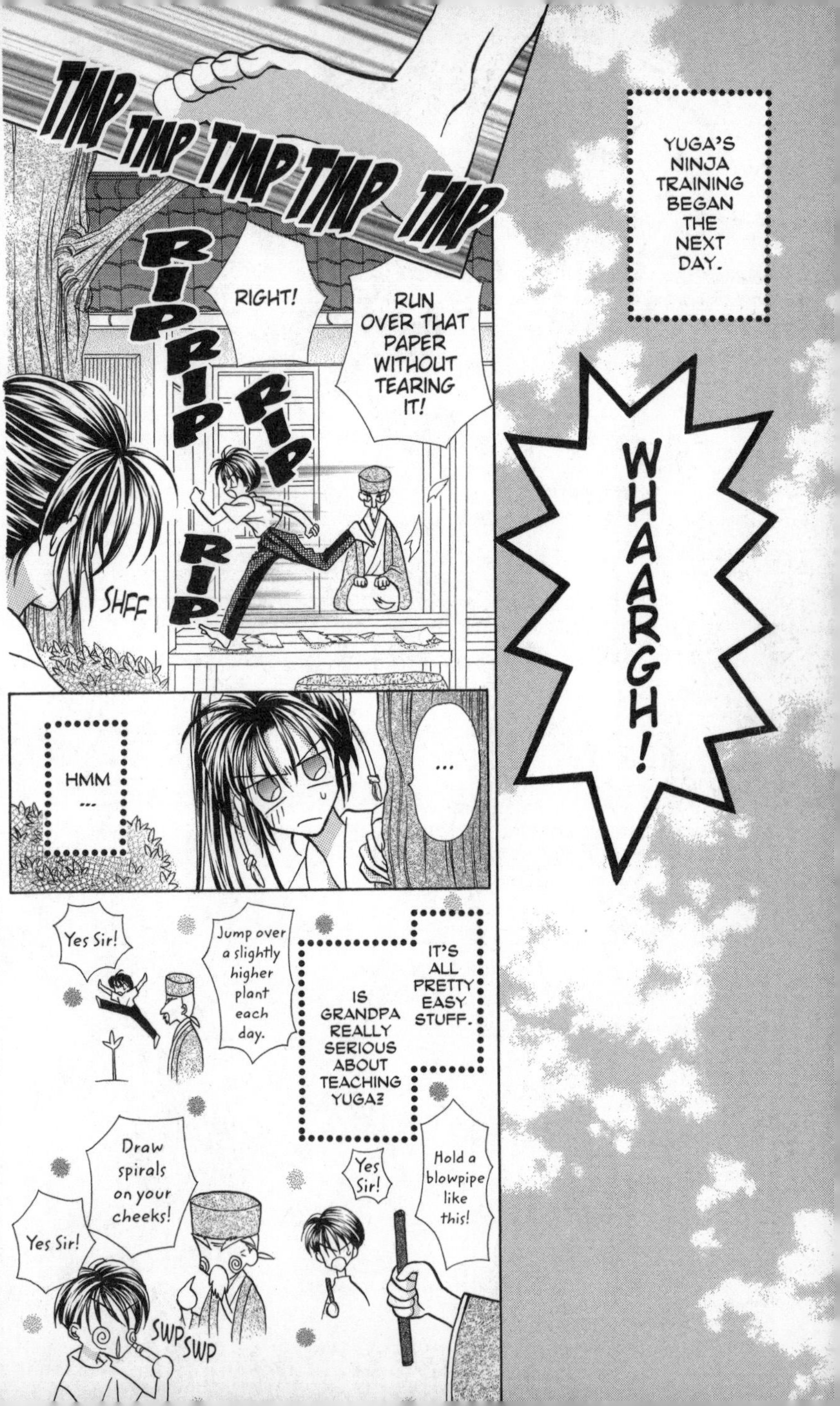
YUGA'S NINJA TRAINING BEGAN THE NEXT DAY.
WHAARGH!
TMP TMP TMP TMP TMP
RUN OVER THAT PAPER WITHOUT TEARING IT!
RIGHT!
RIP RIP RIP RIP
SHFF
...
HMM...
IT'S ALL PRETTY EASY STUFF.
IS GRANDPA REALLY SERIOUS ABOUT TEACHING YUGA?
Jump over a slightly higher plant each day.
Yes Sir!
Hold a blowpipe like this!
Yes Sir!
Draw spirals on your cheeks!
Yes Sir!
SWP SWP

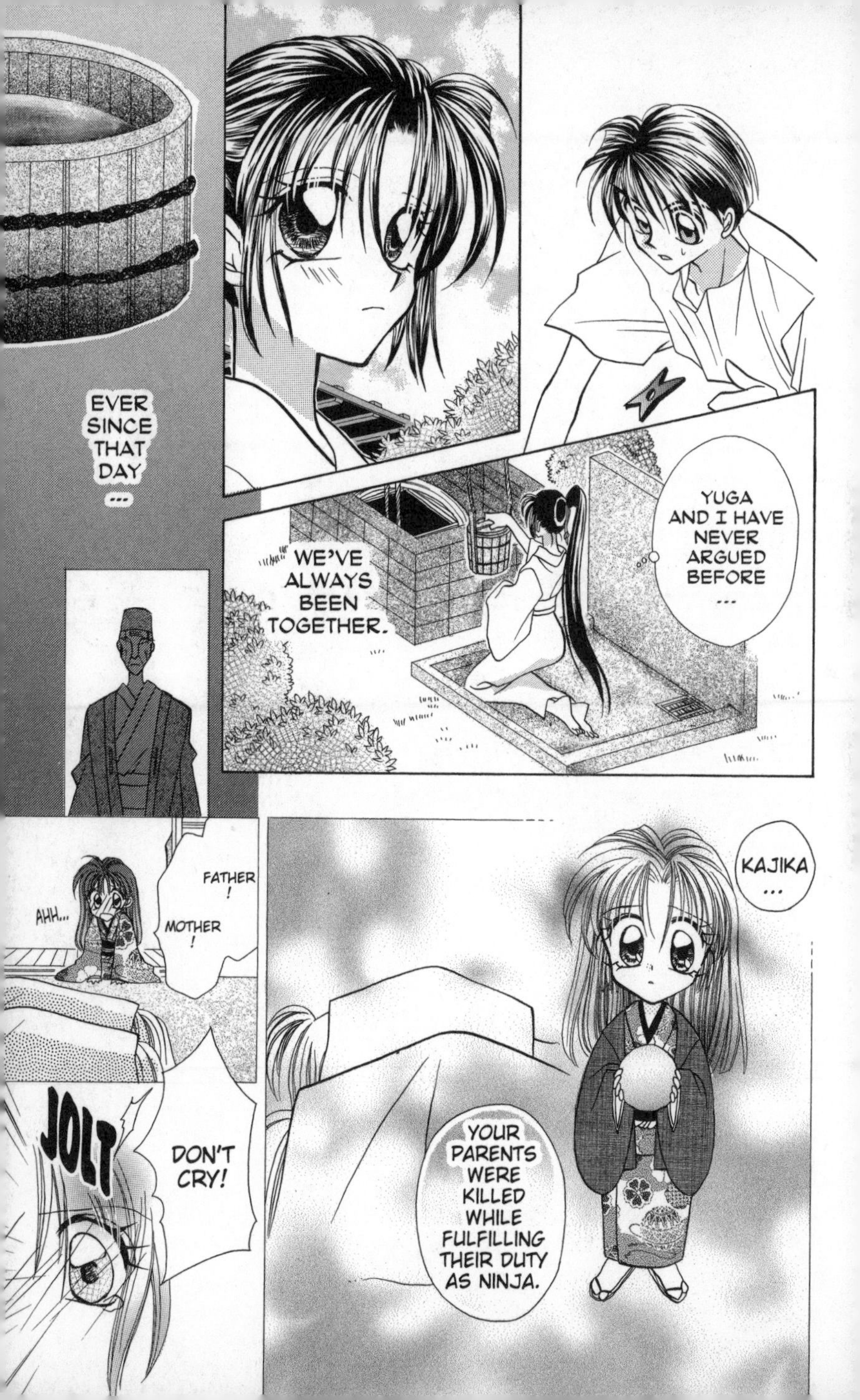
YUGA AND I HAVE NEVER ARGUED BEFORE ...
WE'VE ALWAYS BEEN TOGETHER.
EVER SINCE THAT DAY ---
KAJIKA ...
YOUR PARENTS WERE KILLED WHILE FULFILLING THEIR DUTY AS NINJA.
FATHER!
MOTHER!
AHH...
JOLT
DON'T CRY!

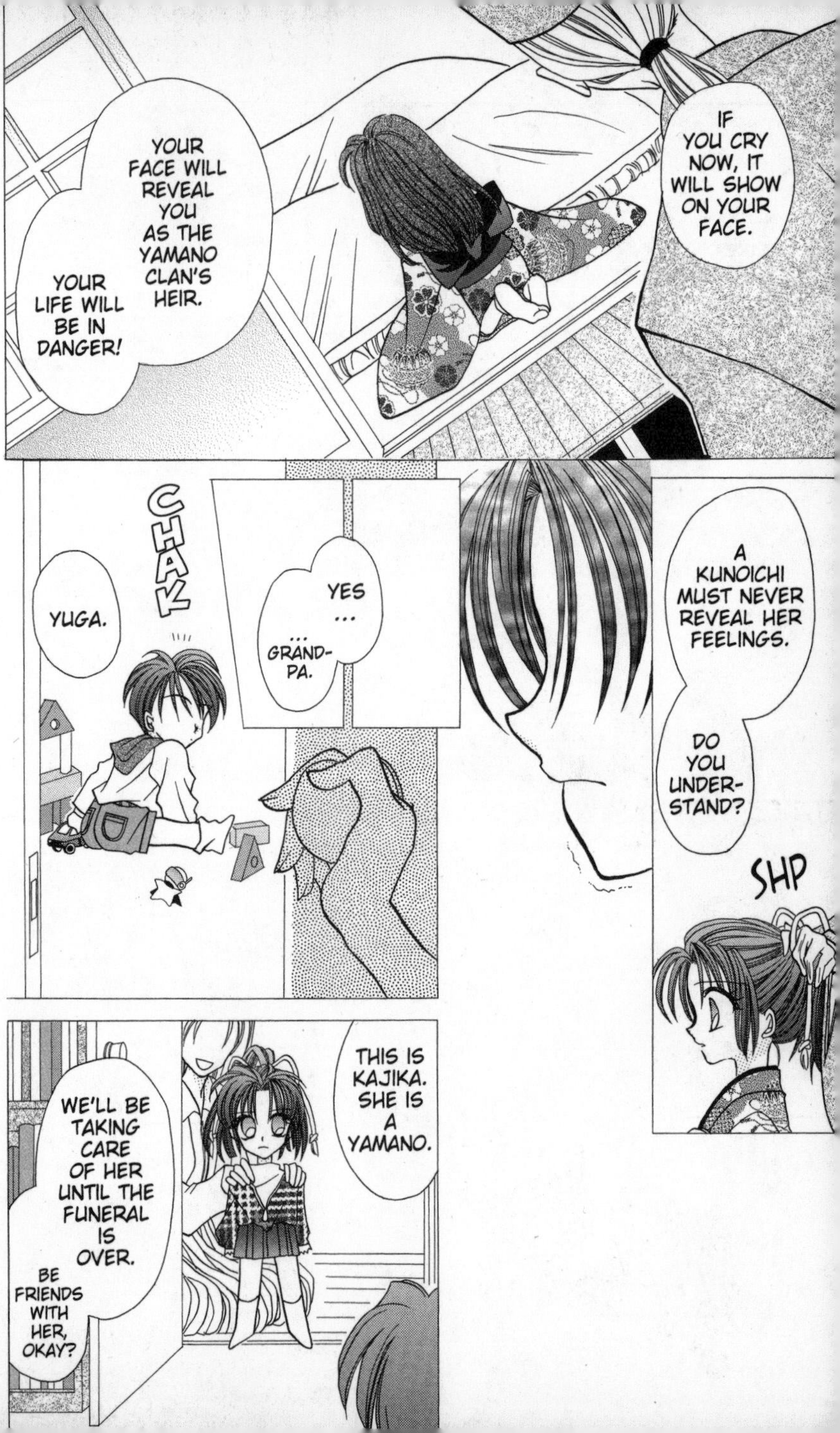
IF YOU CRY NOW, IT WILL SHOW ON YOUR FACE.
YOUR FACE WILL REVEAL YOU AS THE YAMANO CLAN'S HEIR.
YOUR LIFE WILL BE IN DANGER!
A KUNOICHI MUST NEVER REVEAL HER FEELINGS.
DO YOU UNDER-STAND?
SHP
CHAK
YES ... ... GRAND-PA.
YUGA.
THIS IS KAJIKA. SHE IS A YAMANO.
WE'LL BE TAKING CARE OF HER UNTIL THE FUNERAL IS OVER.
BE FRIENDS WITH HER, OKAY?

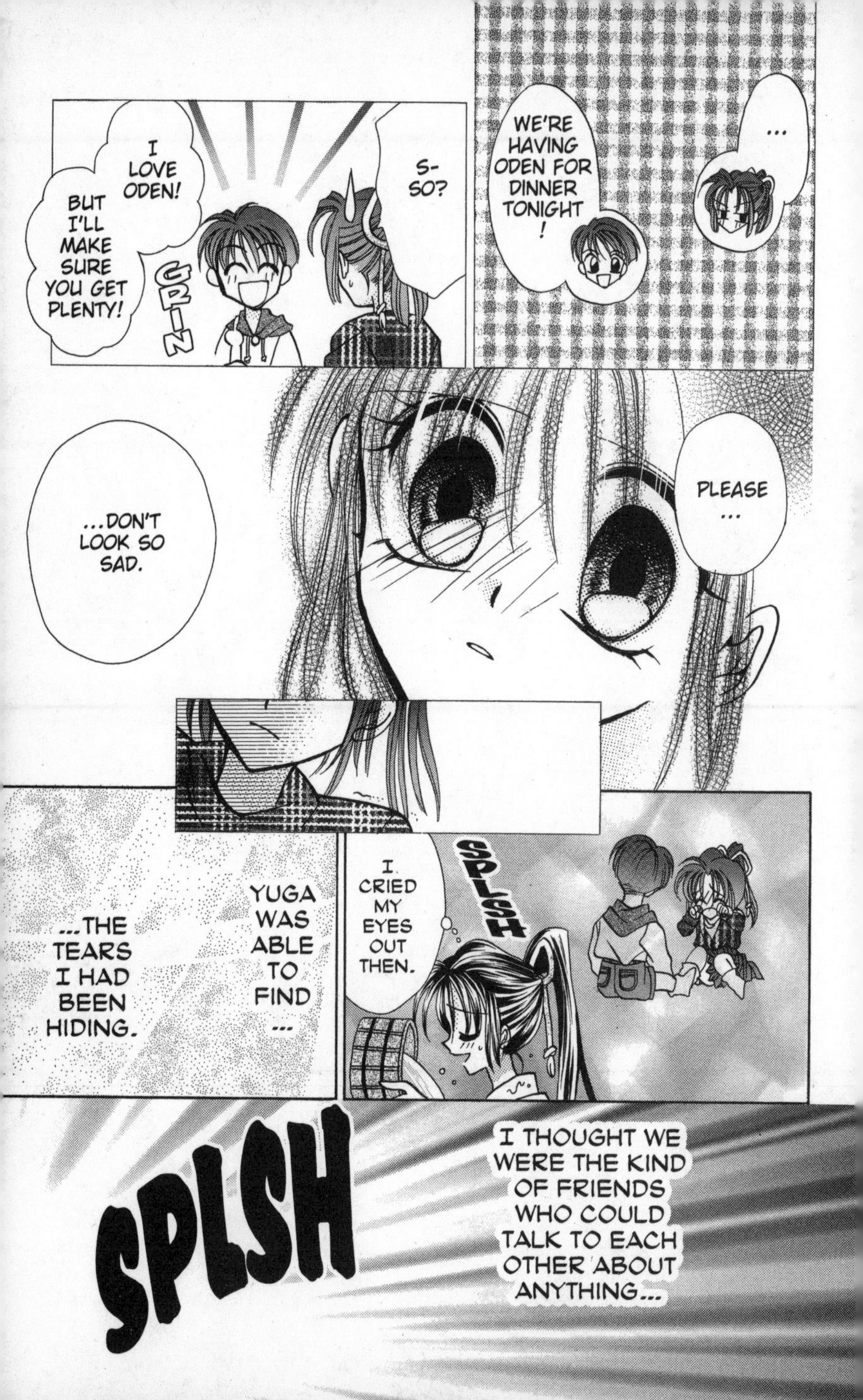
...
WE'RE HAVING ODEN FOR DINNER TONIGHT!
S-SO?
I LOVE ODEN!
BUT I'LL MAKE SURE YOU GET PLENTY!
GRIN
PLEASE...
...DON'T LOOK SO SAD.
SPLSH
I CRIED MY EYES OUT THEN.
YUGA WAS ABLE TO FIND...
...THE TEARS I HAD BEEN HIDING.
I THOUGHT WE WERE THE KIND OF FRIENDS WHO COULD TALK TO EACH OTHER ABOUT ANYTHING...
SPLSH

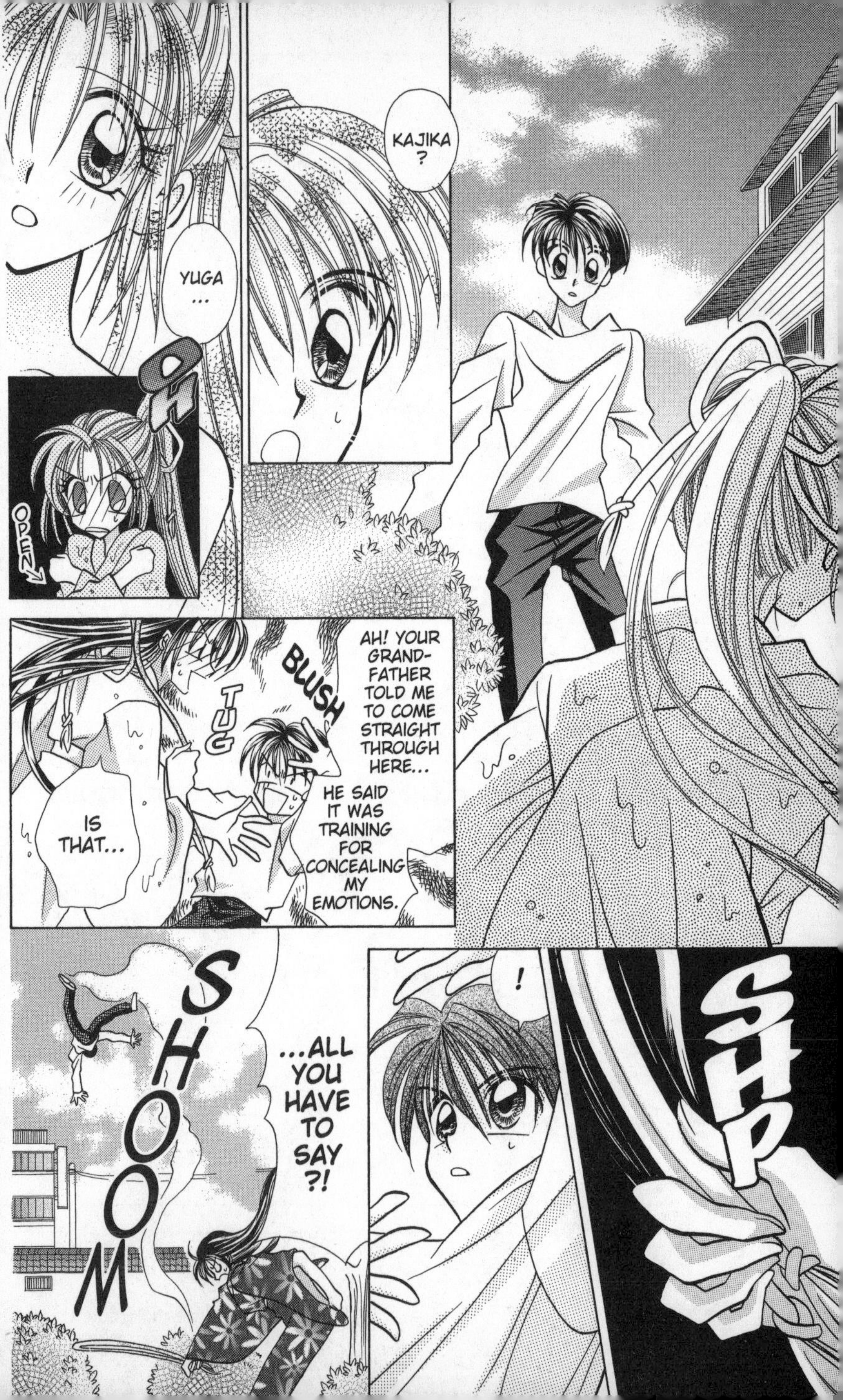
KAJIKA?
YUGA...
OH
OPEN
AH! YOUR GRAND-FATHER TOLD ME TO COME STRAIGHT THROUGH HERE...
HE SAID IT WAS TRAINING FOR CONCEALING MY EMOTIONS.
BLUSH
TUG
IS THAT...
!
SHP
...ALL YOU HAVE TO SAY?!
SHOOOM

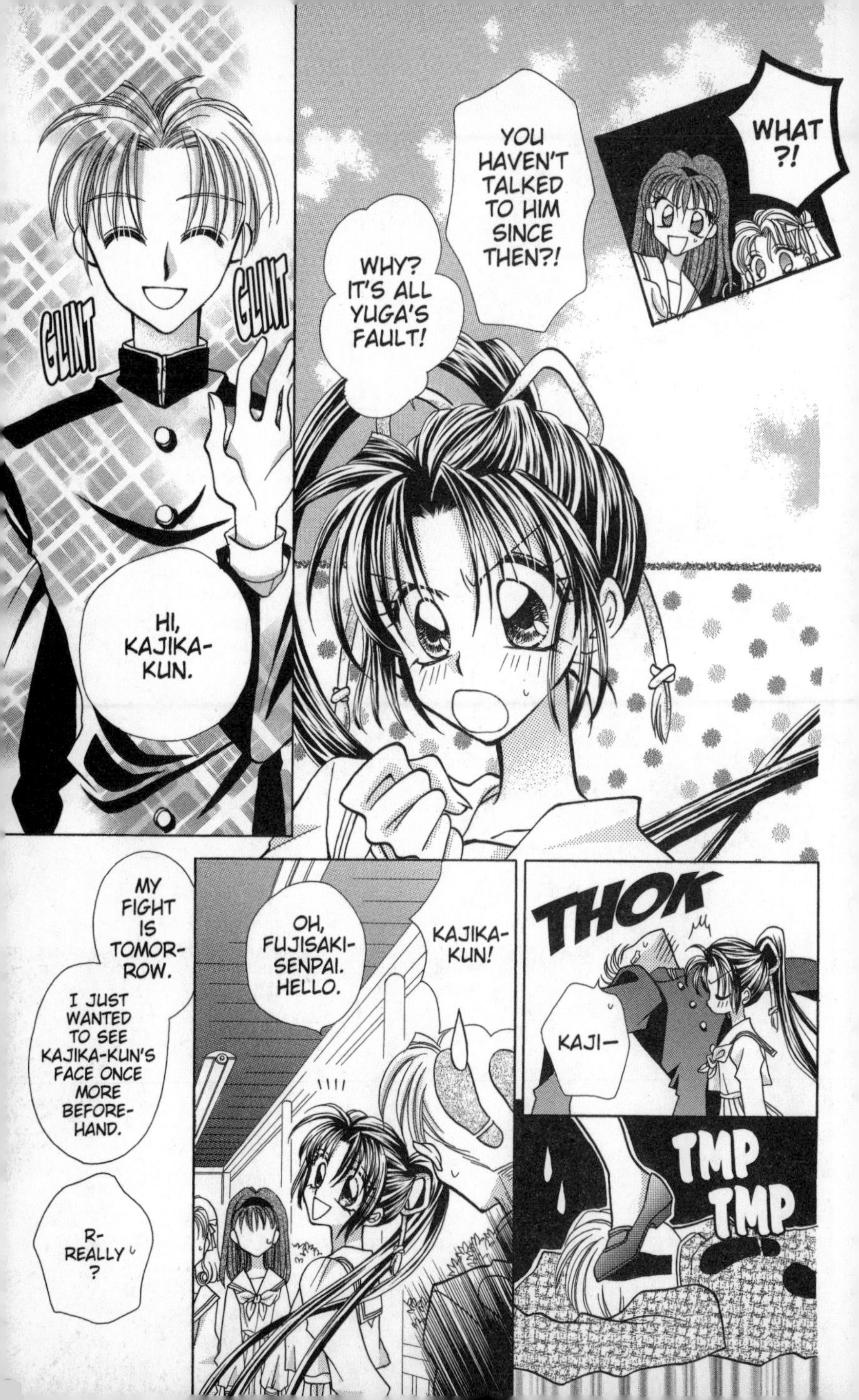
WHAT?!
YOU HAVEN'T TALKED TO HIM SINCE THEN?!
WHY? IT'S ALL YUGA'S FAULT!
GLINT
GLINT
HI, KAJIKA-KUN.
THOK
KAJI—
TMP TMP
KAJIKA-KUN!
OH, FUJISAKI-SENPAI. HELLO.
MY FIGHT IS TOMORROW.
I JUST WANTED TO SEE KAJIKA-KUN'S FACE ONCE MORE BEFOREHAND.
R-REALLY?

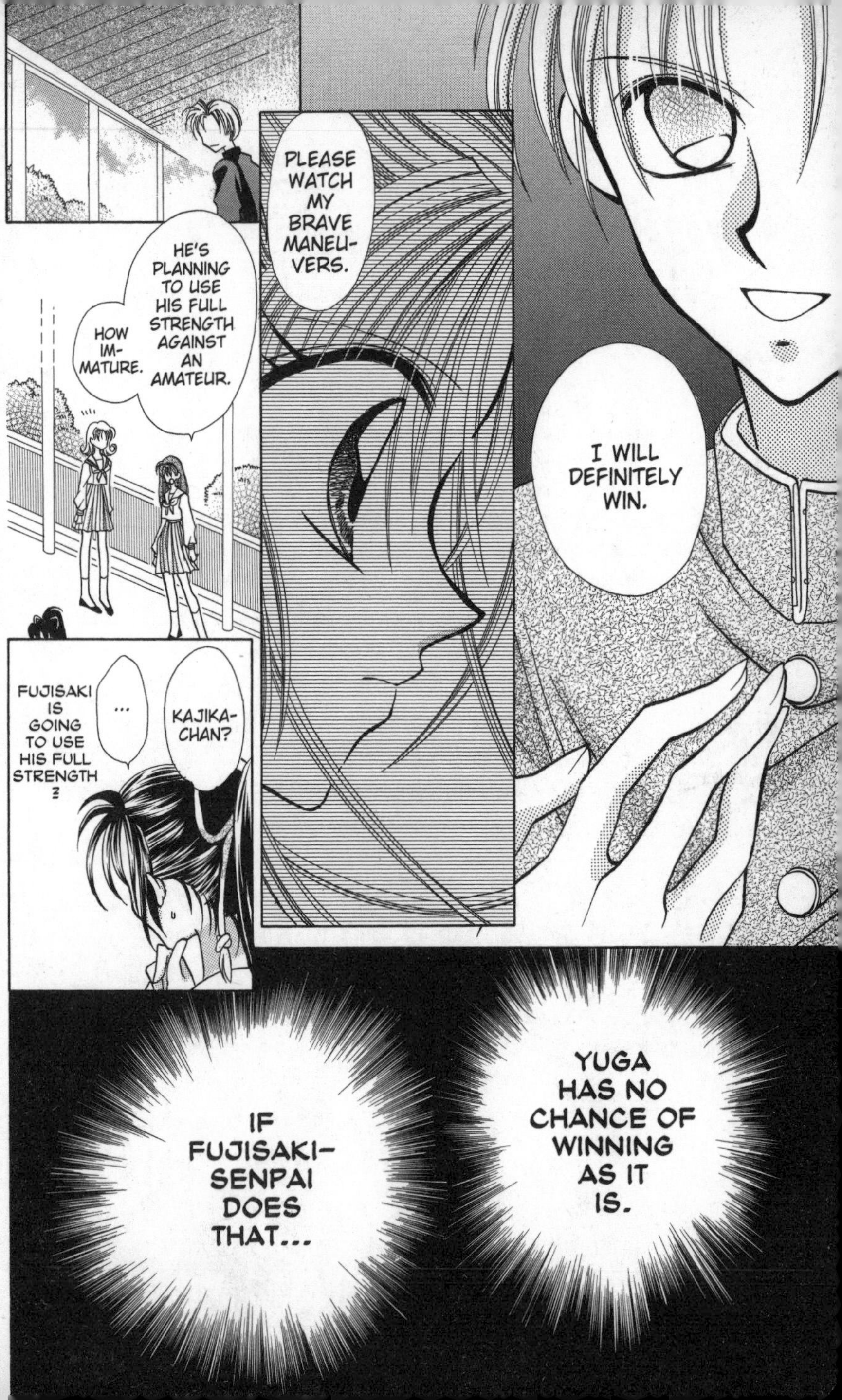
I WILL DEFINITELY WIN.
PLEASE WATCH MY BRAVE MANEU-VERS.
HE'S PLANNING TO USE HIS FULL STRENGTH AGAINST AN AMATEUR.
HOW IM-MATURE.
KAJIKA-CHAN?
...
FUJISAKI IS GOING TO USE HIS FULL STRENGTH?
YUGA HAS NO CHANCE OF WINNING AS IT IS.
IF FUJISAKI-SENPAI DOES THAT...

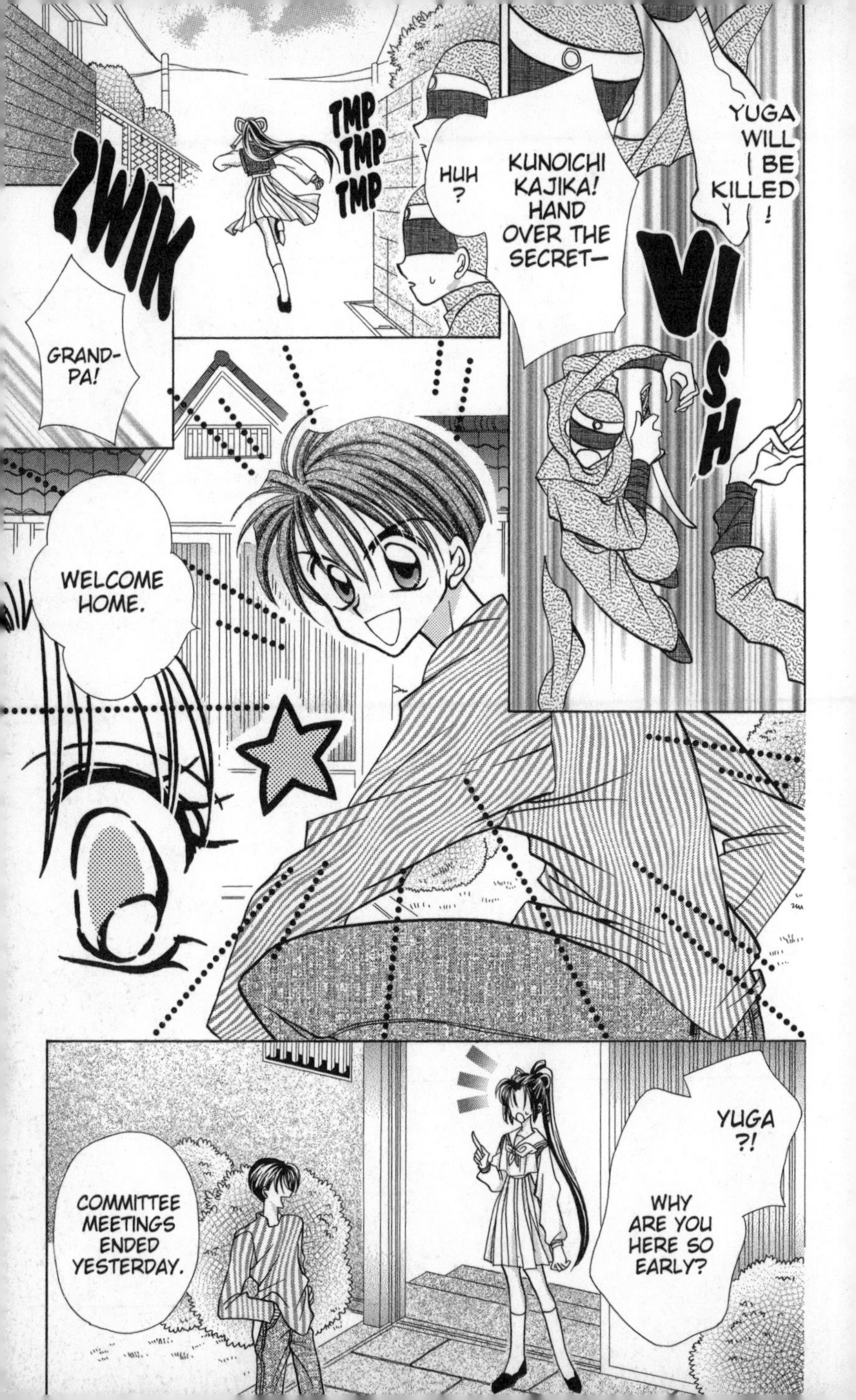
YUGA WILL BE KILLED!
VISH
KUNOICHI KAJIKA! HAND OVER THE SECRET—
HUH?
TMP TMP TMP
ZWIK
GRAND-PA!
WELCOME HOME.
YUGA?!
WHY ARE YOU HERE SO EARLY?
COMMITTEE MEETINGS ENDED YESTERDAY.

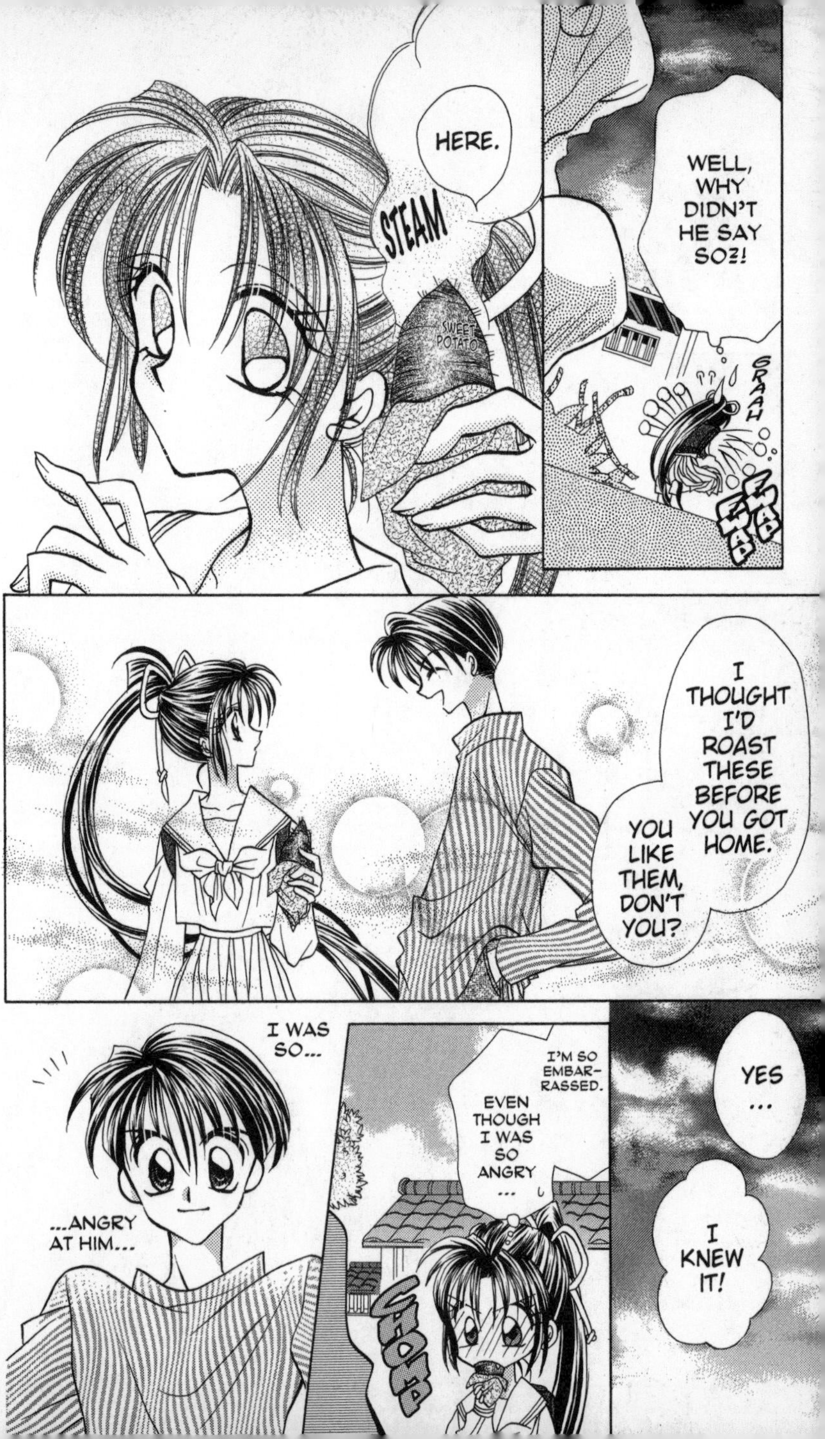
WELL, WHY DIDN'T HE SAY SO?!
GRAAH
GWAP GWAP
HERE.
STEAM
SWEET POTATO
I THOUGHT I'D ROAST THESE BEFORE YOU GOT HOME.
YOU LIKE THEM, DON'T YOU?
YES...
I KNEW IT!
I'M SO EMBARRASSED.
EVEN THOUGH I WAS SO ANGRY...
CHOMP
I WAS SO...
...ANGRY AT HIM...

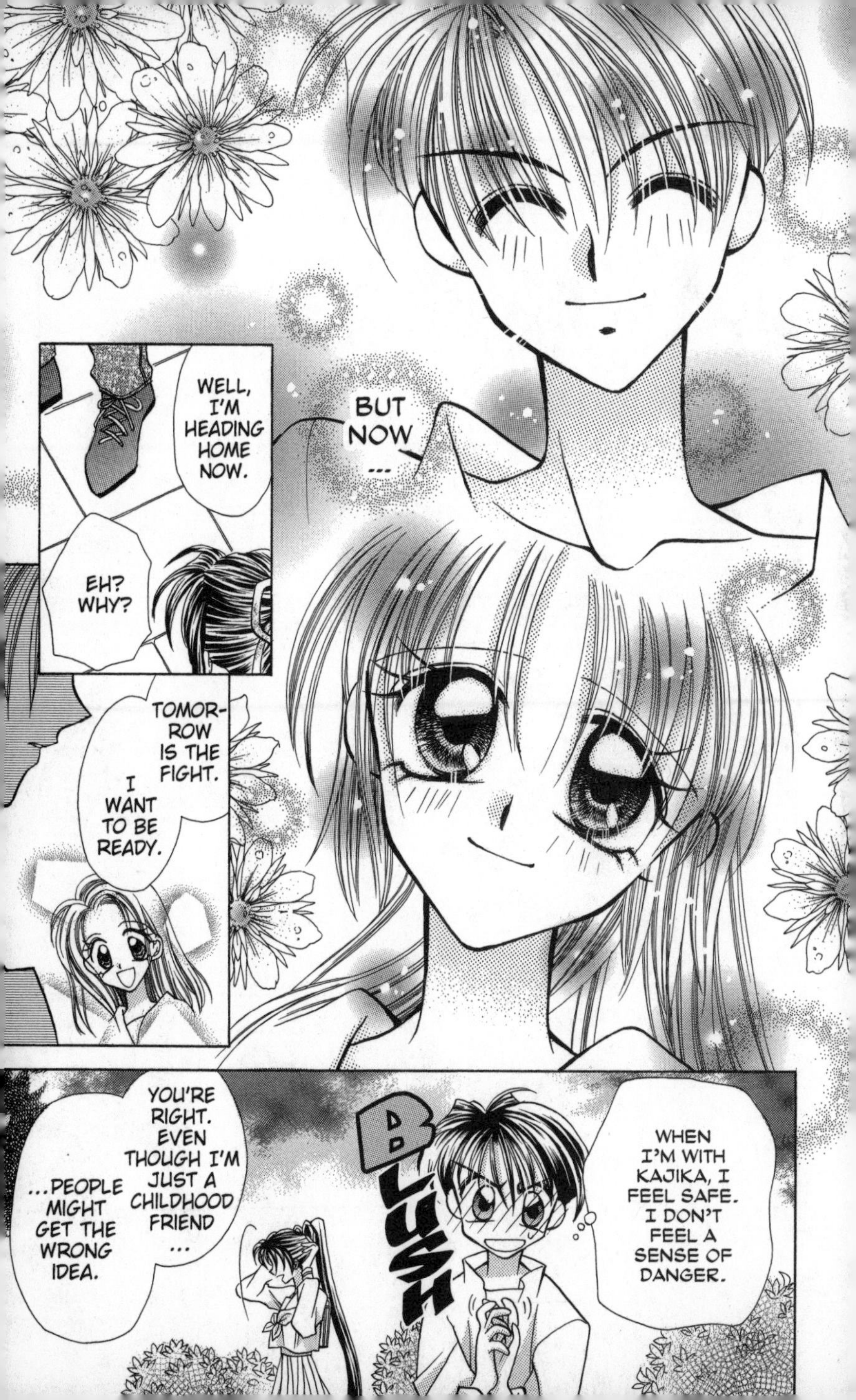
BUT NOW ...
WELL, I'M HEADING HOME NOW.
EH? WHY?
TOMORROW IS THE FIGHT.
I WANT TO BE READY.
WHEN I'M WITH KAJIKA, I FEEL SAFE. I DON'T FEEL A SENSE OF DANGER.
BLUSH
YOU'RE RIGHT. EVEN THOUGH I'M JUST A CHILDHOOD FRIEND ...
...PEOPLE MIGHT GET THE WRONG IDEA.

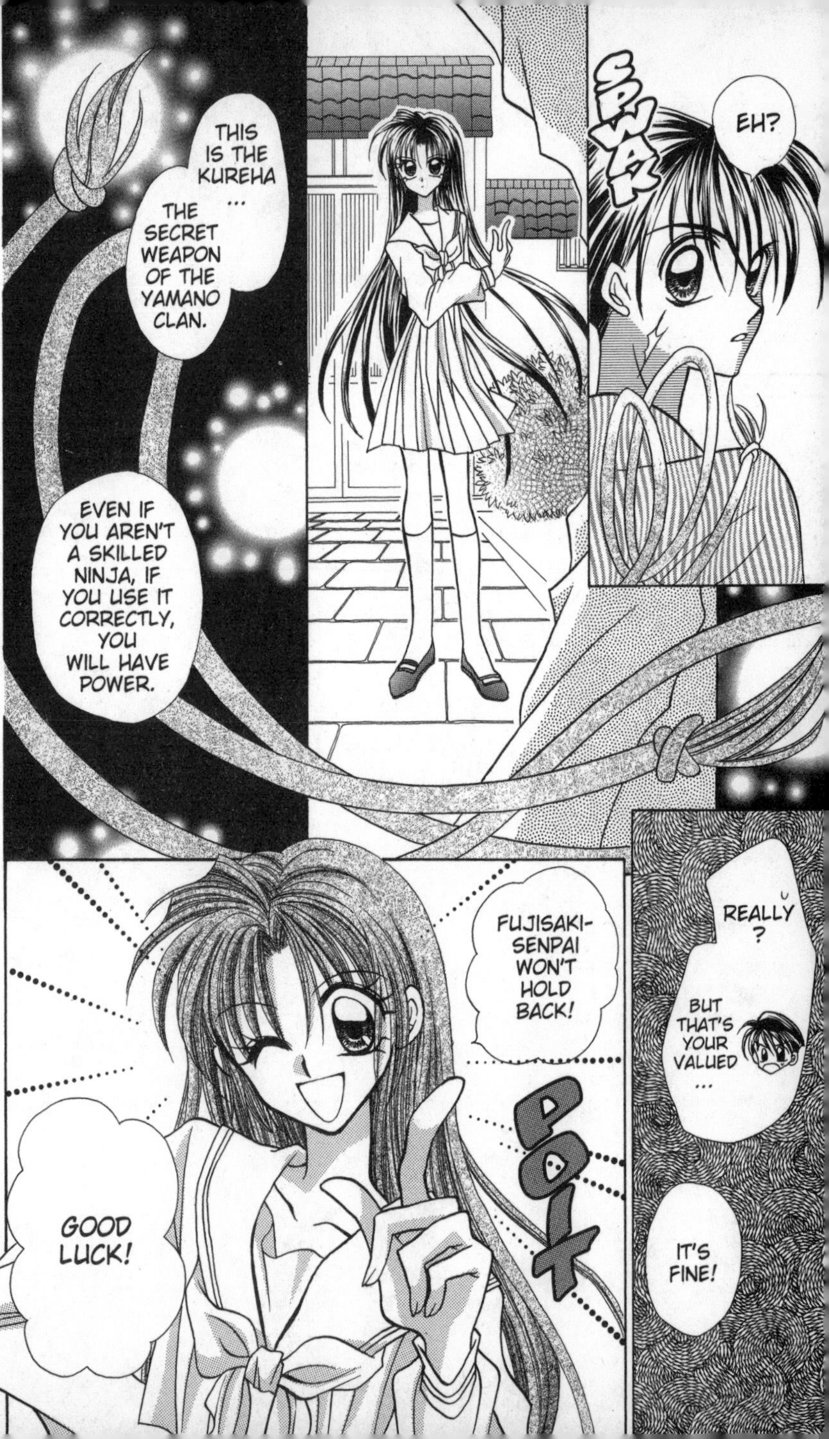
SPWAK
EH?
THIS IS THE KUREHA ...
THE SECRET WEAPON OF THE YAMANO CLAN.
EVEN IF YOU AREN'T A SKILLED NINJA, IF YOU USE IT CORRECTLY, YOU WILL HAVE POWER.
REALLY?
BUT THAT'S YOUR VALUED ...
IT'S FINE!
FUJISAKI-SENPAI WON'T HOLD BACK!
POK
GOOD LUCK!

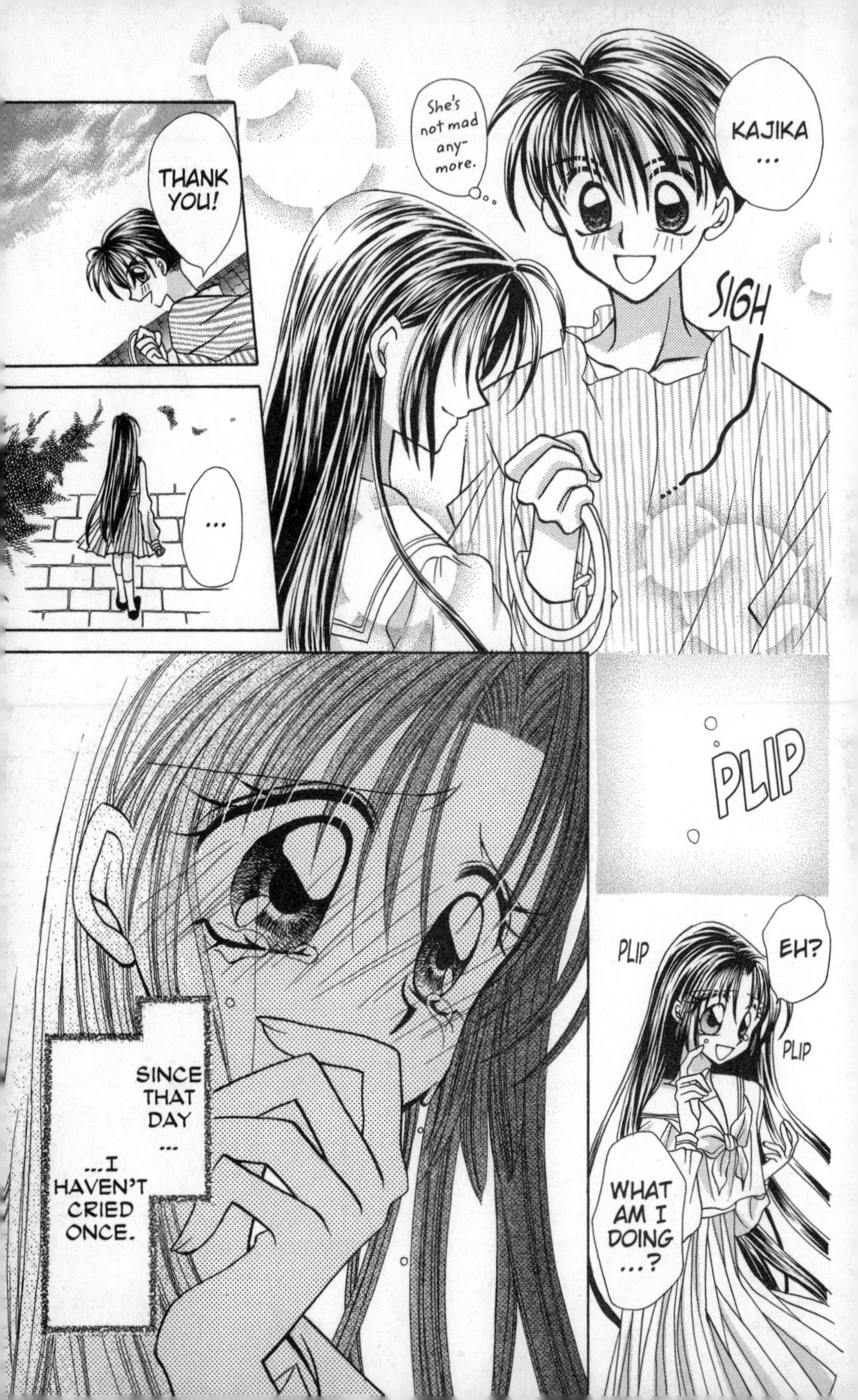
KAJIKA ...
She's not mad any-more.
SIGH
THANK YOU!
...
PLIP
EH?
PLIP
PLIP
WHAT AM I DOING ...?
SINCE THAT DAY ...
...I HAVEN'T CRIED ONCE.

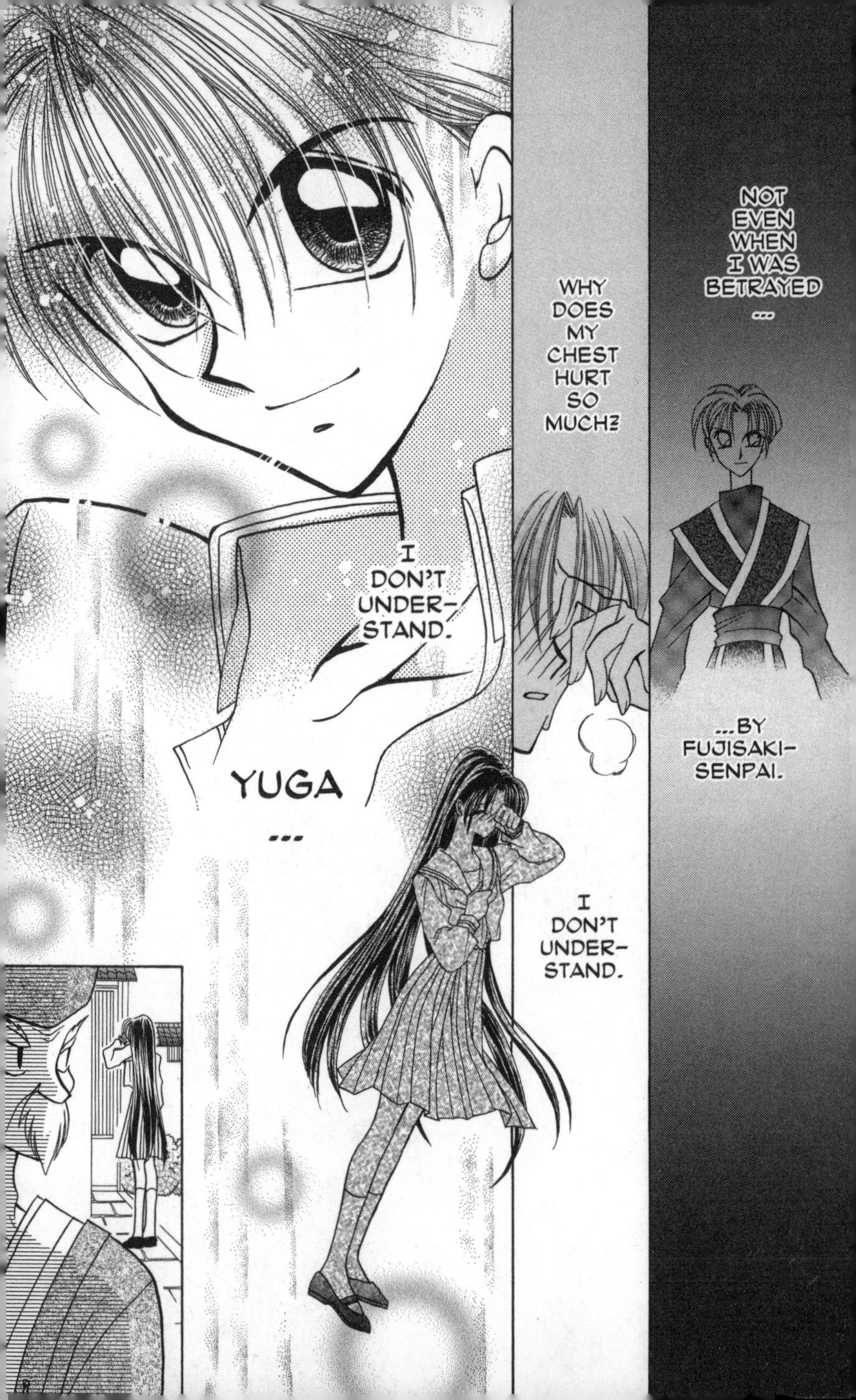
NOT EVEN WHEN I WAS BETRAYED ...
...BY FUJISAKI-SENPAI.
WHY DOES MY CHEST HURT SO MUCH?
I DON'T UNDERSTAND.
I DON'T UNDER-STAND.
YUGA ...

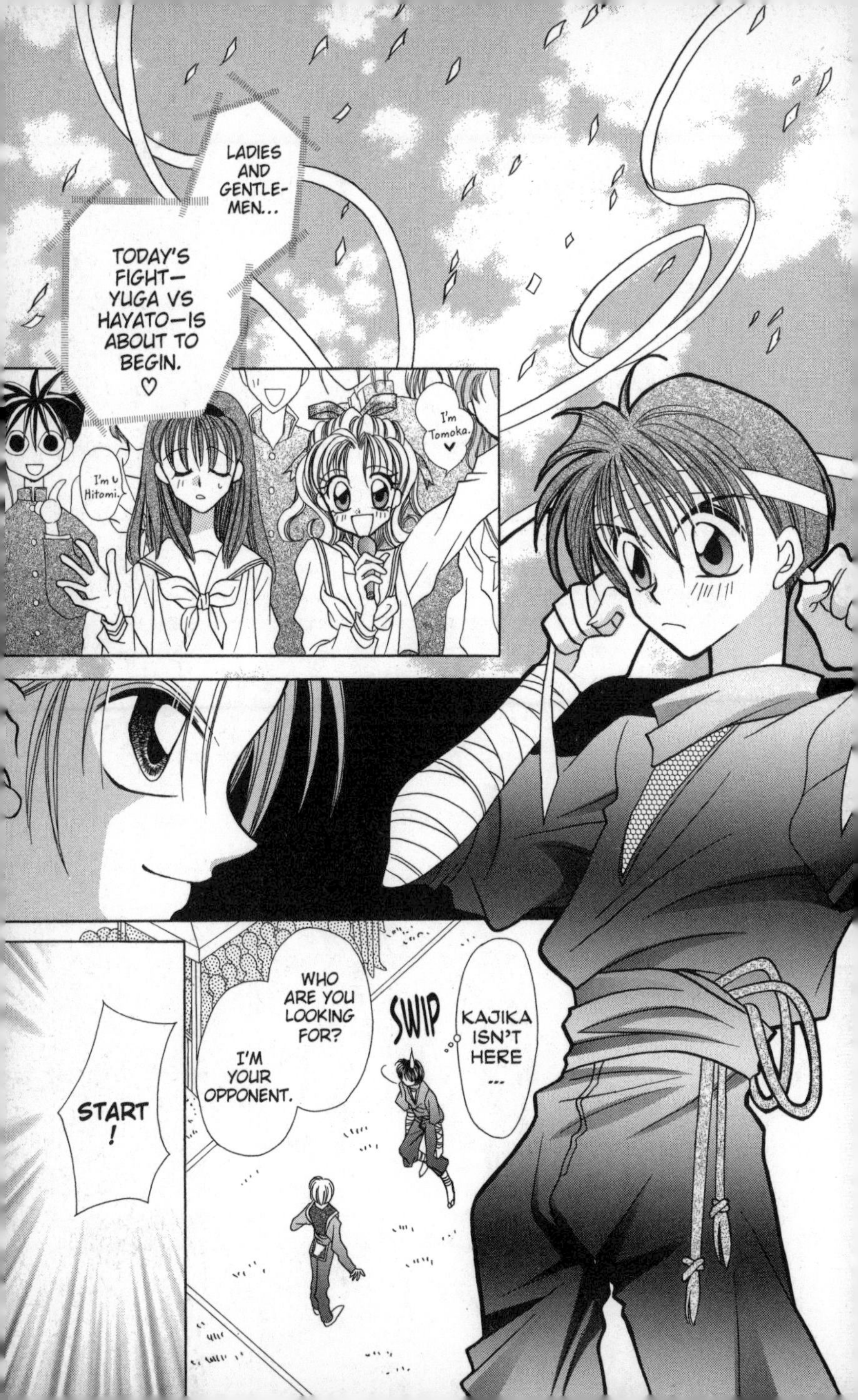
LADIES AND GENTLE-MEN...
TODAY'S FIGHT—YUGA VS HAYATO—IS ABOUT TO BEGIN. ♡
I'm Tomoka. ♥
I'm Hitomi.
KAJIKA ISN'T HERE ...
SWIP
WHO ARE YOU LOOKING FOR?
I'M YOUR OPPONENT.
START!

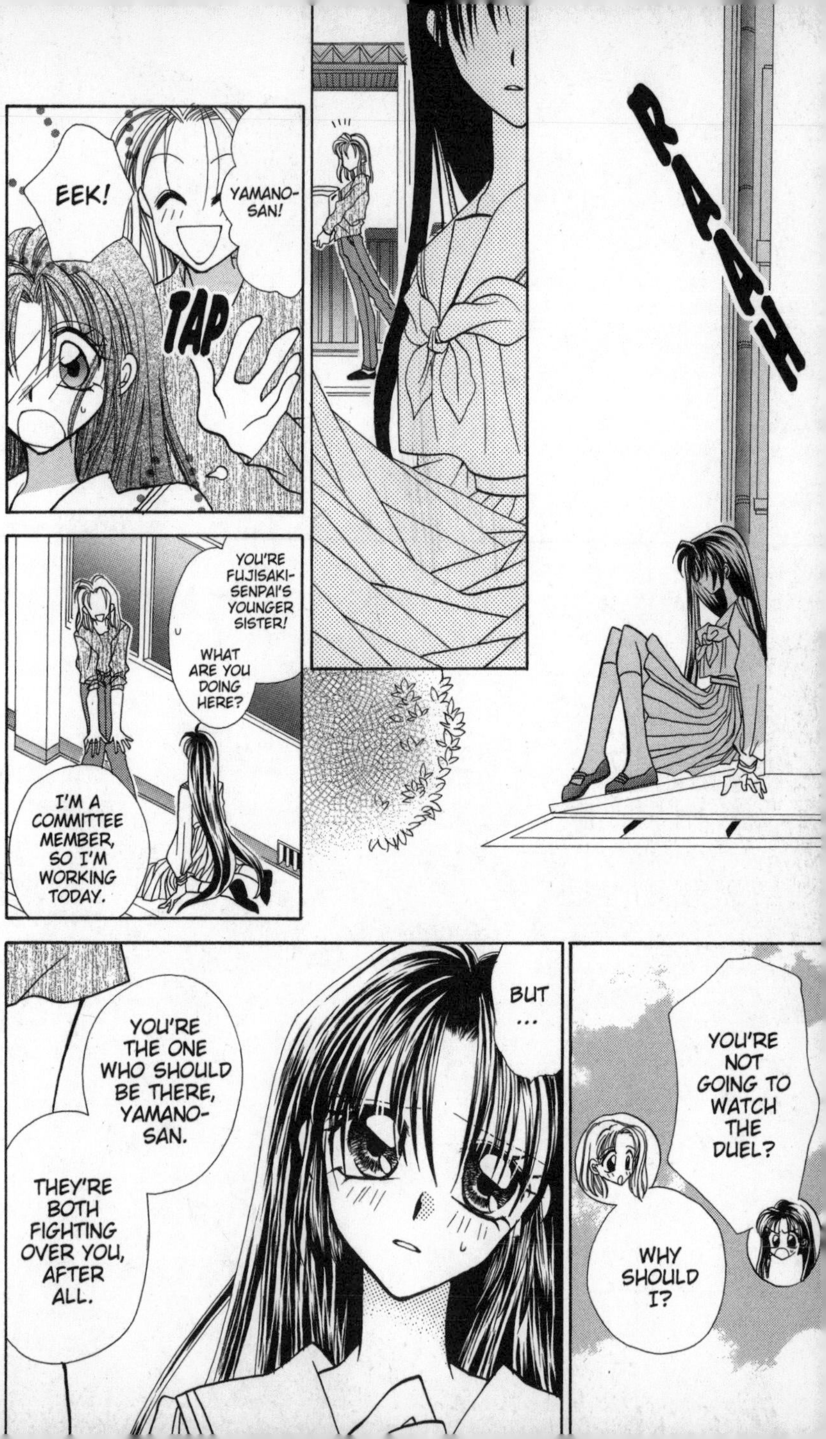
RAAAH
YAMANO-SAN!
TAP
EEK!
YOU'RE FUJISAKI-SENPAI'S YOUNGER SISTER!
WHAT ARE YOU DOING HERE?
I'M A COMMITTEE MEMBER, SO I'M WORKING TODAY.
YOU'RE NOT GOING TO WATCH THE DUEL?
WHY SHOULD I?
BUT ...
YOU'RE THE ONE WHO SHOULD BE THERE, YAMANO-SAN.
THEY'RE BOTH FIGHTING OVER YOU, AFTER ALL.

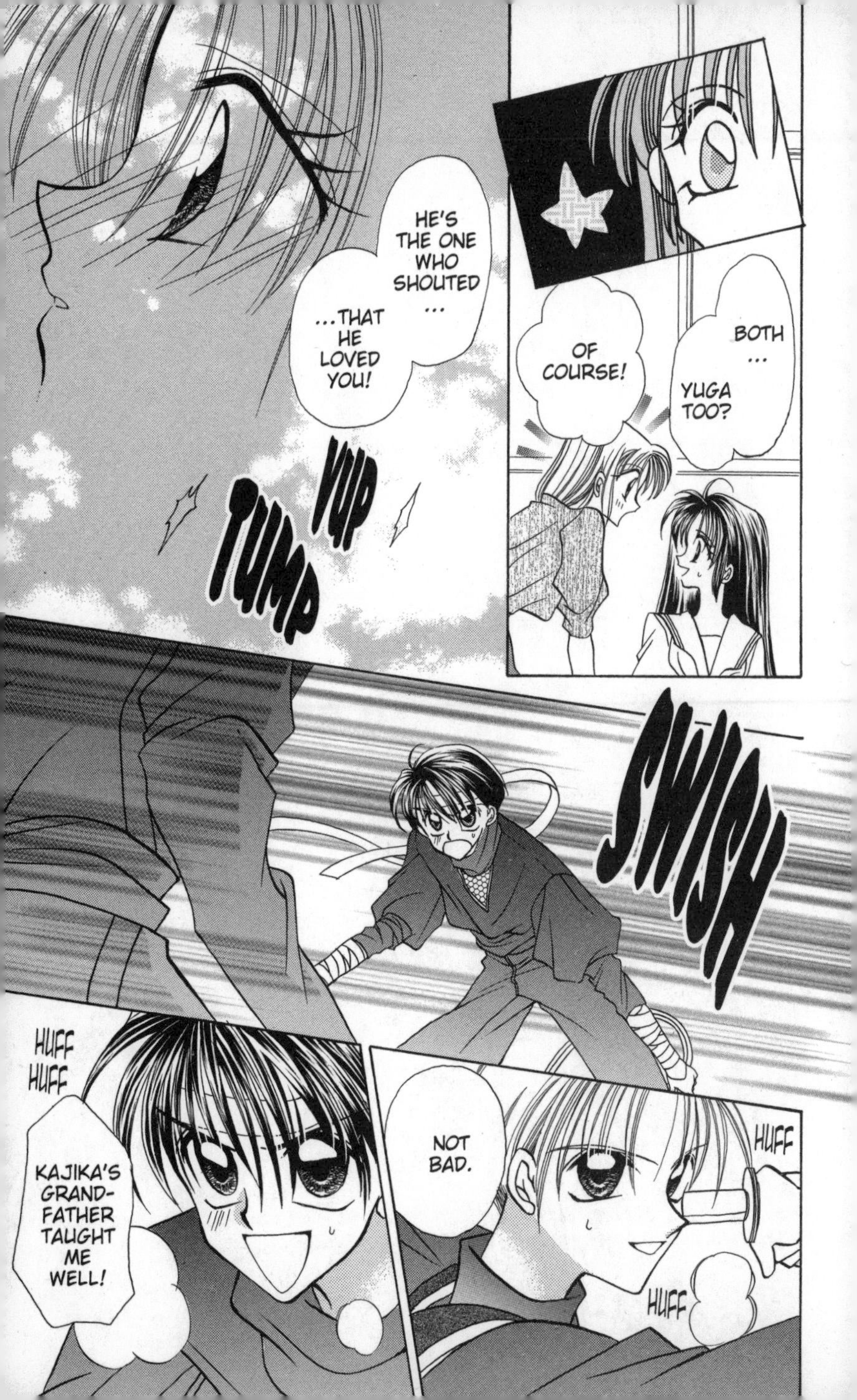
BOTH... YUGA TOO?
OF COURSE!
HE'S THE ONE WHO SHOUTED...
...THAT HE LOVED YOU!
VUP
TUMP
SWISH
NOT BAD.
HUFF
HUFF
HUFF HUFF
KAJIKA'S GRAND-FATHER TAUGHT ME WELL!

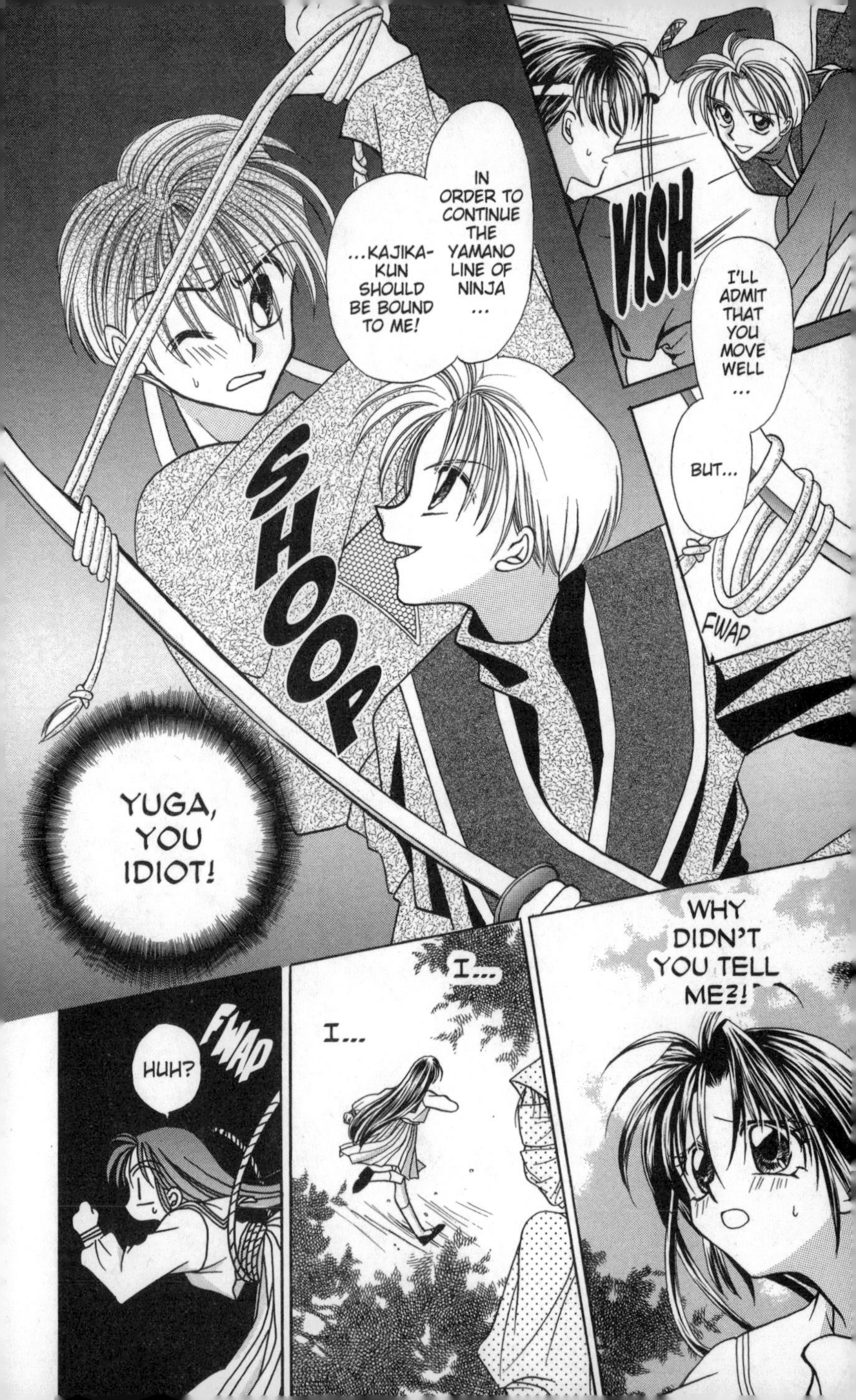
VISH
I'LL ADMIT THAT YOU MOVE WELL ...
BUT...
FWAP
IN ORDER TO CONTINUE THE YAMANO LINE OF NINJA ...
...KAJIKA-KUN SHOULD BE BOUND TO ME!
SHOOP
YUGA, YOU IDIOT!
WHY DIDN'T YOU TELL ME?!
I...
I...
FWAP
HUH?

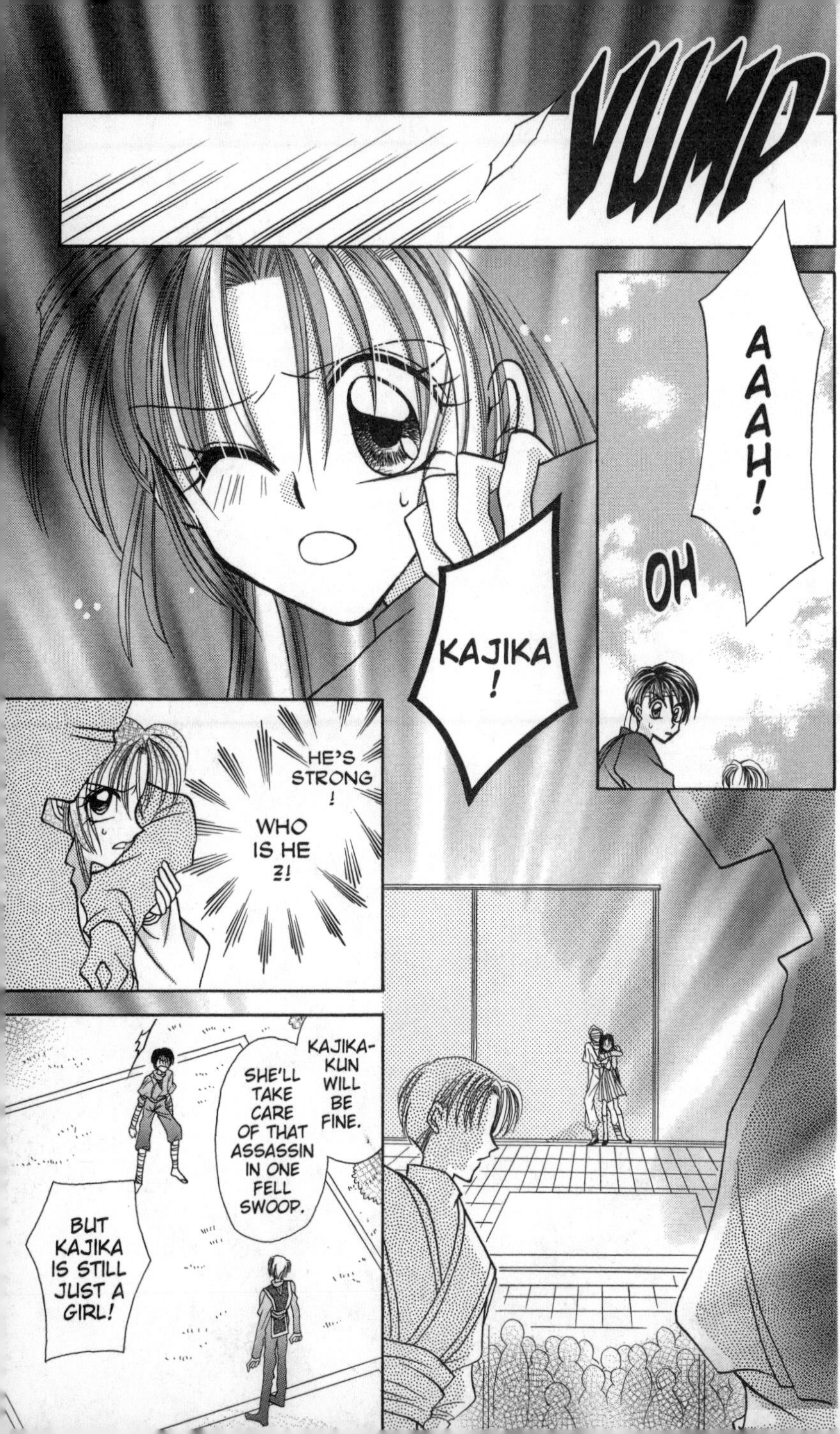
VUMP
AAAAH!
OH
KAJIKA!
HE'S STRONG!
WHO IS HE?!
KAJIKA-KUN WILL BE FINE.
SHE'LL TAKE CARE OF THAT ASSASSIN IN ONE FELL SWOOP.
BUT KAJIKA IS STILL JUST A GIRL!

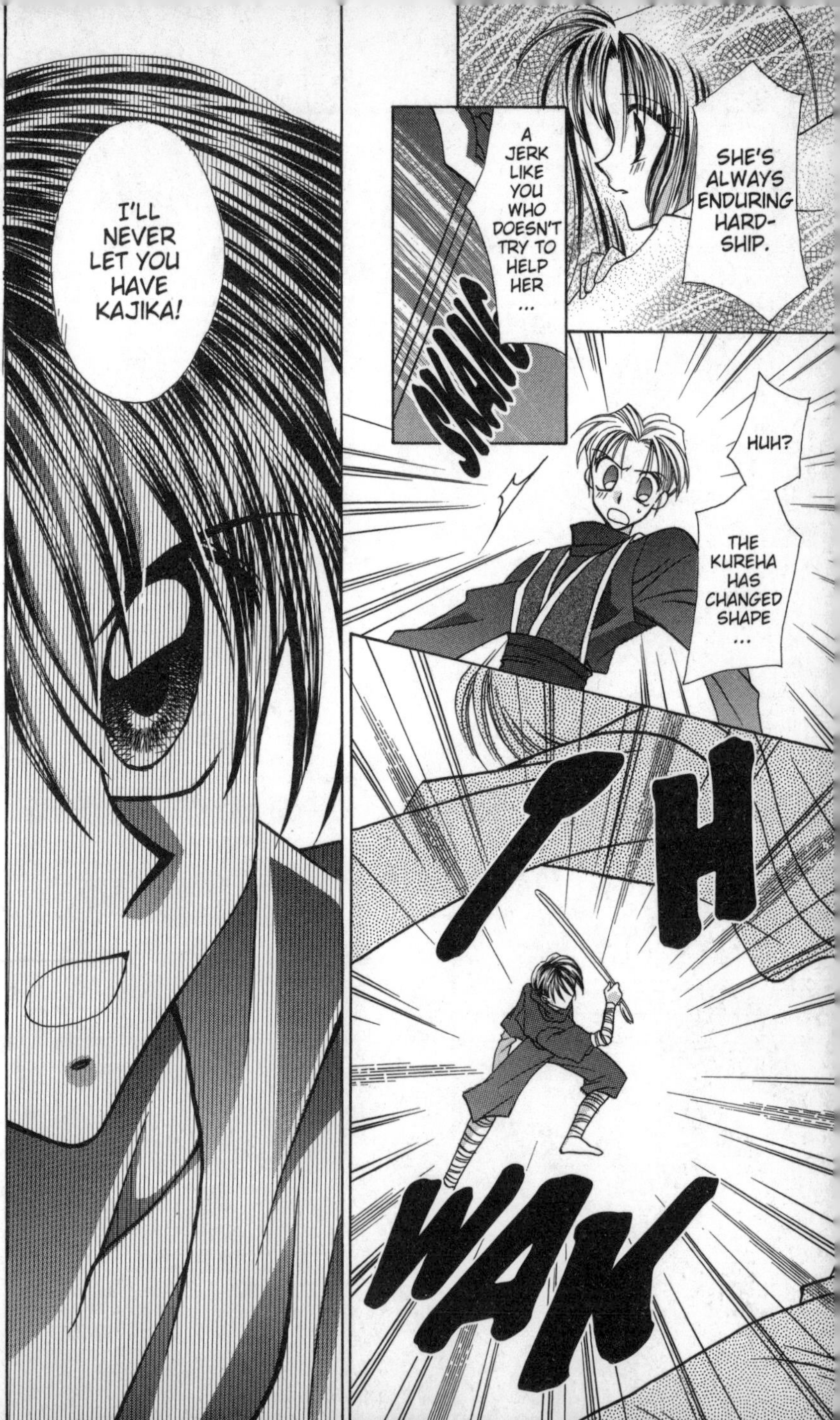
SHE'S ALWAYS ENDURING HARD-SHIP.
A JERK LIKE YOU WHO DOESN'T TRY TO HELP HER ...
HUH?
THE KUREHA HAS CHANGED SHAPE ...
I'LL NEVER LET YOU HAVE KAJIKA!

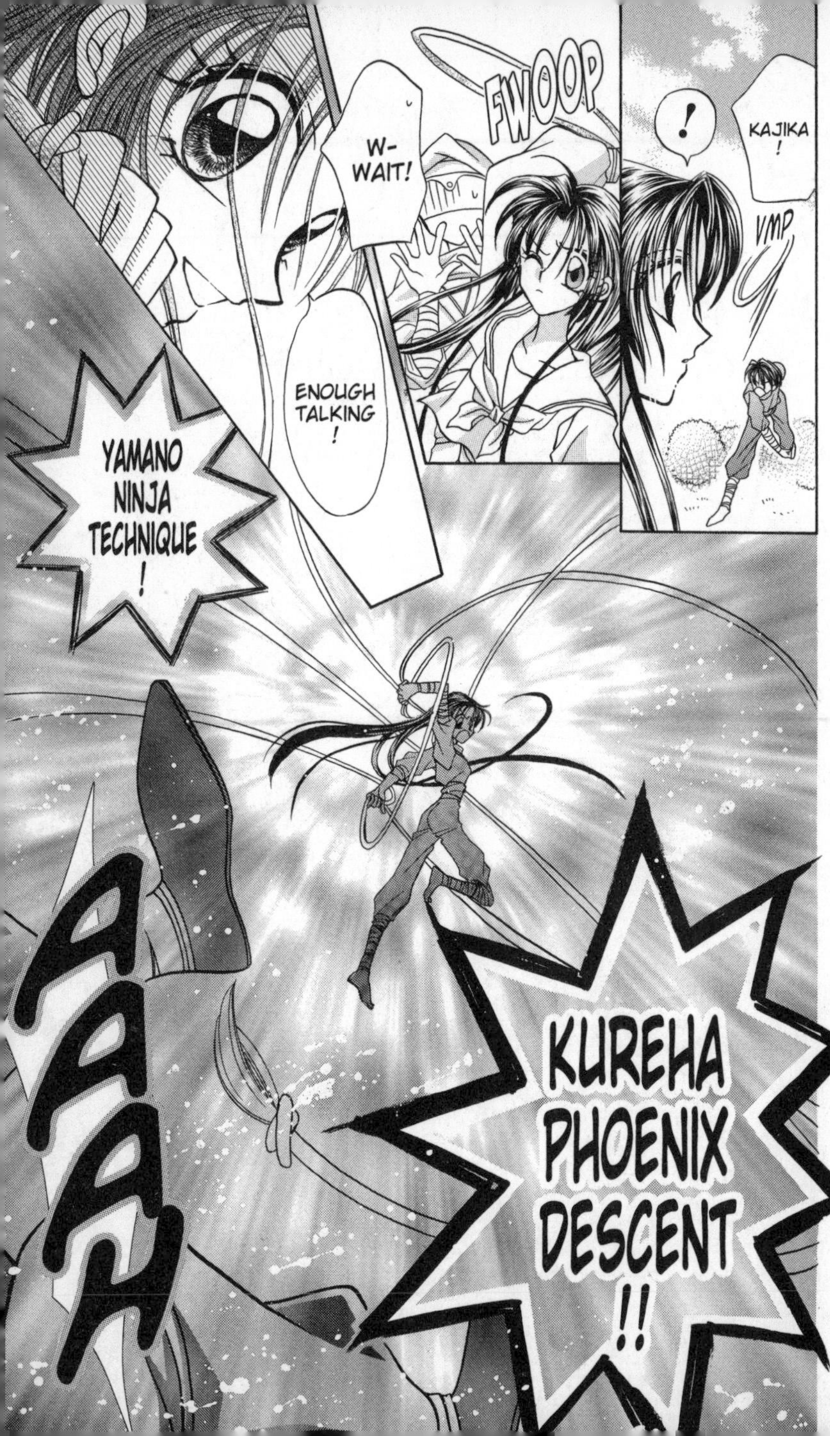
KAJIKA!
!
VMP
FWOOP
W-WAIT!
ENOUGH TALKING!
YAMANO NINJA TECHNIQUE!
KUREHA PHOENIX DESCENT!!

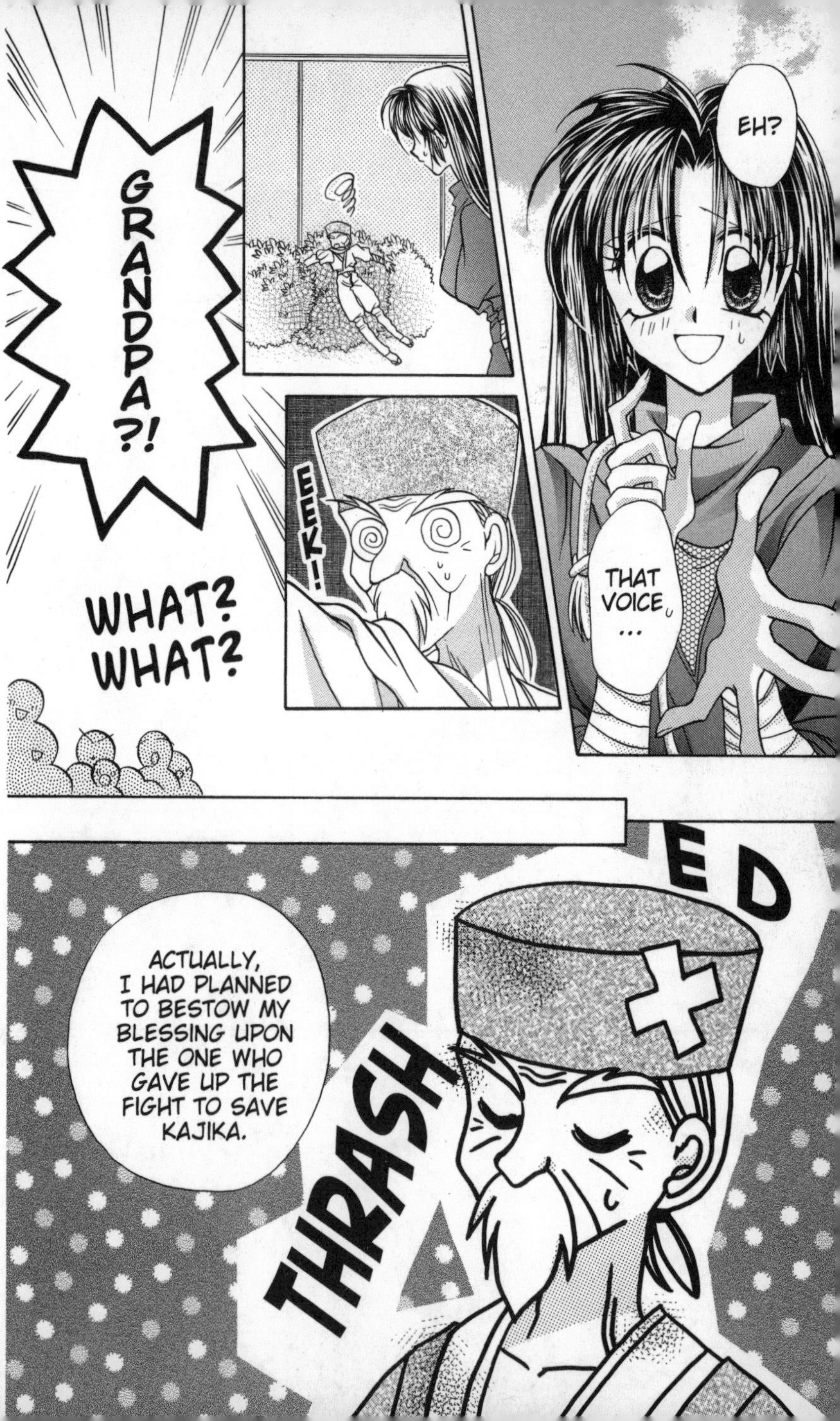
EH?
THAT VOICE ...
EEEK!
GRANDPA?!
WHAT? WHAT?
ED
ACTUALLY, I HAD PLANNED TO BESTOW MY BLESSING UPON THE ONE WHO GAVE UP THE FIGHT TO SAVE KAJIKA.
THRASH

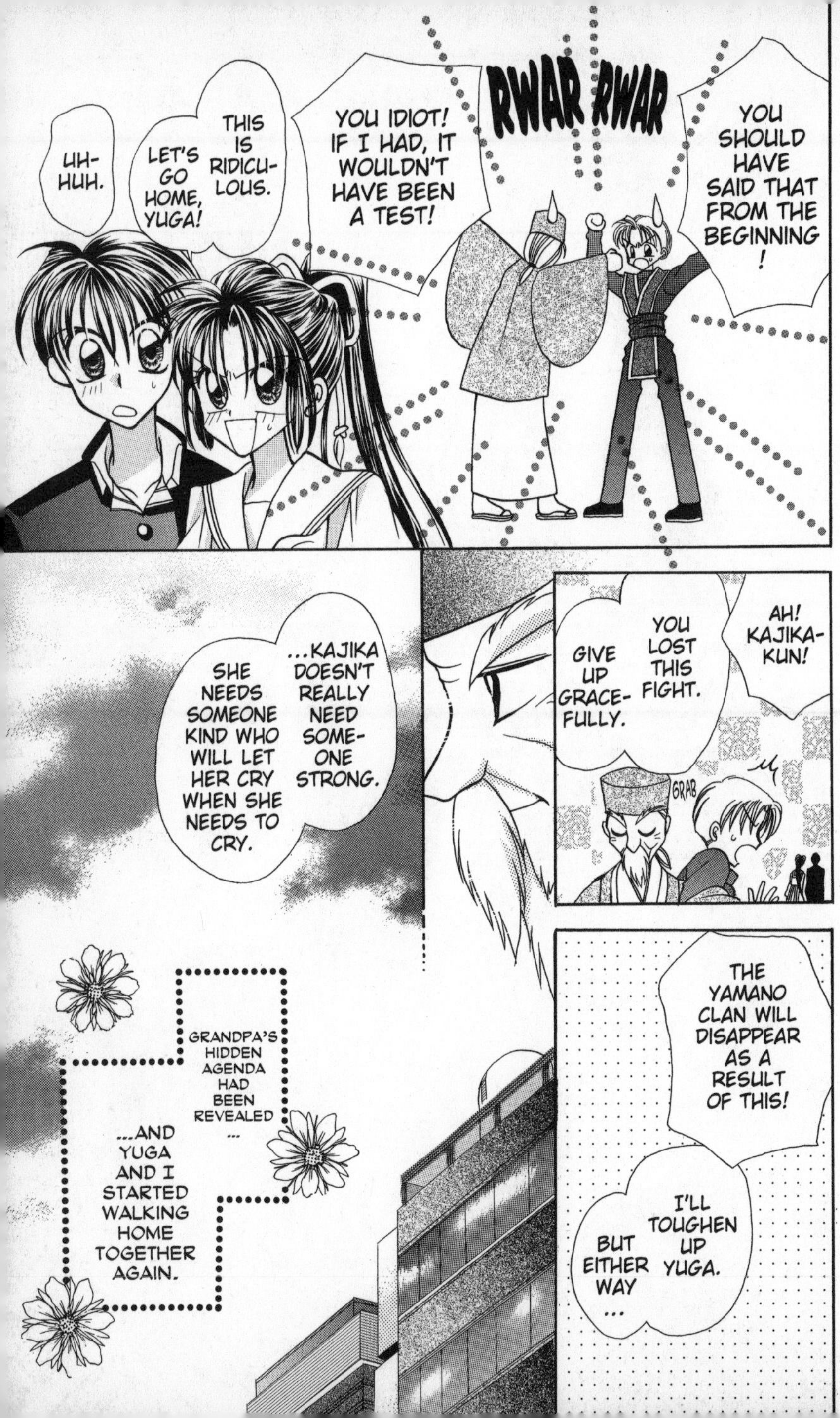
YOU SHOULD HAVE SAID THAT FROM THE BEGINNING!
RWAR RWAR
YOU IDIOT! IF I HAD, IT WOULDN'T HAVE BEEN A TEST!
THIS IS RIDICULOUS. LET'S GO HOME, YUGA!
UH-HUH.
AH! KAJIKA-KUN!
YOU LOST THIS FIGHT. GIVE UP GRACEFULLY.
GRAB
THE YAMANO CLAN WILL DISAPPEAR AS A RESULT OF THIS!
I'LL TOUGHEN UP YUGA. BUT EITHER WAY ...
...KAJIKA DOESN'T REALLY NEED SOMEONE STRONG. SHE NEEDS SOMEONE KIND WHO WILL LET HER CRY WHEN SHE NEEDS TO CRY.
GRANDPA'S HIDDEN AGENDA HAD BEEN REVEALED ... ...AND YUGA AND I STARTED WALKING HOME TOGETHER AGAIN.

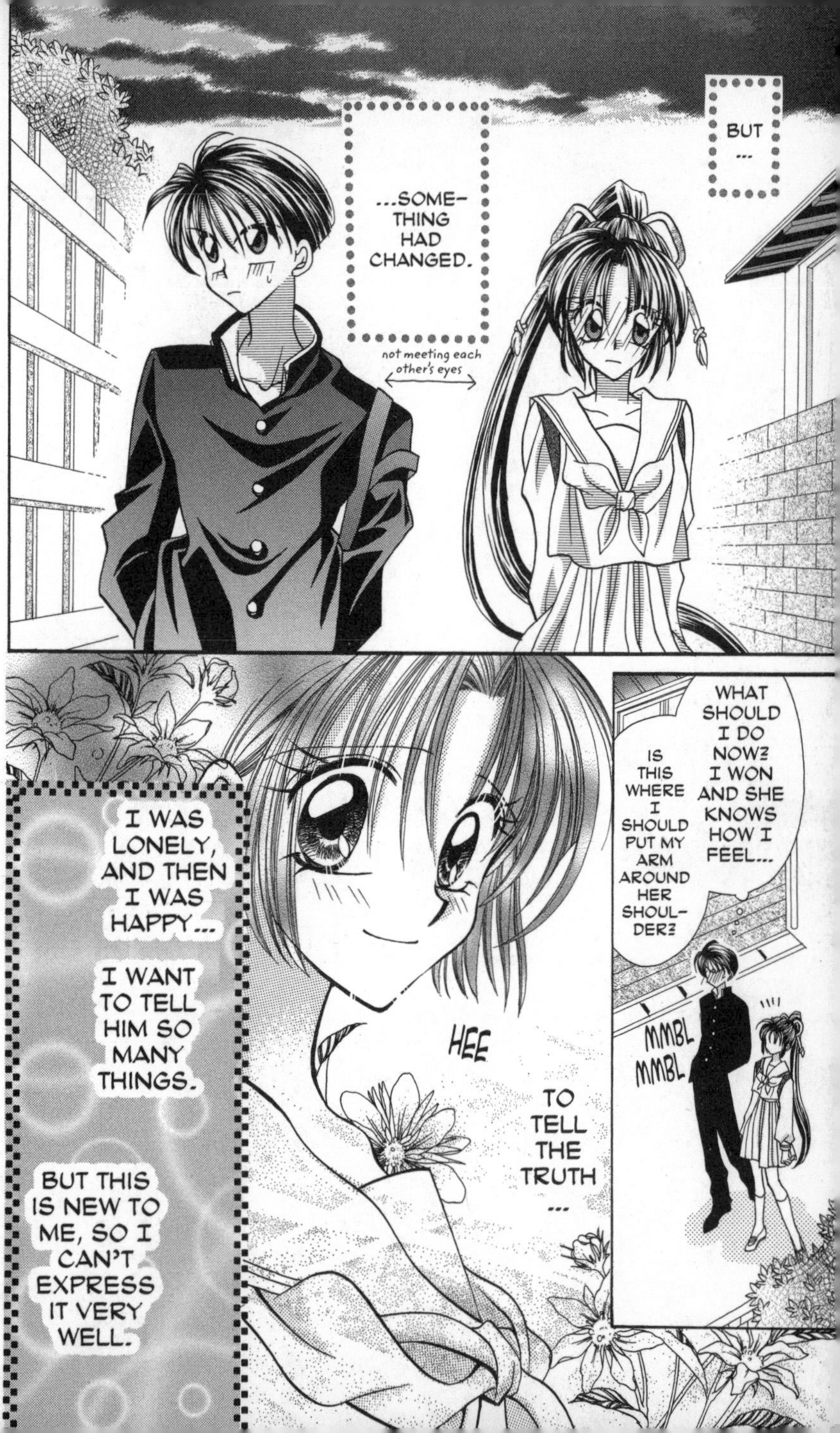
BUT ...
...SOME-THING HAD CHANGED.
not meeting each other's eyes
WHAT SHOULD I DO NOW? I WON AND SHE KNOWS HOW I FEEL...
IS THIS WHERE I SHOULD PUT MY ARM AROUND HER SHOUL-DER?
MMBL MMBL
TO TELL THE TRUTH ...
HEE
I WAS LONELY, AND THEN I WAS HAPPY...
I WANT TO TELL HIM SO MANY THINGS.
BUT THIS IS NEW TO ME, SO I CAN'T EXPRESS IT VERY WELL.

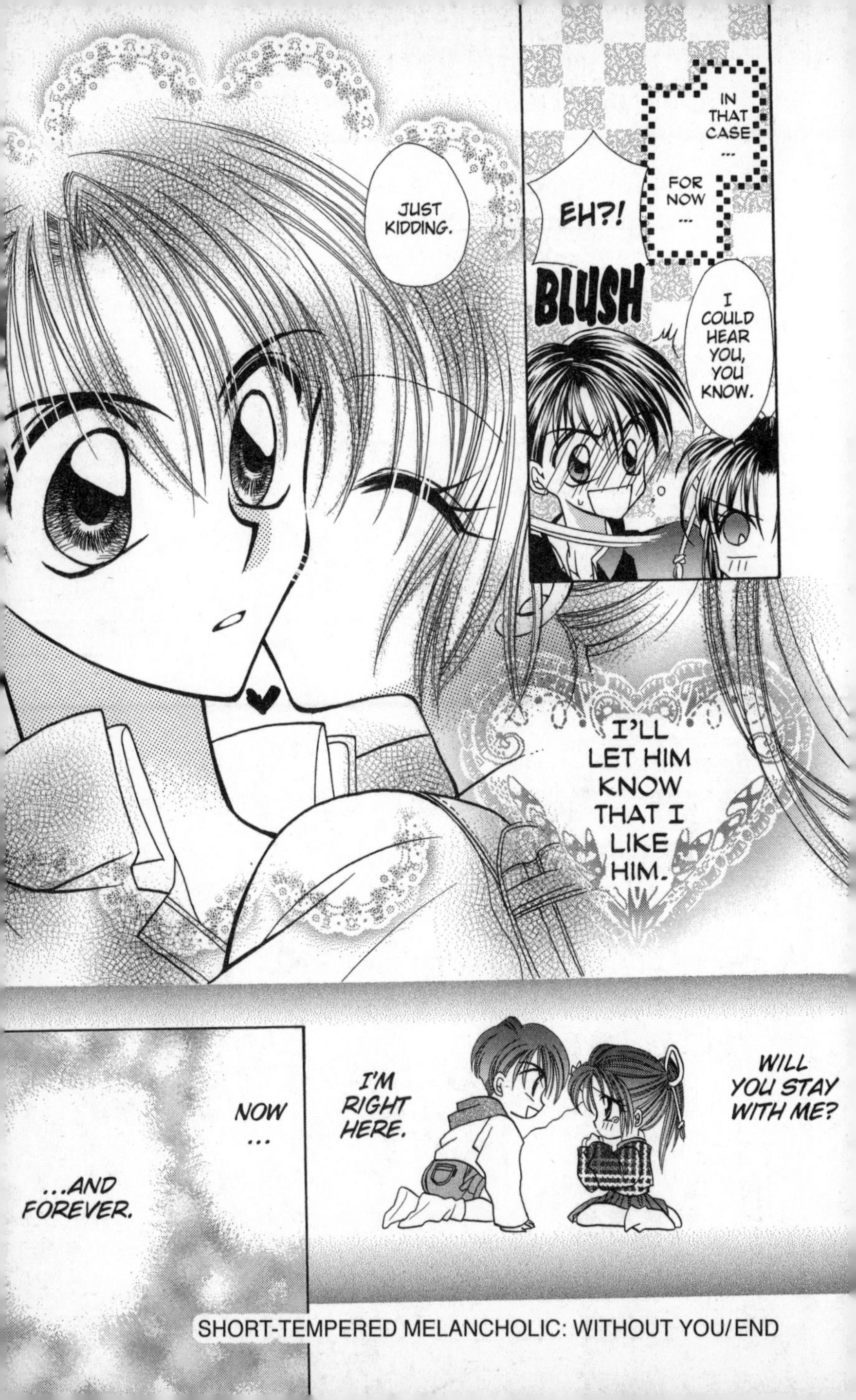
IN THAT CASE...
FOR NOW...
EH?!
BLUSH
I COULD HEAR YOU, YOU KNOW.
JUST KIDDING.
I'LL LET HIM KNOW THAT I LIKE HIM.
WILL YOU STAY WITH ME?
I'M RIGHT HERE.
NOW...
...AND FOREVER.
SHORT-TEMPERED MELANCHOLIC: WITHOUT YOU/END

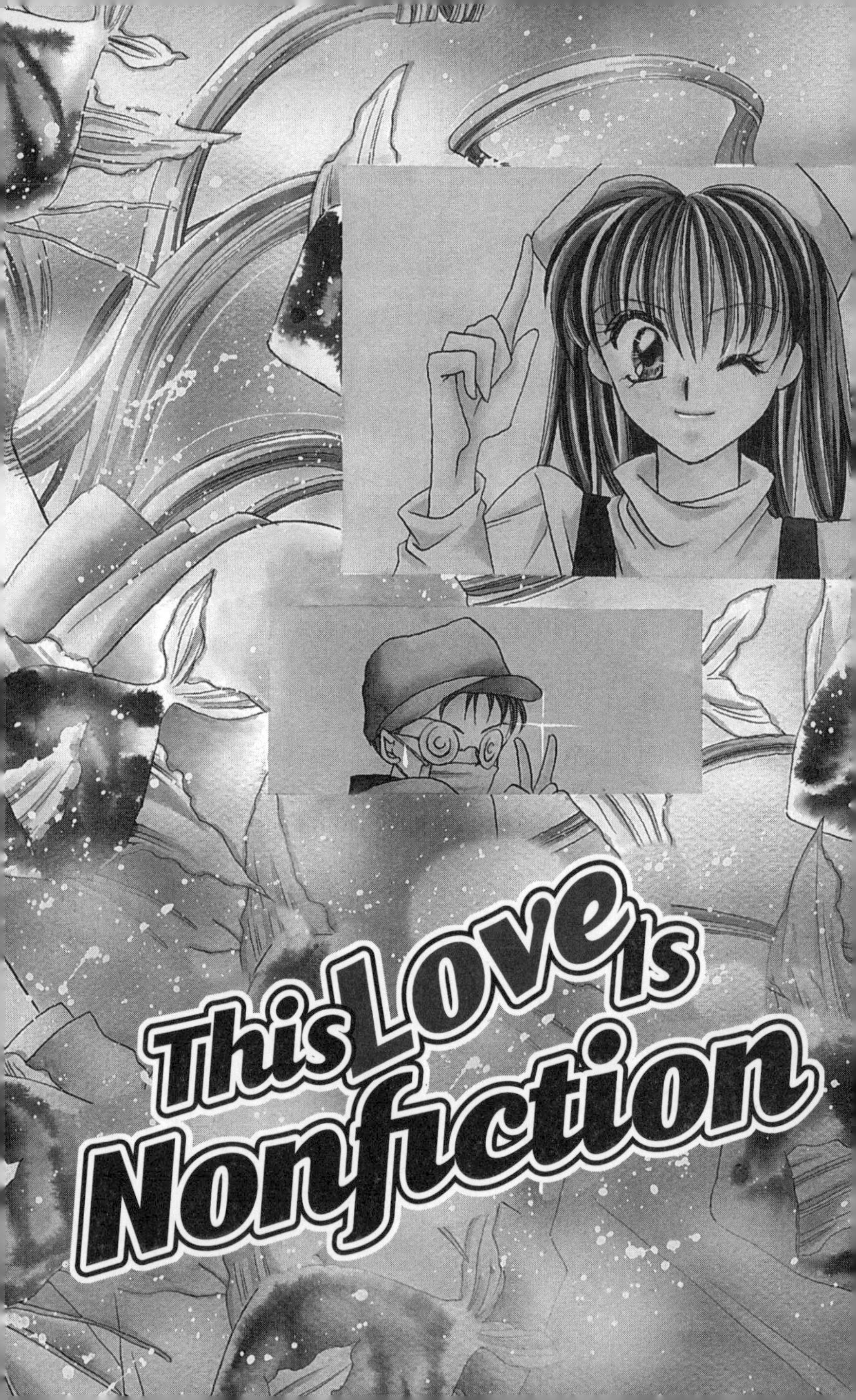
This Love Is Nonfiction

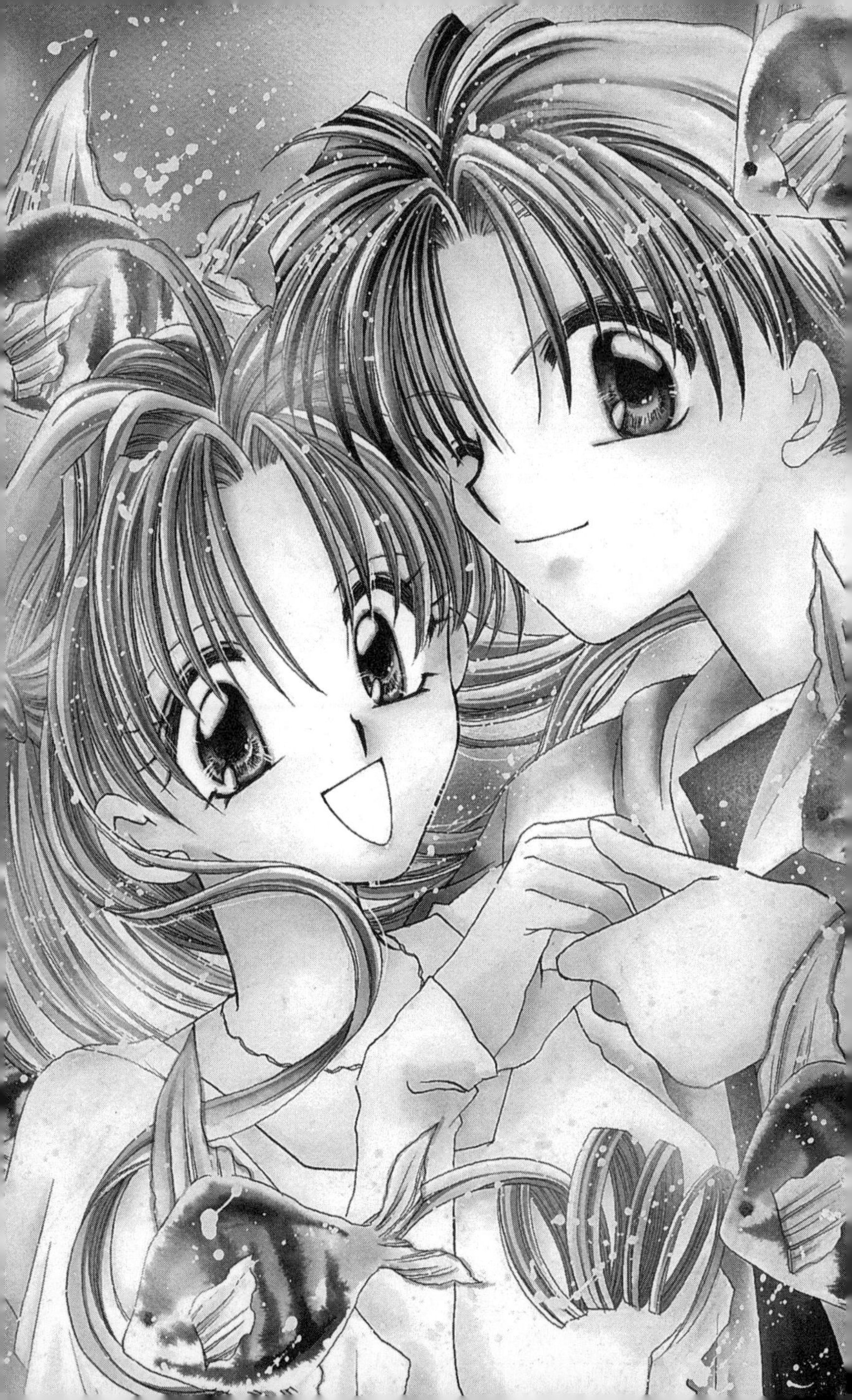

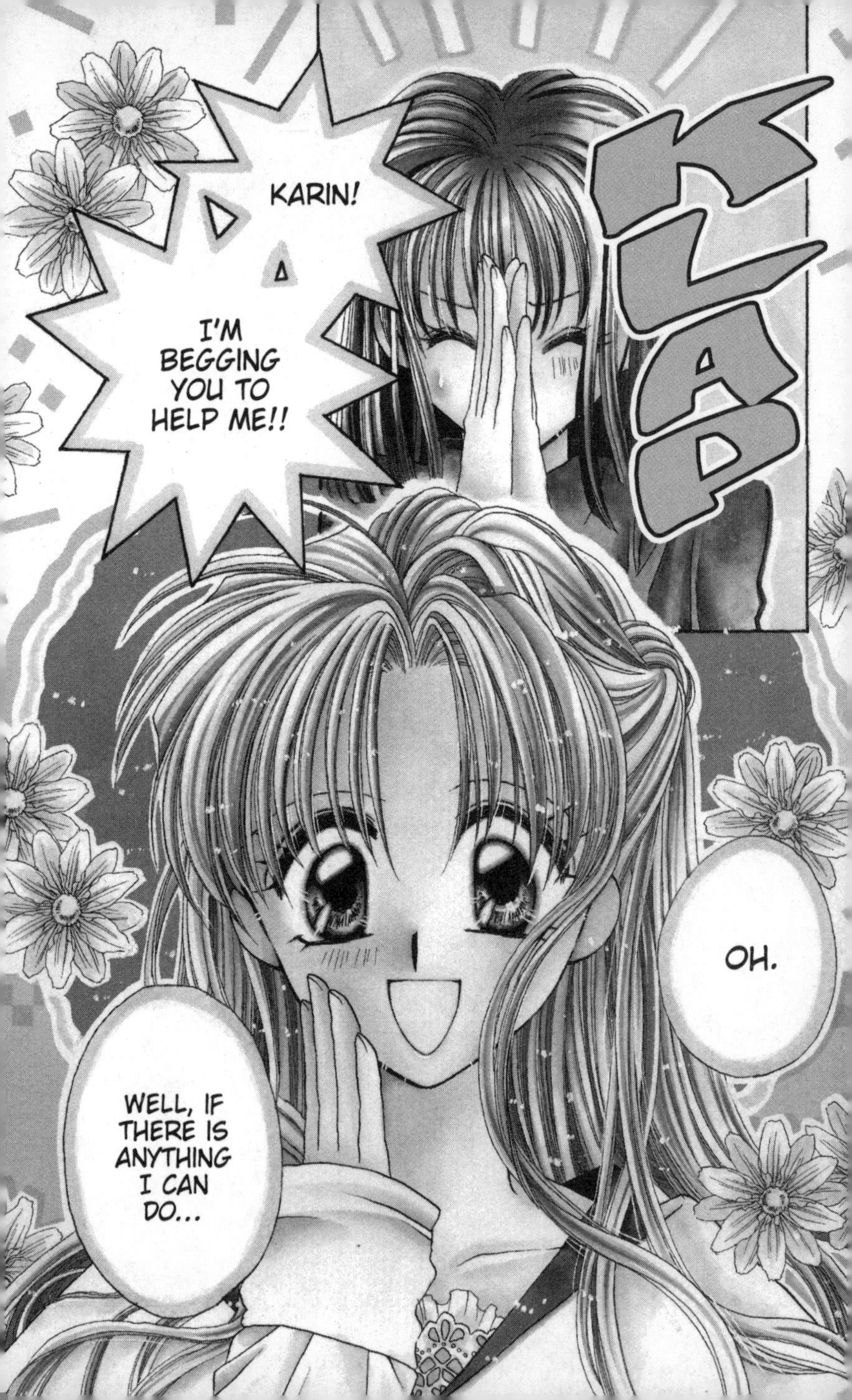
KLAP
KARIN!
I'M BEGGING YOU TO HELP ME!!
OH.
WELL, IF THERE IS ANYTHING I CAN DO...

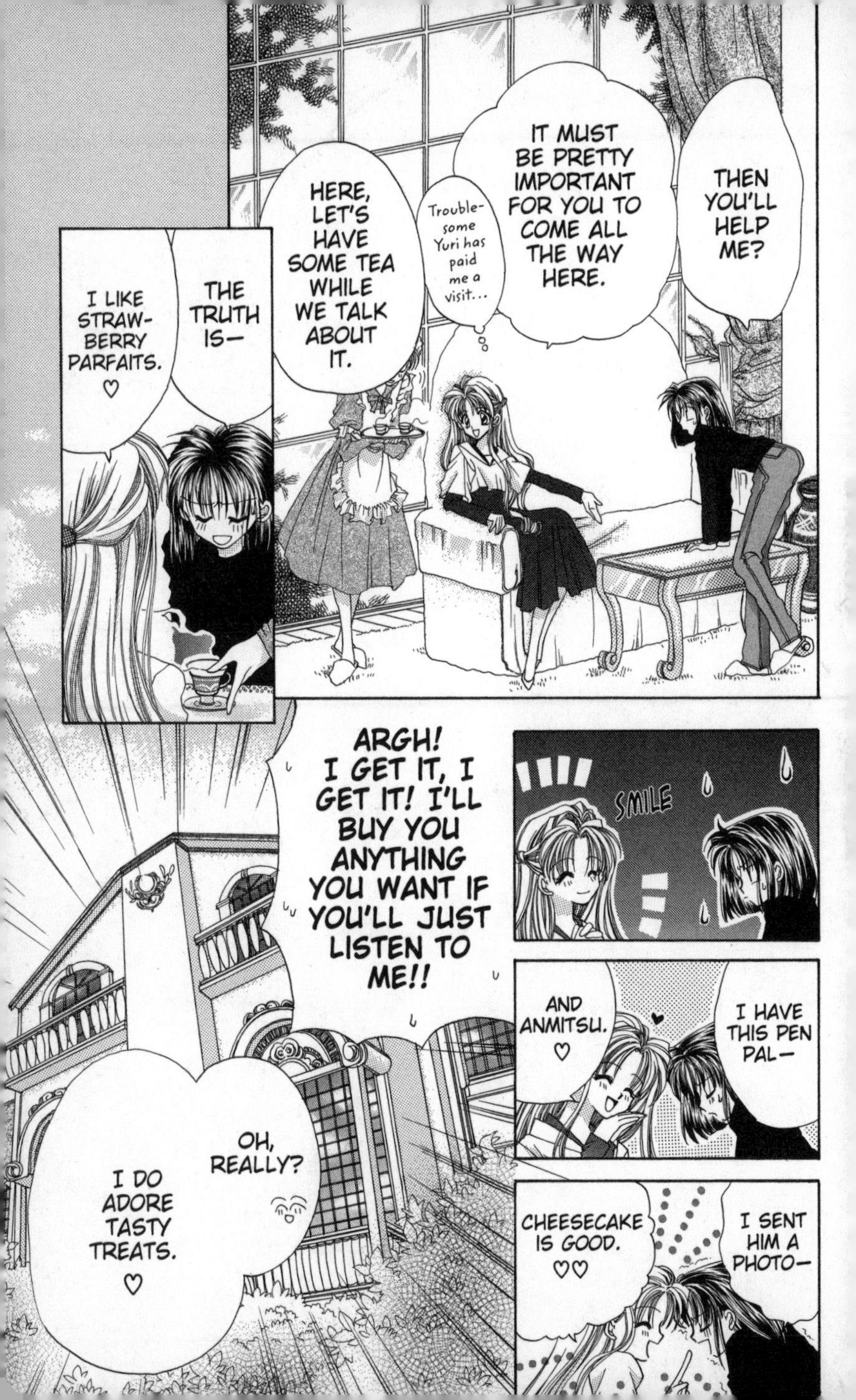
THEN YOU'LL HELP ME?
IT MUST BE PRETTY IMPORTANT FOR YOU TO COME ALL THE WAY HERE.
Trouble-some Yuri has paid me a visit...
HERE, LET'S HAVE SOME TEA WHILE WE TALK ABOUT IT.
THE TRUTH IS—
I LIKE STRAW-BERRY PARFAITS. ♡
SMILE
I HAVE THIS PEN PAL—
AND ANMITSU. ♡
I SENT HIM A PHOTO—
CHEESECAKE IS GOOD. ♡♡
ARGH! I GET IT, I GET IT! I'LL BUY YOU ANYTHING YOU WANT IF YOU'LL JUST LISTEN TO ME!!
OH, REALLY?
I DO ADORE TASTY TREATS. ♡

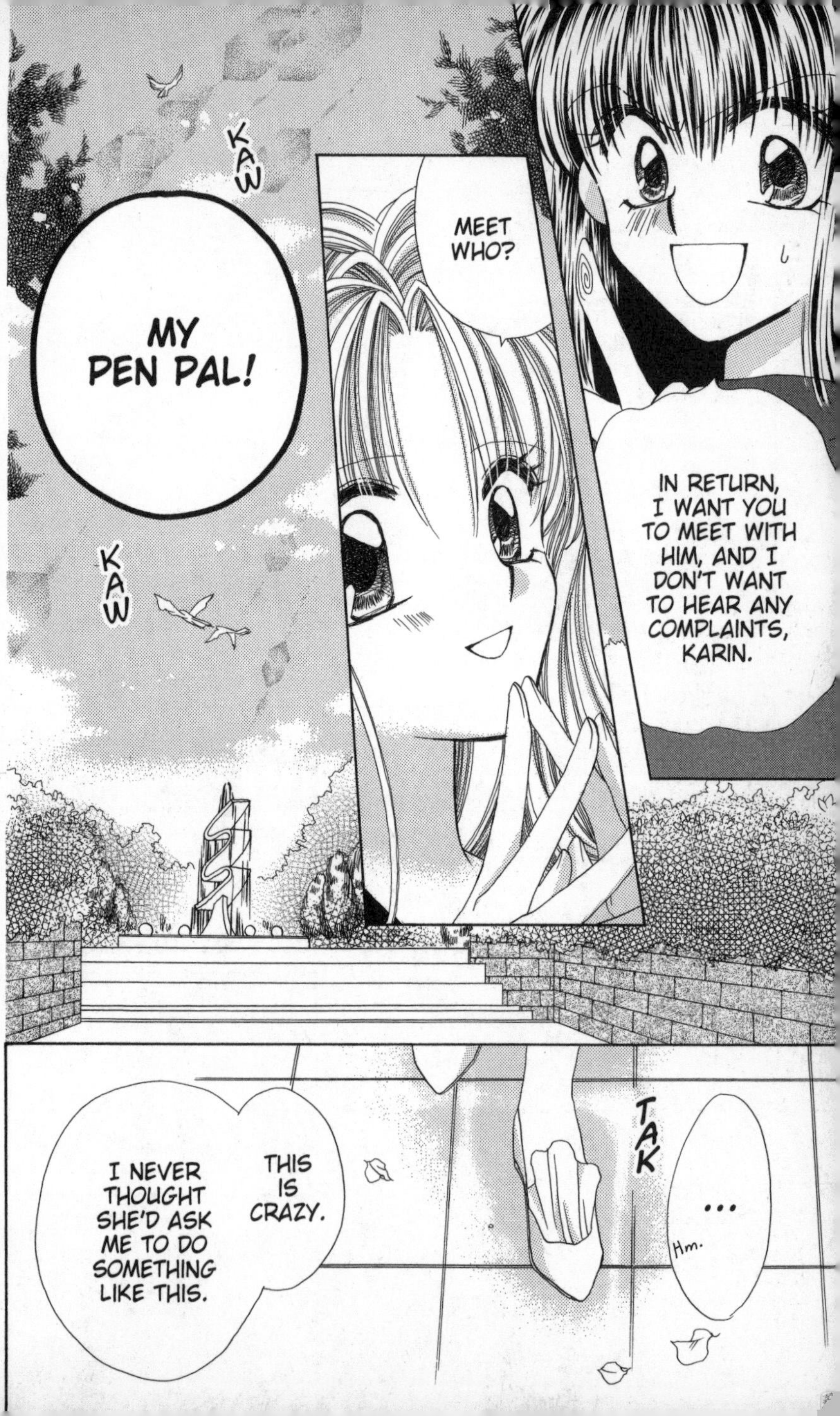

IN RETURN, I WANT YOU TO MEET WITH HIM, AND I DON'T WANT TO HEAR ANY COMPLAINTS, KARIN.
MEET WHO?
KAW
MY PEN PAL!
KAW
...
Hm.
TAK
THIS IS CRAZY.
I NEVER THOUGHT SHE'D ASK ME TO DO SOMETHING LIKE THIS.

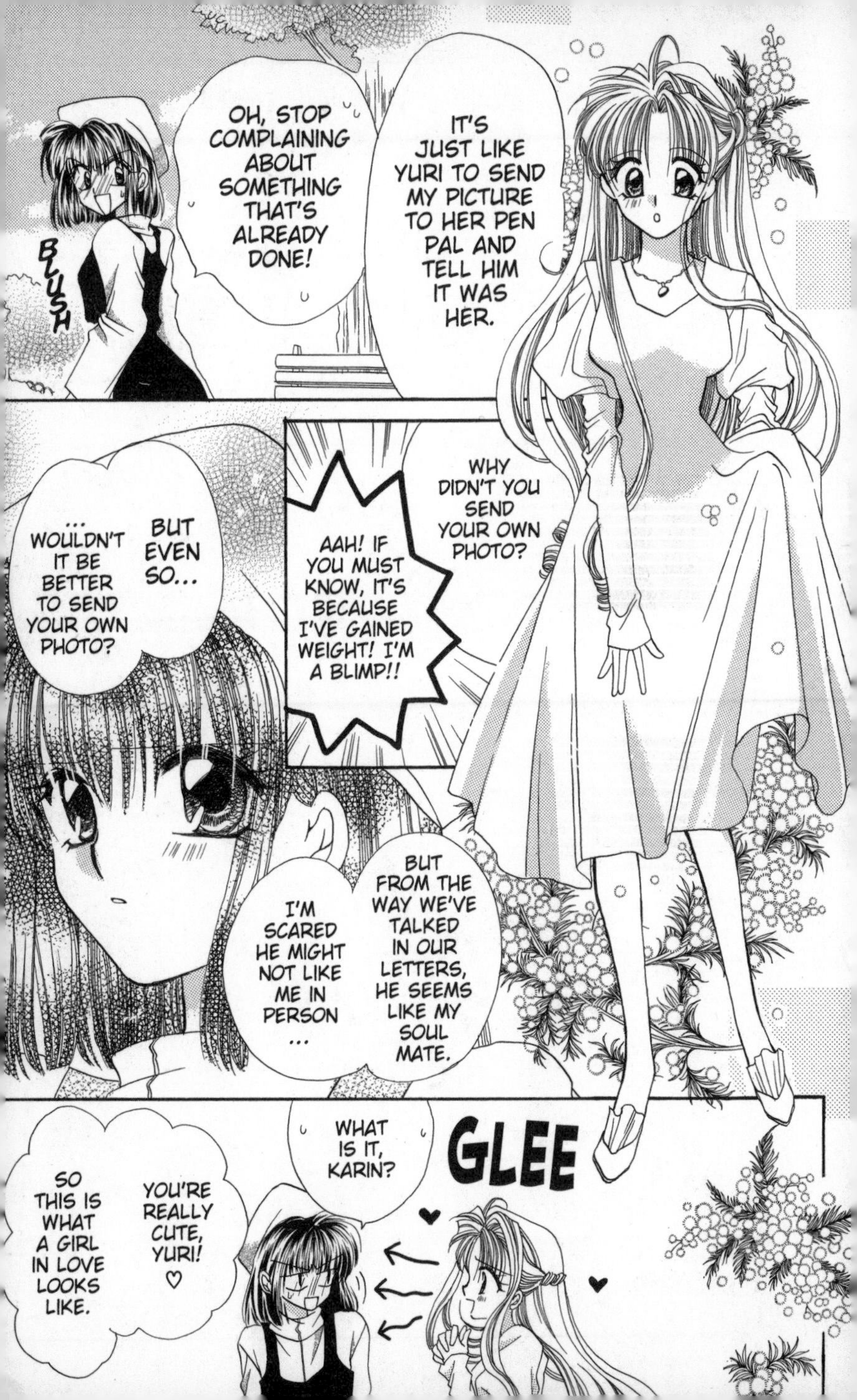
IT'S JUST LIKE YURI TO SEND MY PICTURE TO HER PEN PAL AND TELL HIM IT WAS HER.
OH, STOP COMPLAINING ABOUT SOMETHING THAT'S ALREADY DONE!
BLUSH
WHY DIDN'T YOU SEND YOUR OWN PHOTO?
AAH! IF YOU MUST KNOW, IT'S BECAUSE I'VE GAINED WEIGHT! I'M A BLIMP!!
BUT EVEN SO...
...WOULDN'T IT BE BETTER TO SEND YOUR OWN PHOTO?
BUT FROM THE WAY WE'VE TALKED IN OUR LETTERS, HE SEEMS LIKE MY SOUL MATE.
I'M SCARED HE MIGHT NOT LIKE ME IN PERSON...
GLEE
WHAT IS IT, KARIN?
YOU'RE REALLY CUTE, YURI! ♡
SO THIS IS WHAT A GIRL IN LOVE LOOKS LIKE.

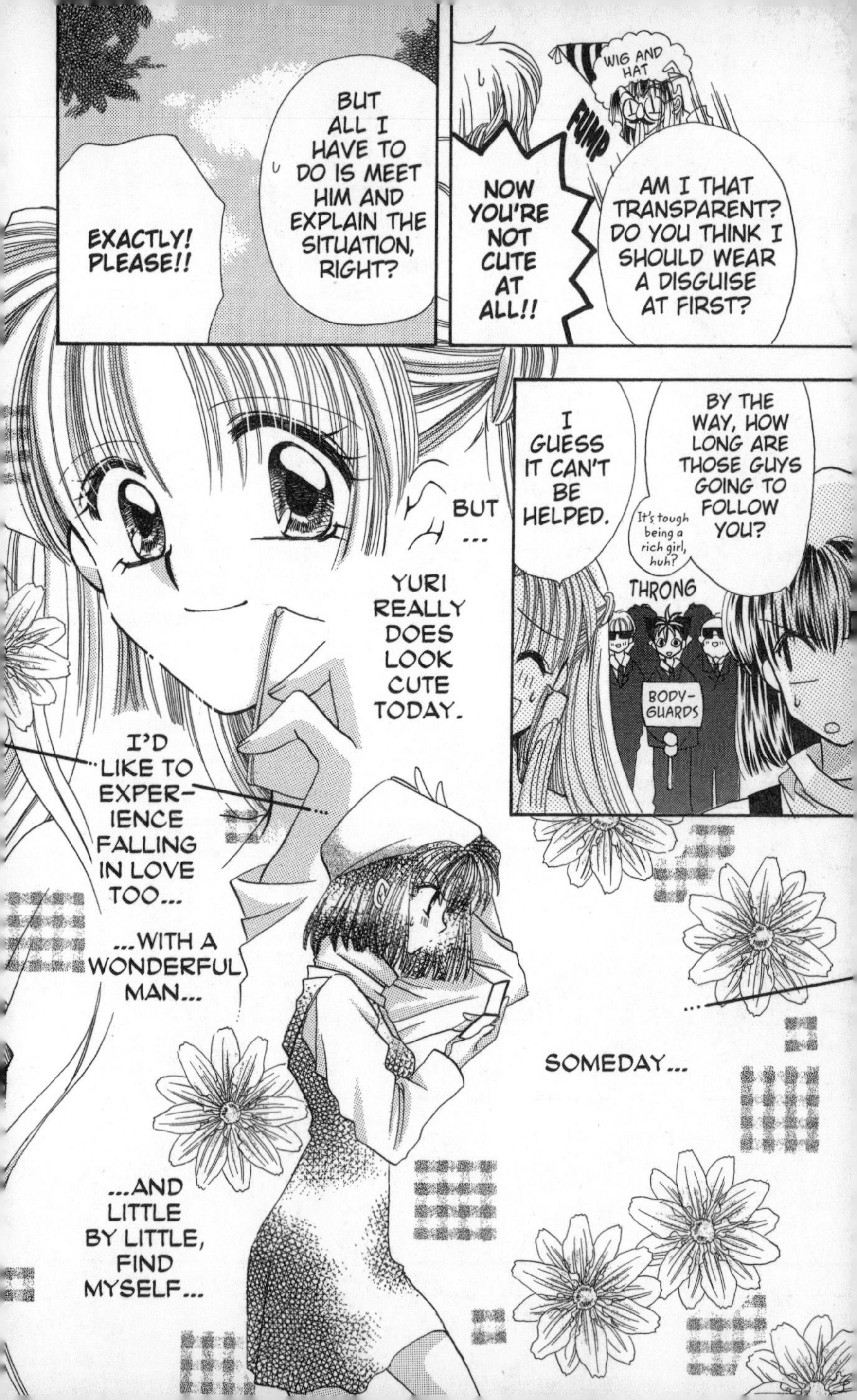
WIG AND HAT
FUMP
AM I THAT TRANSPARENT? DO YOU THINK I SHOULD WEAR A DISGUISE AT FIRST?
NOW YOU'RE NOT CUTE AT ALL!!
BUT ALL I HAVE TO DO IS MEET HIM AND EXPLAIN THE SITUATION, RIGHT?
EXACTLY! PLEASE!!
BY THE WAY, HOW LONG ARE THOSE GUYS GOING TO FOLLOW YOU?
It's tough being a rich girl, huh?
I GUESS IT CAN'T BE HELPED.
THRONG
BODY-GUARDS
BUT ...
YURI REALLY DOES LOOK CUTE TODAY.
...
SOMEDAY...
I'D LIKE TO EXPERIENCE FALLING IN LOVE TOO...
...WITH A WONDERFUL MAN...
...AND LITTLE BY LITTLE, FIND MYSELF...

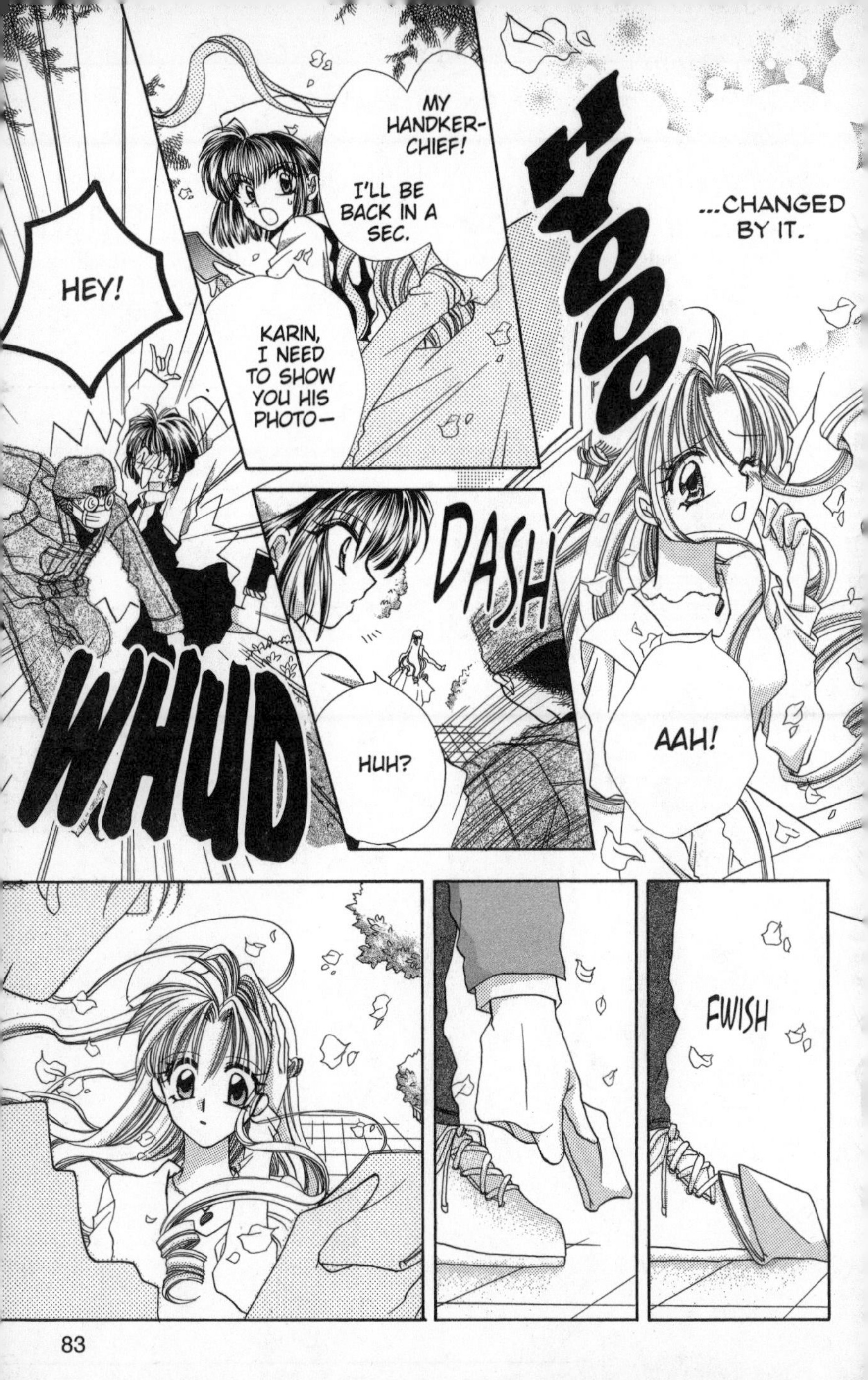
...CHANGED BY IT.
HOOOO
AAH!
MY HANDKERCHIEF!
I'LL BE BACK IN A SEC.
KARIN, I NEED TO SHOW YOU HIS PHOTO—
HEY!
DASH
HUH?
WHUD
FWISH

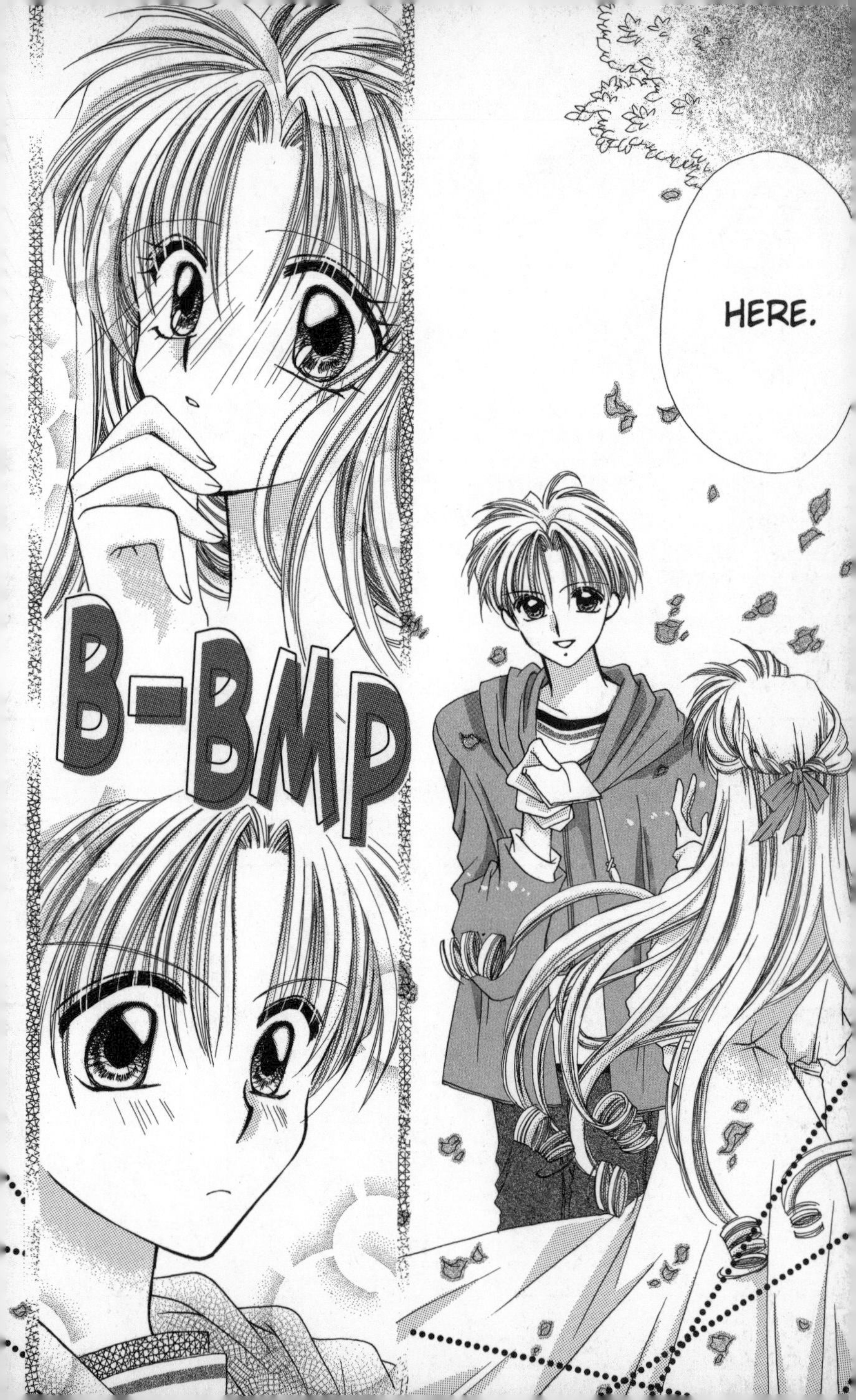
HERE.
B-BMP

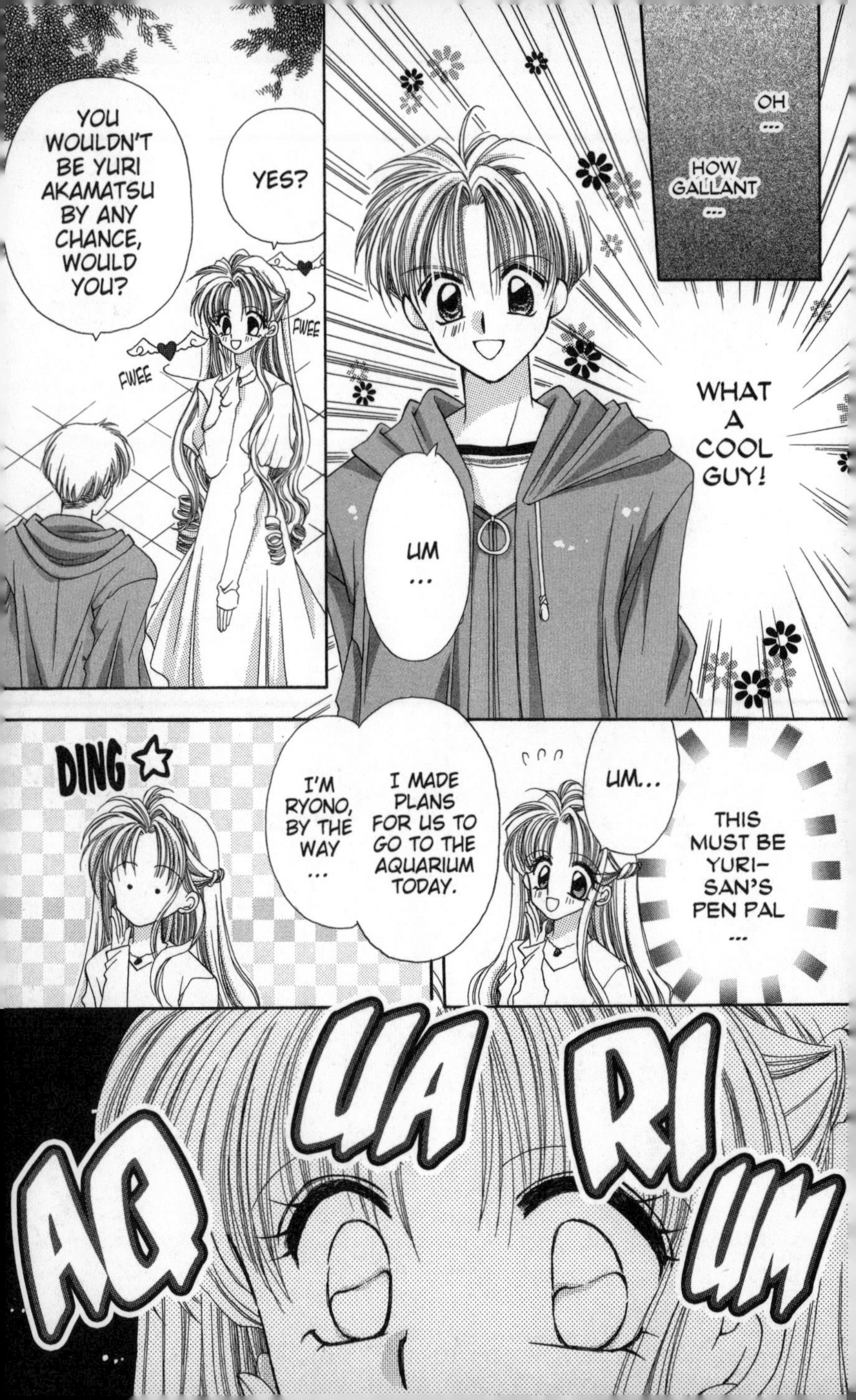
OH ... HOW GALLANT ...
WHAT A COOL GUY!
UM ...
YOU WOULDN'T BE YURI AKAMATSU BY ANY CHANCE, WOULD YOU?
YES?
FWEE
FWEE
UM...
THIS MUST BE YURI-SAN'S PEN PAL ...
I MADE PLANS FOR US TO GO TO THE AQUARIUM TODAY.
I'M RYONO, BY THE WAY ...
DING
AQUARIUM

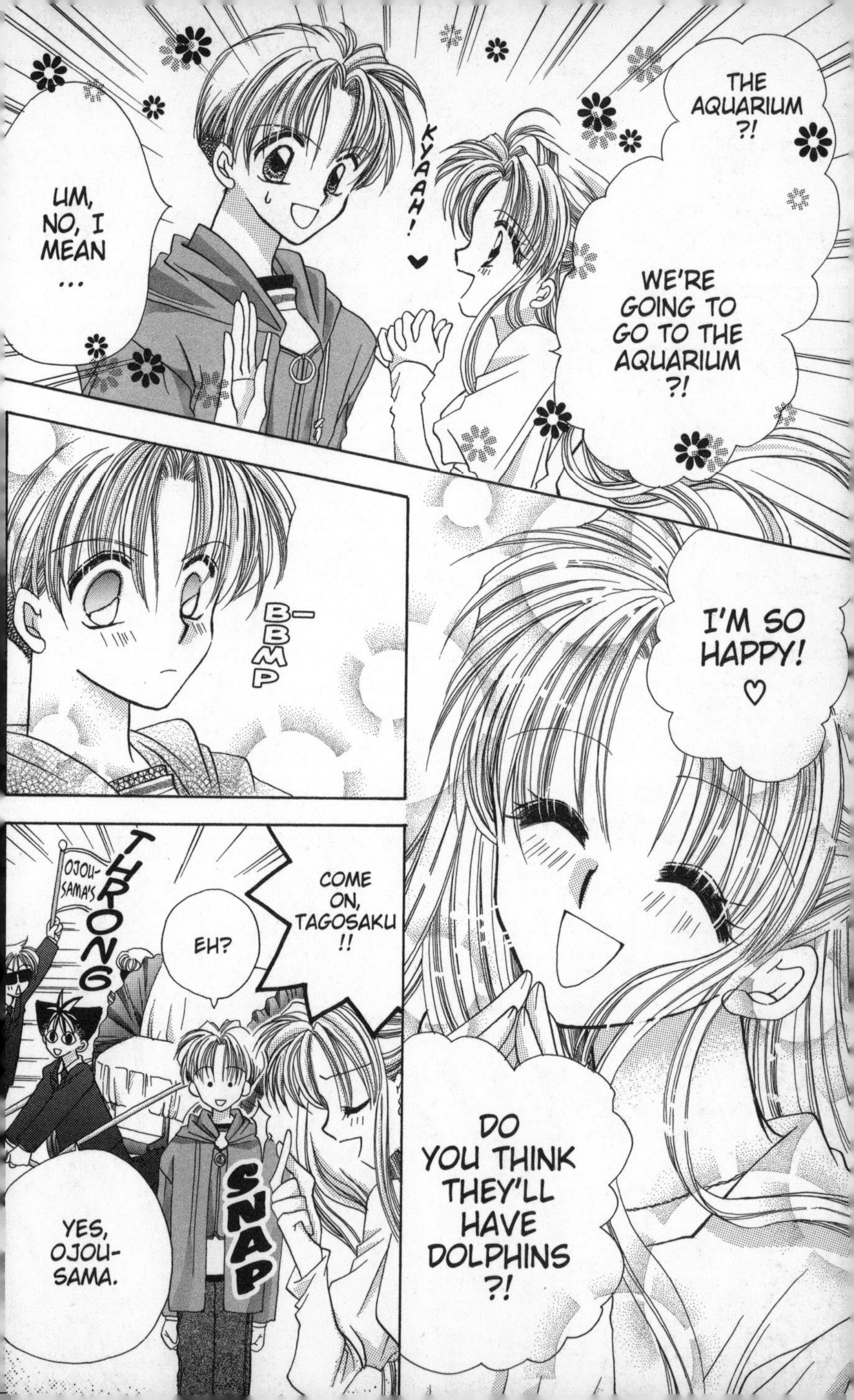
THE AQUARIUM ?!
WE'RE GOING TO GO TO THE AQUARIUM ?!
KYAAH! ♥
UM, NO, I MEAN ...
I'M SO HAPPY! ♡
DO YOU THINK THEY'LL HAVE DOLPHINS ?!
B-BBMP
COME ON, TAGOSAKU !!
EH?
THRONG
OJOU-SAMA'S
SNAP
YES, OJOU-SAMA.

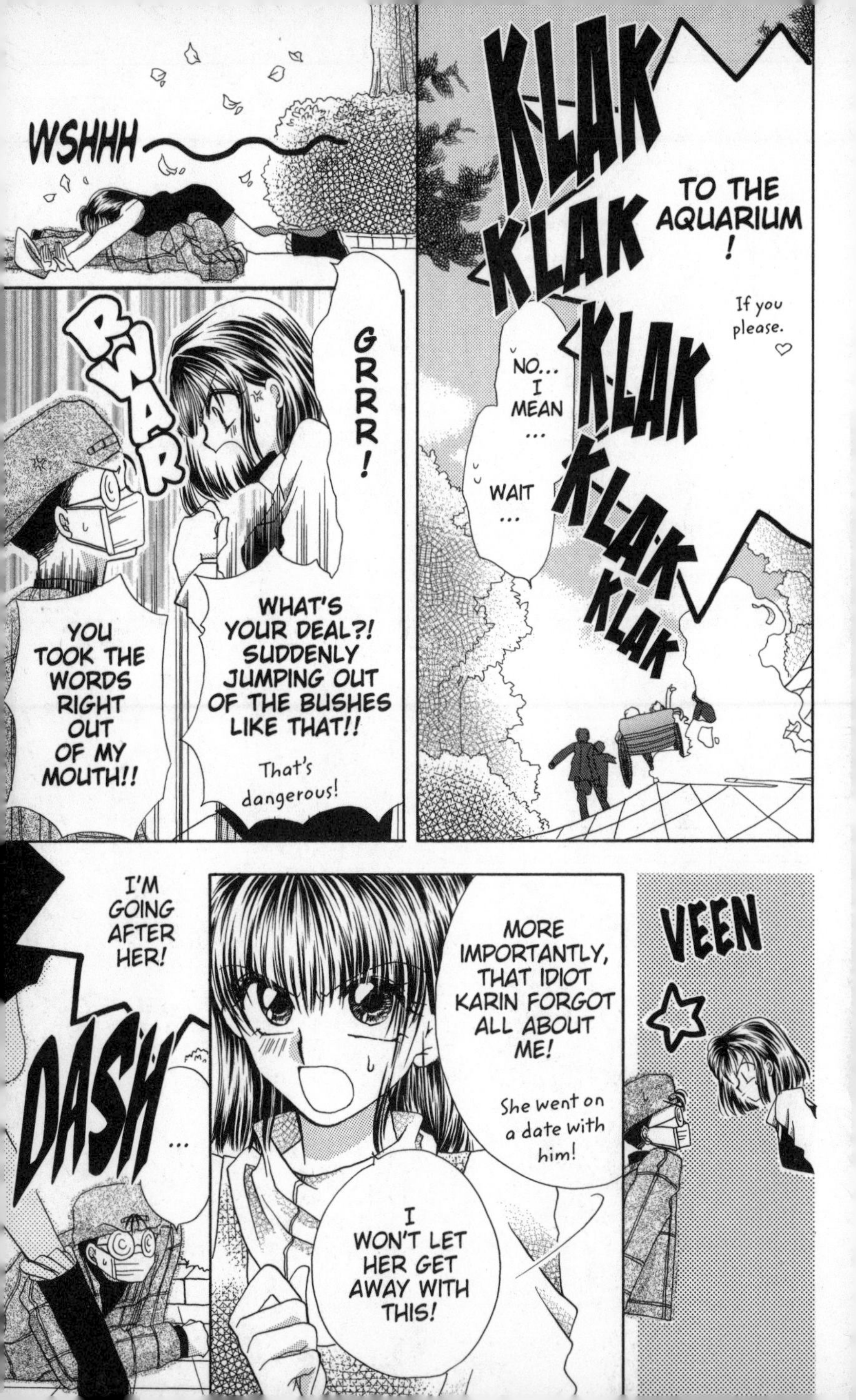
KLAK
TO THE AQUARIUM!
If you please. ♡
NO... I MEAN... WAIT...
KLAK
KLAK
KLAK
KLAK
WSHHH
GRRR!
BWAR
WHAT'S YOUR DEAL?! SUDDENLY JUMPING OUT OF THE BUSHES LIKE THAT!!
That's dangerous!
YOU TOOK THE WORDS RIGHT OUT OF MY MOUTH!!
VEEN
MORE IMPORTANTLY, THAT IDIOT KARIN FORGOT ALL ABOUT ME!
She went on a date with him!
I WON'T LET HER GET AWAY WITH THIS!
I'M GOING AFTER HER!
DASH
...

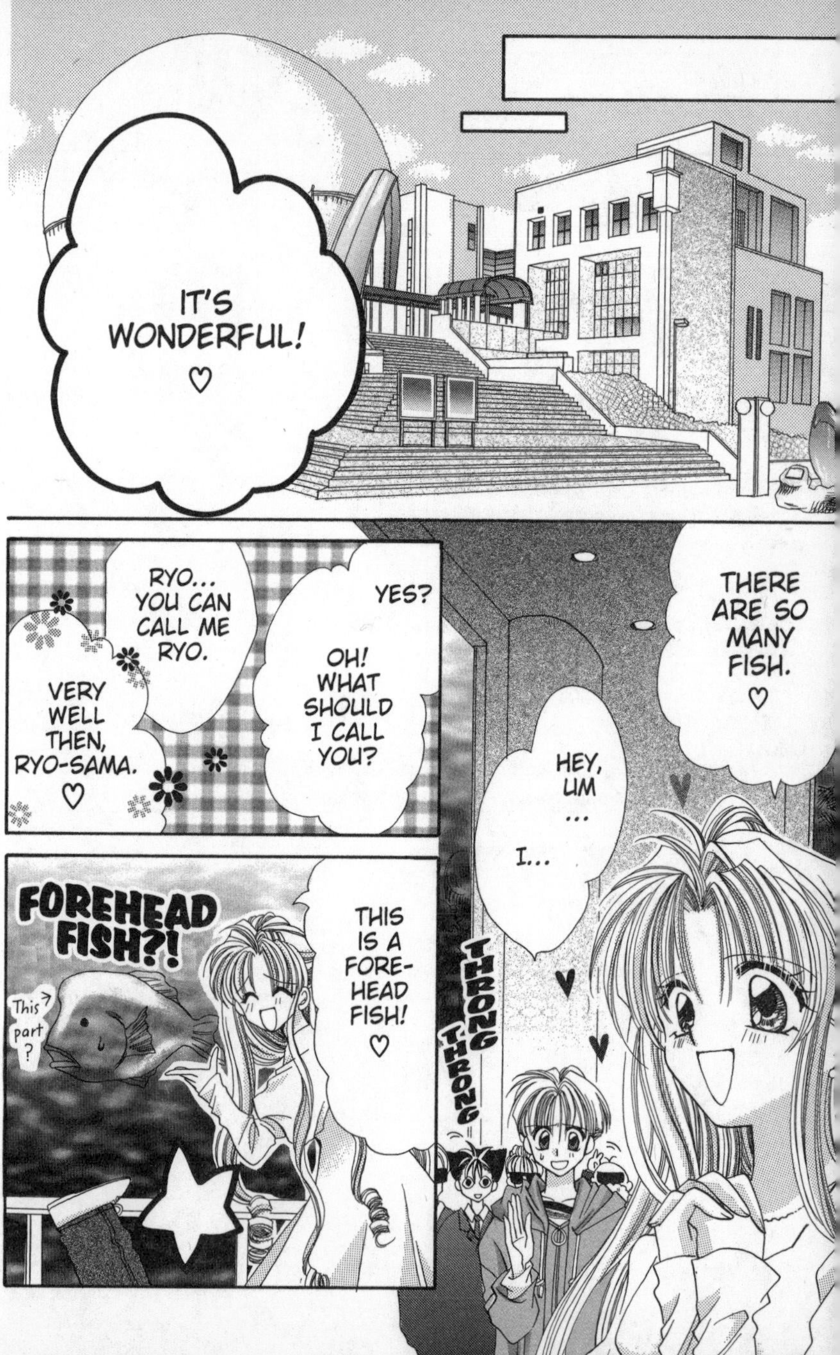
IT'S WONDERFUL! ♡
THERE ARE SO MANY FISH. ♡
HEY, UM ... I...
THRONG THRONG
YES?
OH! WHAT SHOULD I CALL YOU?
RYO... YOU CAN CALL ME RYO.
VERY WELL THEN, RYO-SAMA. ♡
THIS IS A FORE-HEAD FISH! ♡
FOREHEAD FISH?!
This part ?

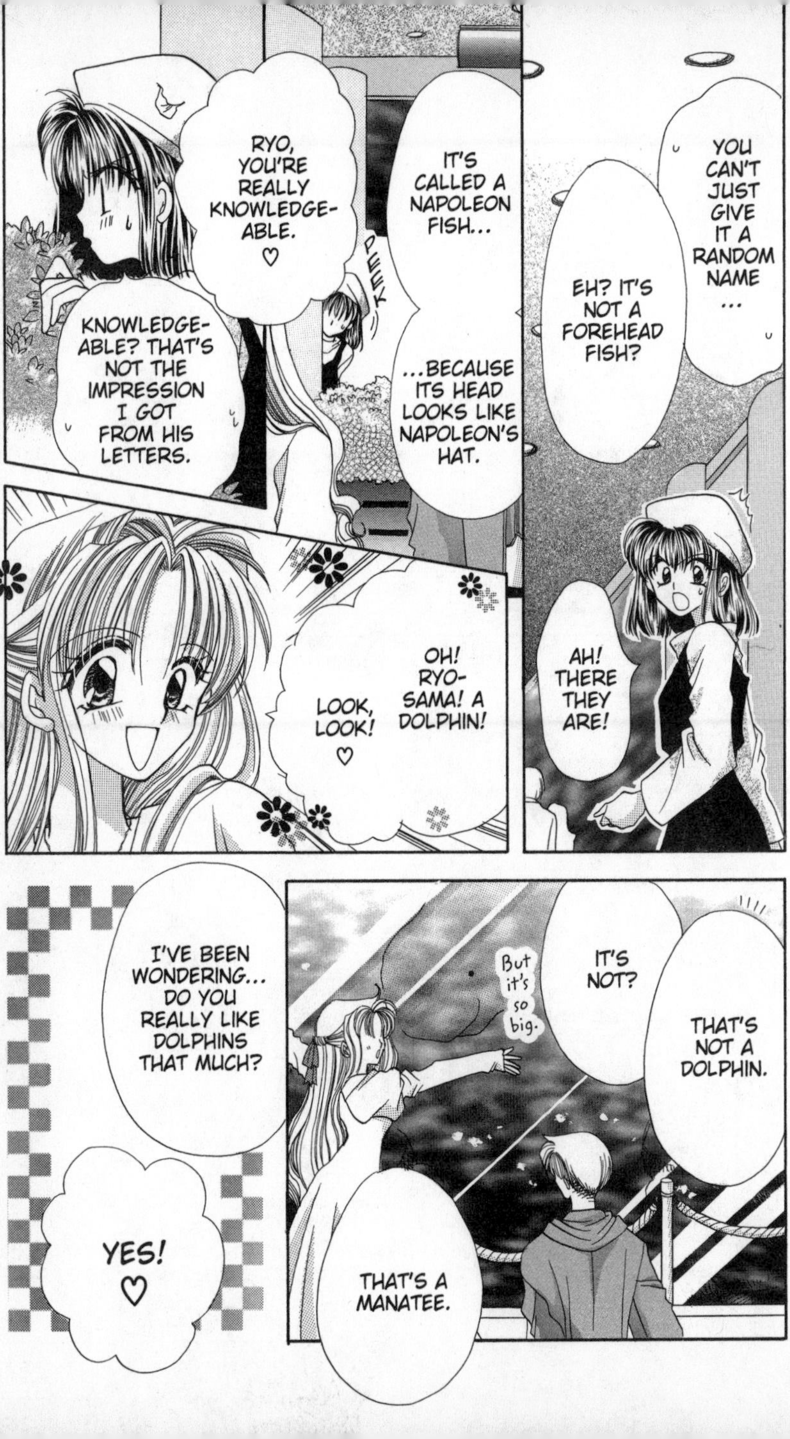
YOU CAN'T JUST GIVE IT A RANDOM NAME...
EH? IT'S NOT A FOREHEAD FISH?
AH! THERE THEY ARE!
IT'S CALLED A NAPOLEON FISH...
...BECAUSE ITS HEAD LOOKS LIKE NAPOLEON'S HAT.
PEEK
RYO, YOU'RE REALLY KNOWLEDGE-ABLE. ♡
KNOWLEDGE-ABLE? THAT'S NOT THE IMPRESSION I GOT FROM HIS LETTERS.
OH! RYO-SAMA! A DOLPHIN!
LOOK, LOOK! ♡
THAT'S NOT A DOLPHIN.
IT'S NOT?
But it's so big.
THAT'S A MANATEE.
I'VE BEEN WONDERING... DO YOU REALLY LIKE DOLPHINS THAT MUCH?
YES! ♡

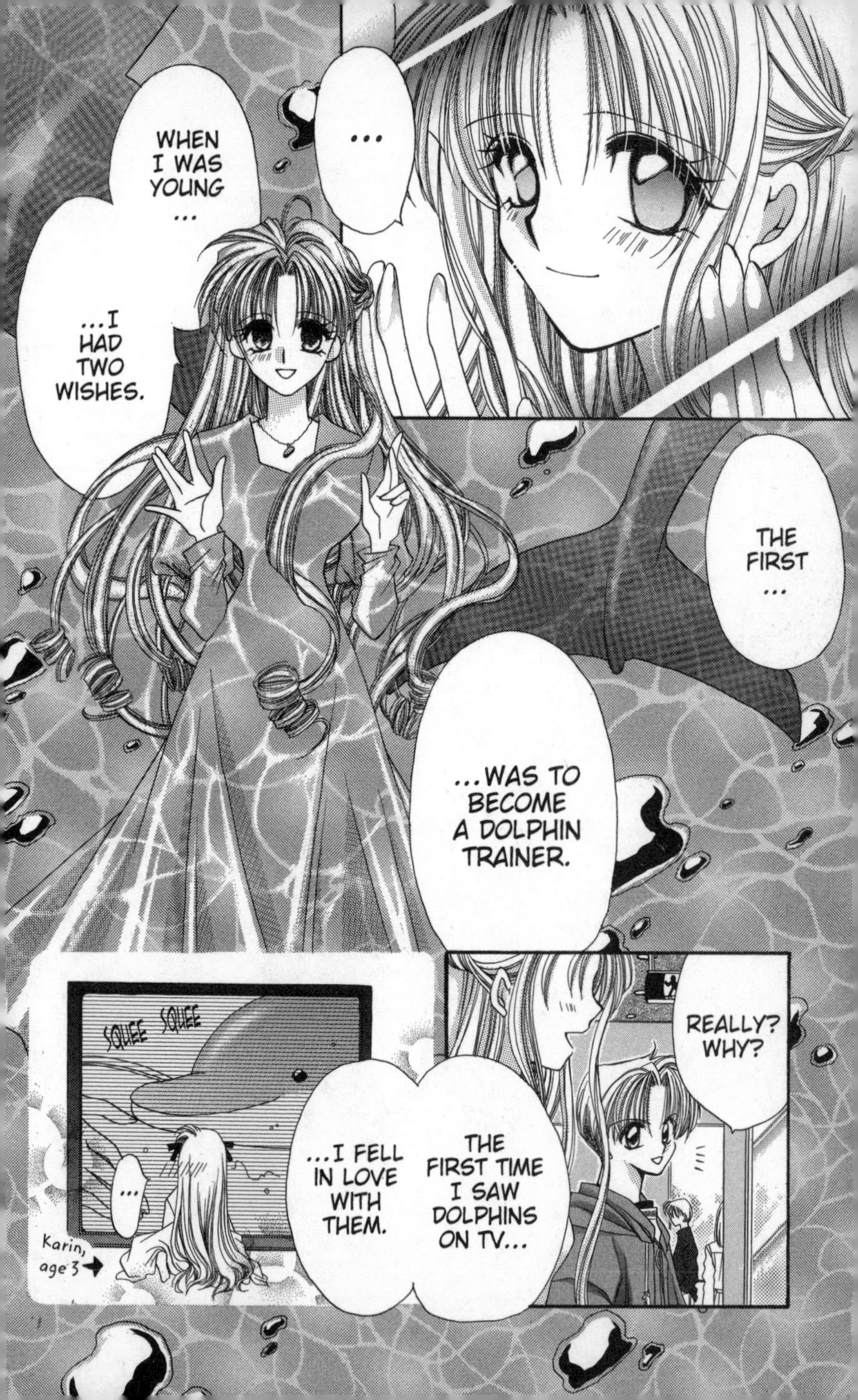
...
WHEN I WAS YOUNG ...
...I HAD TWO WISHES.
THE FIRST ...
...WAS TO BECOME A DOLPHIN TRAINER.
REALLY? WHY?
THE FIRST TIME I SAW DOLPHINS ON TV...
...I FELL IN LOVE WITH THEM.
SQUEE SQUEE
...
Karin, age 3

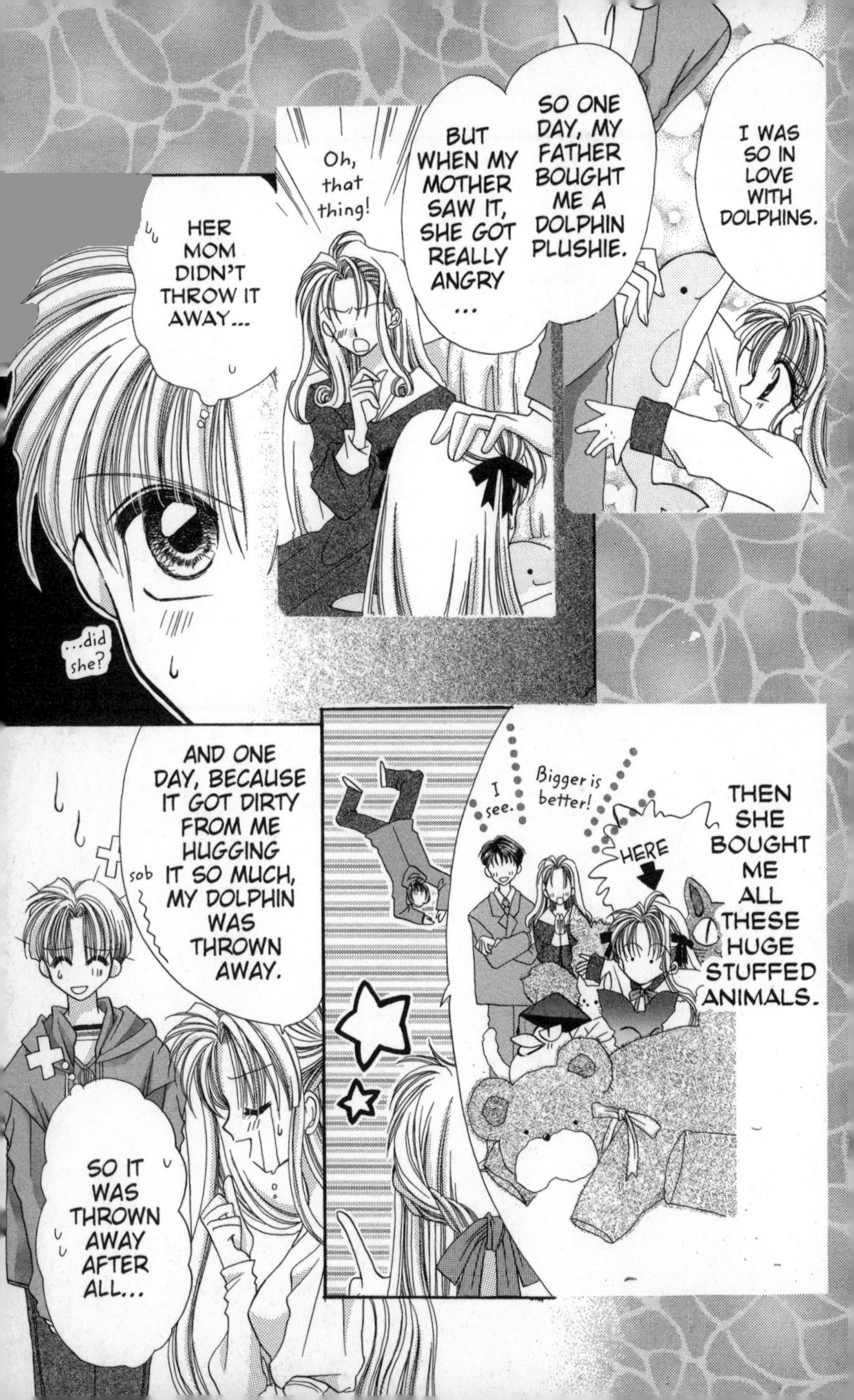
I WAS SO IN LOVE WITH DOLPHINS.
SO ONE DAY, MY FATHER BOUGHT ME A DOLPHIN PLUSHIE.
BUT WHEN MY MOTHER SAW IT, SHE GOT REALLY ANGRY ...
Oh, that thing!
HER MOM DIDN'T THROW IT AWAY...
...did she?
THEN SHE BOUGHT ME ALL THESE HUGE STUFFED ANIMALS.
HERE
Bigger is better!
I see.
AND ONE DAY, BECAUSE IT GOT DIRTY FROM ME HUGGING IT SO MUCH, MY DOLPHIN WAS THROWN AWAY.
sob
SO IT WAS THROWN AWAY AFTER ALL...

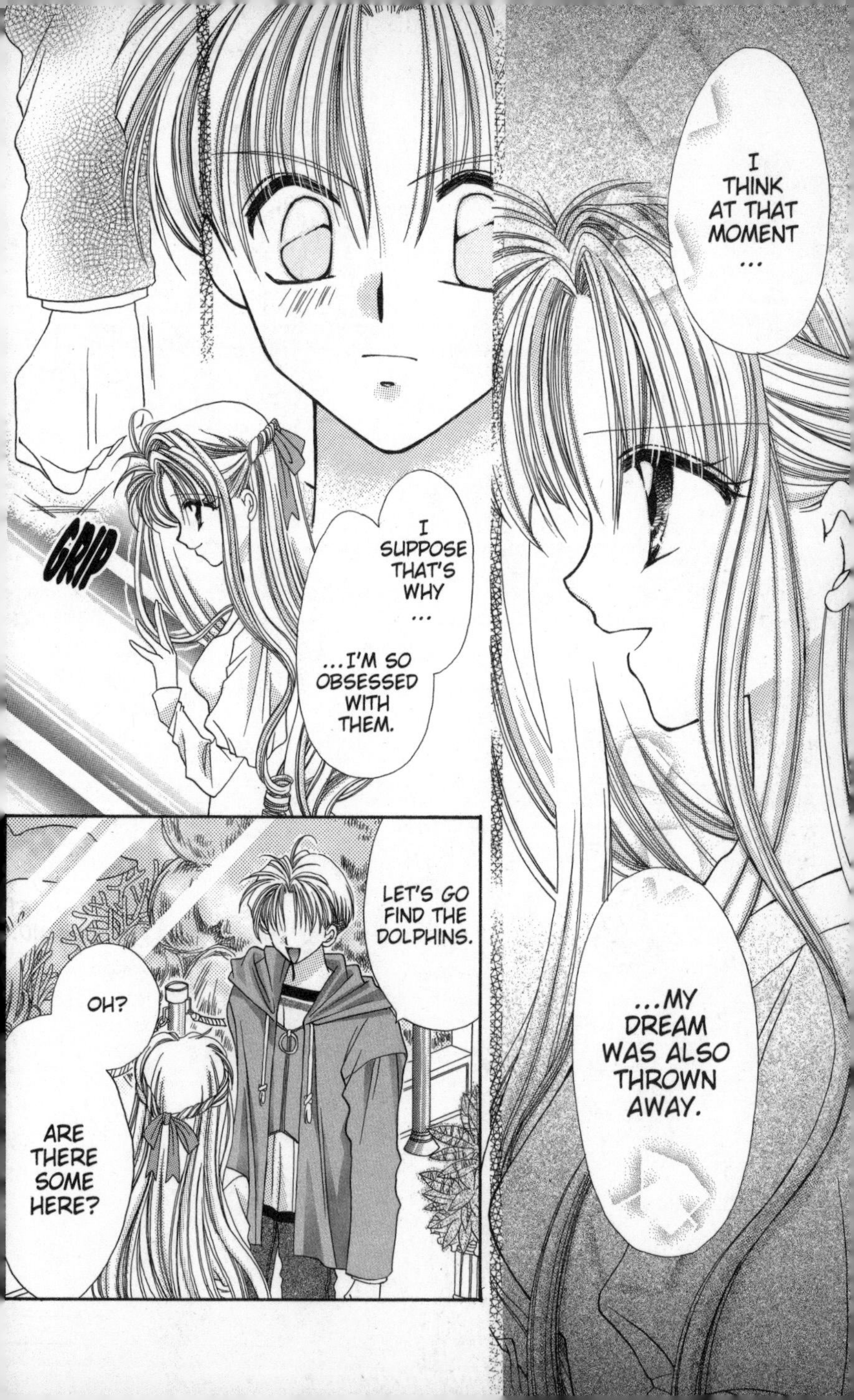
I THINK AT THAT MOMENT ...
...MY DREAM WAS ALSO THROWN AWAY.
I SUPPOSE THAT'S WHY ...
...I'M SO OBSESSED WITH THEM.
GRIP
LET'S GO FIND THE DOLPHINS.
OH?
ARE THERE SOME HERE?

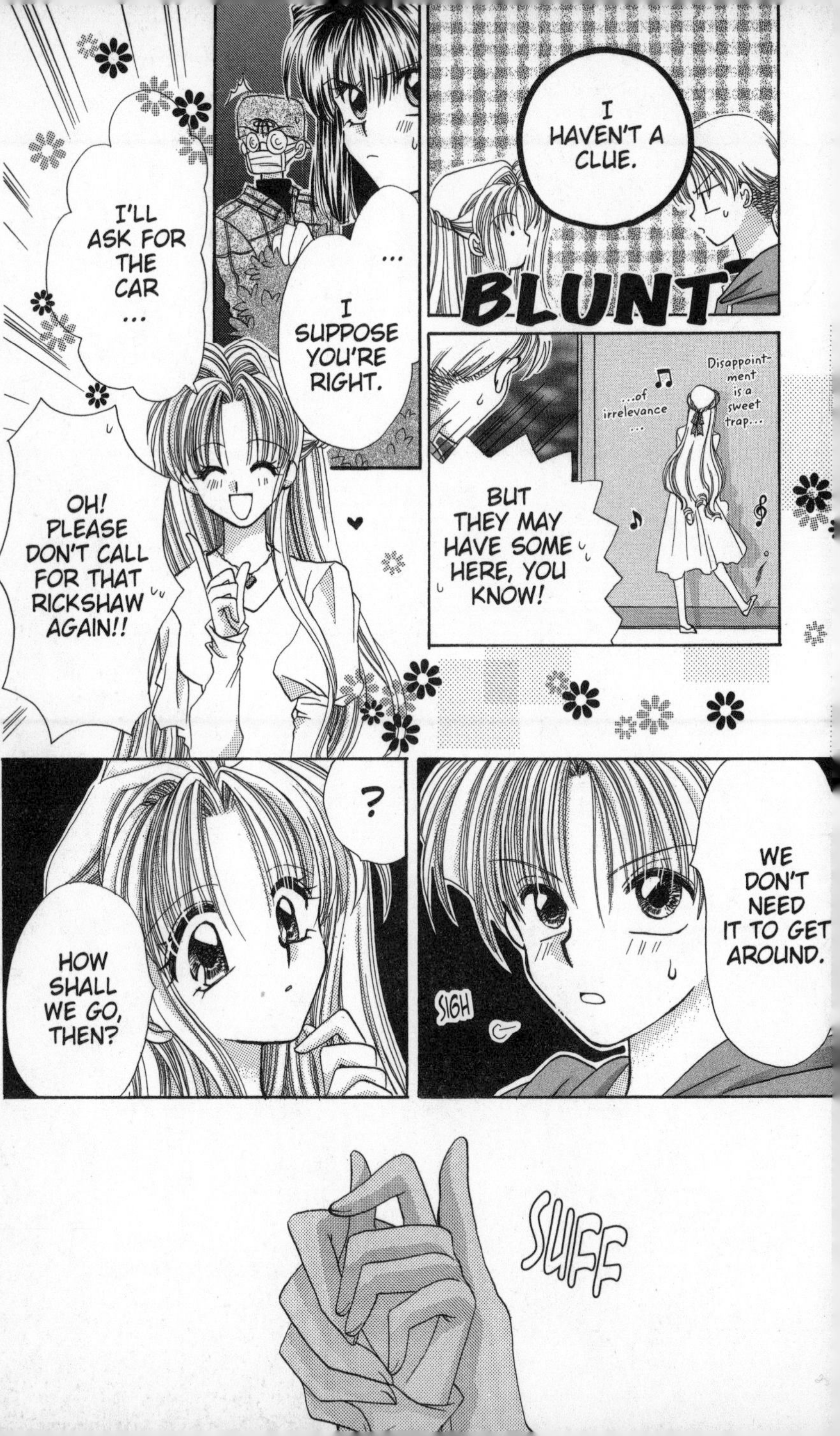
I HAVEN'T A CLUE.
BLUNT
Disappointment is a sweet trap...
...of irrelevance...
BUT THEY MAY HAVE SOME HERE, YOU KNOW!
...
I SUPPOSE YOU'RE RIGHT.
I'LL ASK FOR THE CAR ...
OH! PLEASE DON'T CALL FOR THAT RICKSHAW AGAIN!!
WE DON'T NEED IT TO GET AROUND.
SIGH
?
HOW SHALL WE GO, THEN?
SUFF

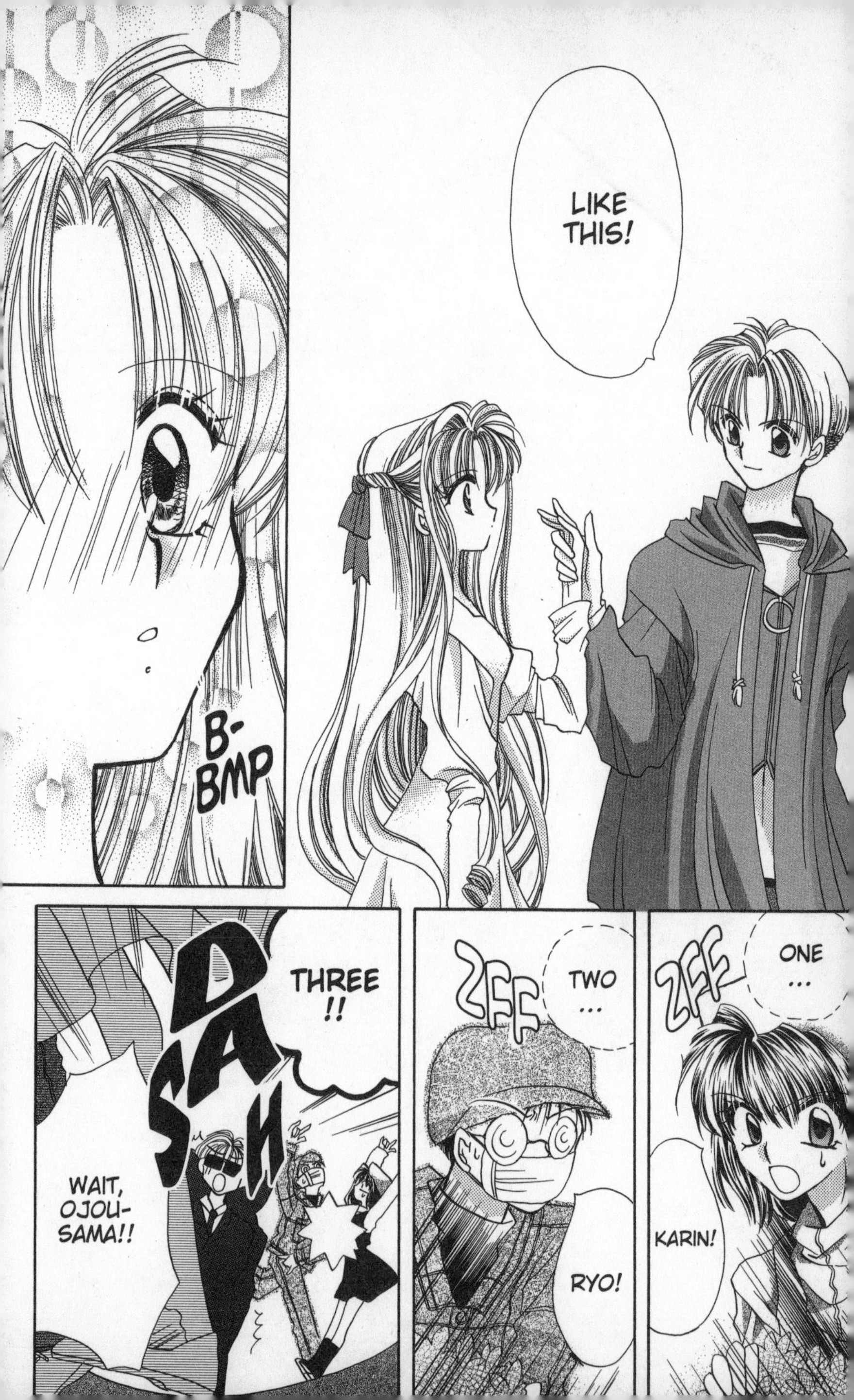
LIKE THIS!
B-BMP
ONE ...
ZFF
KARIN!
TWO ...
ZFF
RYO!
THREE !!
DASH
WAIT, OJOU-SAMA!!

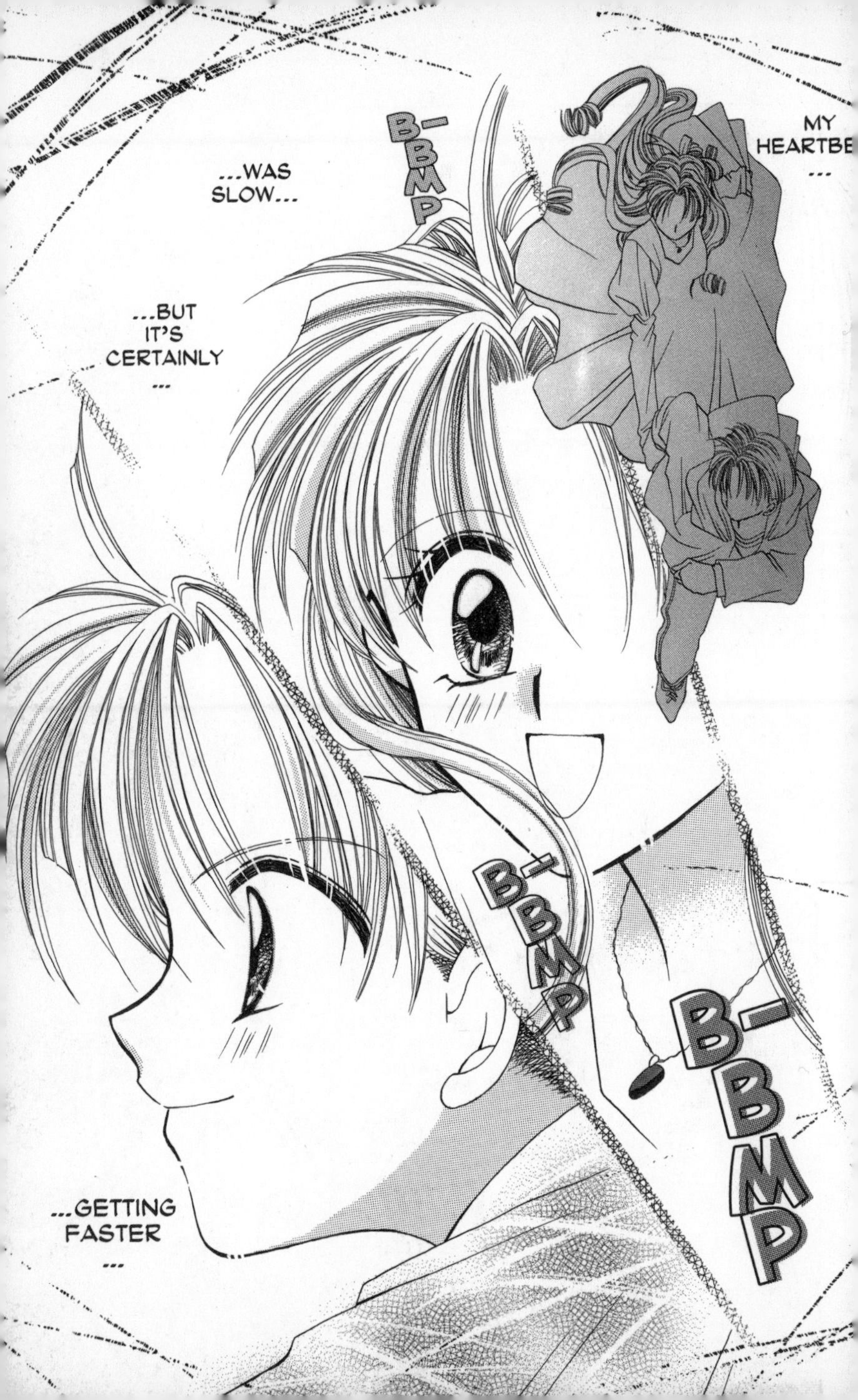
MY HEARTBE ...
B-BMP
...WAS SLOW...
...BUT IT'S CERTAINLY ...
B-BMP
B-BMP
...GETTING FASTER ...

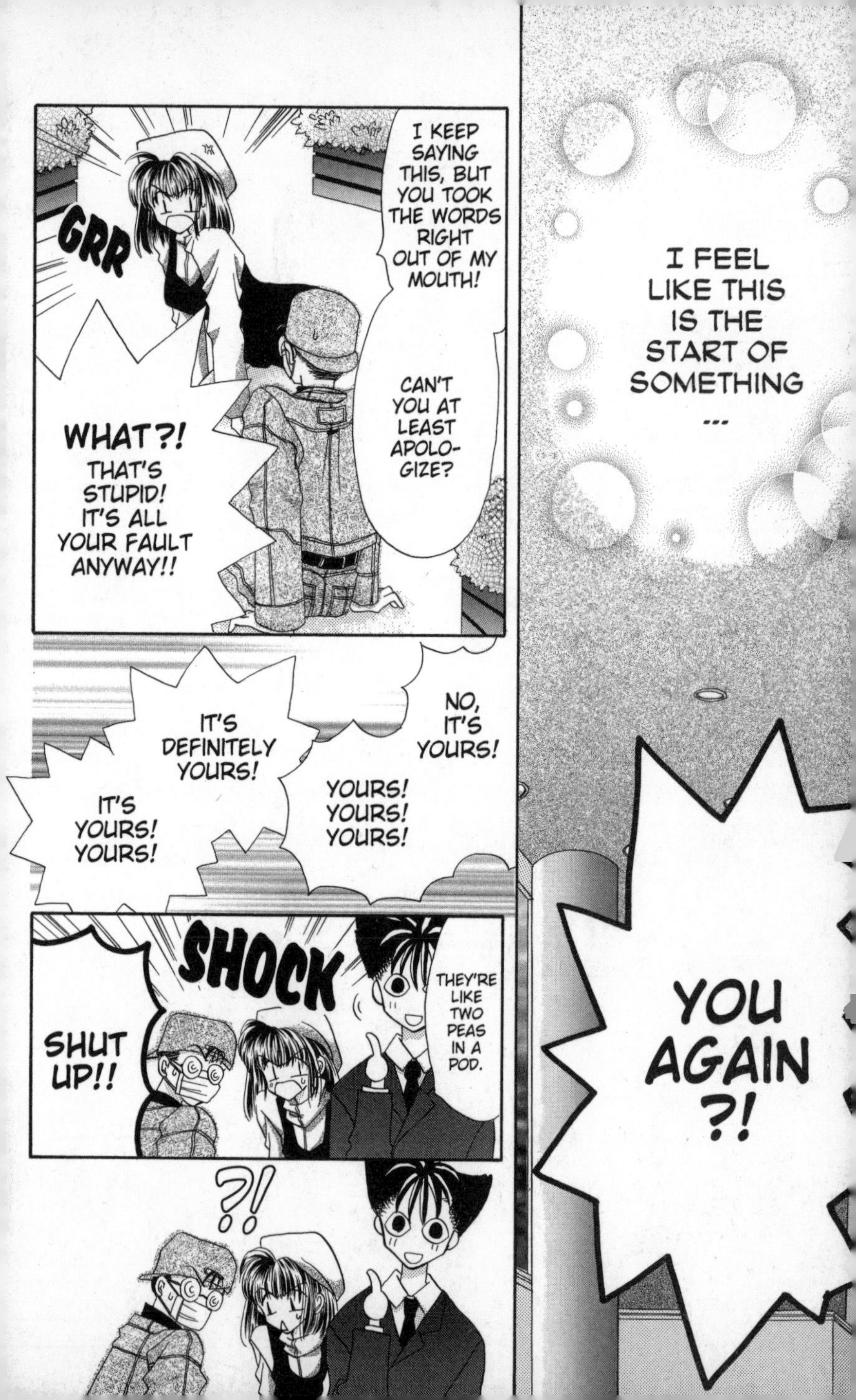
I FEEL LIKE THIS IS THE START OF SOMETHING ...
YOU AGAIN?!
I KEEP SAYING THIS, BUT YOU TOOK THE WORDS RIGHT OUT OF MY MOUTH!
GRR
CAN'T YOU AT LEAST APOLOGIZE?
WHAT?! THAT'S STUPID! IT'S ALL YOUR FAULT ANYWAY!!
NO, IT'S YOURS!
IT'S DEFINITELY YOURS!
YOURS! YOURS! YOURS!
IT'S YOURS! YOURS!
THEY'RE LIKE TWO PEAS IN A POD.
SHOCK
SHUT UP!!
?!

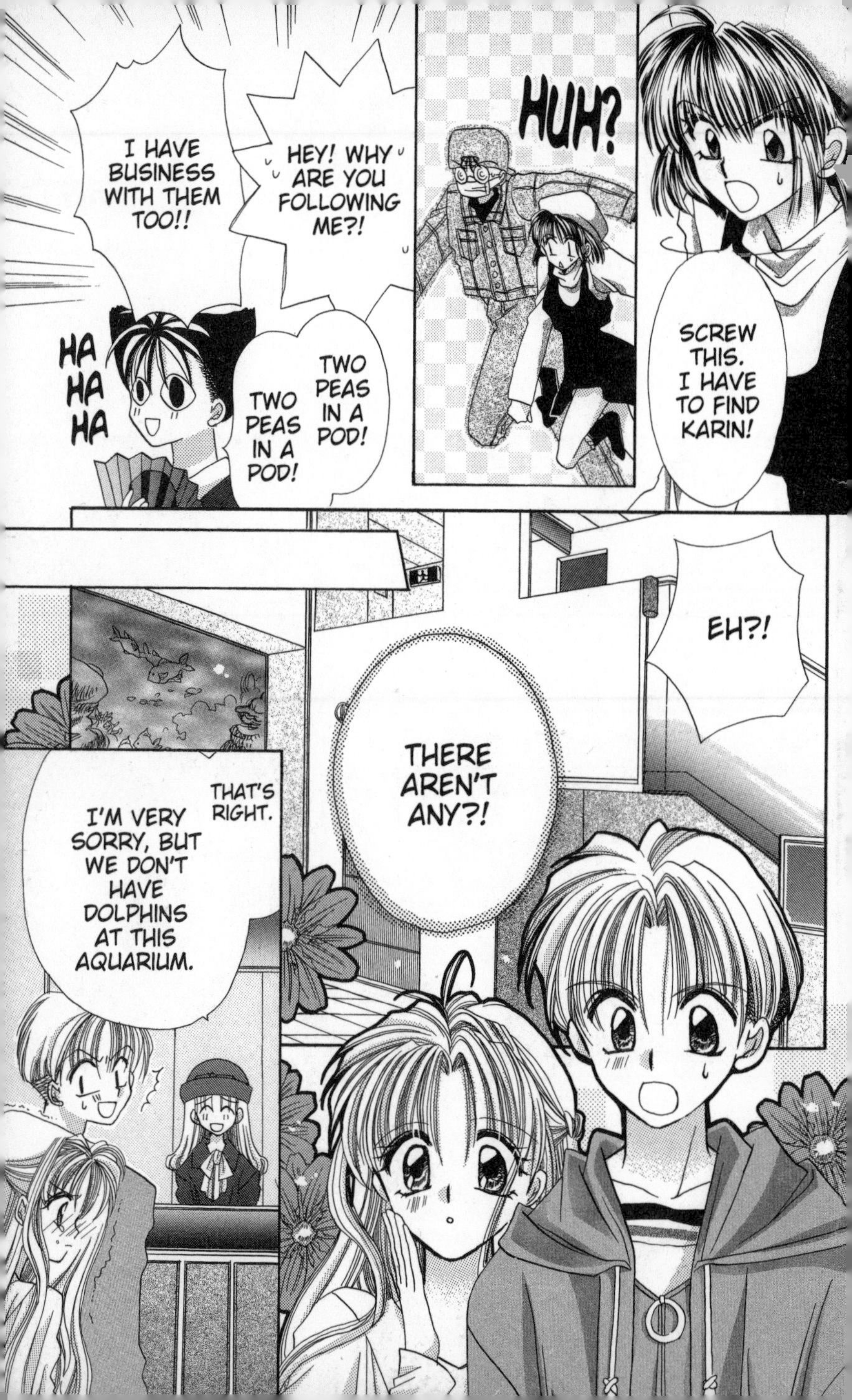
SCREW THIS. I HAVE TO FIND KARIN!
HUH?
HEY! WHY ARE YOU FOLLOWING ME?!
I HAVE BUSINESS WITH THEM TOO!!
TWO PEAS IN A POD!
TWO PEAS IN A POD!
HA HA HA
EH?!
THERE AREN'T ANY?!
THAT'S RIGHT.
I'M VERY SORRY, BUT WE DON'T HAVE DOLPHINS AT THIS AQUARIUM.

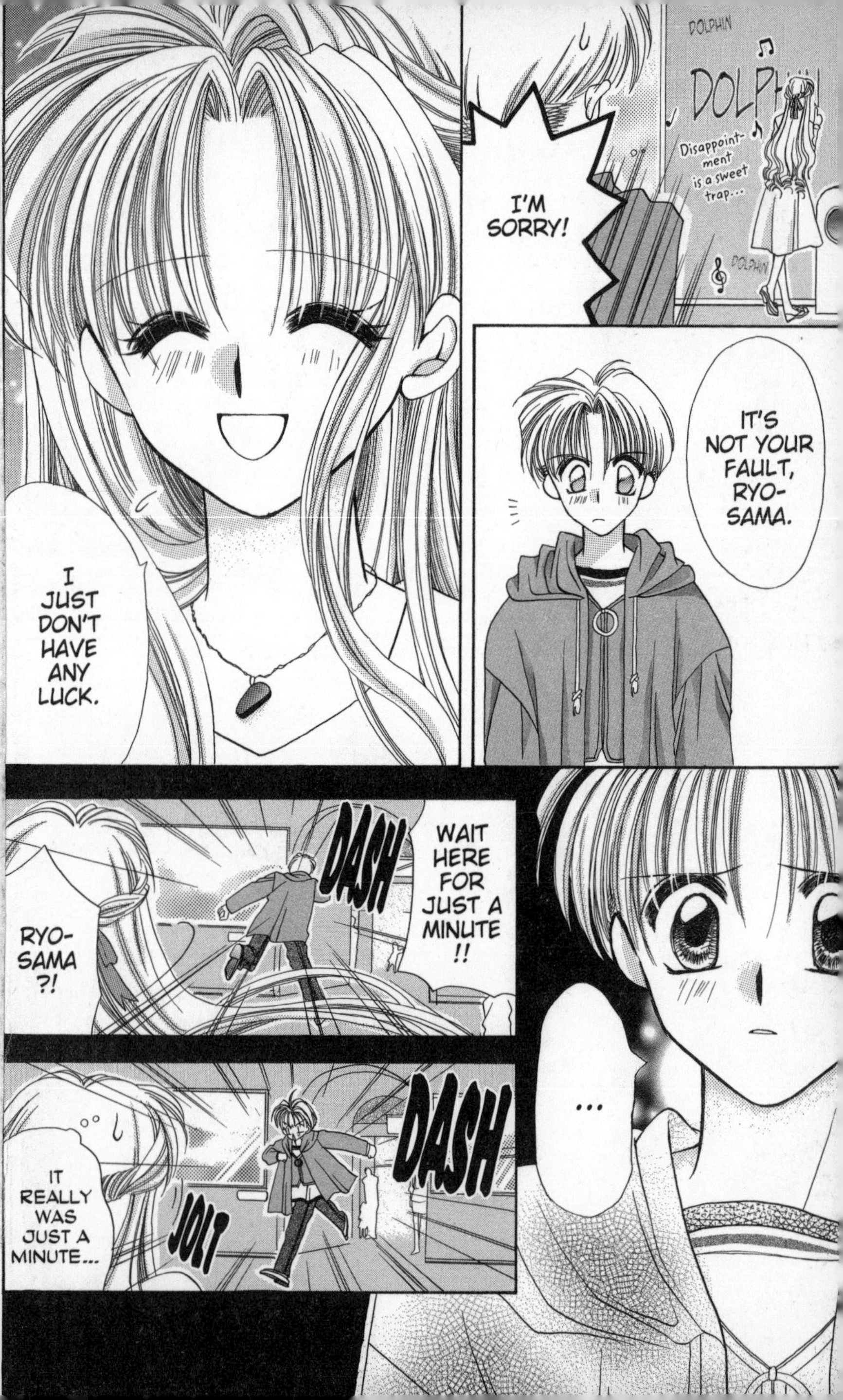
DOLPHIN
DOLPHIN
Disappointment is a sweet trap...
DOLPHIN
I'M SORRY!
IT'S NOT YOUR FAULT, RYO-SAMA.
I JUST DON'T HAVE ANY LUCK.
...
WAIT HERE FOR JUST A MINUTE!!
DASH
RYO-SAMA?!
DASH
JOLT
IT REALLY WAS JUST A MINUTE...

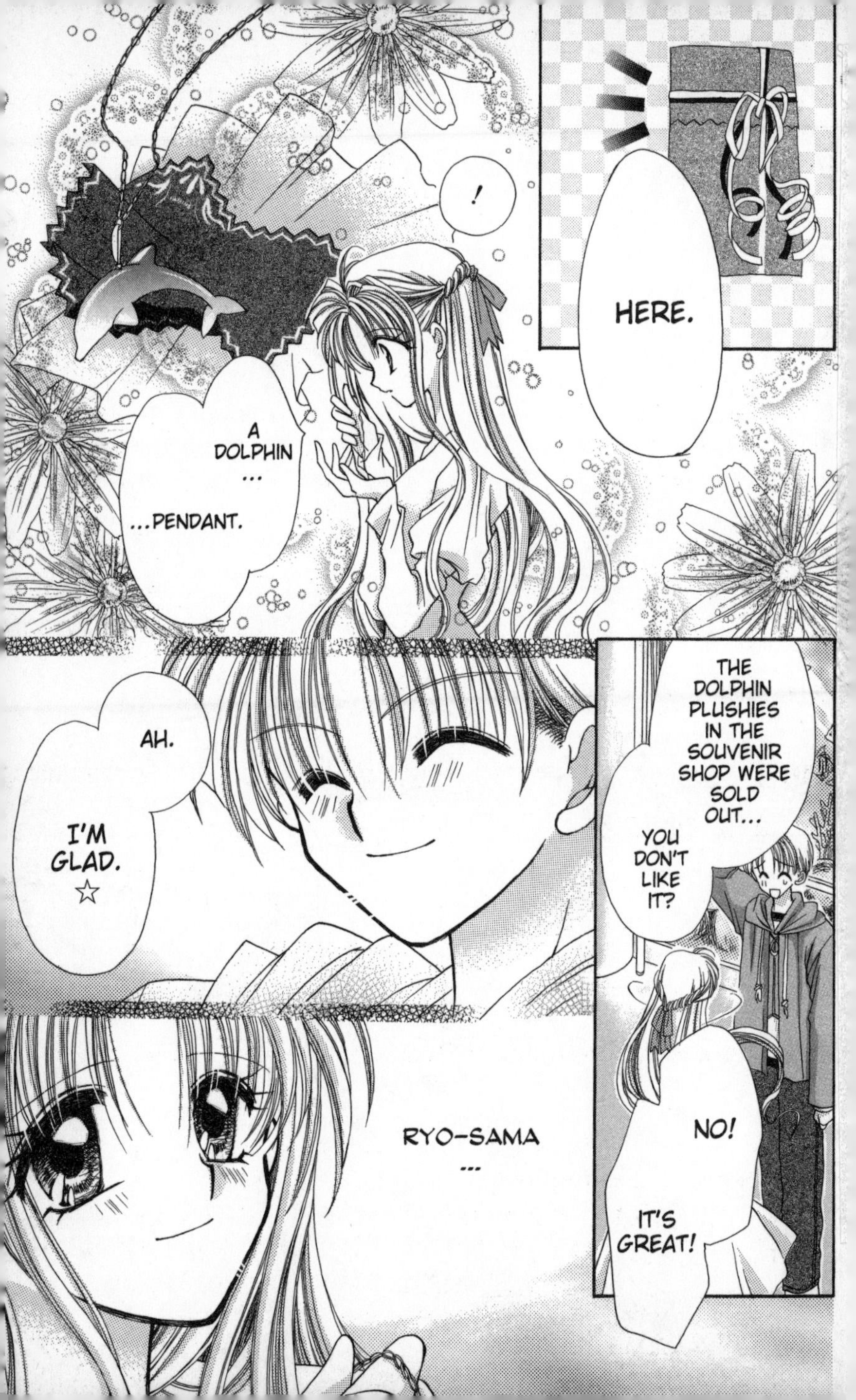
HERE.
!
A DOLPHIN ...
...PENDANT.
THE DOLPHIN PLUSHIES IN THE SOUVENIR SHOP WERE SOLD OUT...
YOU DON'T LIKE IT?
NO!
IT'S GREAT!
AH.
I'M GLAD. ☆
RYO-SAMA ...

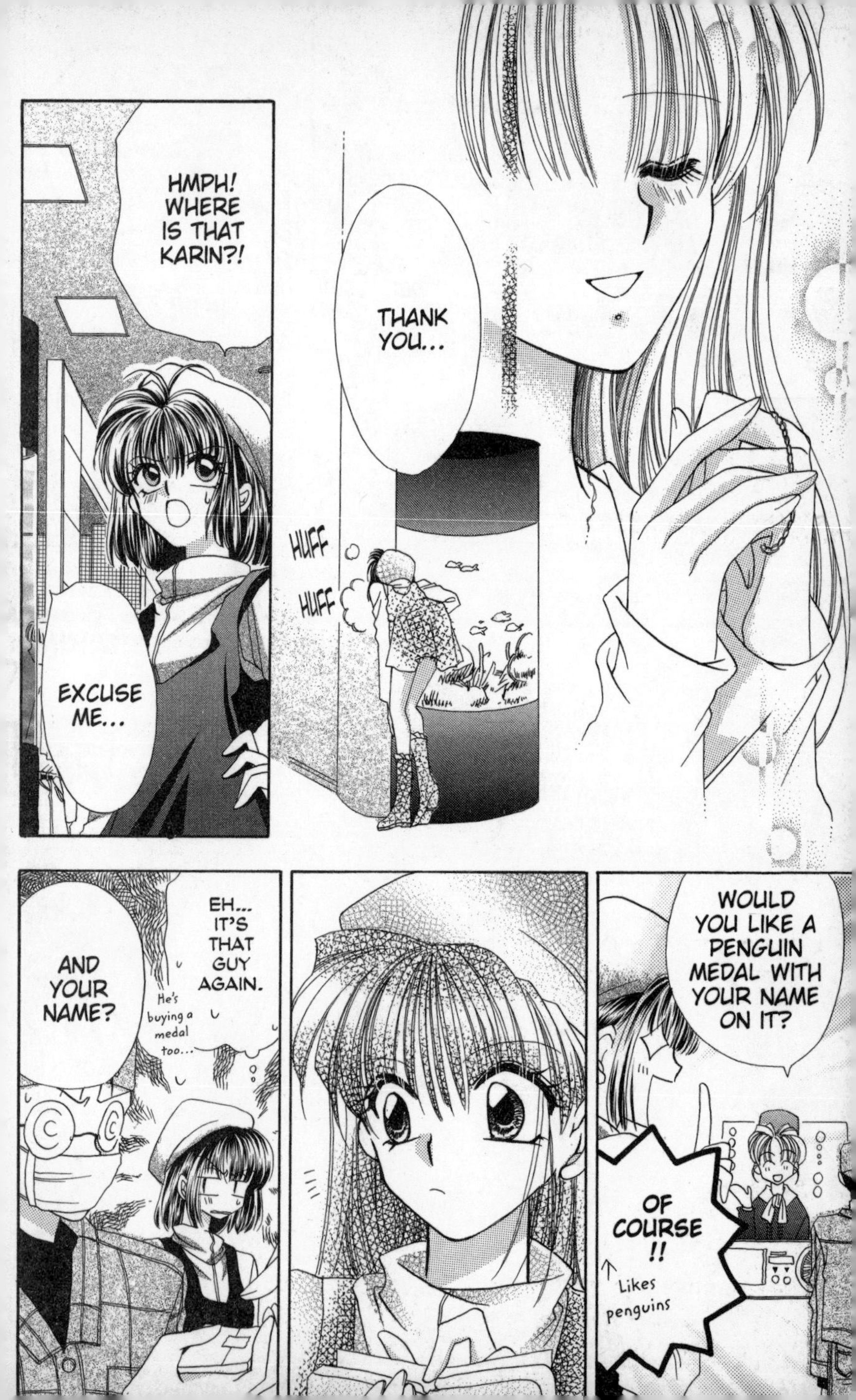
THANK YOU...
HUFF
HUFF
HMPH! WHERE IS THAT KARIN?!
EXCUSE ME...
WOULD YOU LIKE A PENGUIN MEDAL WITH YOUR NAME ON IT?
OF COURSE!!
↑ Likes penguins
EH... IT'S THAT GUY AGAIN.
He's buying a medal too...
AND YOUR NAME?

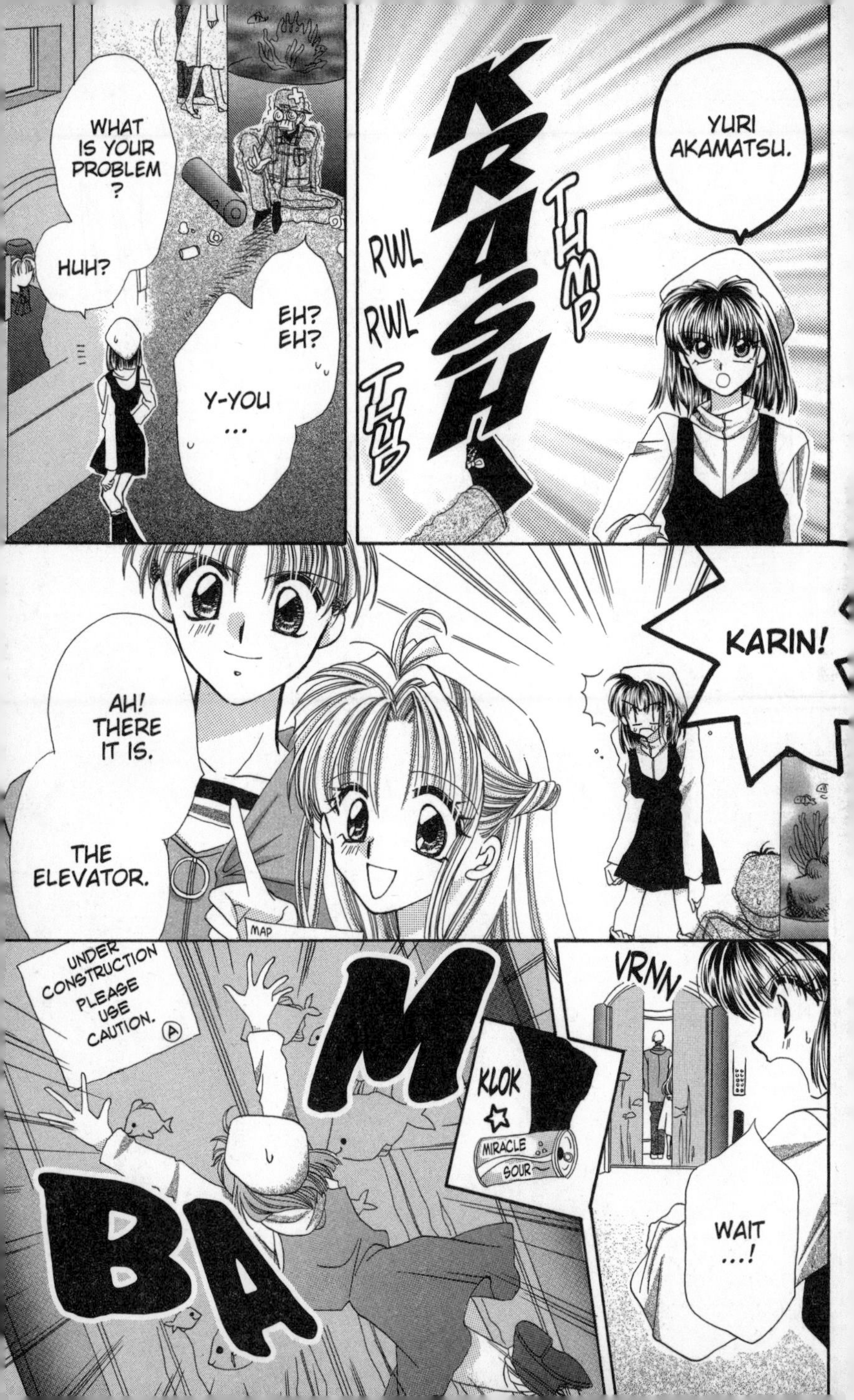
YURI AKAMATSU.
KRASH
THUMP
RWL RWL
THUD
WHAT IS YOUR PROBLEM?
HUH?
EH? EH?
Y-YOU...
KARIN!
AH! THERE IT IS.
THE ELEVATOR.
MAP
VRNN
WAIT...!
UNDER CONSTRUCTION PLEASE USE CAUTION.
BAM
KLOK
MIRACLE SOUR

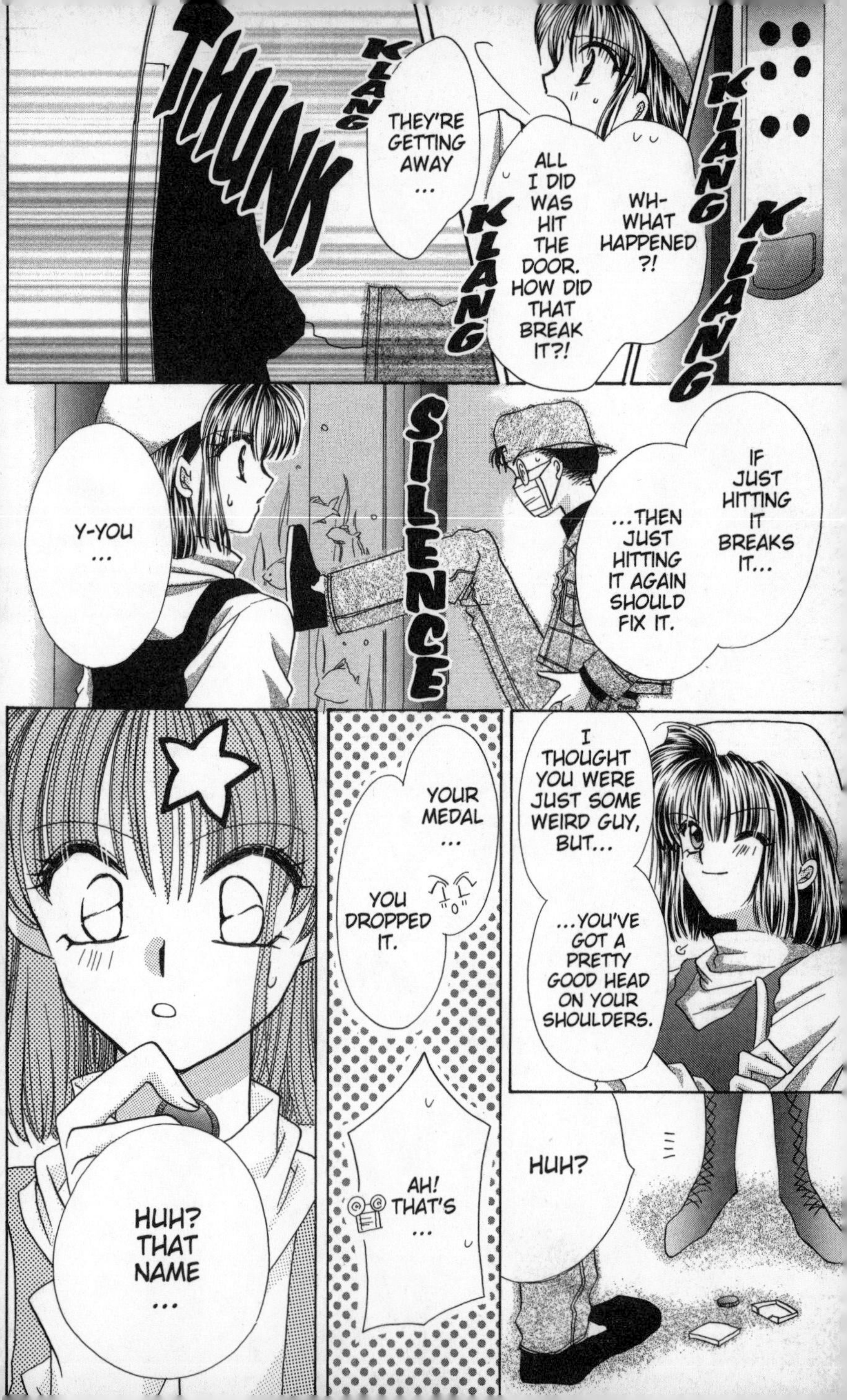
KLANG
KLANG
WH-WHAT HAPPENED?!
ALL I DID WAS HIT THE DOOR. HOW DID THAT BREAK IT?!
KLANG
THEY'RE GETTING AWAY...
KLANG
THUNK
IF JUST HITTING IT BREAKS IT...
...THEN JUST HITTING IT AGAIN SHOULD FIX IT.
SILENCE
Y-YOU...
I THOUGHT YOU WERE JUST SOME WEIRD GUY, BUT...
...YOU'VE GOT A PRETTY GOOD HEAD ON YOUR SHOULDERS.
HUH?
YOUR MEDAL...
YOU DROPPED IT.
AH! THAT'S...
HUH? THAT NAME...

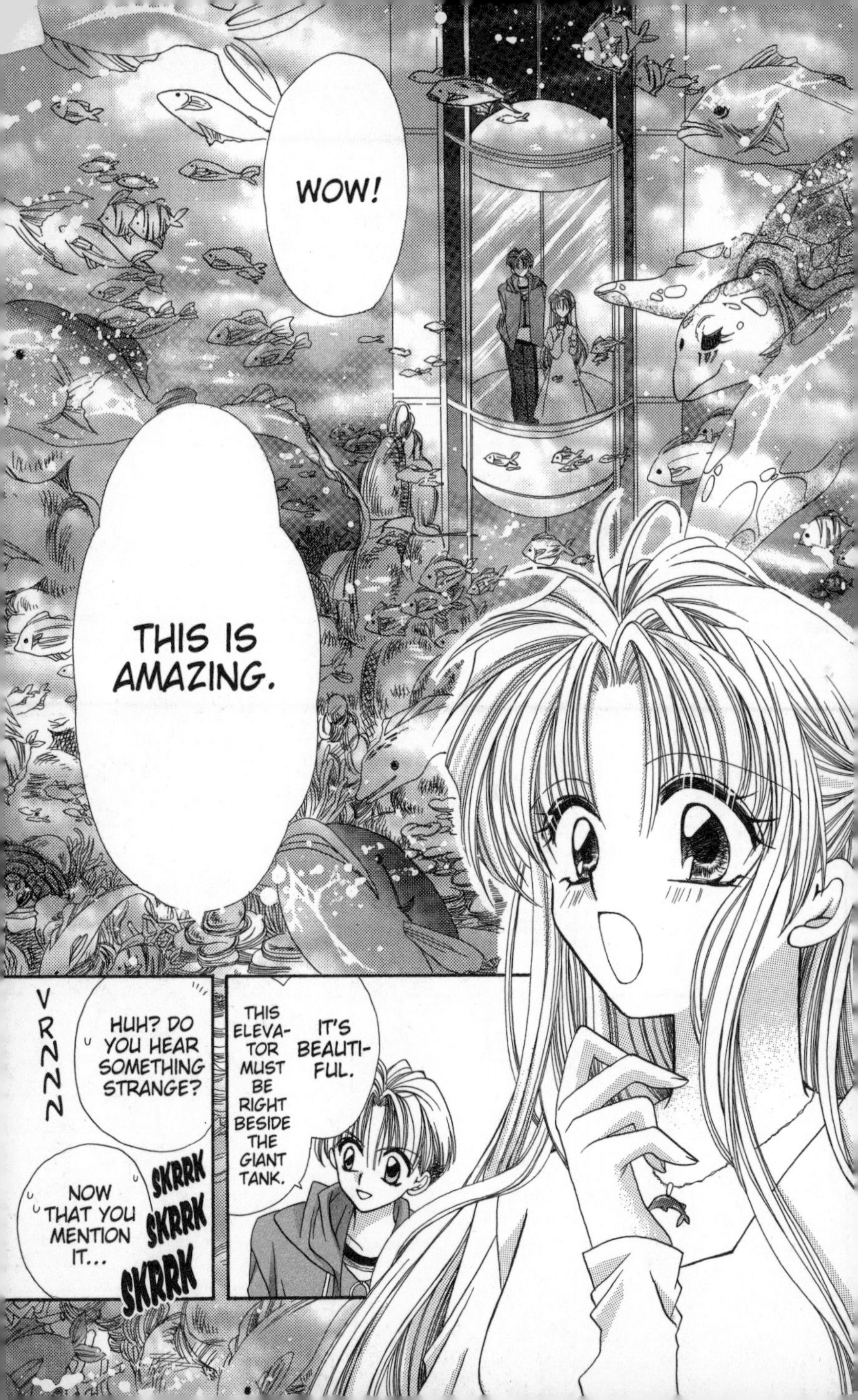
WOW!
THIS IS AMAZING.
IT'S BEAUTIFUL.
THIS ELEVATOR MUST BE RIGHT BESIDE THE GIANT TANK.
VRNNN
HUH? DO YOU HEAR SOMETHING STRANGE?
SKRRK SKRRK SKRRK
NOW THAT YOU MENTION IT...

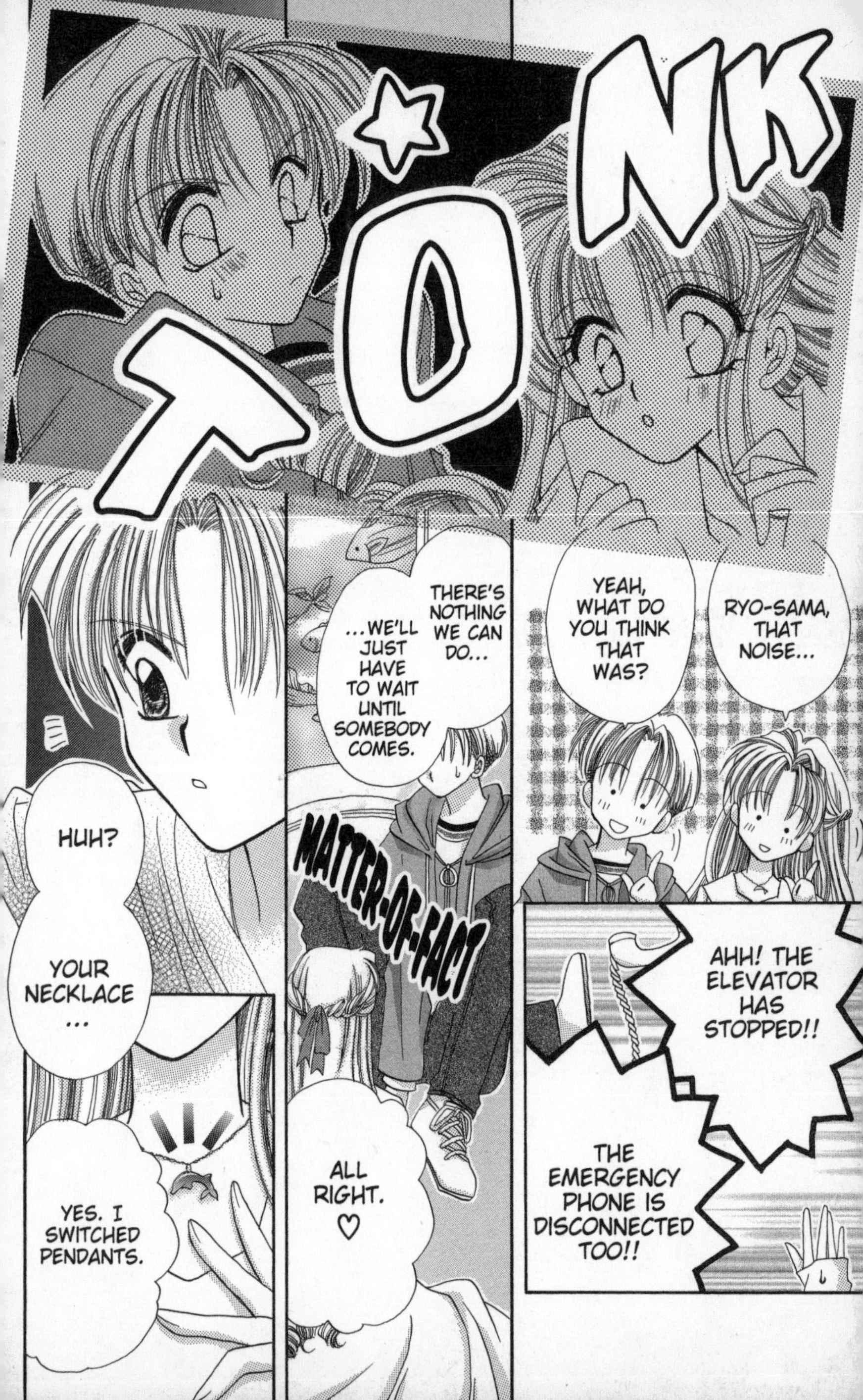
TONK
RYO-SAMA, THAT NOISE...
YEAH, WHAT DO YOU THINK THAT WAS?
AHH! THE ELEVATOR HAS STOPPED!!
THE EMERGENCY PHONE IS DISCONNECTED TOO!!
THERE'S NOTHING WE CAN DO...
...WE'LL JUST HAVE TO WAIT UNTIL SOMEBODY COMES.
MATTER-OF-FACT
ALL RIGHT. ♡
HUH?
YOUR NECKLACE ...
YES. I SWITCHED PENDANTS.

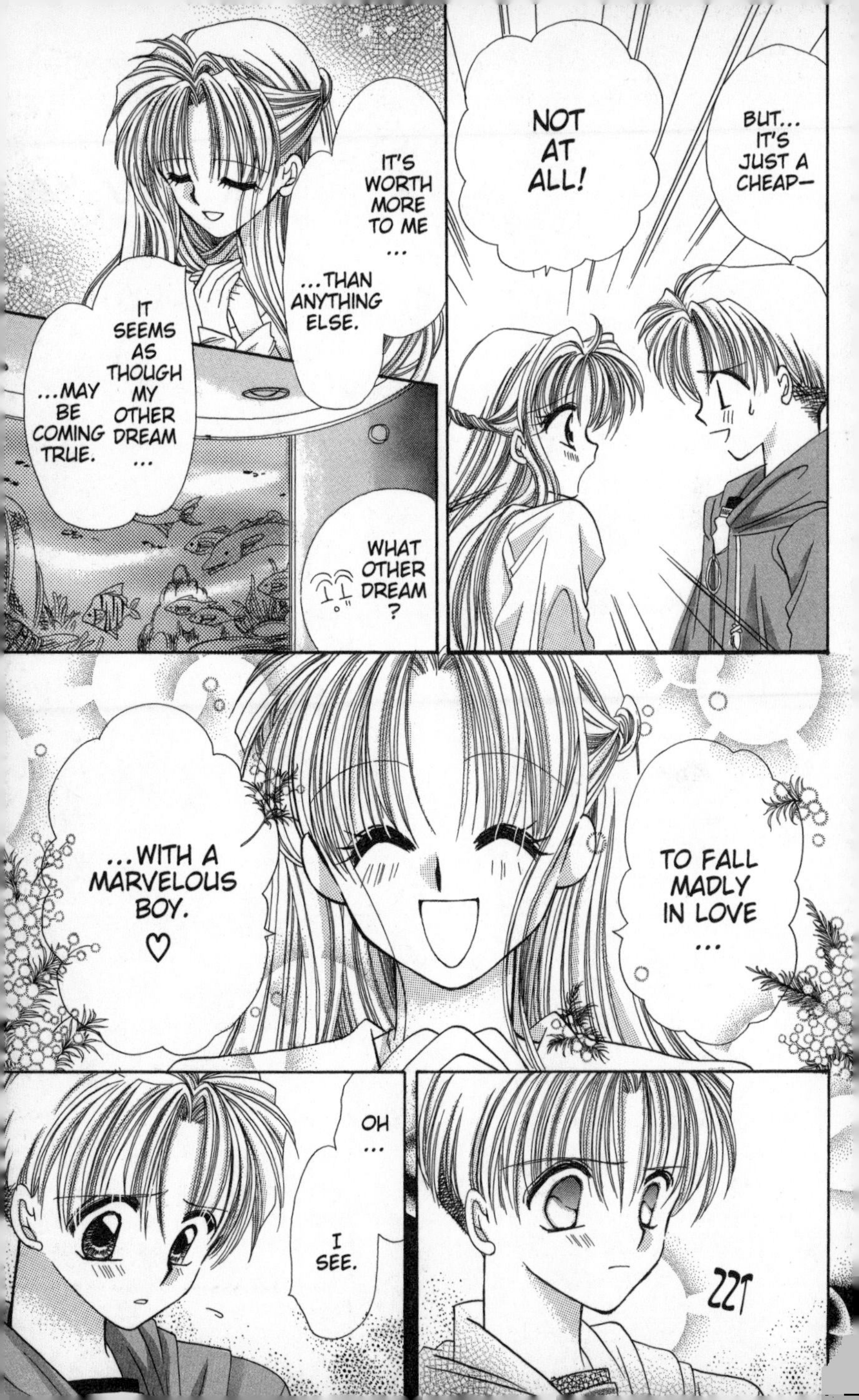

BUT... IT'S JUST A CHEAP—
NOT AT ALL!
IT'S WORTH MORE TO ME ...
...THAN ANYTHING ELSE.
IT SEEMS AS THOUGH MY OTHER DREAM ...
...MAY BE COMING TRUE.
WHAT OTHER DREAM ?
TO FALL MADLY IN LOVE ...
...WITH A MARVELOUS BOY. ♡
OH ... I SEE.

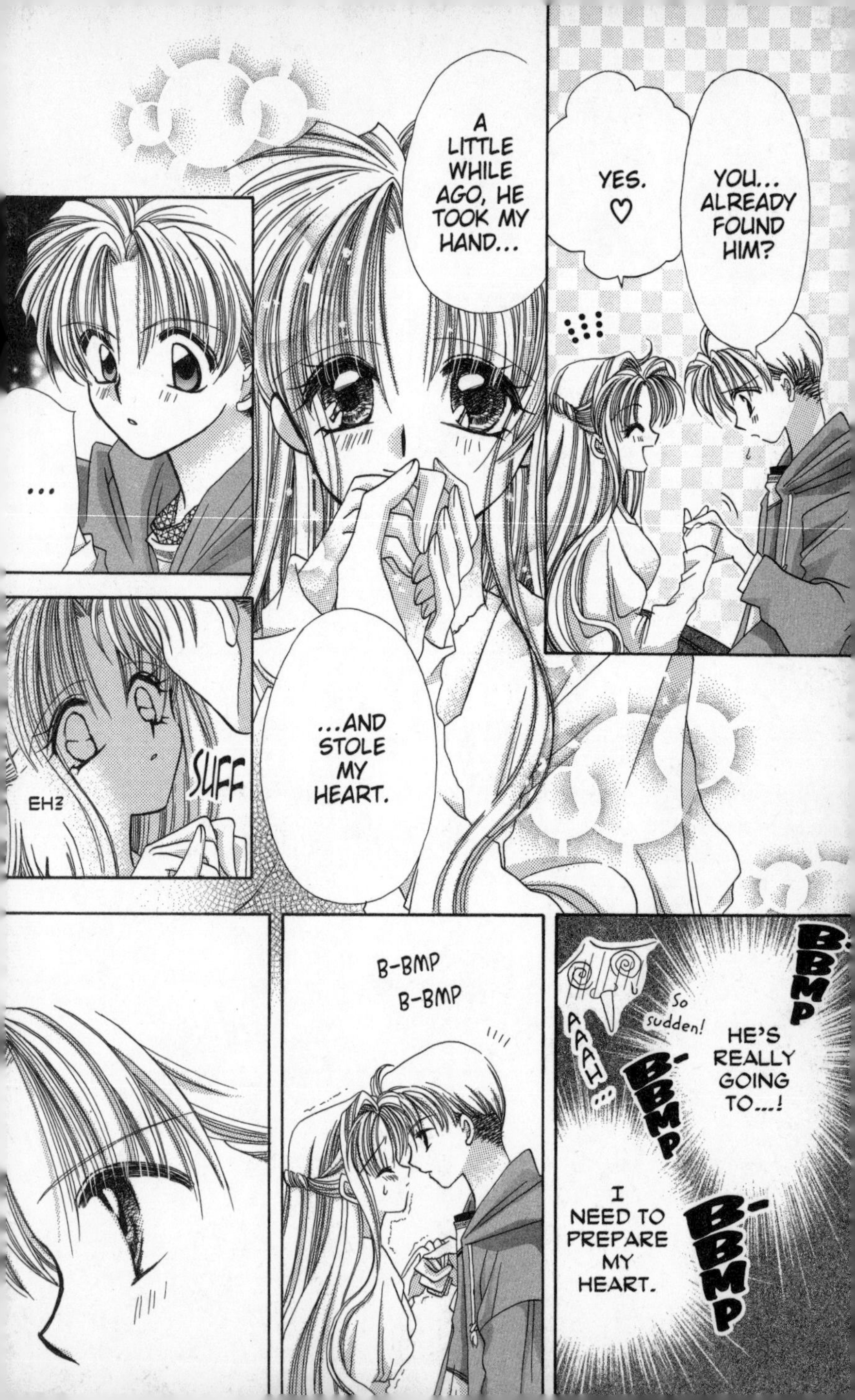
YOU... ALREADY FOUND HIM?
YES. ♡
A LITTLE WHILE AGO, HE TOOK MY HAND...
...AND STOLE MY HEART.
...
SUFF
EH?
B-BBMP
So sudden!
AAAH...
HE'S REALLY GOING TO...!
B-BBMP
I NEED TO PREPARE MY HEART.
B-BBMP
B-BMP
B-BMP

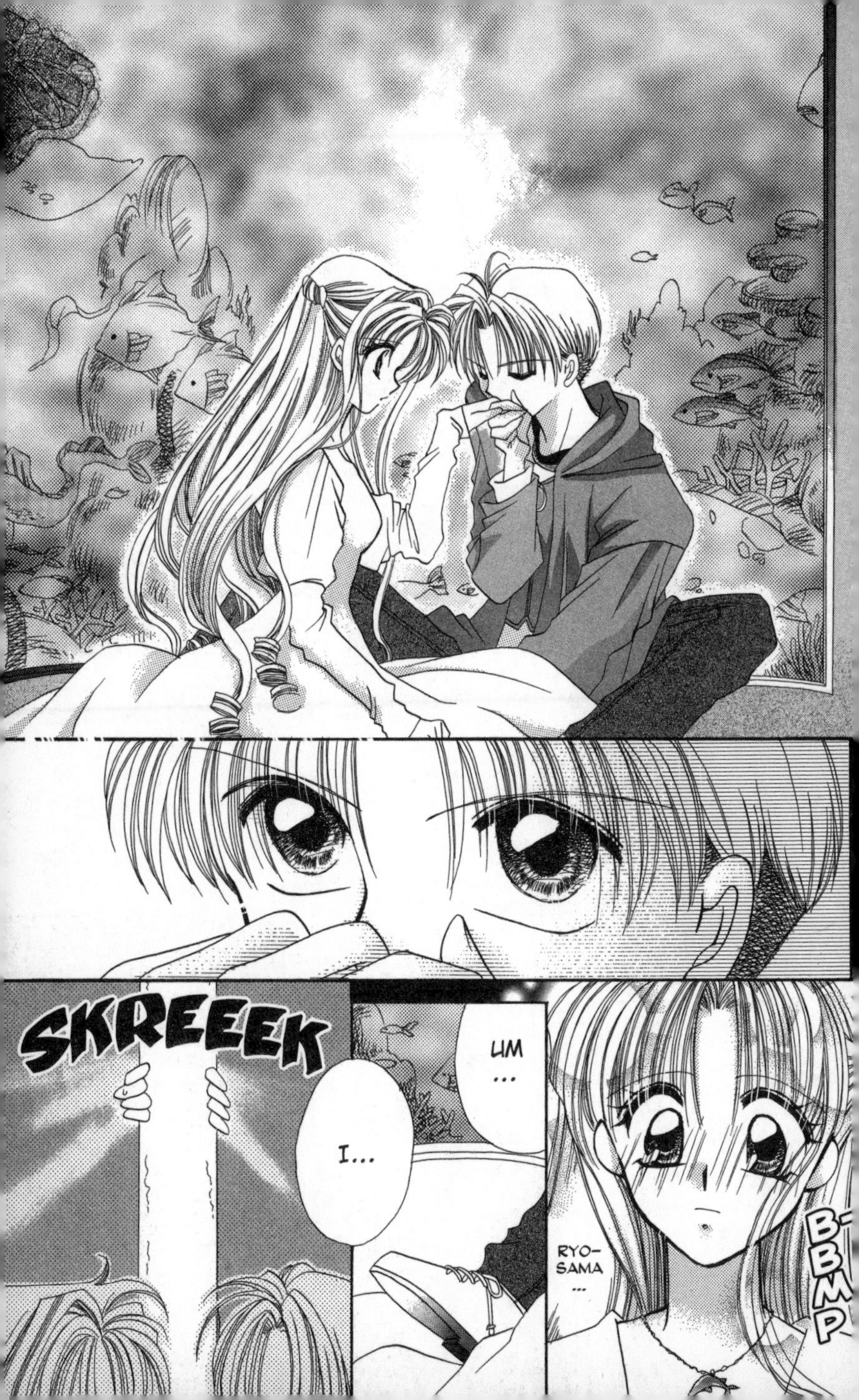
B-BBMP
RYO-SAMA ...
UM ...
I...
SKREEEK

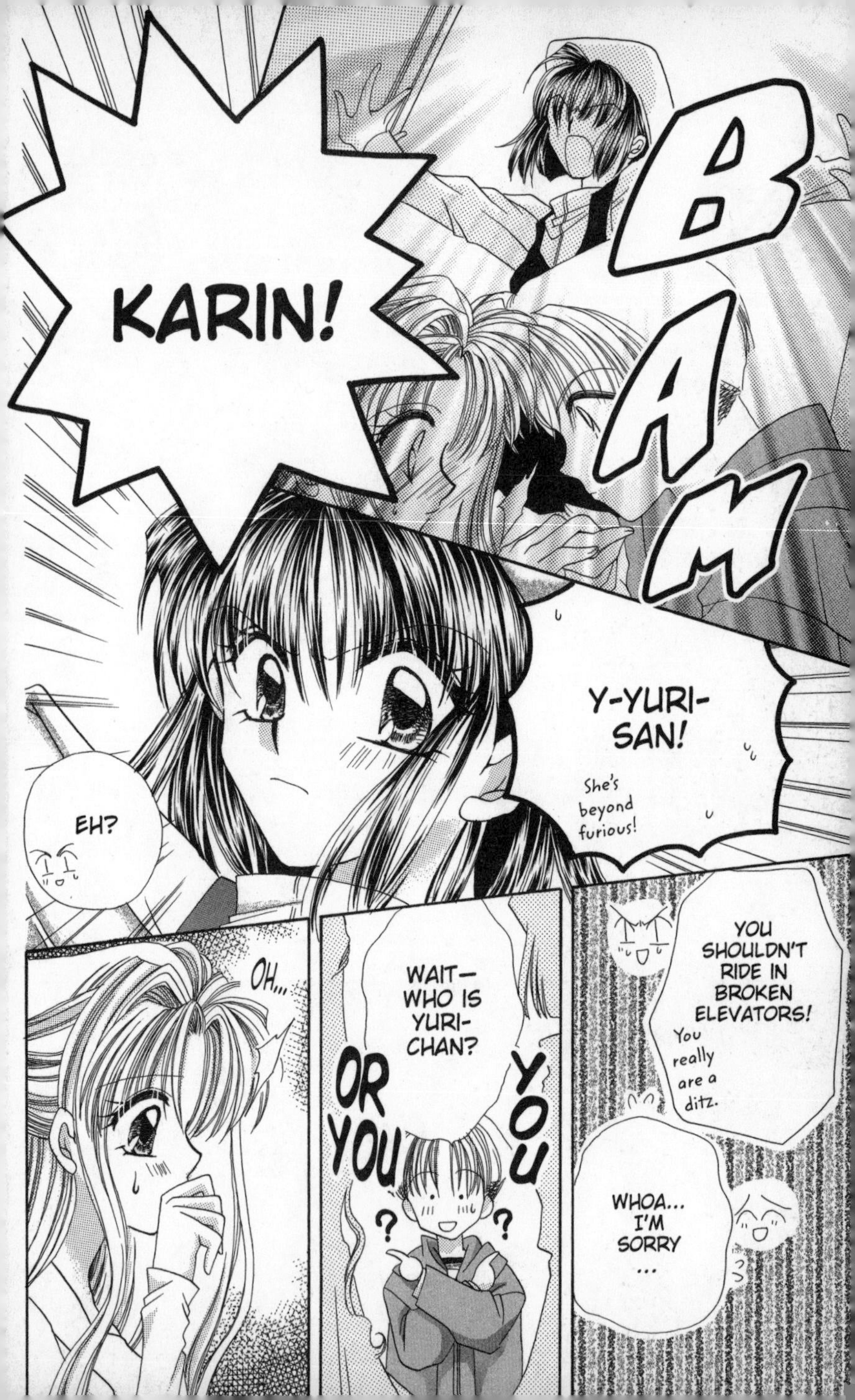
BAM
KARIN!
Y-YURI-SAN!
She's beyond furious!
EH?
YOU SHOULDN'T RIDE IN BROKEN ELEVATORS!
You really are a ditz.
WHOA... I'M SORRY ...
WAIT—WHO IS YURI-CHAN?
YOU
OR YOU
OH...

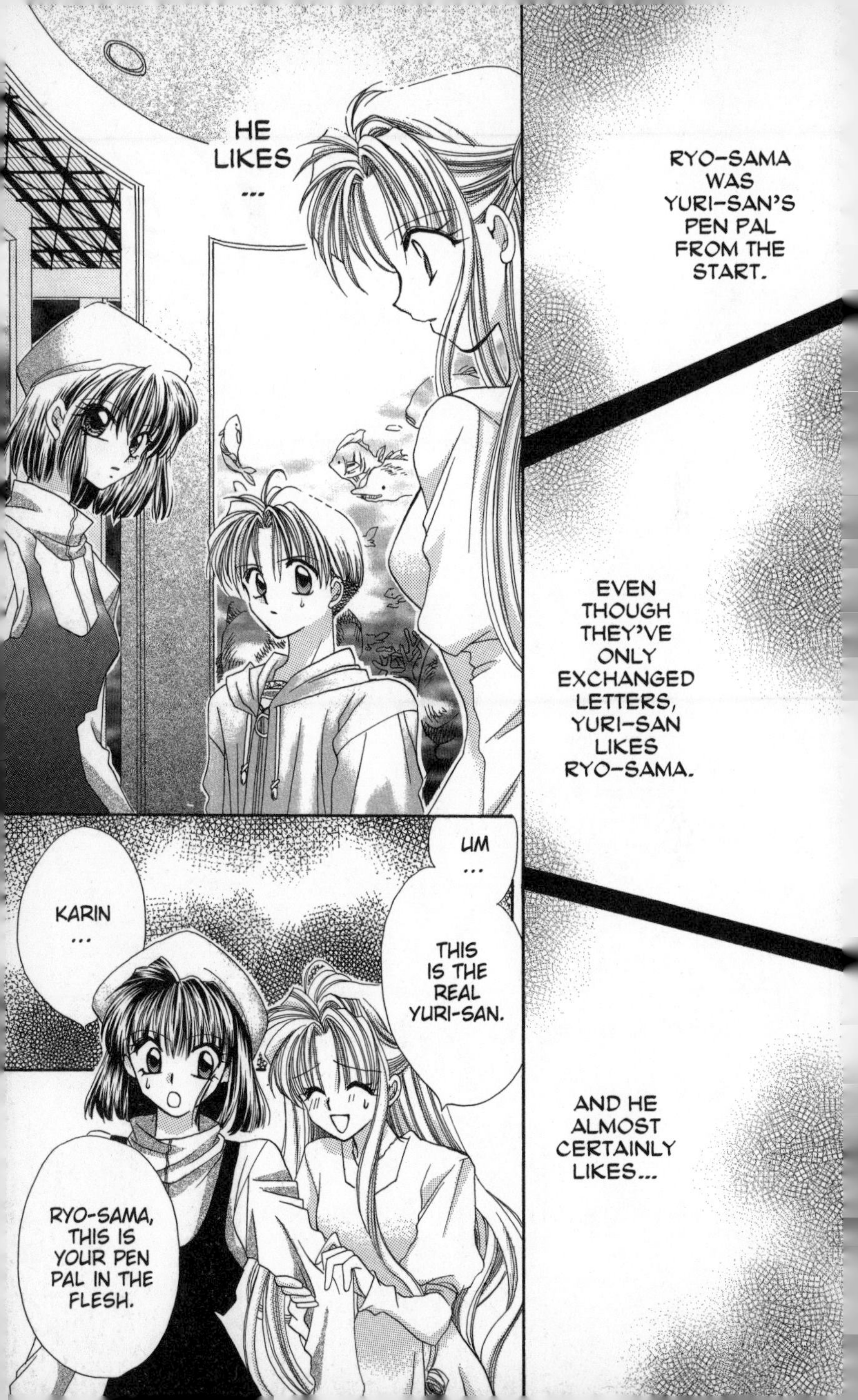
RYO-SAMA WAS YURI-SAN'S PEN PAL FROM THE START.
EVEN THOUGH THEY'VE ONLY EXCHANGED LETTERS, YURI-SAN LIKES RYO-SAMA.
AND HE ALMOST CERTAINLY LIKES...
HE LIKES ...
UM ...
THIS IS THE REAL YURI-SAN.
KARIN ...
RYO-SAMA, THIS IS YOUR PEN PAL IN THE FLESH.

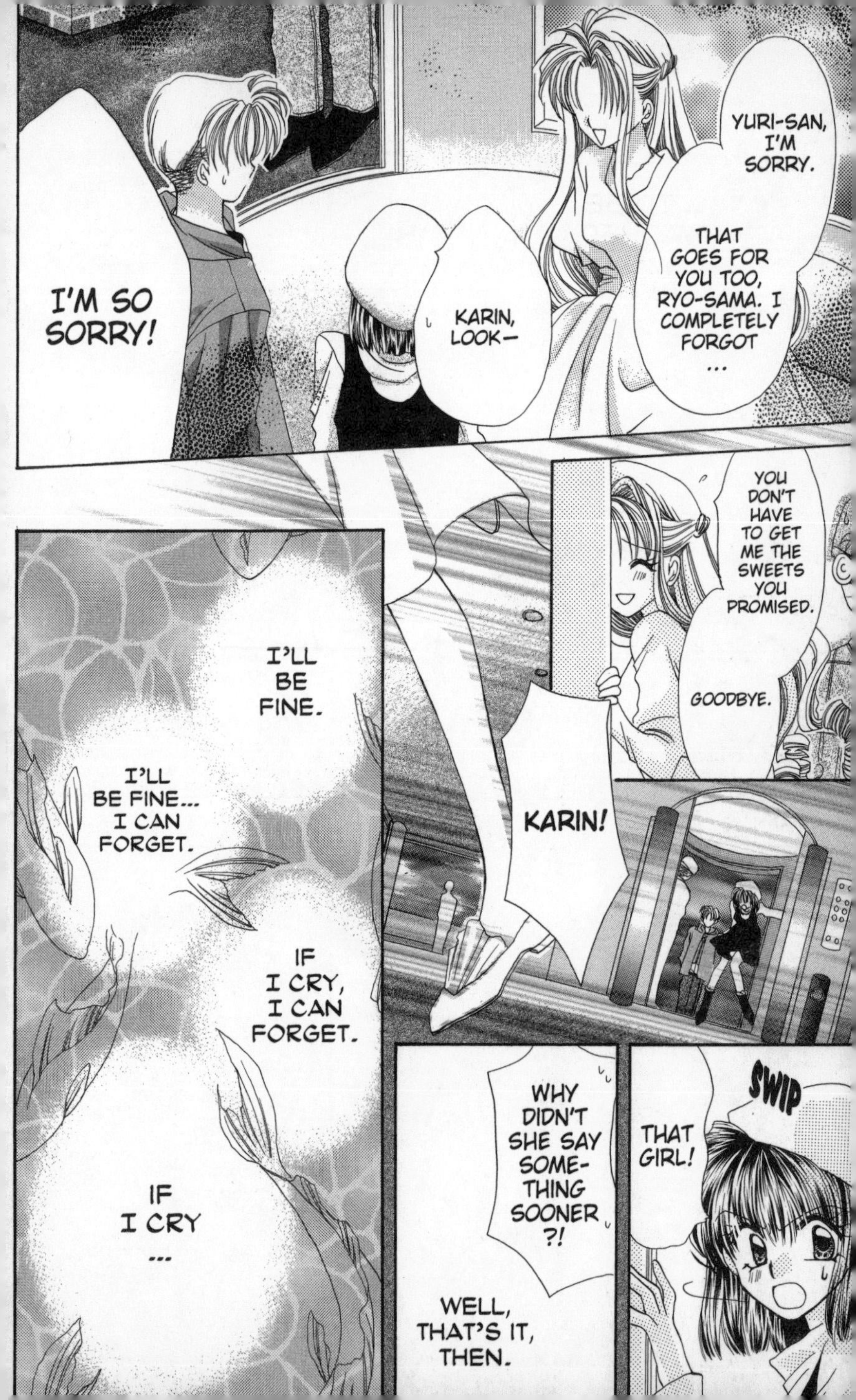
YURI-SAN, I'M SORRY.
THAT GOES FOR YOU TOO, RYO-SAMA. I COMPLETELY FORGOT ...
KARIN, LOOK—
I'M SO SORRY!
YOU DON'T HAVE TO GET ME THE SWEETS YOU PROMISED.
GOODBYE.
KARIN!
SWIP
THAT GIRL!
WHY DIDN'T SHE SAY SOME-THING SOONER ?!
WELL, THAT'S IT, THEN.
I'LL BE FINE.
I'LL BE FINE... I CAN FORGET.
IF I CRY, I CAN FORGET.
IF I CRY ...

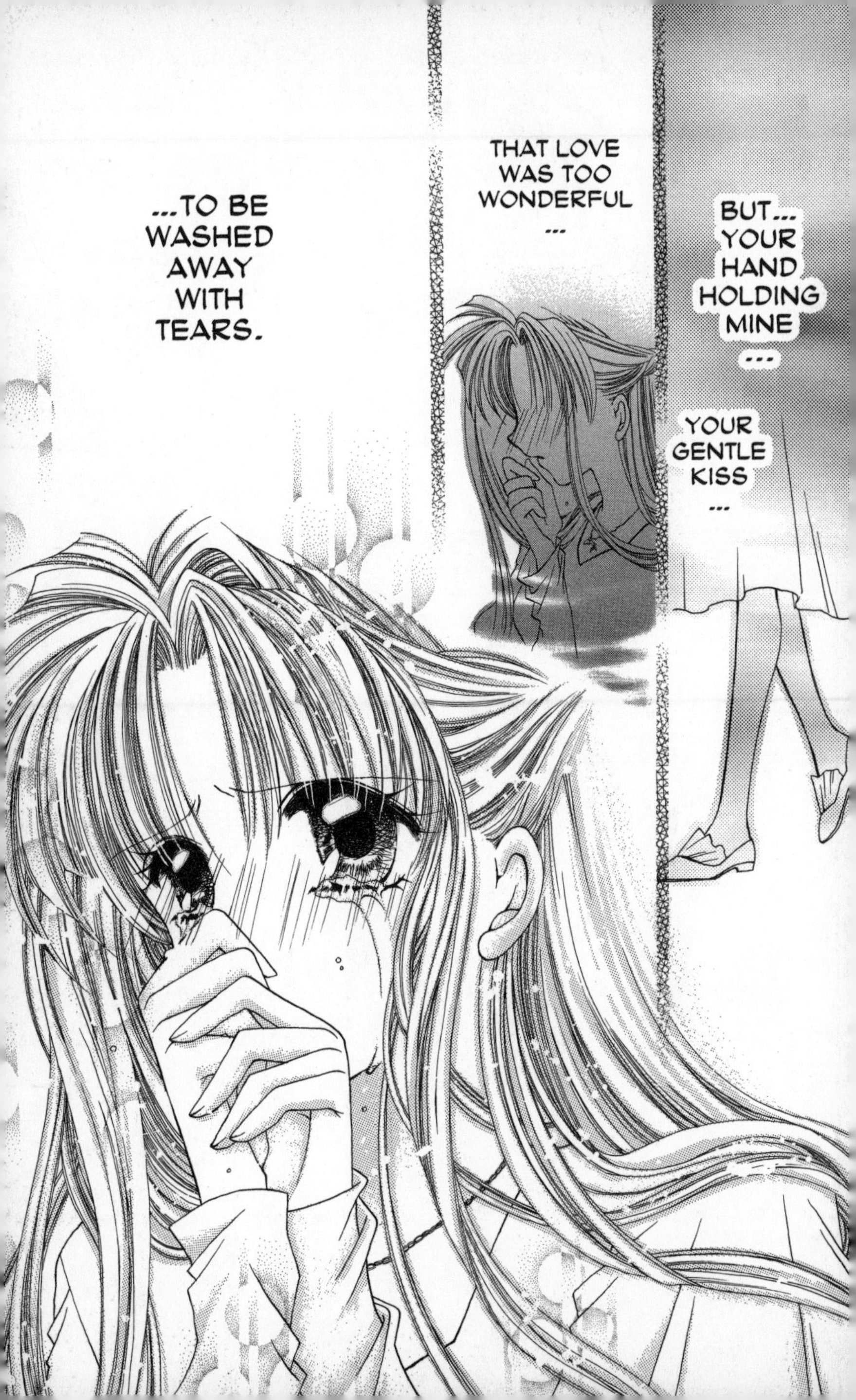
BUT... YOUR HAND HOLDING MINE ...
YOUR GENTLE KISS ...
THAT LOVE WAS TOO WONDERFUL ...
...TO BE WASHED AWAY WITH TEARS.

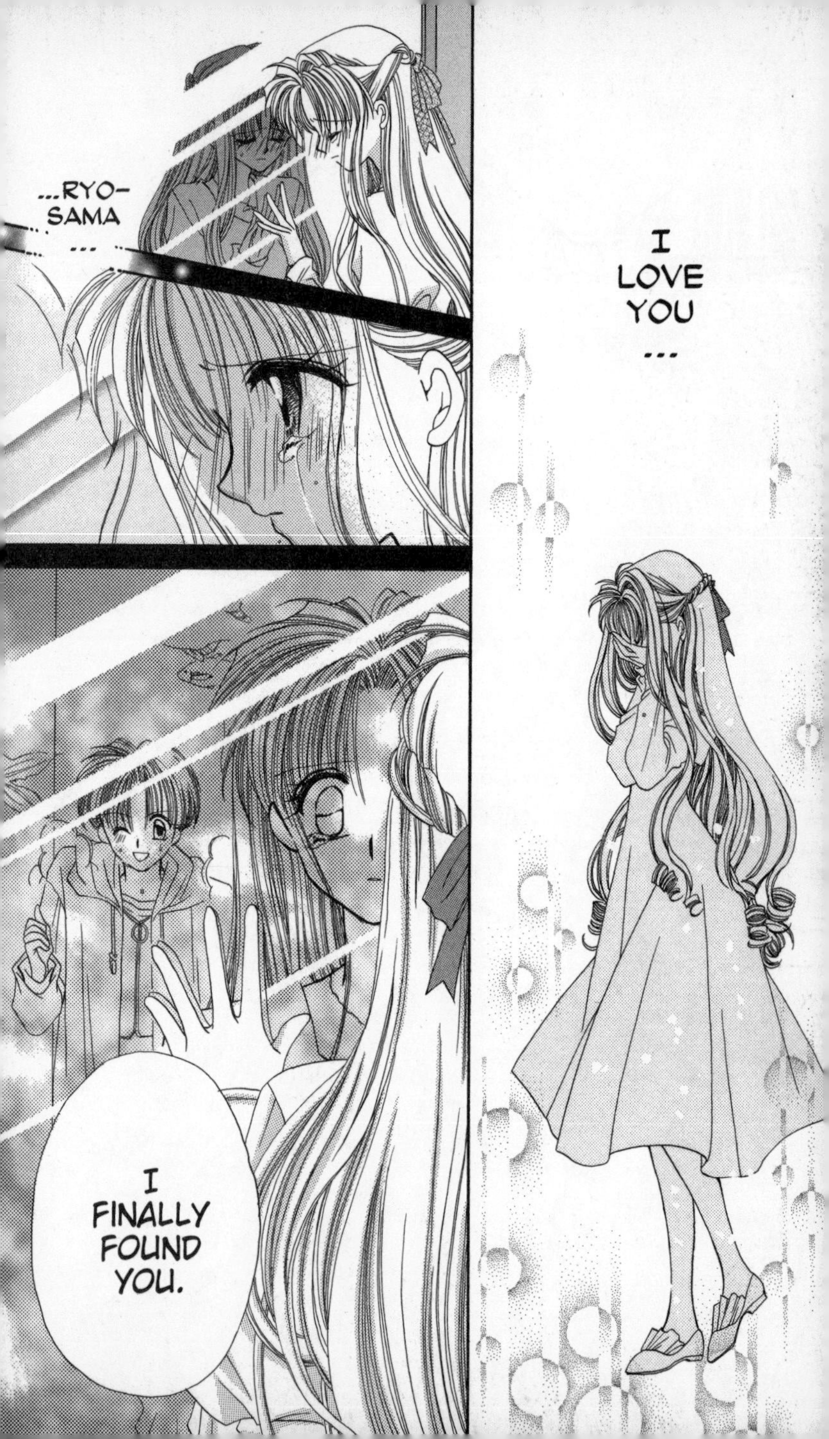
I LOVE YOU ...
...RYO-SAMA ...
I FINALLY FOUND YOU.

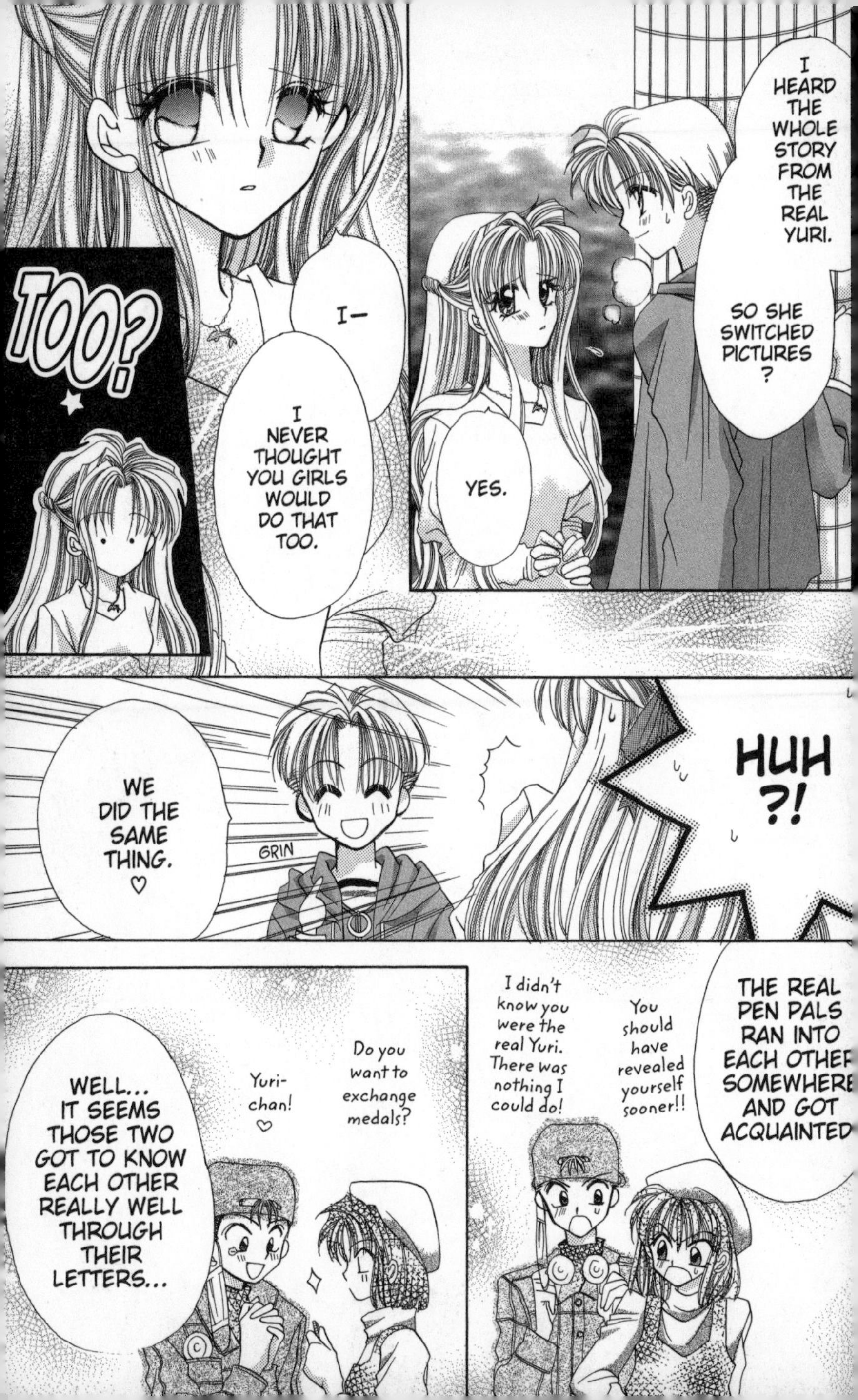
I HEARD THE WHOLE STORY FROM THE REAL YURI.
SO SHE SWITCHED PICTURES?
YES.
I—
I NEVER THOUGHT YOU GIRLS WOULD DO THAT TOO.
TOO?
HUH?!
WE DID THE SAME THING. ♡
GRIN
THE REAL PEN PALS RAN INTO EACH OTHER SOMEWHERE AND GOT ACQUAINTED
You should have revealed yourself sooner!!
I didn't know you were the real Yuri. There was nothing I could do!
WELL... IT SEEMS THOSE TWO GOT TO KNOW EACH OTHER REALLY WELL THROUGH THEIR LETTERS...
Do you want to exchange medals?
Yuri-chan! ♡

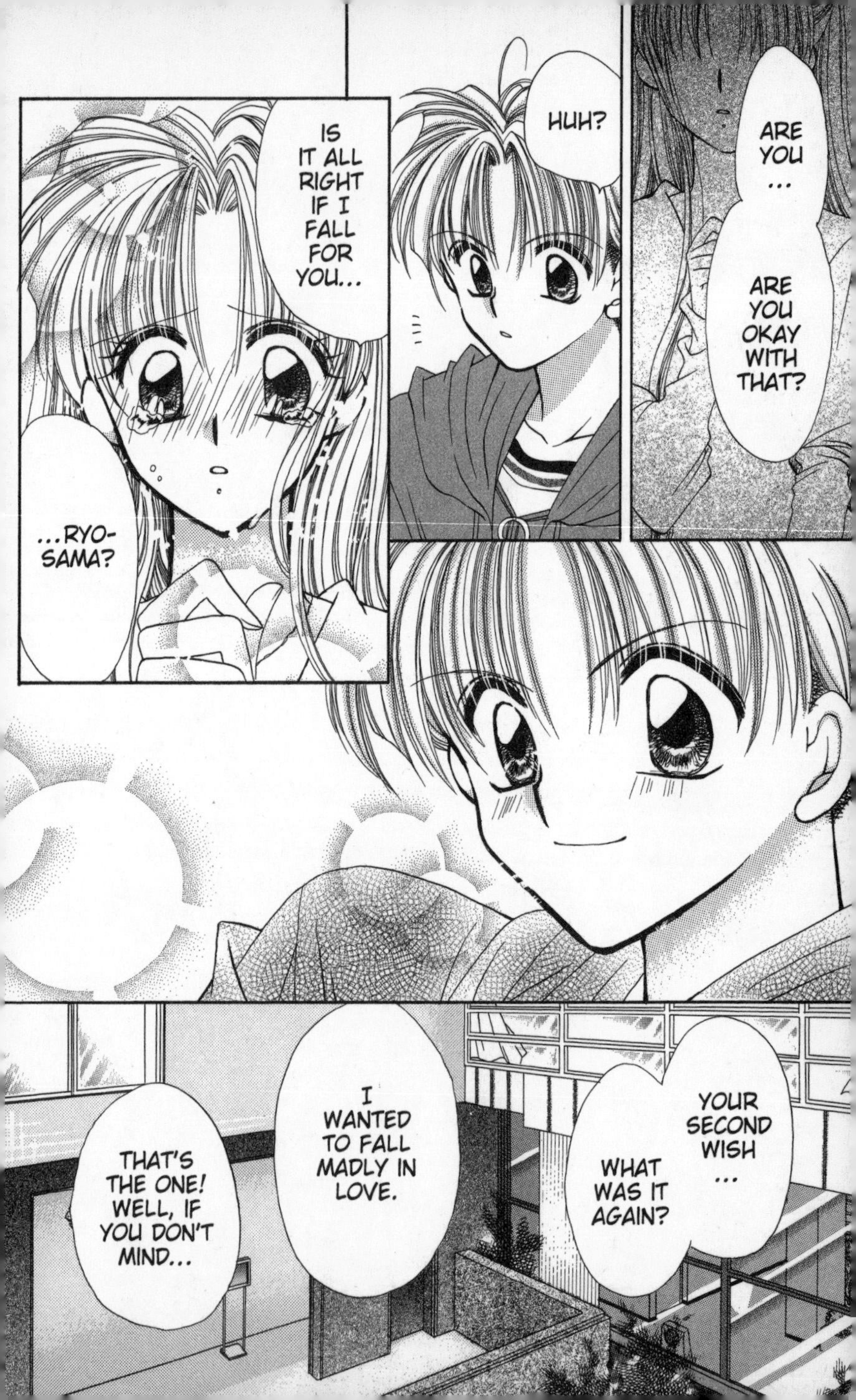
ARE YOU ...
ARE YOU OKAY WITH THAT?
HUH?
IS IT ALL RIGHT IF I FALL FOR YOU...
...RYO-SAMA?
YOUR SECOND WISH ...
WHAT WAS IT AGAIN?
I WANTED TO FALL MADLY IN LOVE.
THAT'S THE ONE! WELL, IF YOU DON'T MIND...

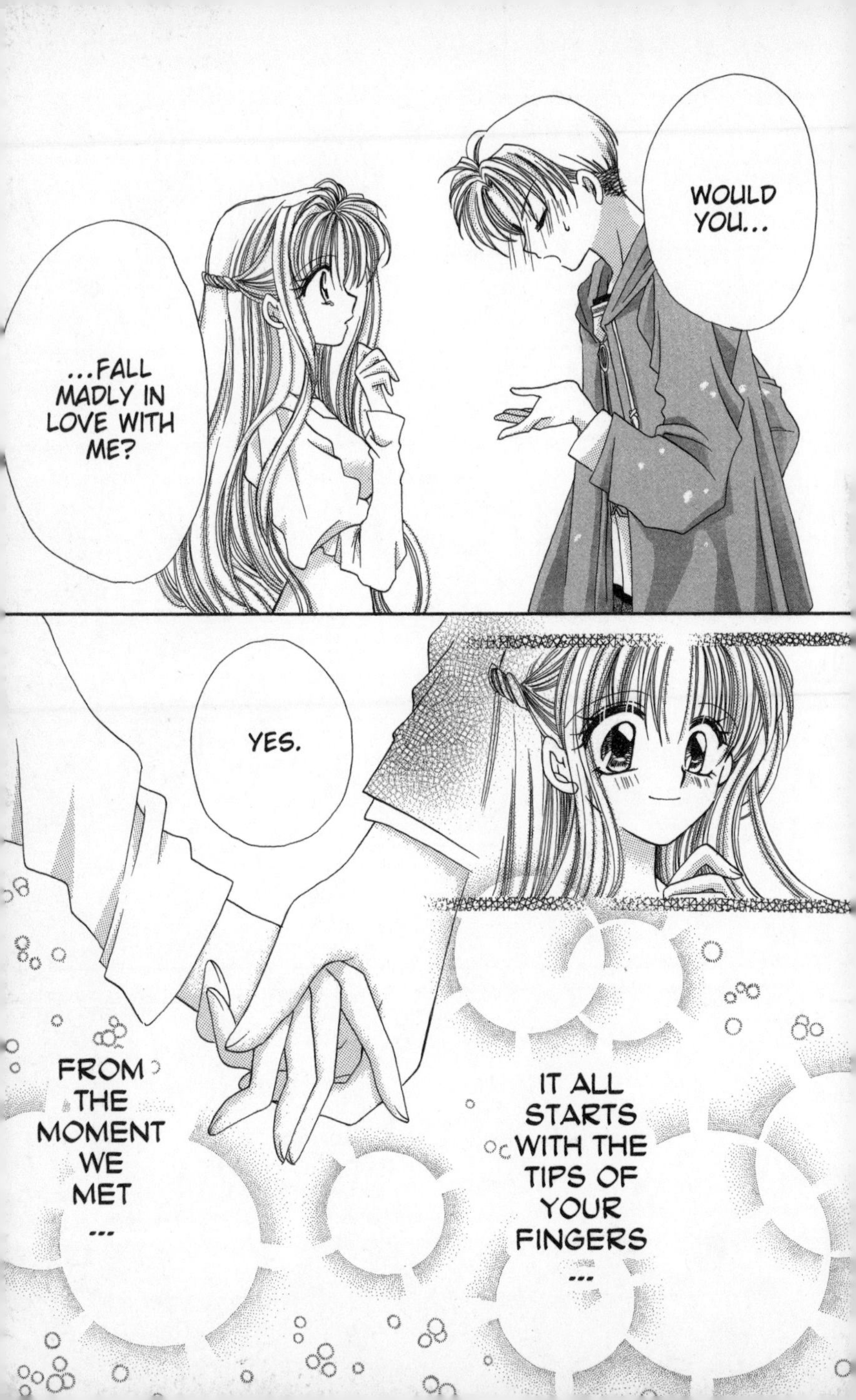
WOULD YOU...
...FALL MADLY IN LOVE WITH ME?
YES.
IT ALL STARTS WITH THE TIPS OF YOUR FINGERS...
FROM THE MOMENT WE MET...

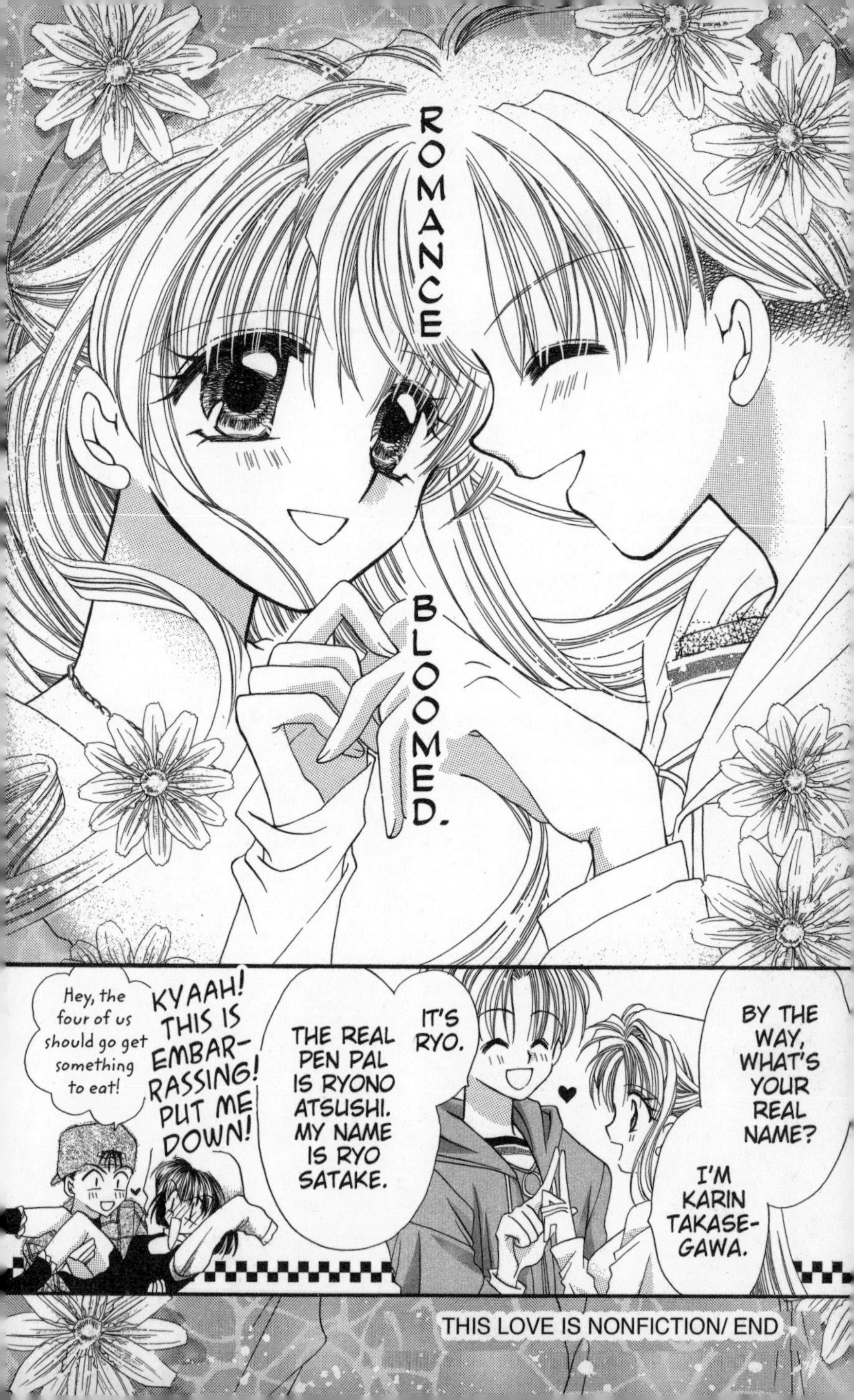
ROMANCE BLOOMED.
BY THE WAY, WHAT'S YOUR REAL NAME?
I'M KARIN TAKASE-GAWA.
IT'S RYO.
THE REAL PEN PAL IS RYONO ATSUSHI. MY NAME IS RYO SATAKE.
KYAAH! THIS IS EMBAR-RASSING! PUT ME DOWN!
Hey, the four of us should go get something to eat!
THIS LOVE IS NONFICTION/ END

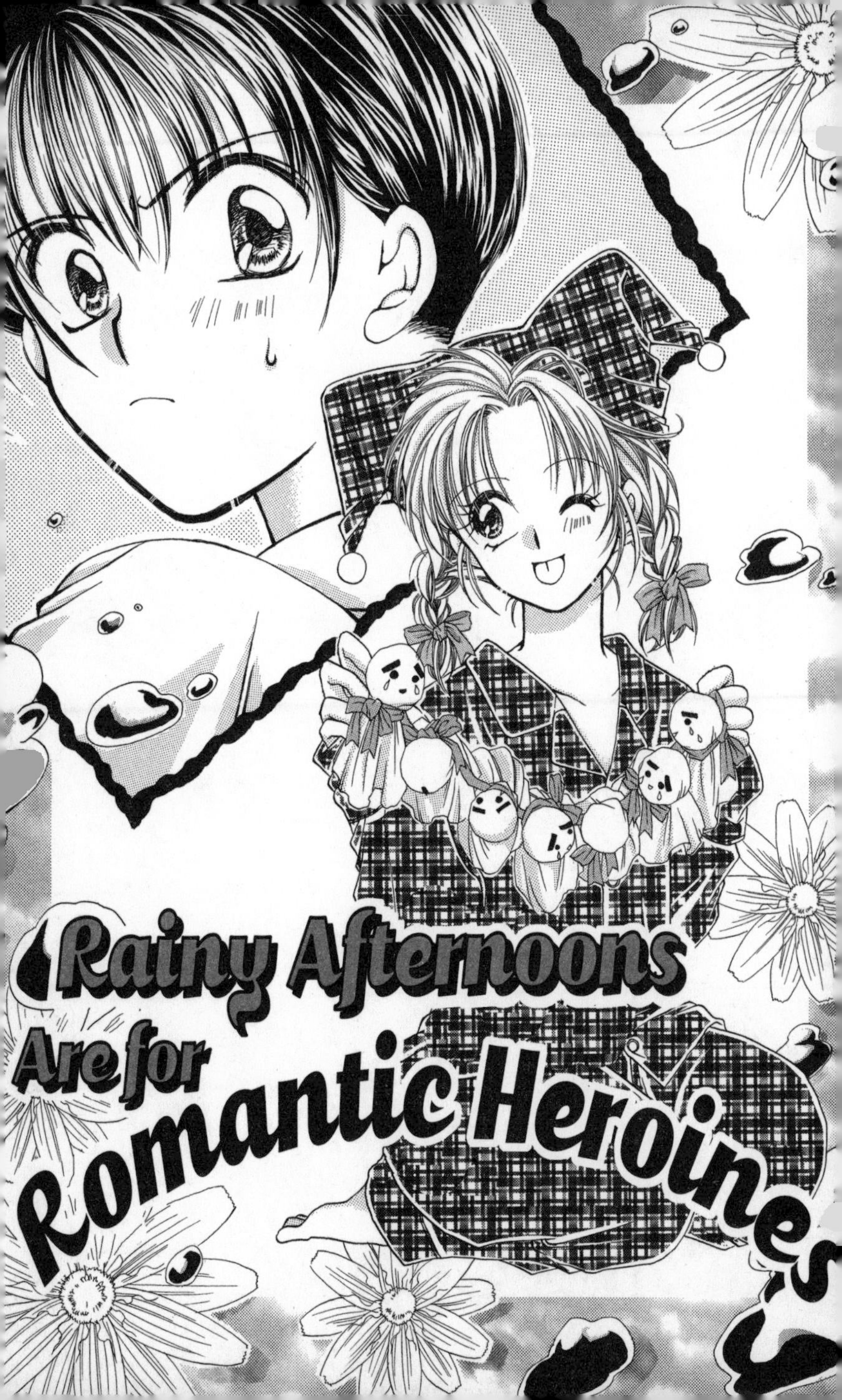
Rainy Afternoons
Are for
Romantic Heroines

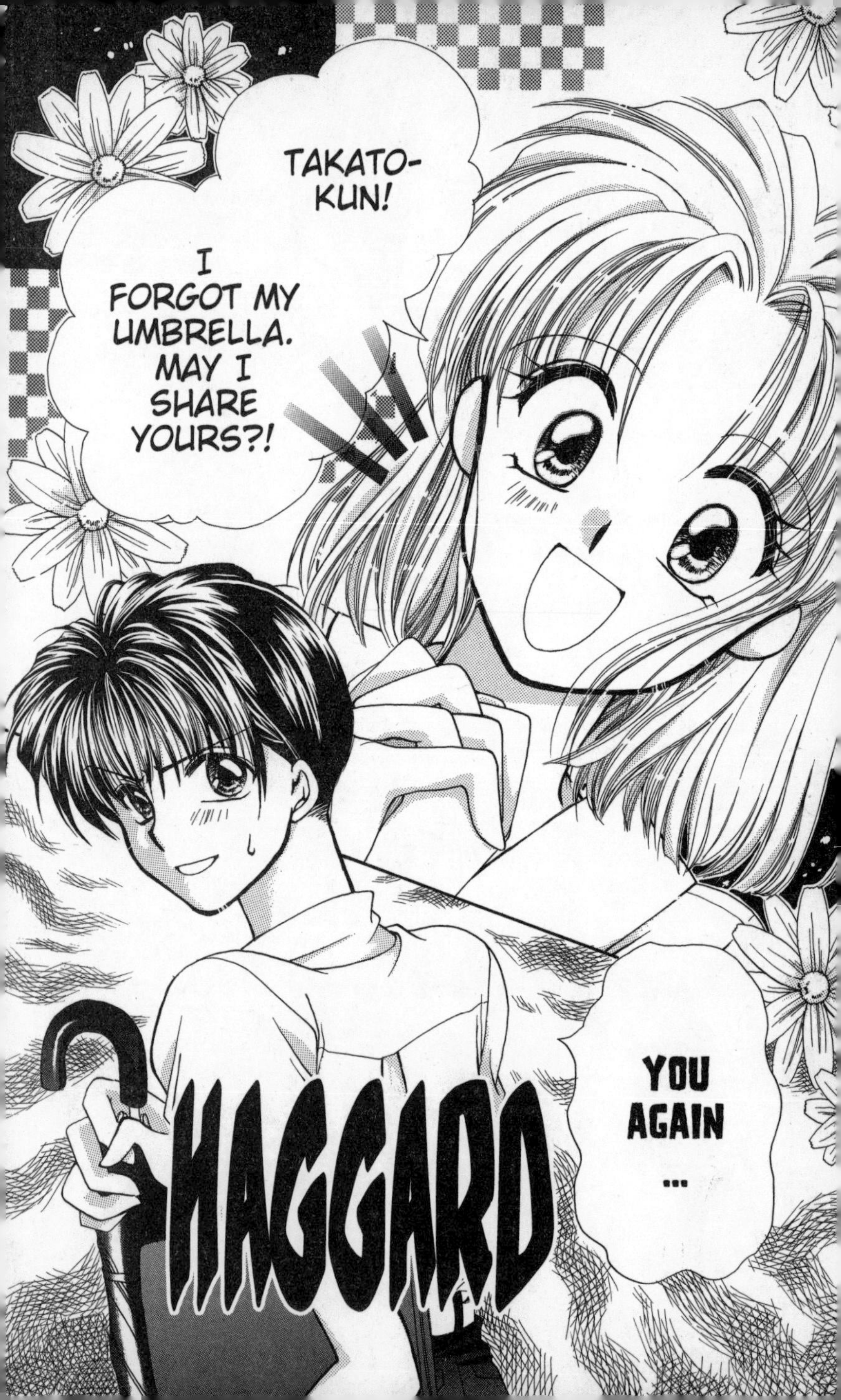
TAKATO-KUN!
I FORGOT MY UMBRELLA. MAY I SHARE YOURS?!
YOU AGAIN ...
HAGGARD

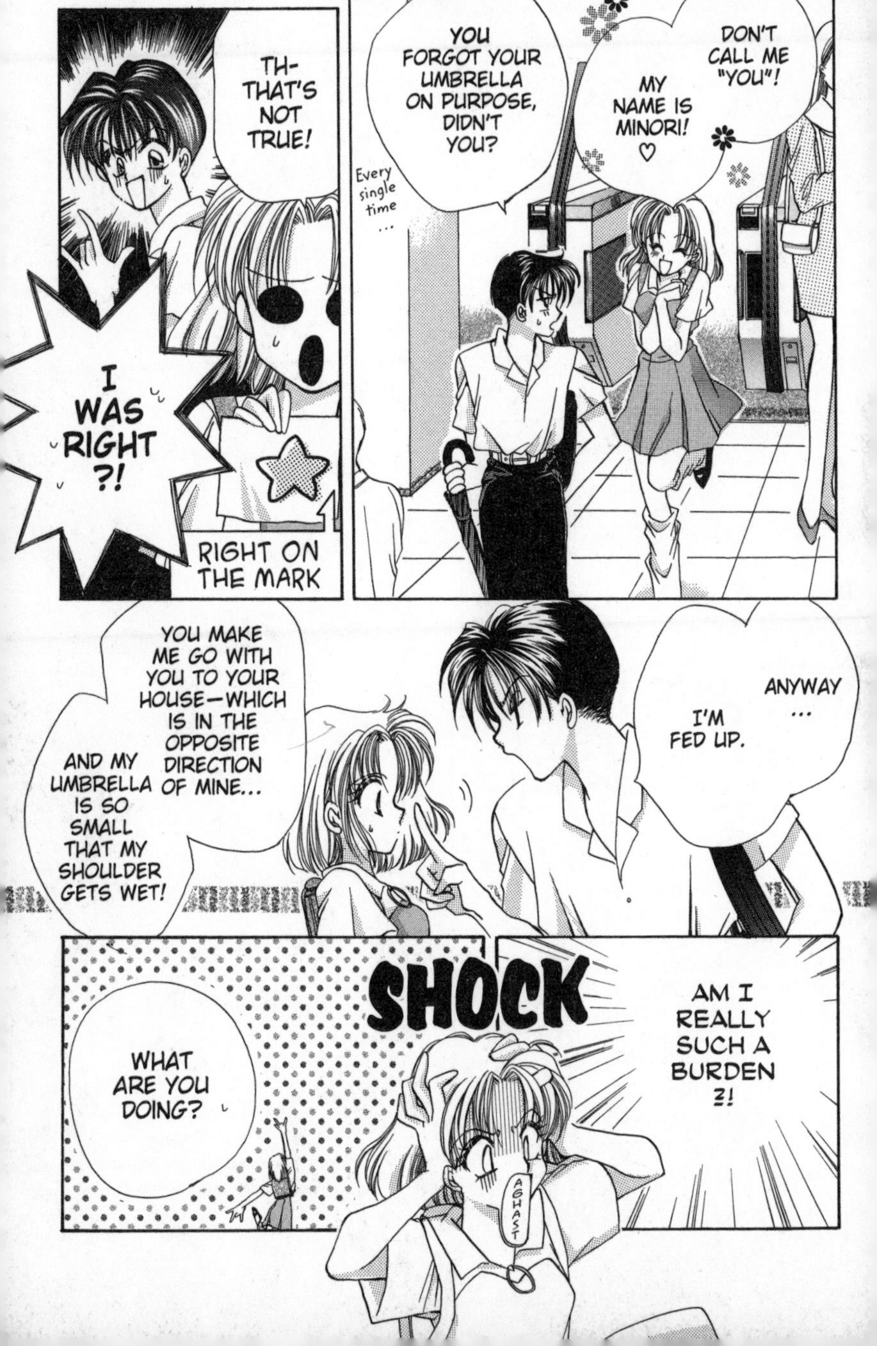
DON'T CALL ME "YOU"!
MY NAME IS MINORI! ♡
YOU FORGOT YOUR UMBRELLA ON PURPOSE, DIDN'T YOU?
Every single time ...
TH- THAT'S NOT TRUE!
I WAS RIGHT ?!
RIGHT ON THE MARK
ANYWAY ...
I'M FED UP.
YOU MAKE ME GO WITH YOU TO YOUR HOUSE—WHICH IS IN THE OPPOSITE DIRECTION OF MINE...
AND MY UMBRELLA IS SO SMALL THAT MY SHOULDER GETS WET!
SHOCK
AM I REALLY SUCH A BURDEN ?!
AGHAST
WHAT ARE YOU DOING?

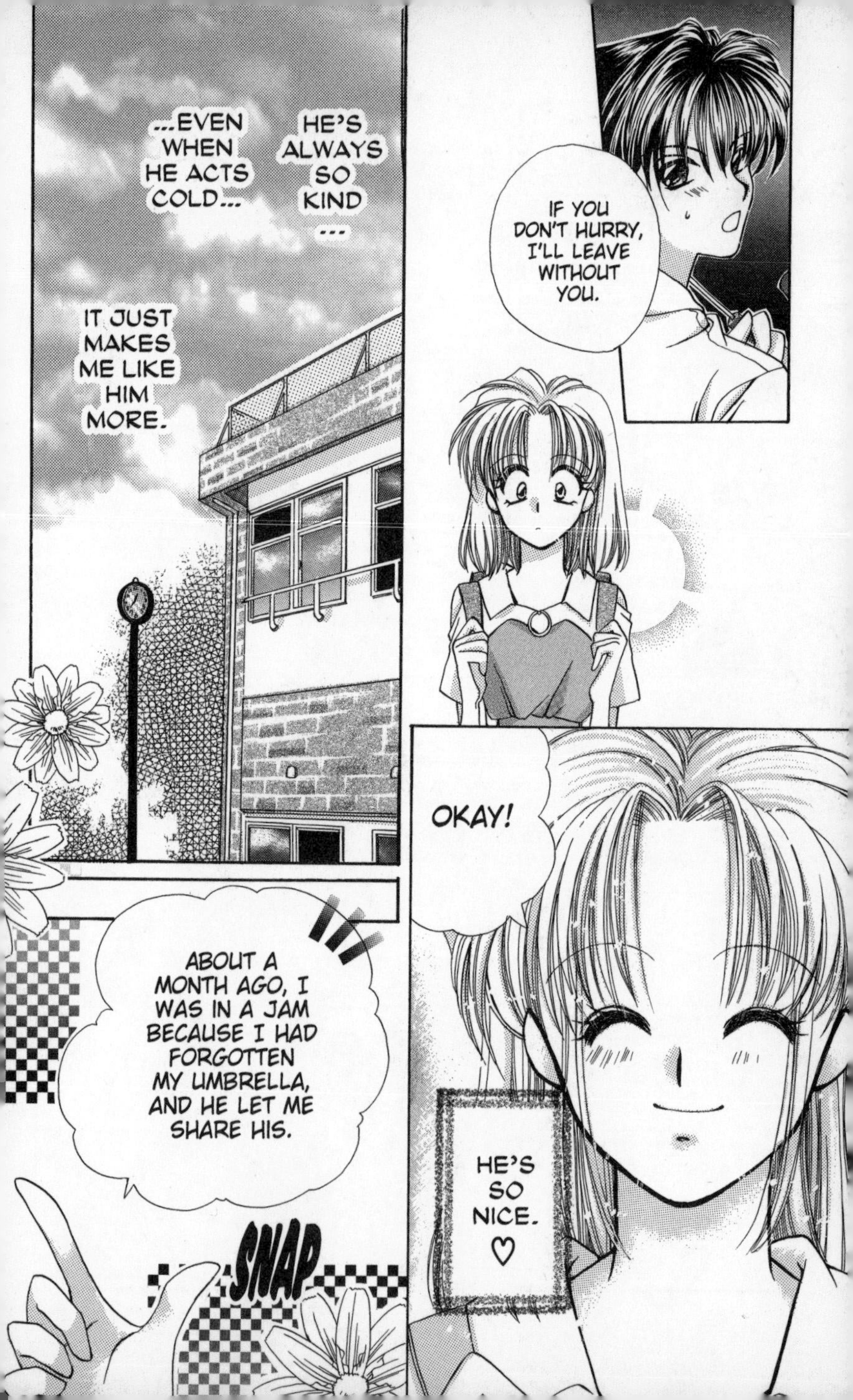
IF YOU DON'T HURRY, I'LL LEAVE WITHOUT YOU.
OKAY!
HE'S SO NICE. ♡
HE'S ALWAYS SO KIND ...
...EVEN WHEN HE ACTS COLD...
IT JUST MAKES ME LIKE HIM MORE.
ABOUT A MONTH AGO, I WAS IN A JAM BECAUSE I HAD FORGOTTEN MY UMBRELLA, AND HE LET ME SHARE HIS.
SNAP

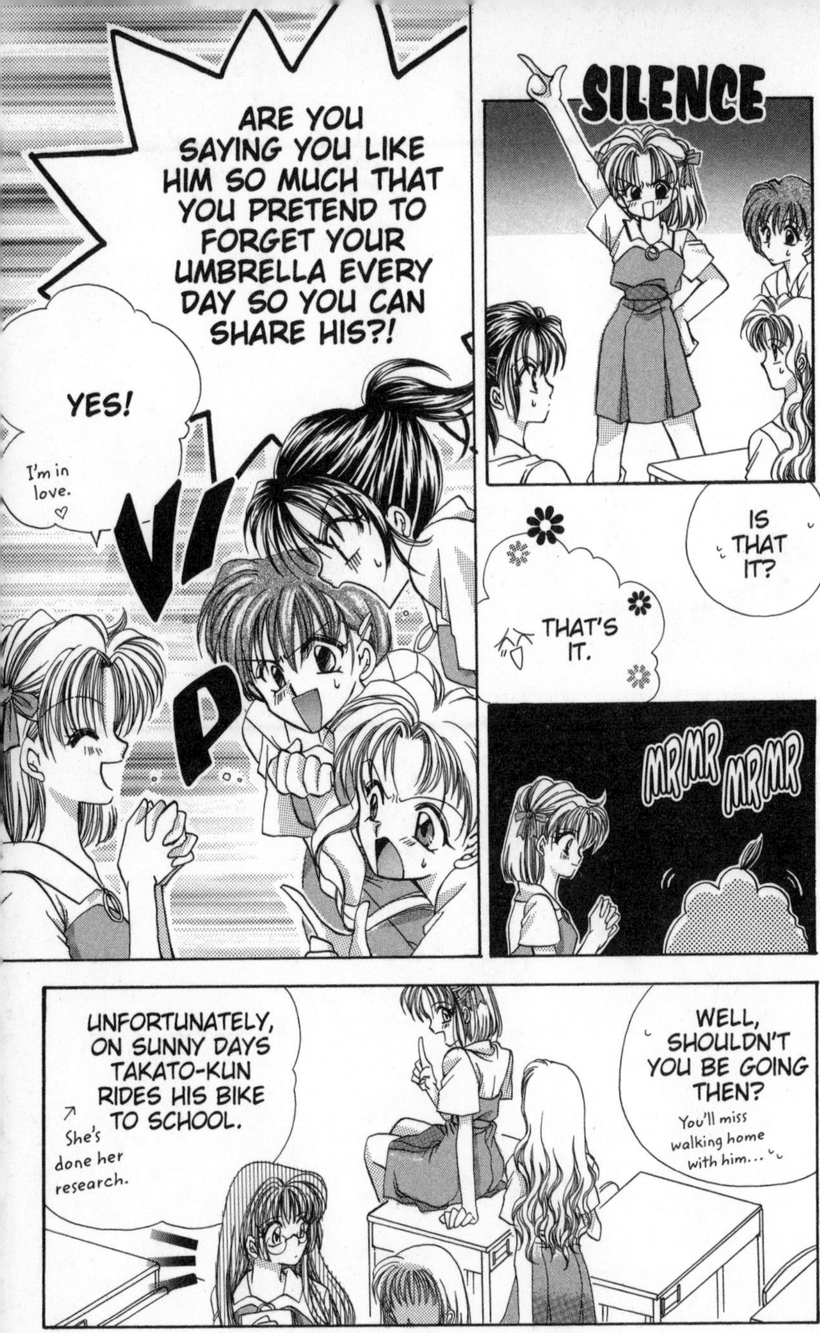
SILENCE
IS THAT IT?
THAT'S IT.
MRMR MRMR
ARE YOU SAYING YOU LIKE HIM SO MUCH THAT YOU PRETEND TO FORGET YOUR UMBRELLA EVERY DAY SO YOU CAN SHARE HIS?!
YES!
I'm in love.
WELL, SHOULDN'T YOU BE GOING THEN?
You'll miss walking home with him...
UNFORTUNATELY, ON SUNNY DAYS TAKATO-KUN RIDES HIS BIKE TO SCHOOL.
She's done her research.

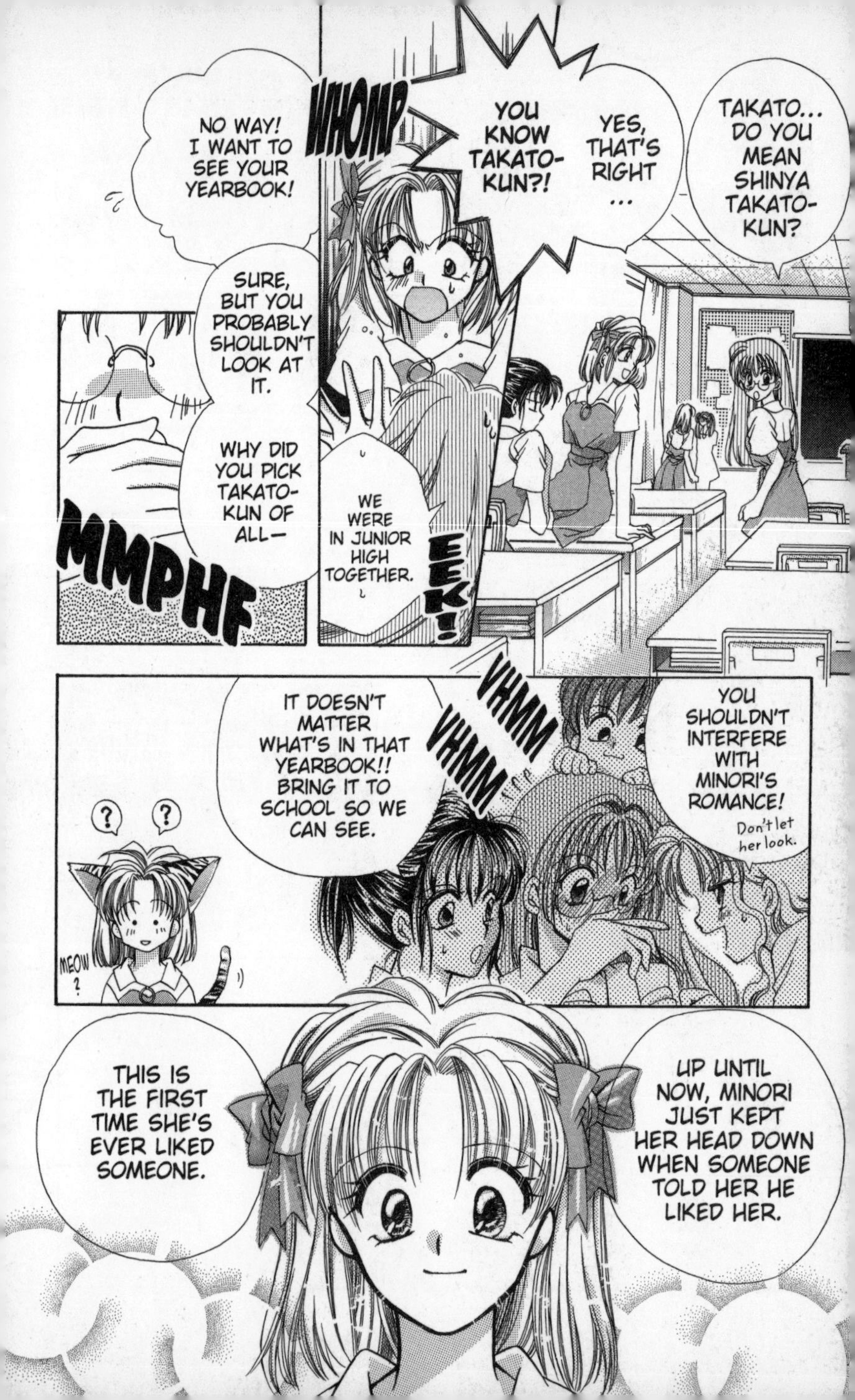
TAKATO... DO YOU MEAN SHINYA TAKATO-KUN?
YES, THAT'S RIGHT...
YOU KNOW TAKATO-KUN?!
WHOMP
WE WERE IN JUNIOR HIGH TOGETHER.
EEK!
NO WAY! I WANT TO SEE YOUR YEARBOOK!
SURE, BUT YOU PROBABLY SHOULDN'T LOOK AT IT.
WHY DID YOU PICK TAKATO-KUN OF ALL—
MMPHF
YOU SHOULDN'T INTERFERE WITH MINORI'S ROMANCE!
Don't let her look.
VHMM
VHMM
IT DOESN'T MATTER WHAT'S IN THAT YEARBOOK!! BRING IT TO SCHOOL SO WE CAN SEE.
?
?
MEOW ?
UP UNTIL NOW, MINORI JUST KEPT HER HEAD DOWN WHEN SOMEONE TOLD HER HE LIKED HER.
THIS IS THE FIRST TIME SHE'S EVER LIKED SOMEONE.

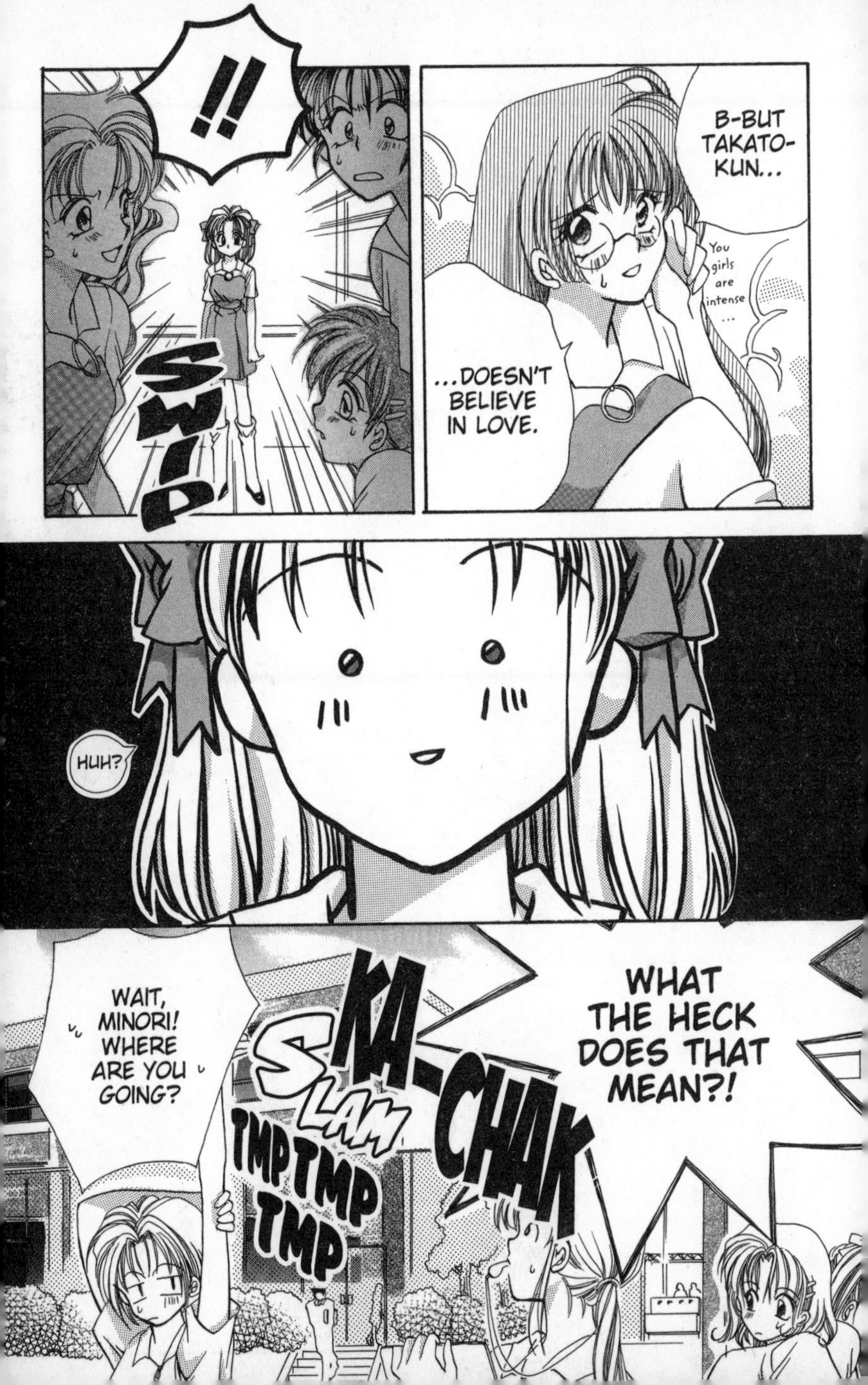
B-BUT TAKATO-KUN...
You girls are intense...
...DOESN'T BELIEVE IN LOVE.
!!
SWIP
HUH?
WHAT THE HECK DOES THAT MEAN?!
KA-CHAK
SLAM
TMP TMP TMP
WAIT, MINORI! WHERE ARE YOU GOING?

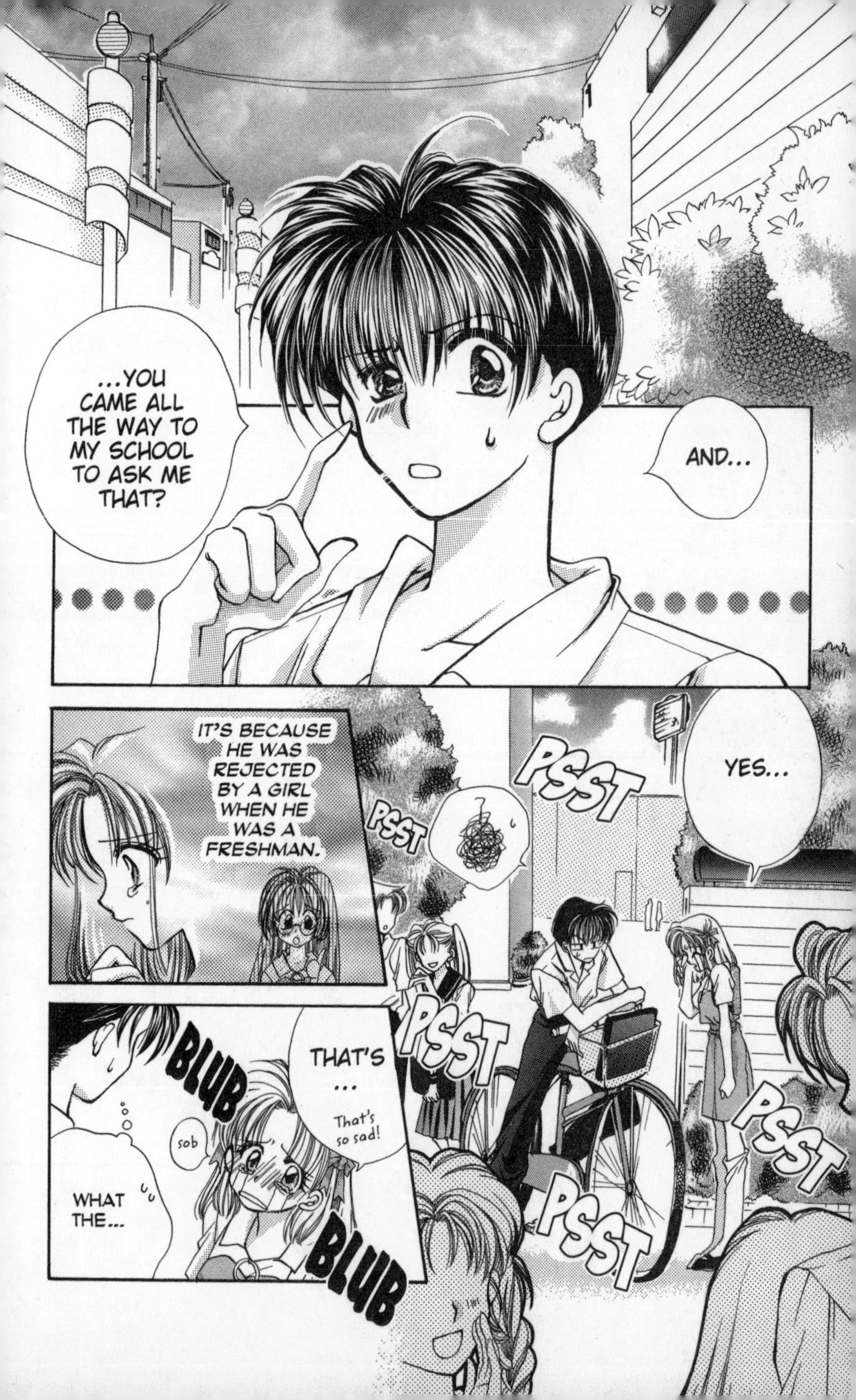
...YOU CAME ALL THE WAY TO MY SCHOOL TO ASK ME THAT?
AND...
YES...
PSST
PSST
PSST
PSST
PSST
PSST
IT'S BECAUSE HE WAS REJECTED BY A GIRL WHEN HE WAS A FRESHMAN.
THAT'S ...
That's so sad!
BLUB
sob
WHAT THE...
BLUB

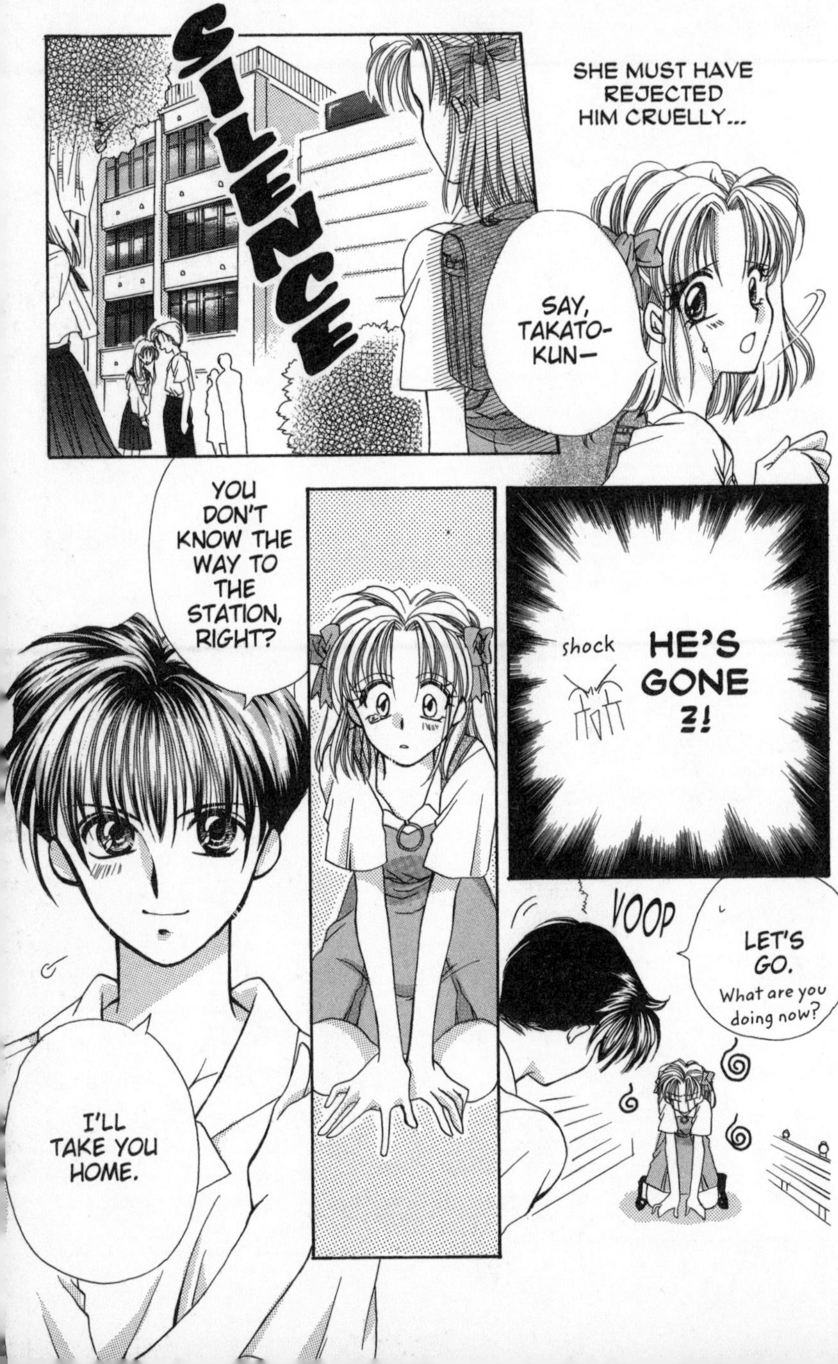
SHE MUST HAVE REJECTED HIM CRUELLY...
SAY, TAKATO-KUN—
SILENCE
shock
HE'S GONE ?!
VOOP
LET'S GO.
What are you doing now?
YOU DON'T KNOW THE WAY TO THE STATION, RIGHT?
I'LL TAKE YOU HOME.

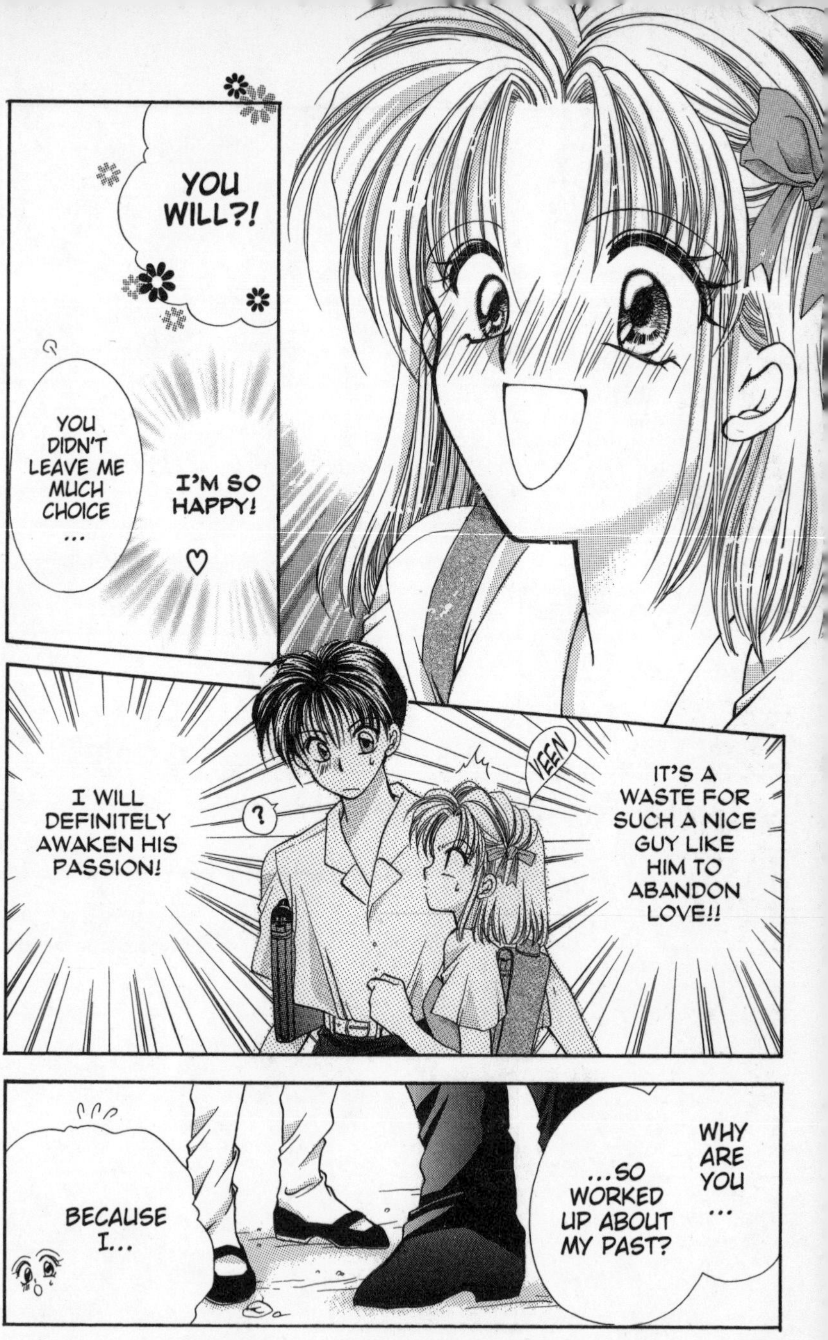
YOU WILL?!
I'M SO HAPPY! ♡
YOU DIDN'T LEAVE ME MUCH CHOICE ...
VEEN
IT'S A WASTE FOR SUCH A NICE GUY LIKE HIM TO ABANDON LOVE!!
?
I WILL DEFINITELY AWAKEN HIS PASSION!
WHY ARE YOU ...
...SO WORKED UP ABOUT MY PAST?
BECAUSE I...

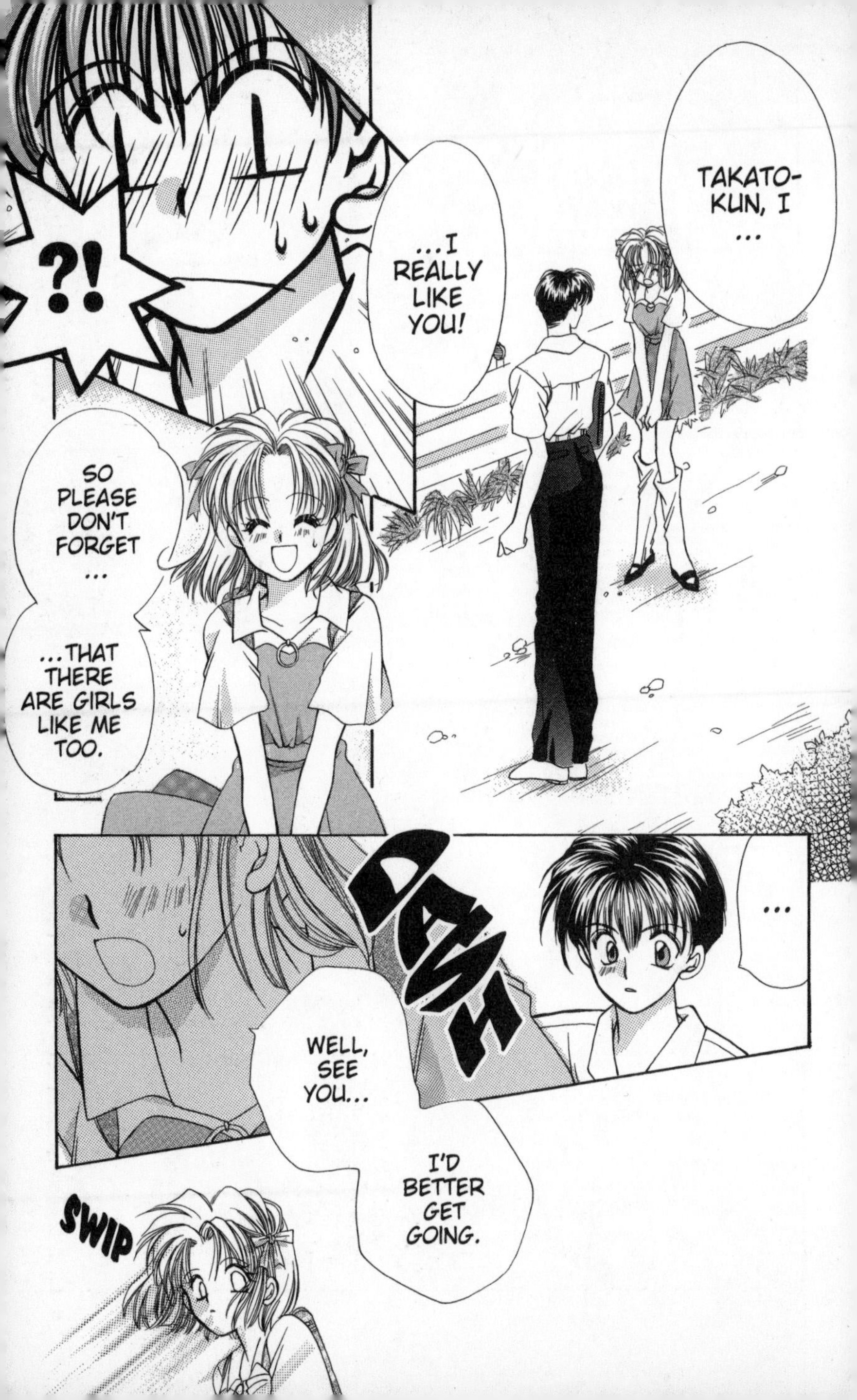
TAKATO-KUN, I ...
...I REALLY LIKE YOU!
?!
SO PLEASE DON'T FORGET ...
...THAT THERE ARE GIRLS LIKE ME TOO.
...
DASH
WELL, SEE YOU...
I'D BETTER GET GOING.
SWIP

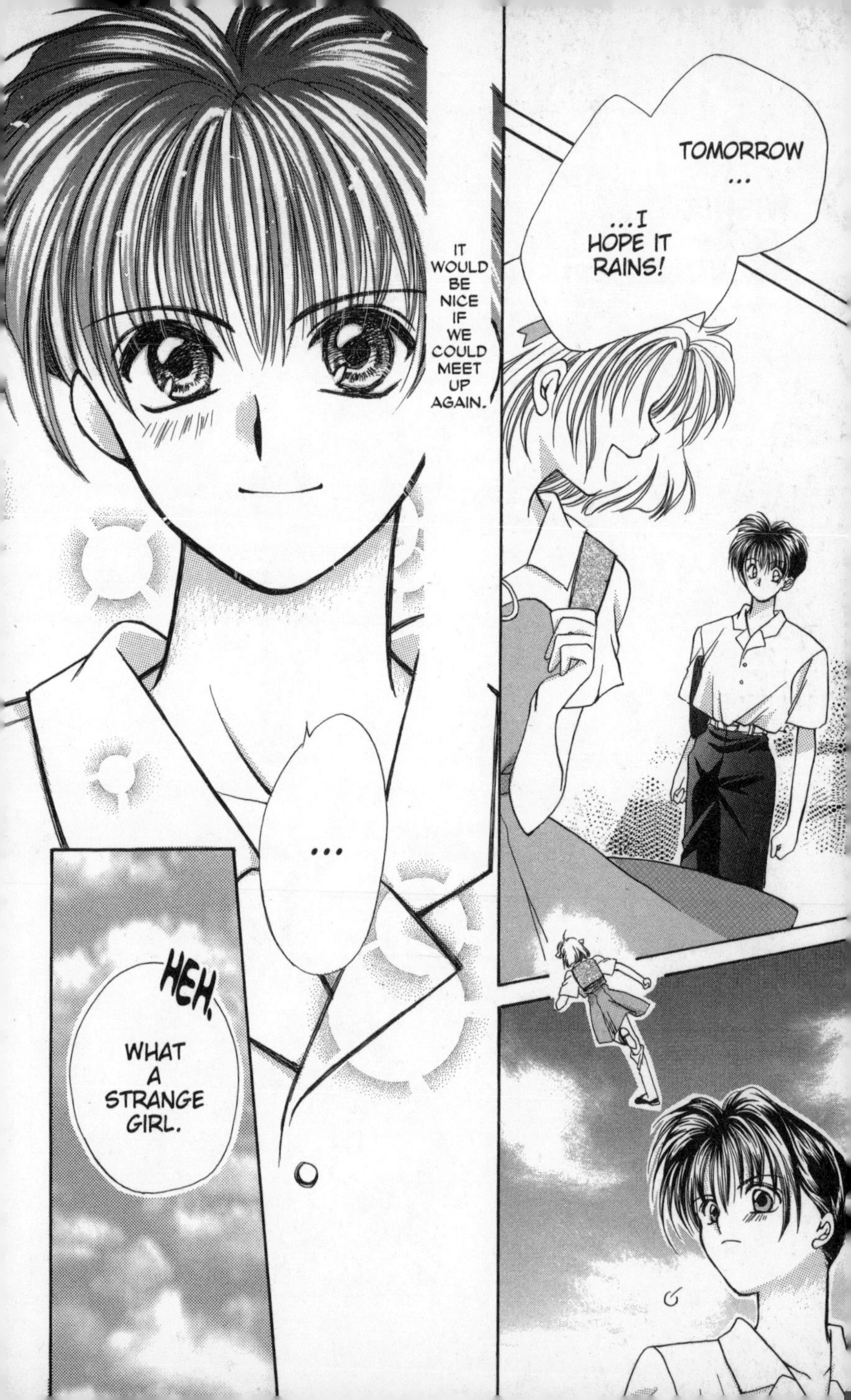
TOMORROW ...
...I HOPE IT RAINS!
IT WOULD BE NICE IF WE COULD MEET UP AGAIN.
...
HEH.
WHAT A STRANGE GIRL.

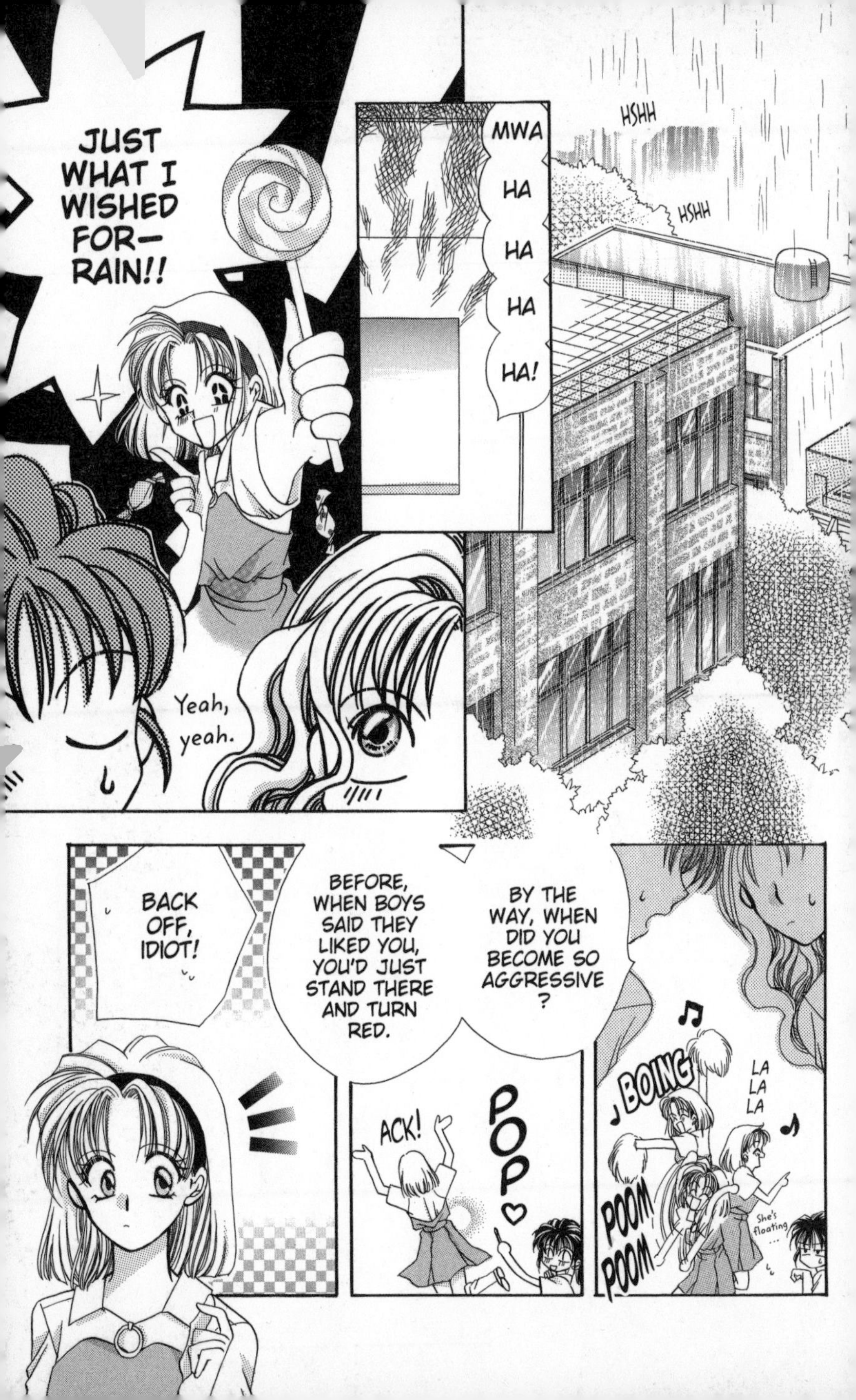
HSHH
HSHH
MWA HA HA HA HA!
JUST WHAT I WISHED FOR—RAIN!!
Yeah, yeah.
BY THE WAY, WHEN DID YOU BECOME SO AGGRESSIVE?
BOING
LA LA LA
POOM POOM
She's floating...
BEFORE, WHEN BOYS SAID THEY LIKED YOU, YOU'D JUST STAND THERE AND TURN RED.
ACK!
POP
BACK OFF, IDIOT!

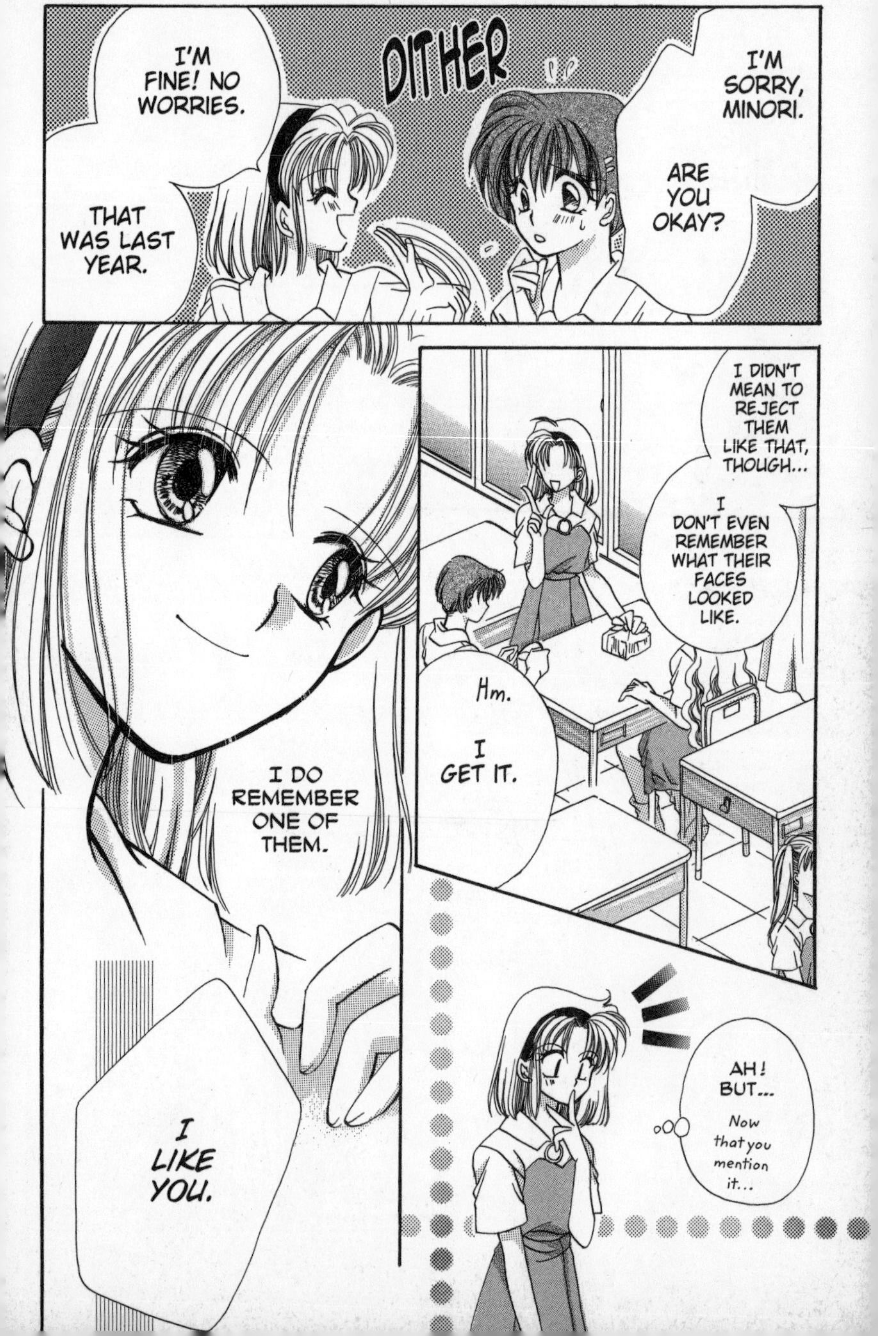
I'M SORRY, MINORI.
ARE YOU OKAY?
DITHER
I'M FINE! NO WORRIES.
THAT WAS LAST YEAR.
I DIDN'T MEAN TO REJECT THEM LIKE THAT, THOUGH...
I DON'T EVEN REMEMBER WHAT THEIR FACES LOOKED LIKE.
Hm.
I GET IT.
AH! BUT...
Now that you mention it...
I DO REMEMBER ONE OF THEM.
I LIKE YOU.

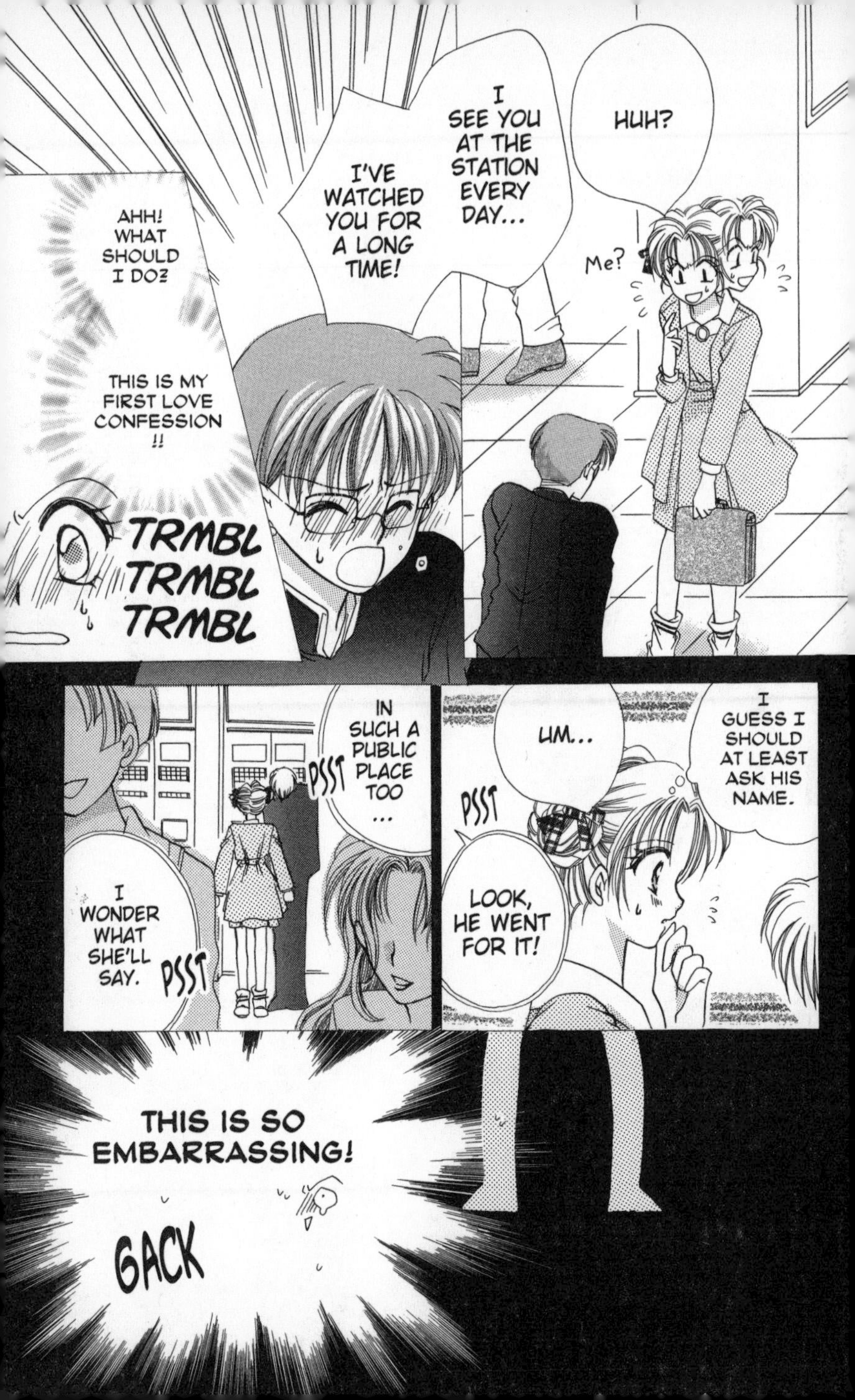
HUH?
Me?
I SEE YOU AT THE STATION EVERY DAY...
I'VE WATCHED YOU FOR A LONG TIME!
AHH! WHAT SHOULD I DO?
THIS IS MY FIRST LOVE CONFESSION !!
TRMBL TRMBL TRMBL
I GUESS I SHOULD AT LEAST ASK HIS NAME.
UM...
PSST
LOOK, HE WENT FOR IT!
IN SUCH A PUBLIC PLACE TOO ...
PSST
I WONDER WHAT SHE'LL SAY.
PSST
THIS IS SO EMBARRASSING!
GACK

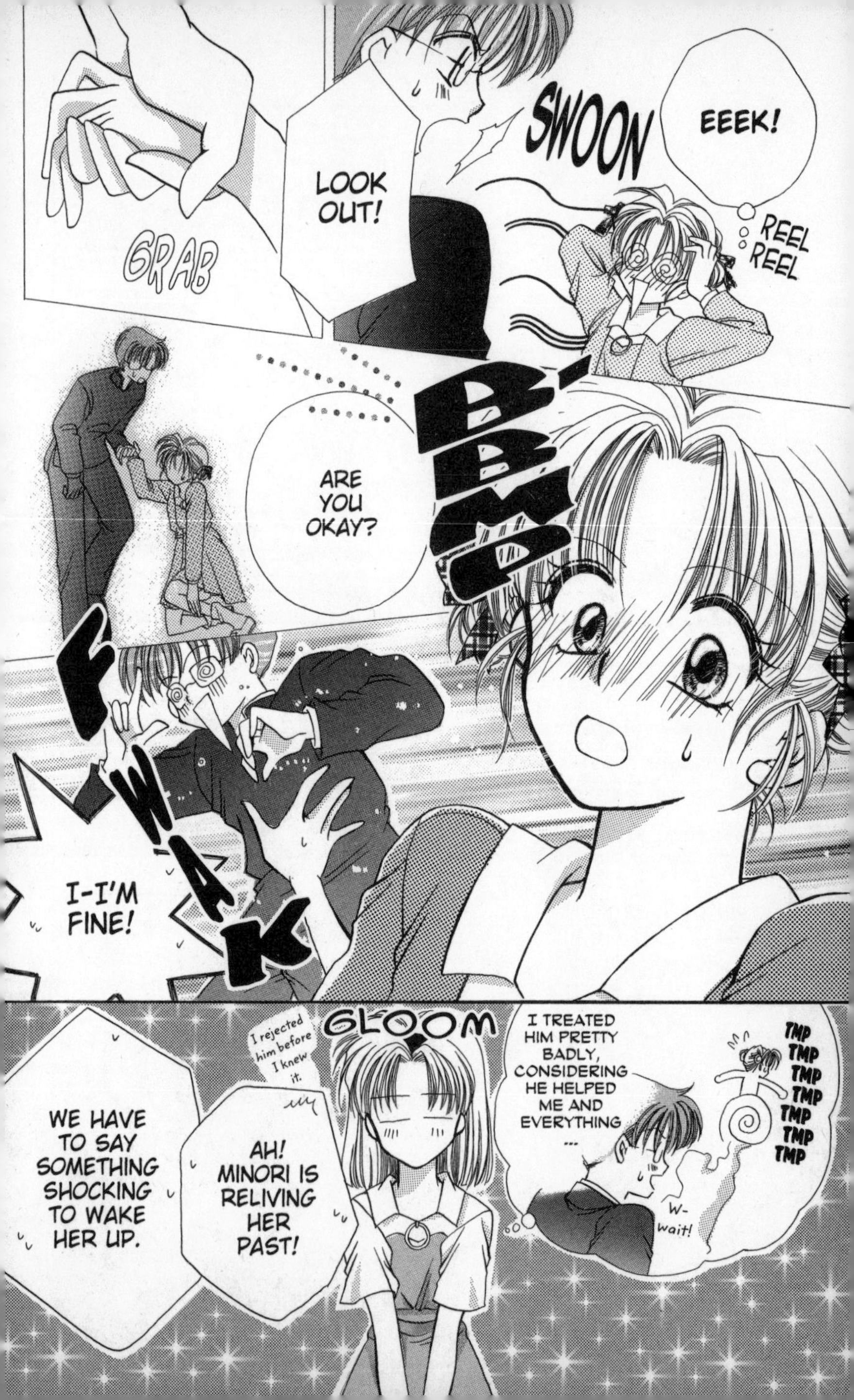
EEEK!
SWOON
REEL REEL
LOOK OUT!
GRAB
B-BMP
ARE YOU OKAY?
FWAK
I-I'M FINE!
TMP TMP TMP TMP TMP TMP TMP
I TREATED HIM PRETTY BADLY, CONSIDERING HE HELPED ME AND EVERYTHING...
W-wait!
GLOOM
I rejected him before I knew it.
AH! MINORI IS RELIVING HER PAST!
WE HAVE TO SAY SOMETHING SHOCKING TO WAKE HER UP.

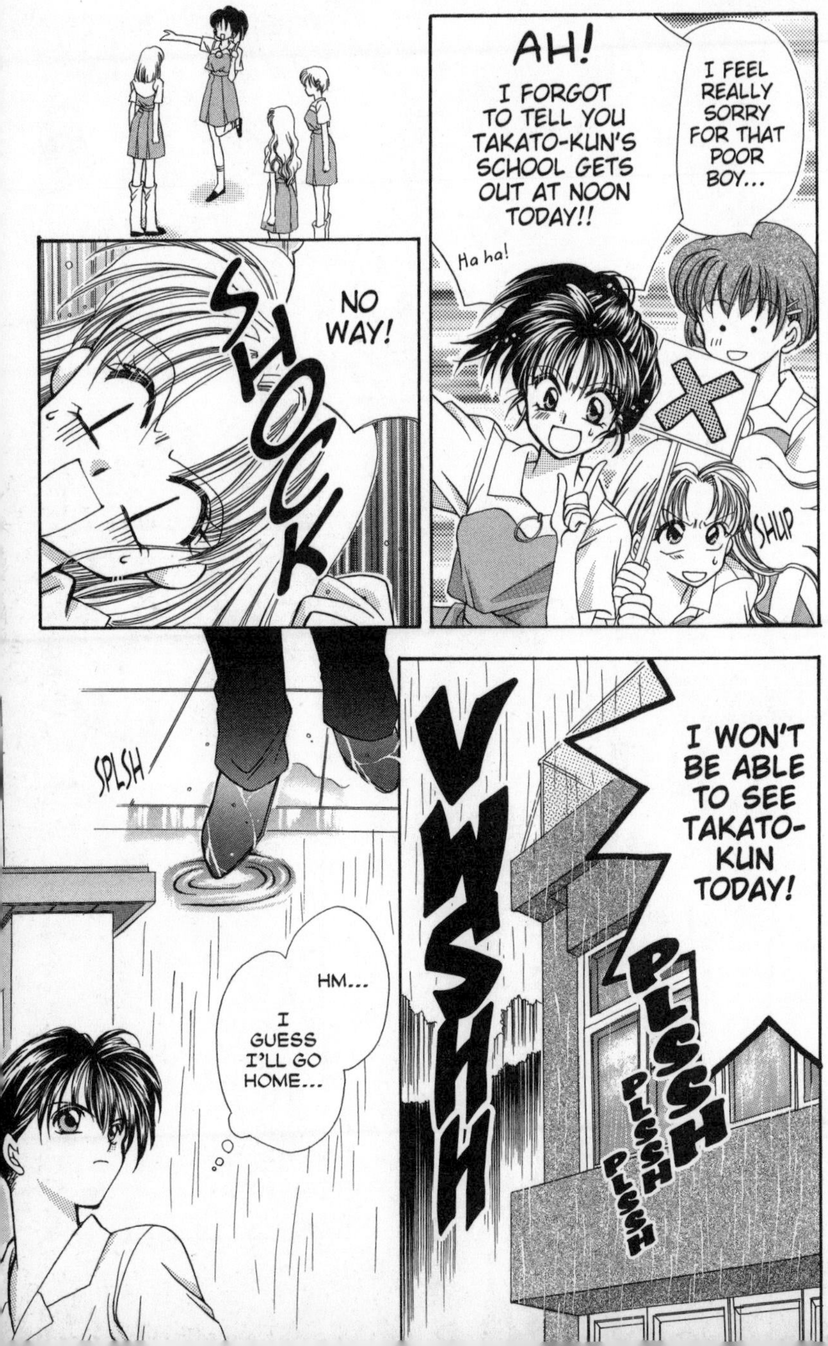
AH!
I FORGOT TO TELL YOU TAKATO-KUN'S SCHOOL GETS OUT AT NOON TODAY!!
I FEEL REALLY SORRY FOR THAT POOR BOY...
Ha ha!
SHUP
NO WAY!
SHOCK
I WON'T BE ABLE TO SEE TAKATO-KUN TODAY!
VWSHH
PLSSH
PLSSH
PLSSH
SPLSH
HM...
I GUESS I'LL GO HOME...

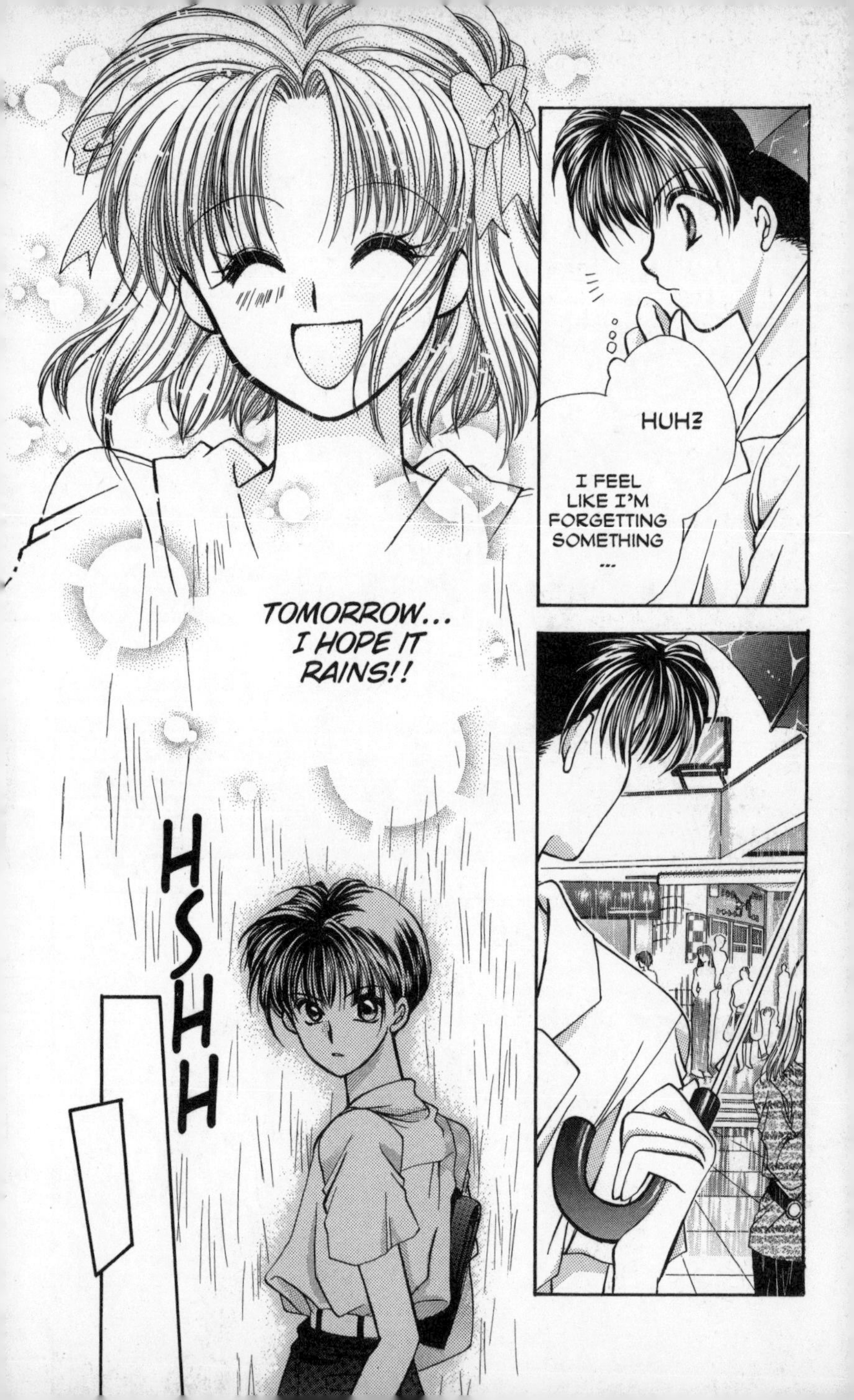
HUH?
I FEEL LIKE I'M FORGETTING SOMETHING ...
TOMORROW... I HOPE IT RAINS!!
HSHH

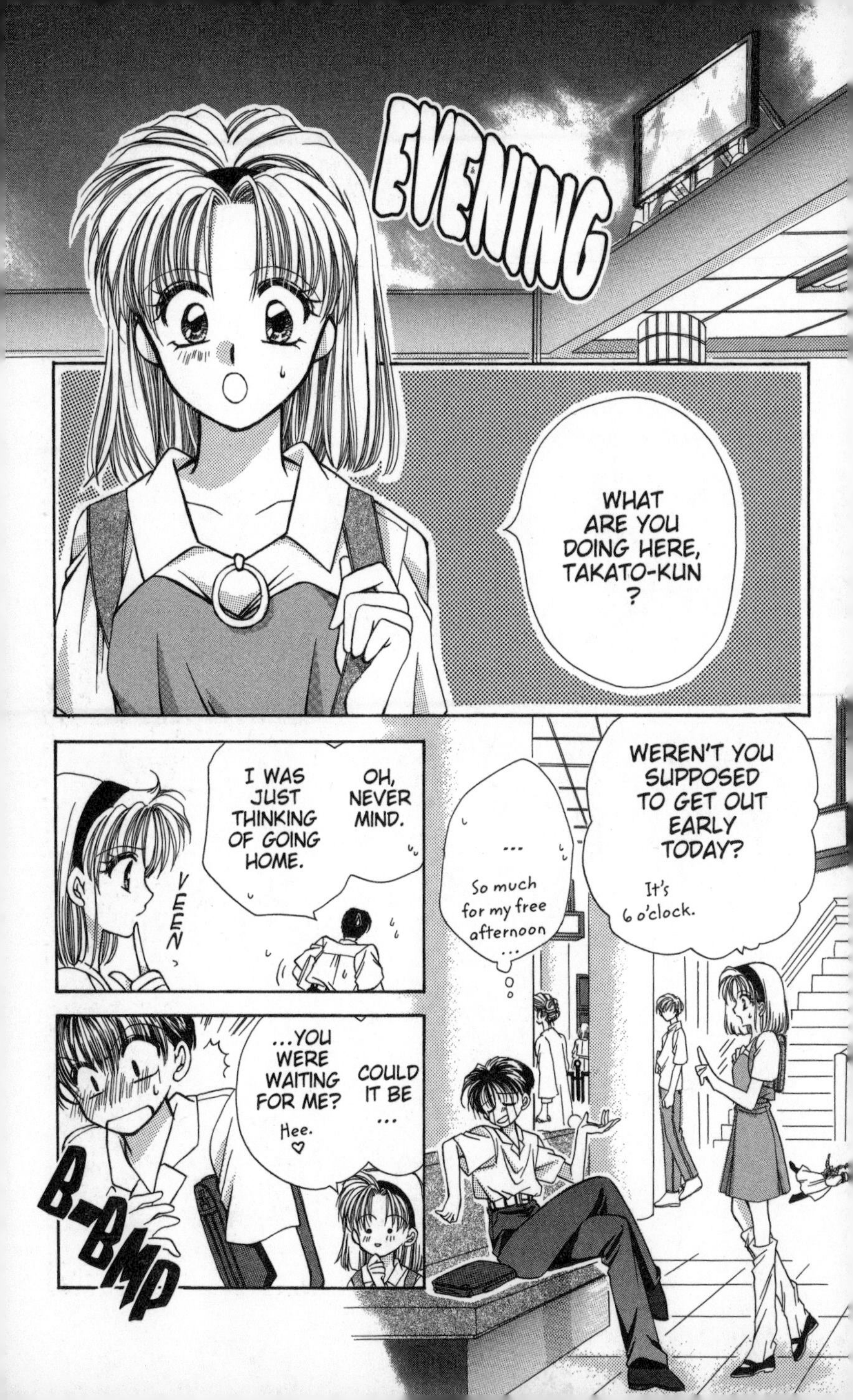
EVENING
WHAT ARE YOU DOING HERE, TAKATO-KUN?
WEREN'T YOU SUPPOSED TO GET OUT EARLY TODAY?
It's 6 o'clock.
...
So much for my free afternoon...
OH, NEVER MIND.
I WAS JUST THINKING OF GOING HOME.
VEEN
COULD IT BE...
...YOU WERE WAITING FOR ME?
Hee. ♡
B-BMP

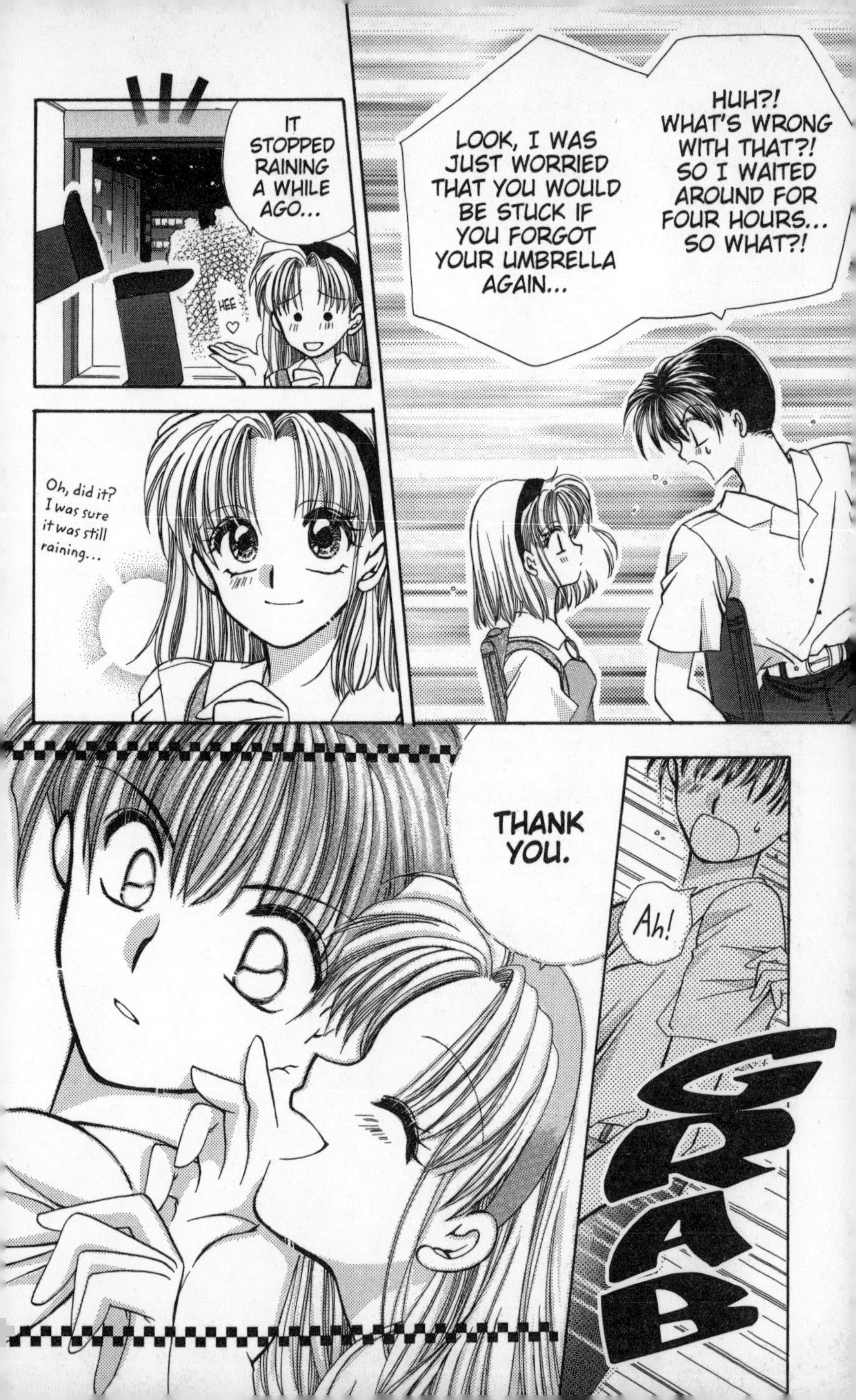
HUH?! WHAT'S WRONG WITH THAT?! SO I WAITED AROUND FOR FOUR HOURS... SO WHAT?!
LOOK, I WAS JUST WORRIED THAT YOU WOULD BE STUCK IF YOU FORGOT YOUR UMBRELLA AGAIN...
IT STOPPED RAINING A WHILE AGO...
HEE ♥
Oh, did it? I was sure it was still raining...
Ah!
GRAB
THANK YOU.

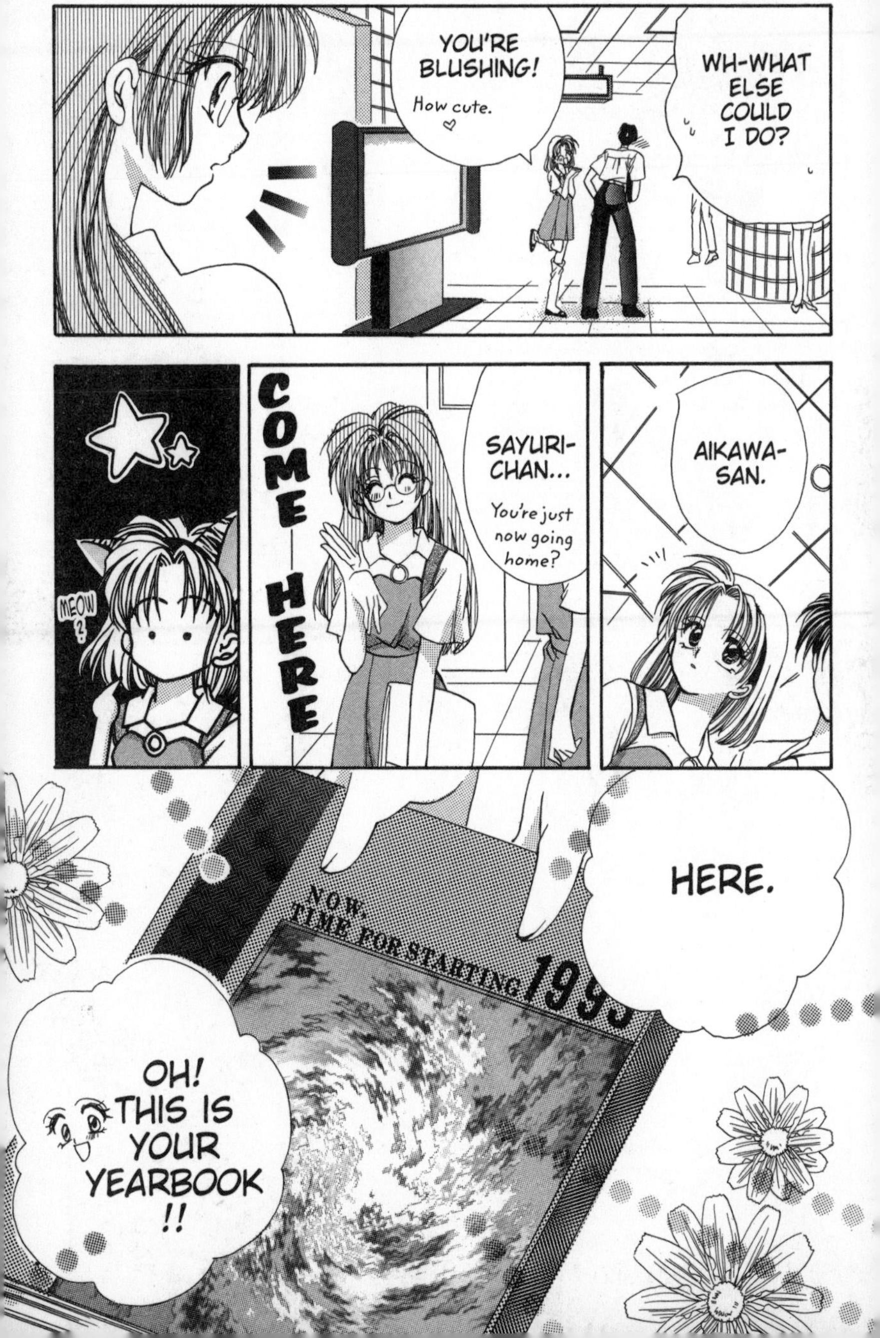
WH-WHAT ELSE COULD I DO?
YOU'RE BLUSHING!
How cute.
AIKAWA-SAN.
SAYURI-CHAN...
You're just now going home?
COME HERE
MEOW?
HERE.
NOW, TIME FOR STARTING
OH! THIS IS YOUR YEARBOOK!!

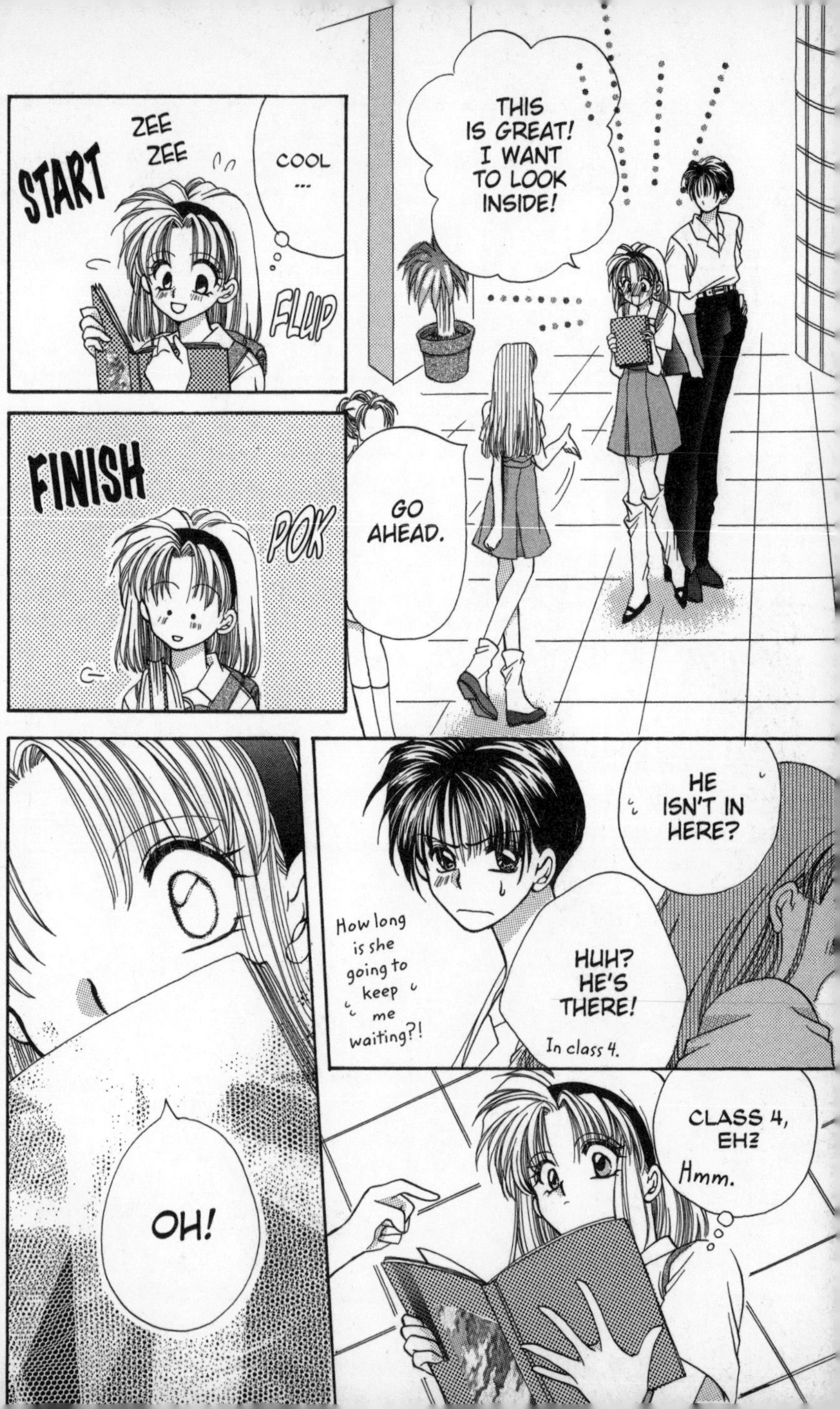
THIS IS GREAT! I WANT TO LOOK INSIDE!
GO AHEAD.
COOL ...
ZEE ZEE
START
FLUP
POK
FINISH
HE ISN'T IN HERE?
HUH? HE'S THERE!
In class 4.
How long is she going to keep me waiting?!
CLASS 4, EH?
Hmm.
OH!

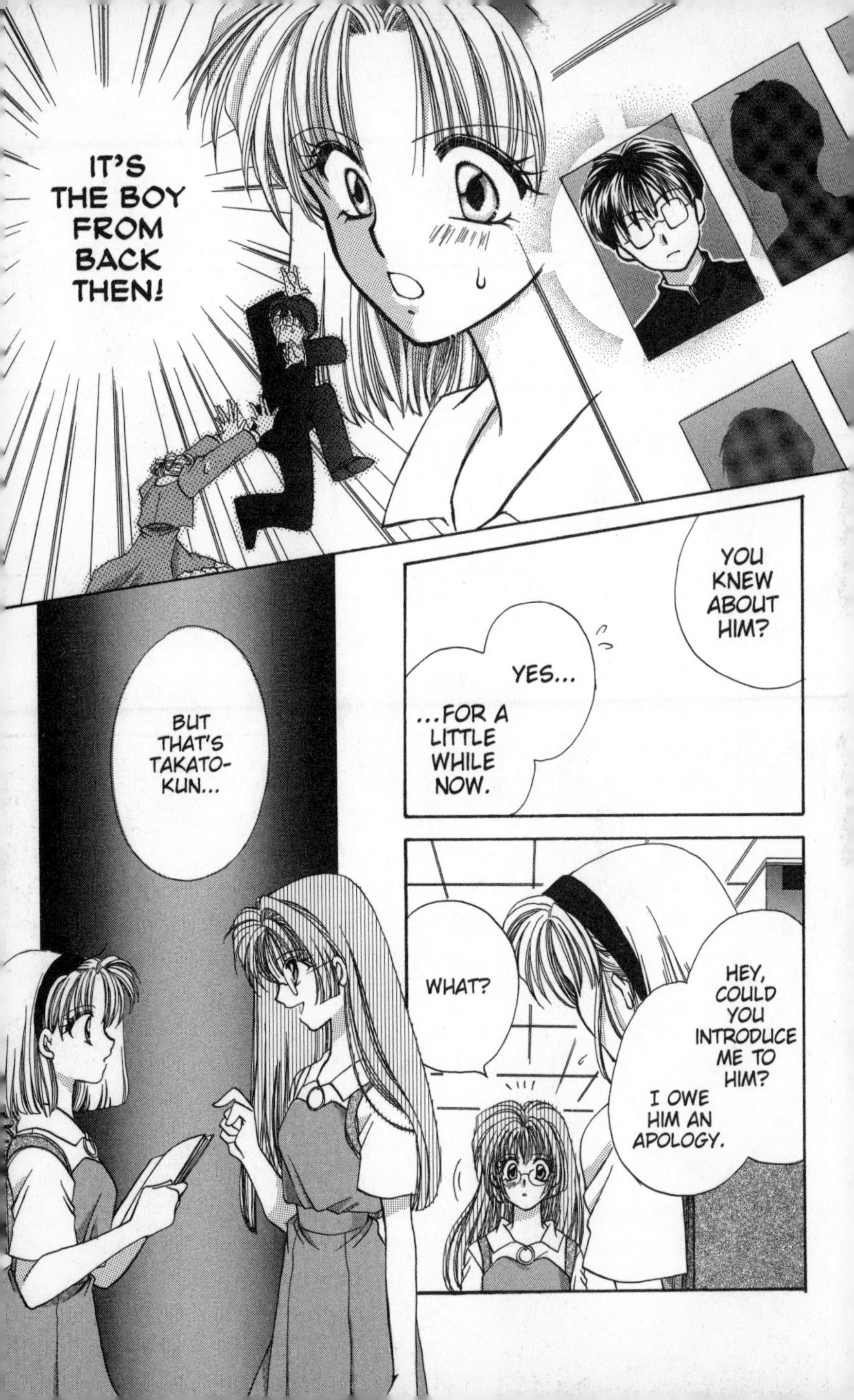
IT'S THE BOY FROM BACK THEN!
YOU KNEW ABOUT HIM?
YES...
...FOR A LITTLE WHILE NOW.
HEY, COULD YOU INTRODUCE ME TO HIM?
I OWE HIM AN APOLOGY.
WHAT?
BUT THAT'S TAKATO-KUN...

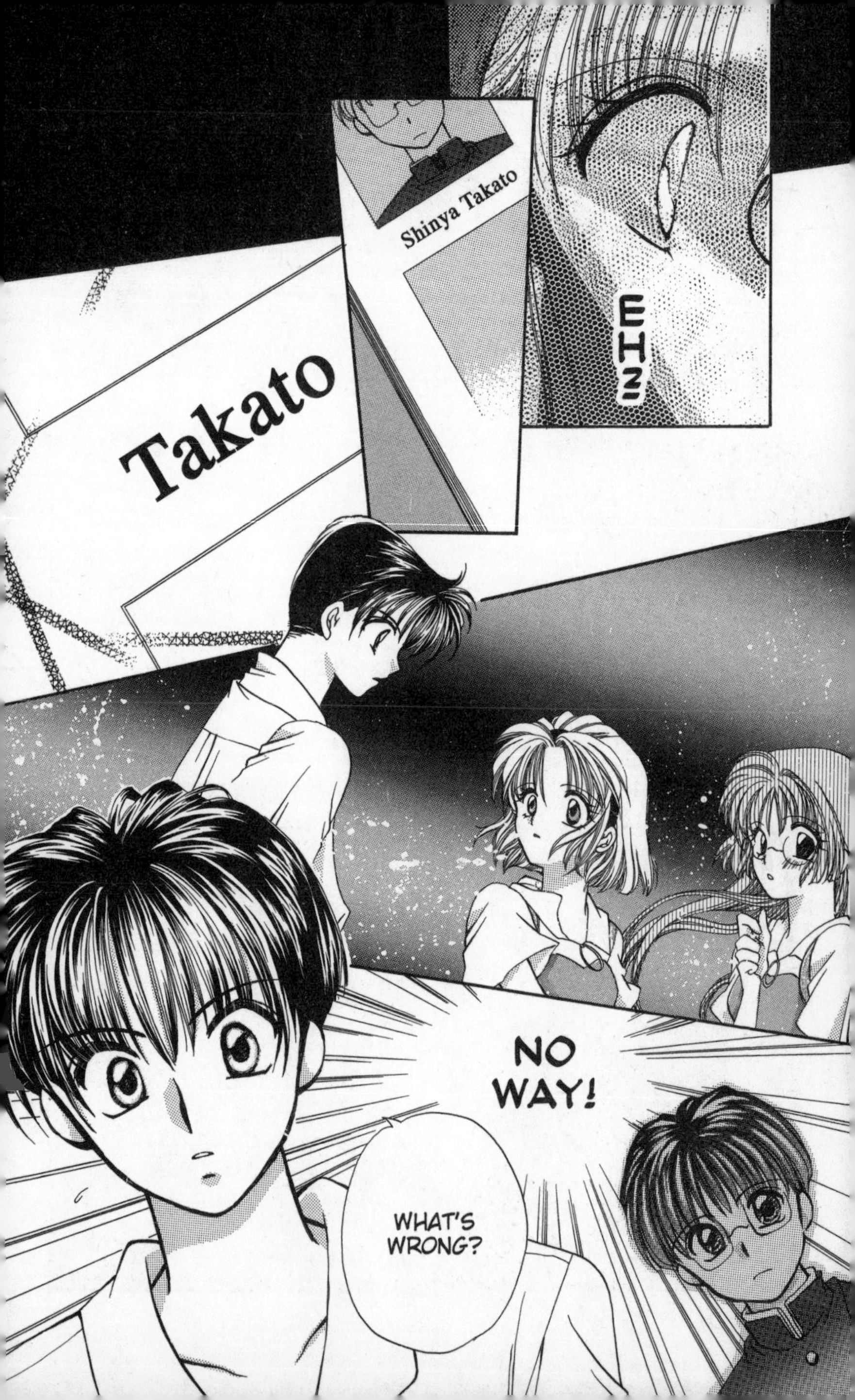
EH?!
Shinya Takato
Takato
NO WAY!
WHAT'S WRONG?

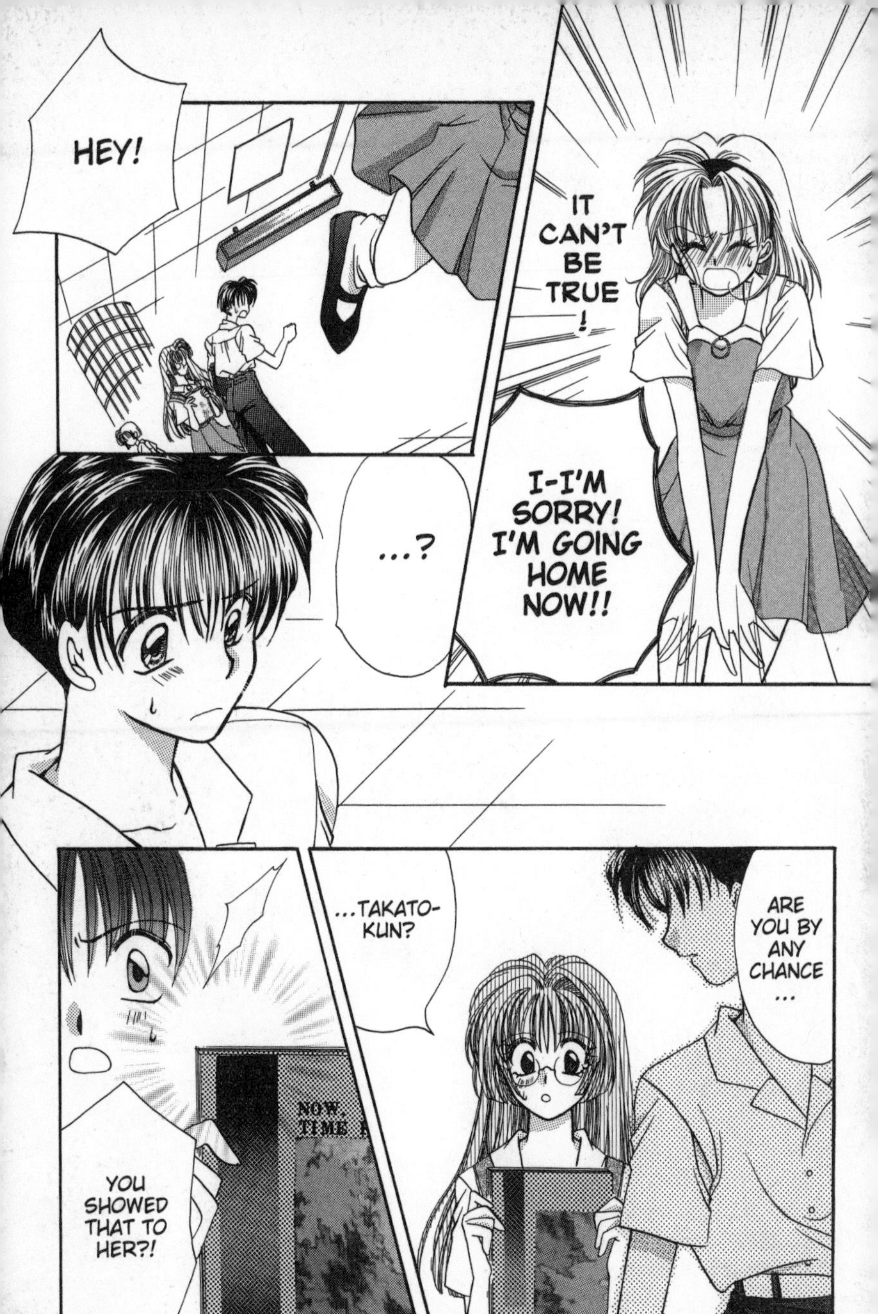
IT CAN'T BE TRUE!
I-I'M SORRY! I'M GOING HOME NOW!!
HEY!
...?
ARE YOU BY ANY CHANCE...
...TAKATO-KUN?
YOU SHOWED THAT TO HER?!

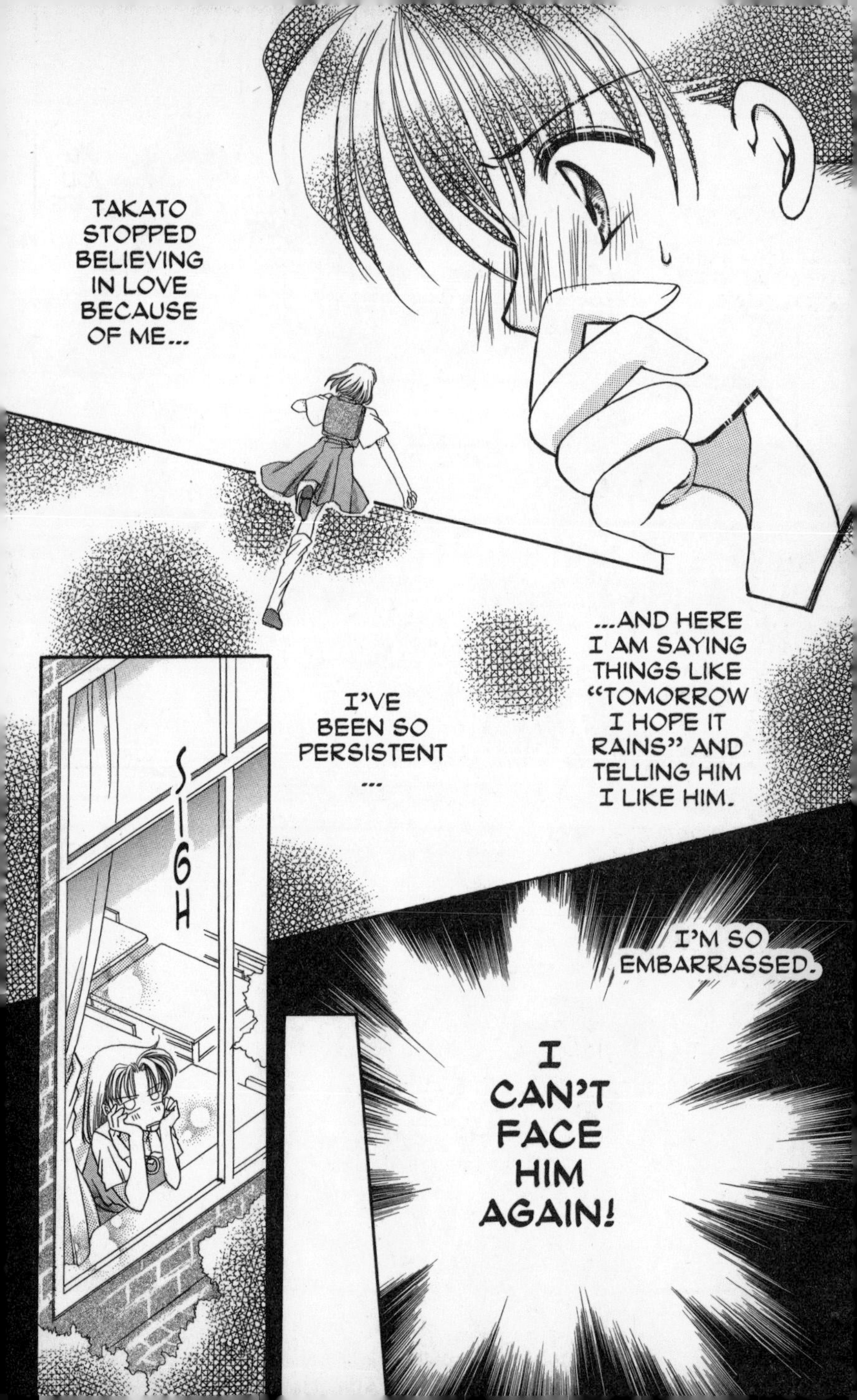

TAKATO STOPPED BELIEVING IN LOVE BECAUSE OF ME...
I'VE BEEN SO PERSISTENT ...
...AND HERE I AM SAYING THINGS LIKE "TOMORROW I HOPE IT RAINS" AND TELLING HIM I LIKE HIM.
I'M SO EMBARRASSED.
I CAN'T FACE HIM AGAIN!
SIGH

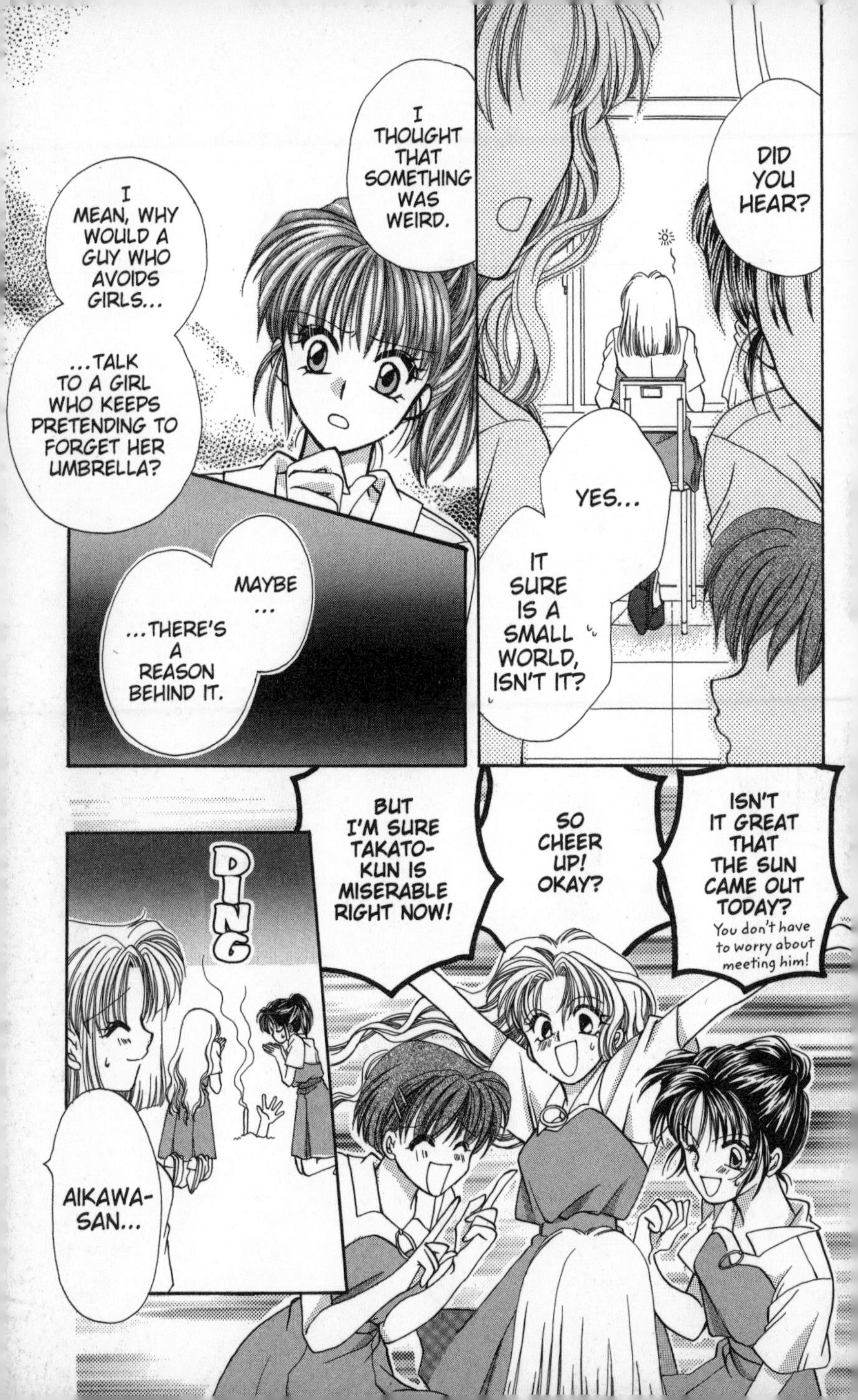
DID YOU HEAR?
YES...
IT SURE IS A SMALL WORLD, ISN'T IT?
I THOUGHT THAT SOMETHING WAS WEIRD.
I MEAN, WHY WOULD A GUY WHO AVOIDS GIRLS...
...TALK TO A GIRL WHO KEEPS PRETENDING TO FORGET HER UMBRELLA?
MAYBE...
...THERE'S A REASON BEHIND IT.
ISN'T IT GREAT THAT THE SUN CAME OUT TODAY?
You don't have to worry about meeting him!
SO CHEER UP! OKAY?
BUT I'M SURE TAKATO-KUN IS MISERABLE RIGHT NOW!
DING
AIKAWA-SAN...

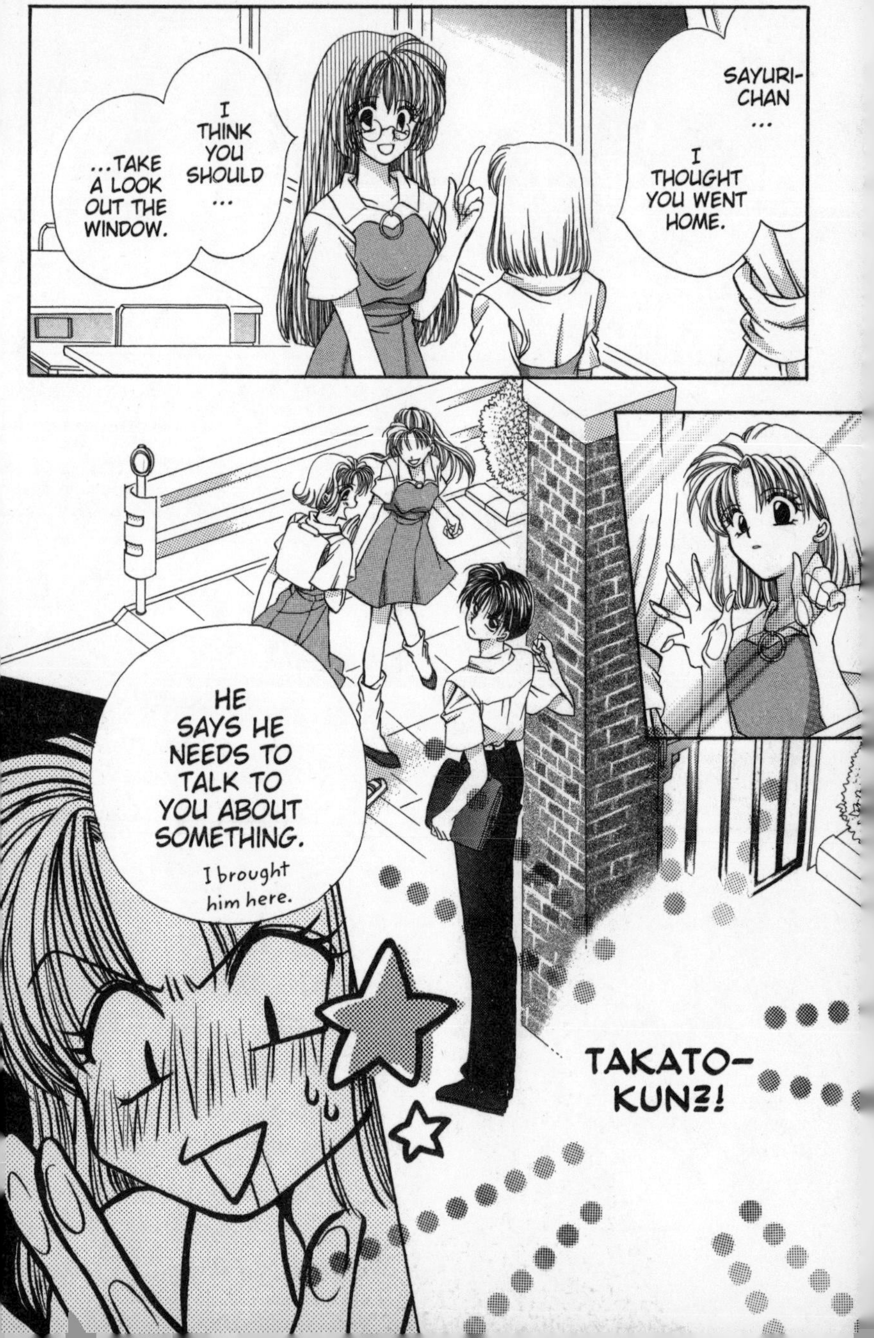
SAYURI-CHAN ...
I THOUGHT YOU WENT HOME.
I THINK YOU SHOULD ...
...TAKE A LOOK OUT THE WINDOW.
TAKATO-KUN?!
HE SAYS HE NEEDS TO TALK TO YOU ABOUT SOMETHING.
I brought him here.

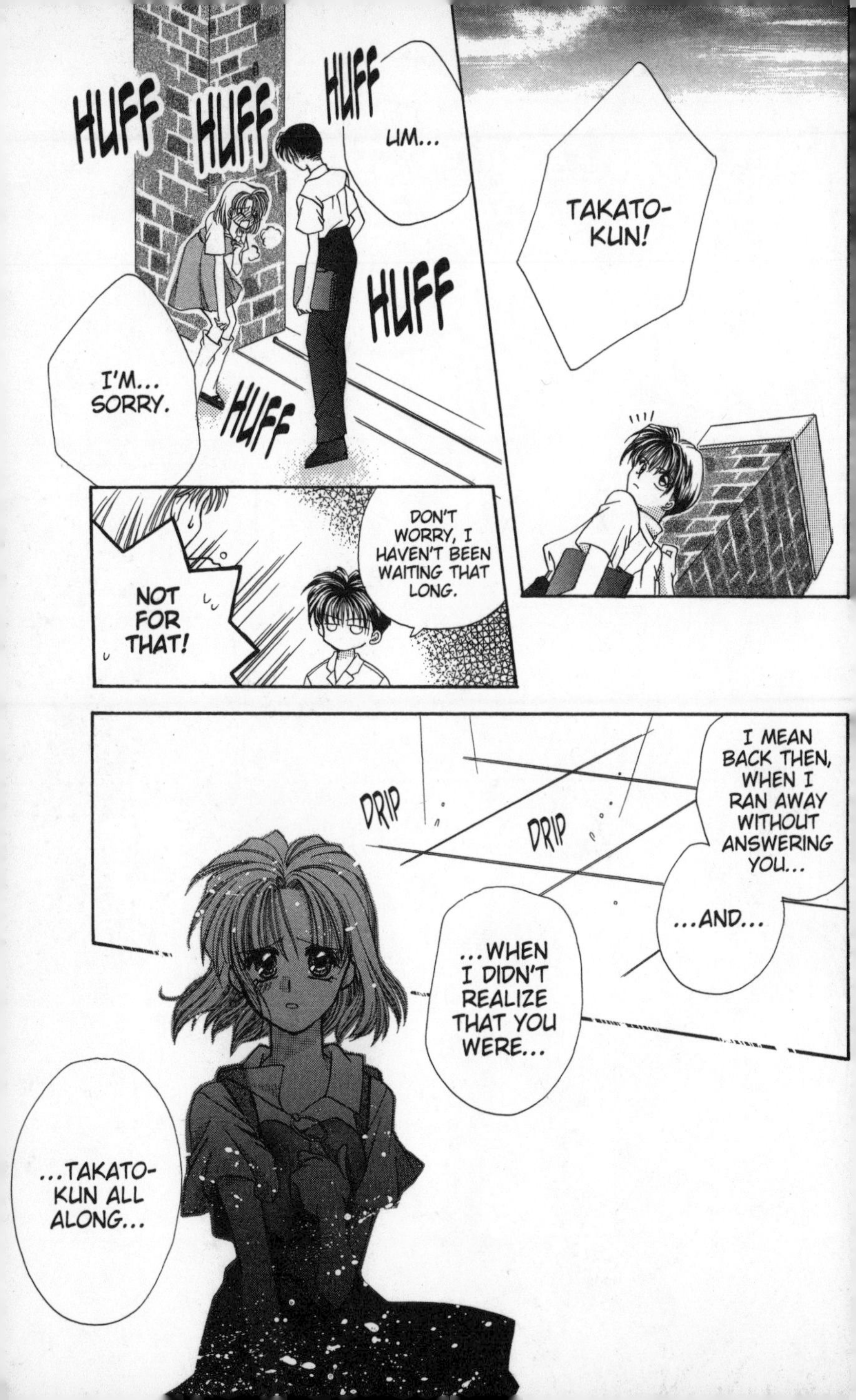
TAKATO-KUN!
HUFF
UM...
HUFF
HUFF
HUFF
I'M... SORRY.
HUFF
DON'T WORRY, I HAVEN'T BEEN WAITING THAT LONG.
NOT FOR THAT!
I MEAN BACK THEN, WHEN I RAN AWAY WITHOUT ANSWERING YOU...
...AND...
DRIP
DRIP
...WHEN I DIDN'T REALIZE THAT YOU WERE...
...TAKATO-KUN ALL ALONG...

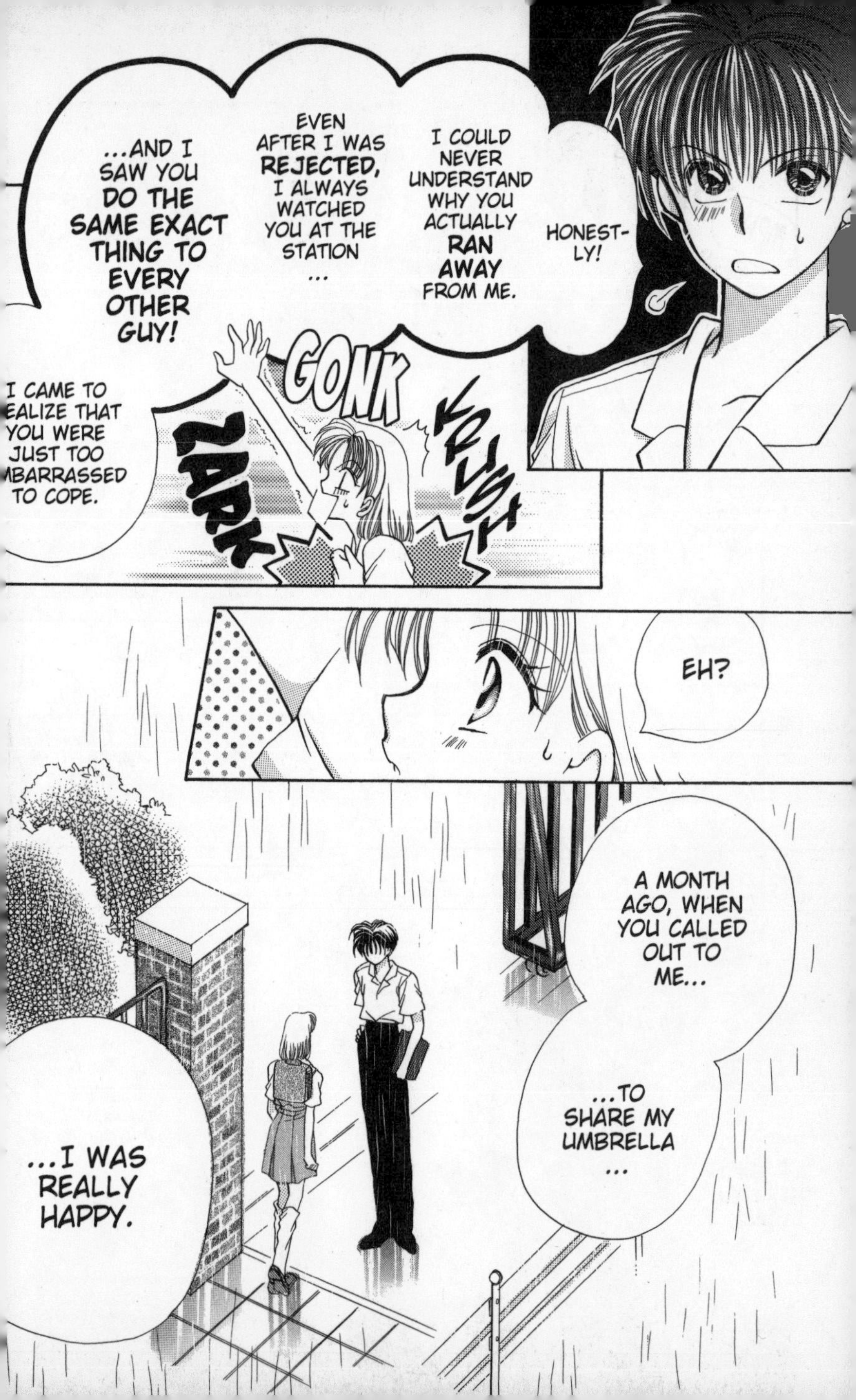
HONEST-LY!
I COULD NEVER UNDERSTAND WHY YOU ACTUALLY RAN AWAY FROM ME.
EVEN AFTER I WAS REJECTED, I ALWAYS WATCHED YOU AT THE STATION ...
...AND I SAW YOU DO THE SAME EXACT THING TO EVERY OTHER GUY!
GONK
ZARK
I CAME TO EALIZE THAT YOU WERE JUST TOO MBARRASSED TO COPE.
EH?
A MONTH AGO, WHEN YOU CALLED OUT TO ME...
...TO SHARE MY UMBRELLA ...
...I WAS REALLY HAPPY.

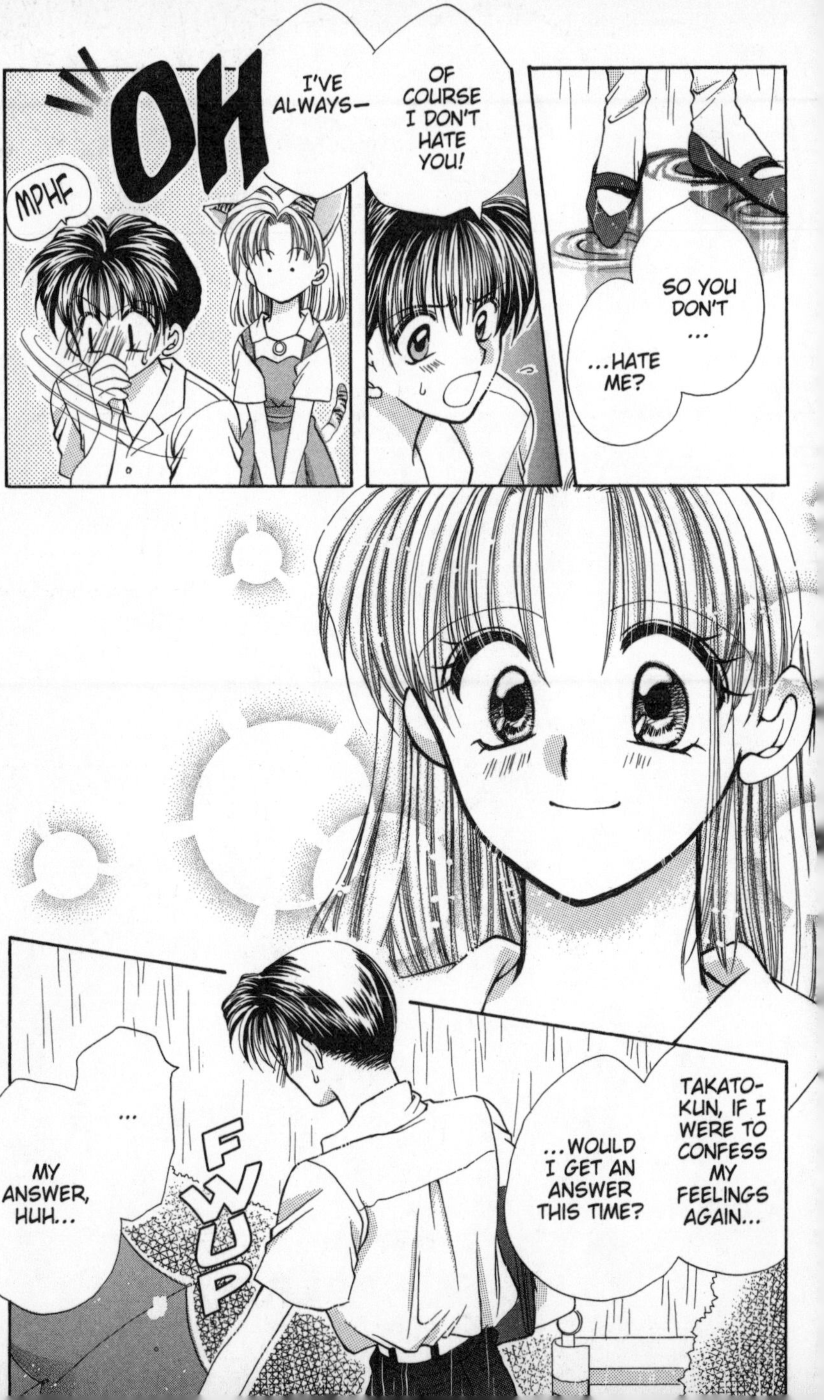
SO YOU DON'T ...
...HATE ME?
OF COURSE I DON'T HATE YOU!
I'VE ALWAYS—
OH
MPHF
TAKATO-KUN, IF I WERE TO CONFESS MY FEELINGS AGAIN...
...WOULD I GET AN ANSWER THIS TIME?
FWUP
...
MY ANSWER, HUH...

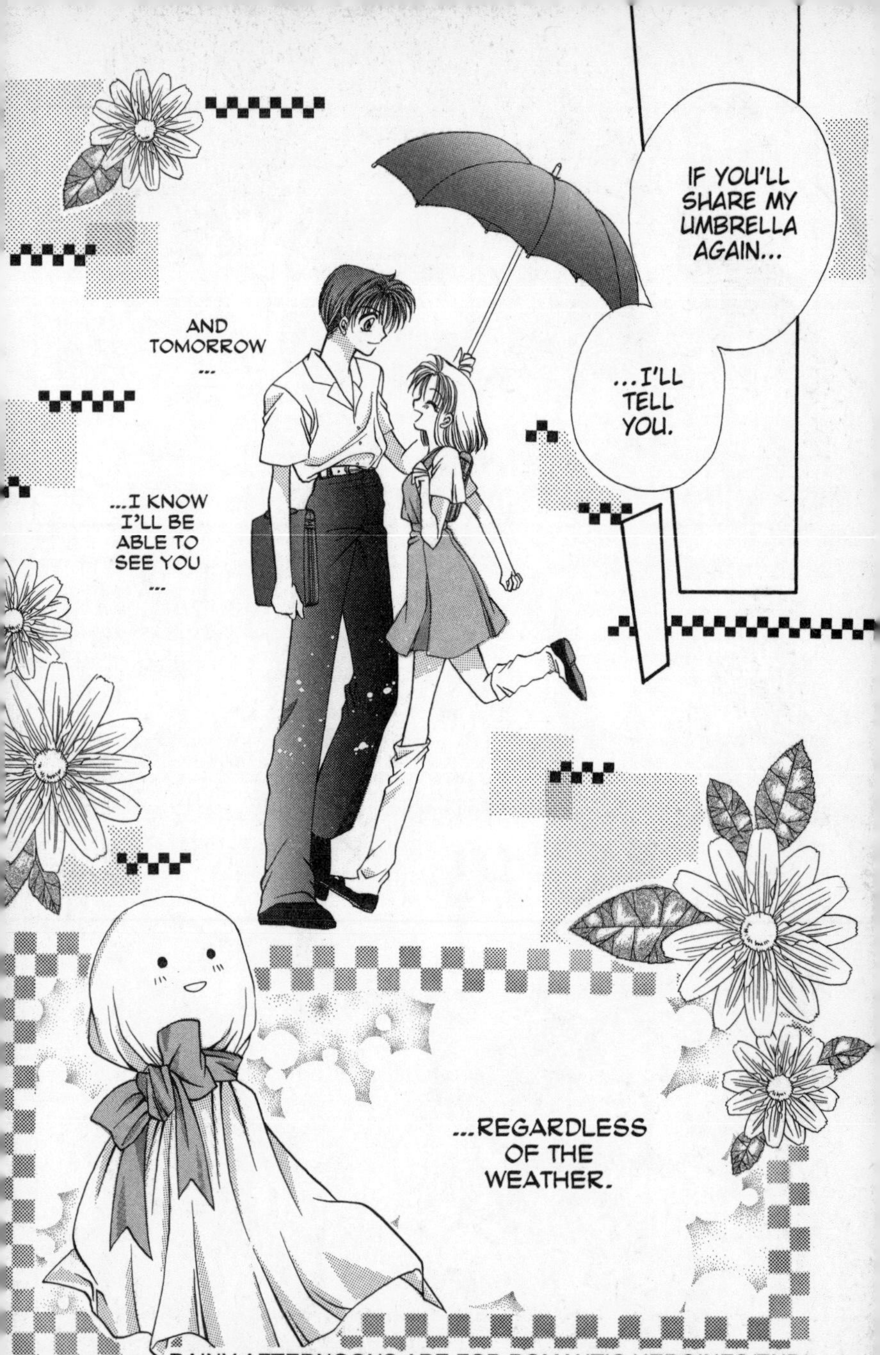
IF YOU'LL SHARE MY UMBRELLA AGAIN...
...I'LL TELL YOU.
AND TOMORROW ...
...I KNOW I'LL BE ABLE TO SEE YOU ...
...REGARDLESS OF THE WEATHER.

RAINY AFTERNOONS ARE FOR ROMANTIC HEROINES/END

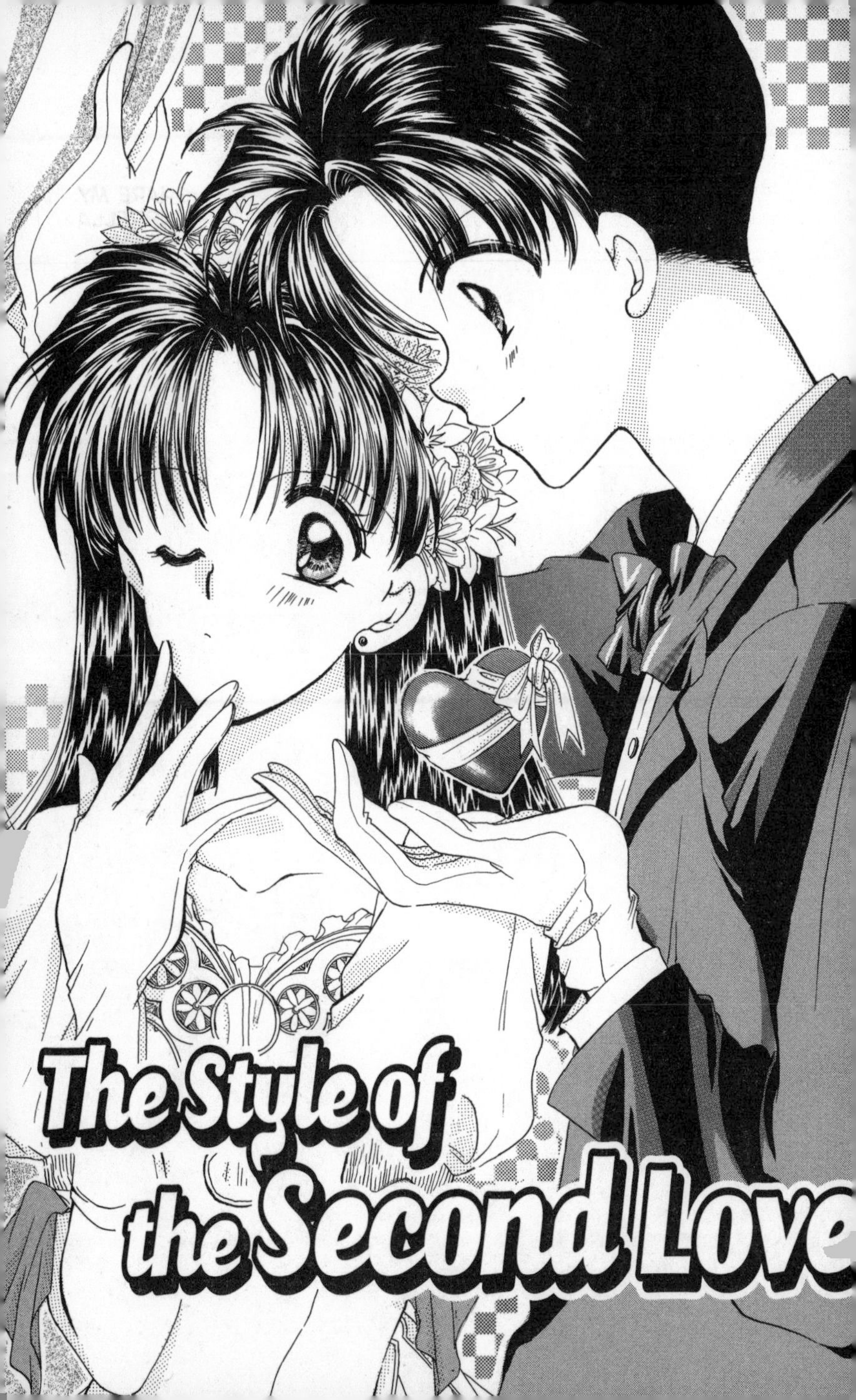
The Style of
the Second Love

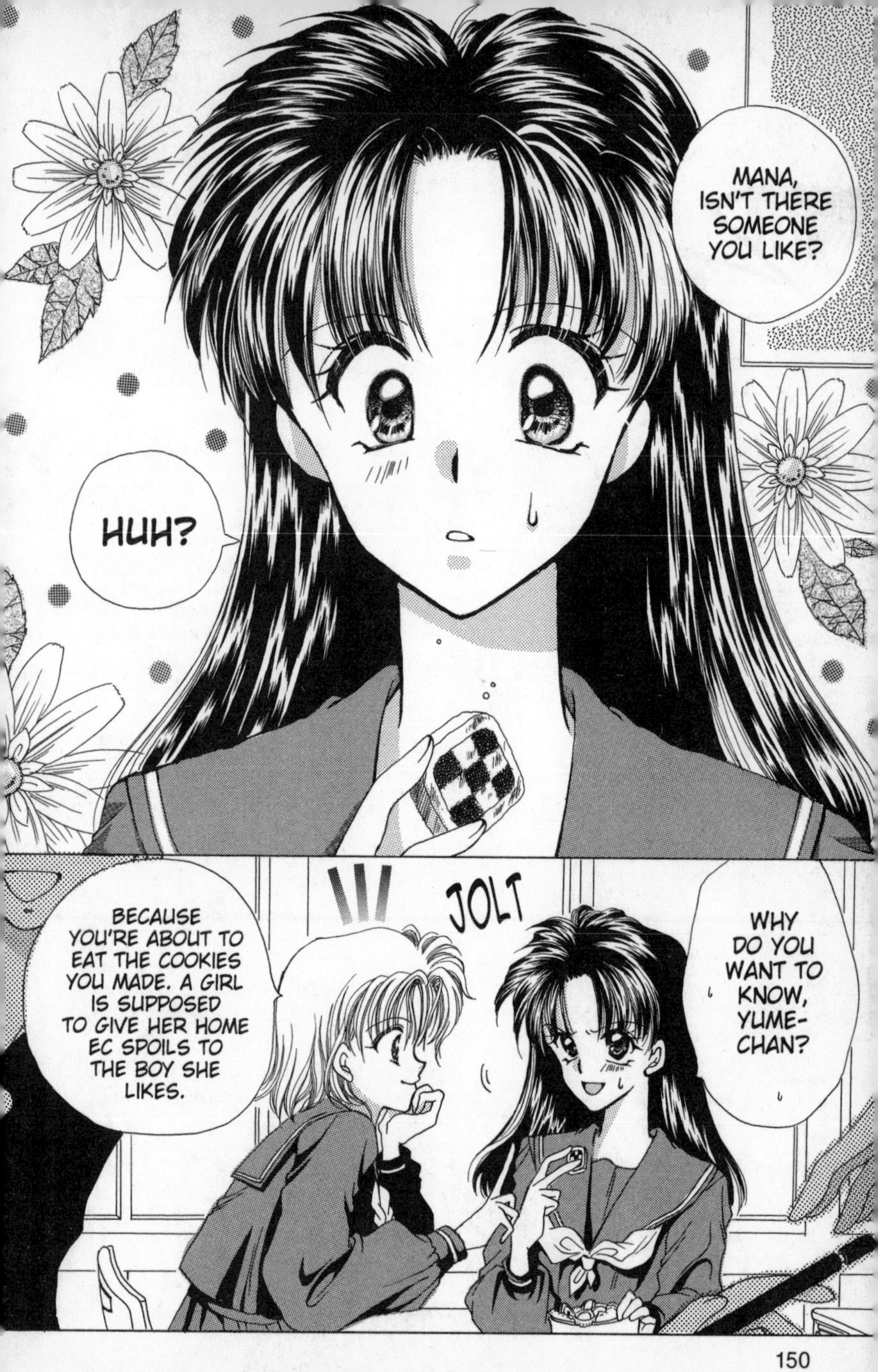
MANA, ISN'T THERE SOMEONE YOU LIKE?
HUH?
WHY DO YOU WANT TO KNOW, YUME-CHAN?
JOLT
BECAUSE YOU'RE ABOUT TO EAT THE COOKIES YOU MADE. A GIRL IS SUPPOSED TO GIVE HER HOME EC SPOILS TO THE BOY SHE LIKES.

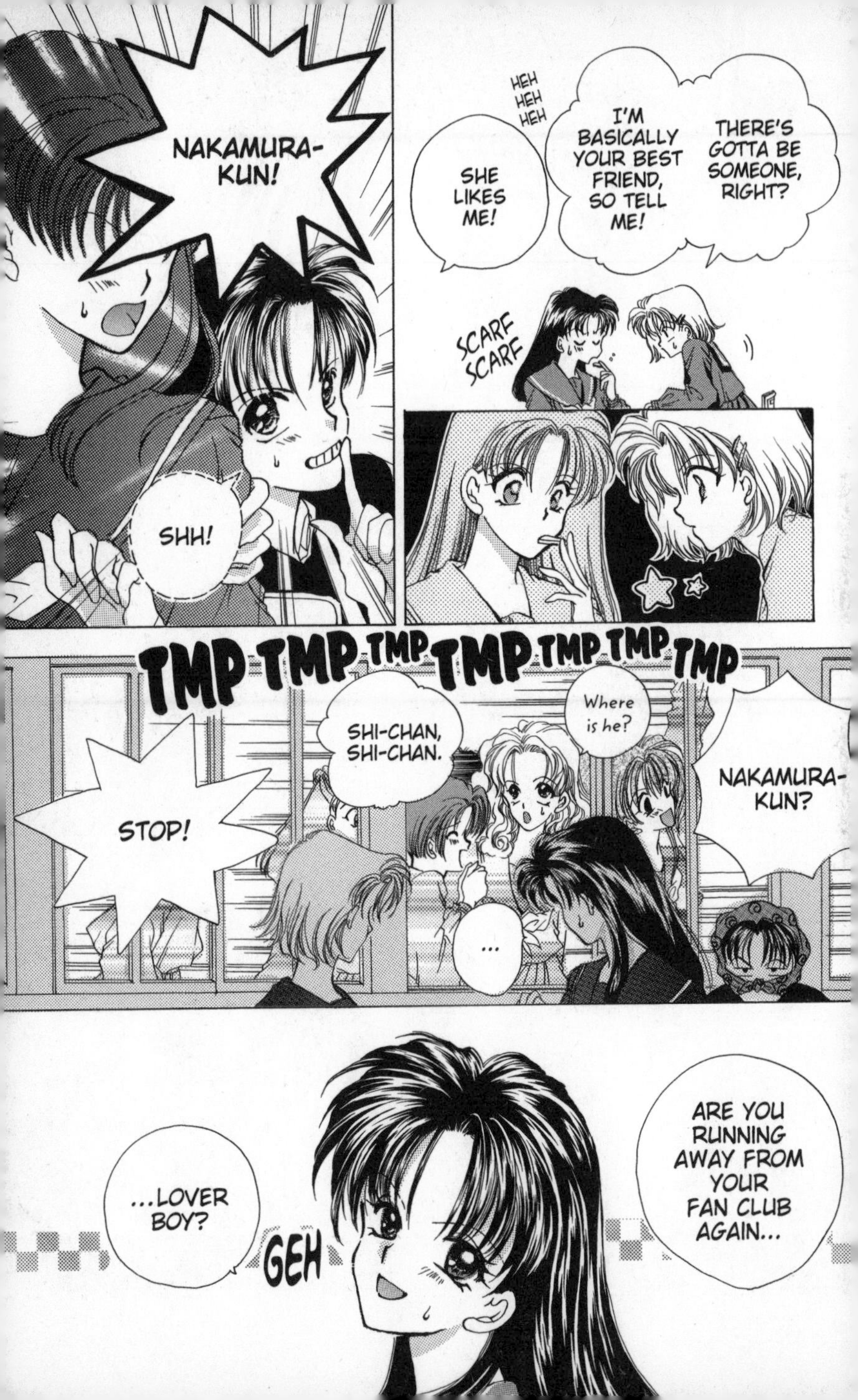
THERE'S GOTTA BE SOMEONE, RIGHT?
I'M BASICALLY YOUR BEST FRIEND, SO TELL ME!
HEH HEH HEH
SHE LIKES ME!
SCARF SCARF
NAKAMURA-KUN!
SHH!
TMP TMP TMP TMP TMP TMP TMP
NAKAMURA-KUN?
Where is he?
SHI-CHAN, SHI-CHAN.
STOP!
...
ARE YOU RUNNING AWAY FROM YOUR FAN CLUB AGAIN...
GEH
...LOVER BOY?

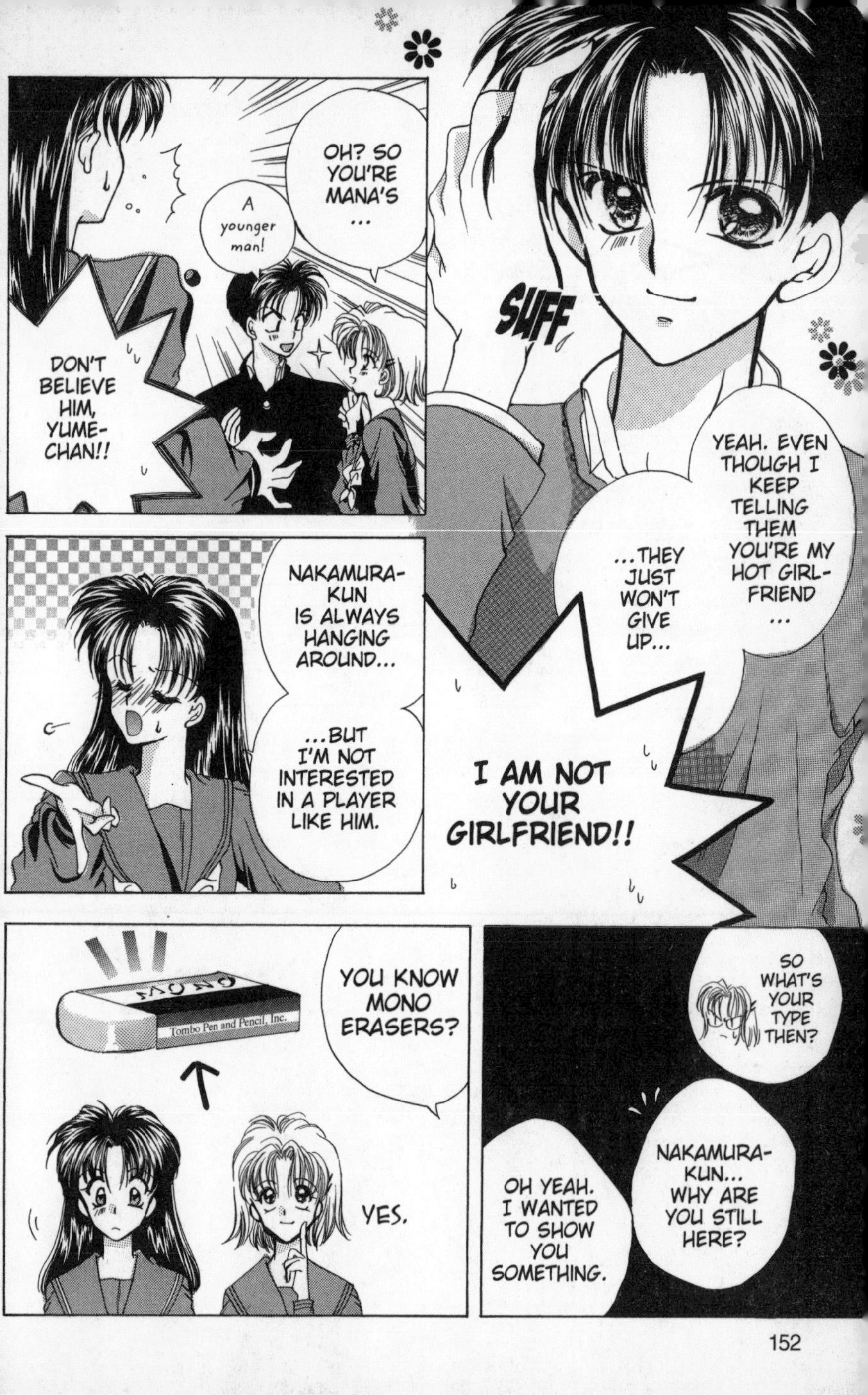

SUFF
YEAH. EVEN THOUGH I KEEP TELLING THEM YOU'RE MY HOT GIRLFRIEND...
...THEY JUST WON'T GIVE UP...
I AM NOT YOUR GIRLFRIEND!!
OH? SO YOU'RE MANA'S ...
A younger man!
DON'T BELIEVE HIM, YUME-CHAN!!
NAKAMURA-KUN IS ALWAYS HANGING AROUND...
...BUT I'M NOT INTERESTED IN A PLAYER LIKE HIM.
SO WHAT'S YOUR TYPE THEN?
NAKAMURA-KUN... WHY ARE YOU STILL HERE?
OH YEAH. I WANTED TO SHOW YOU SOMETHING.
YOU KNOW MONO ERASERS?
MONO
Tombo Pen and Pencil, Inc.
YES.

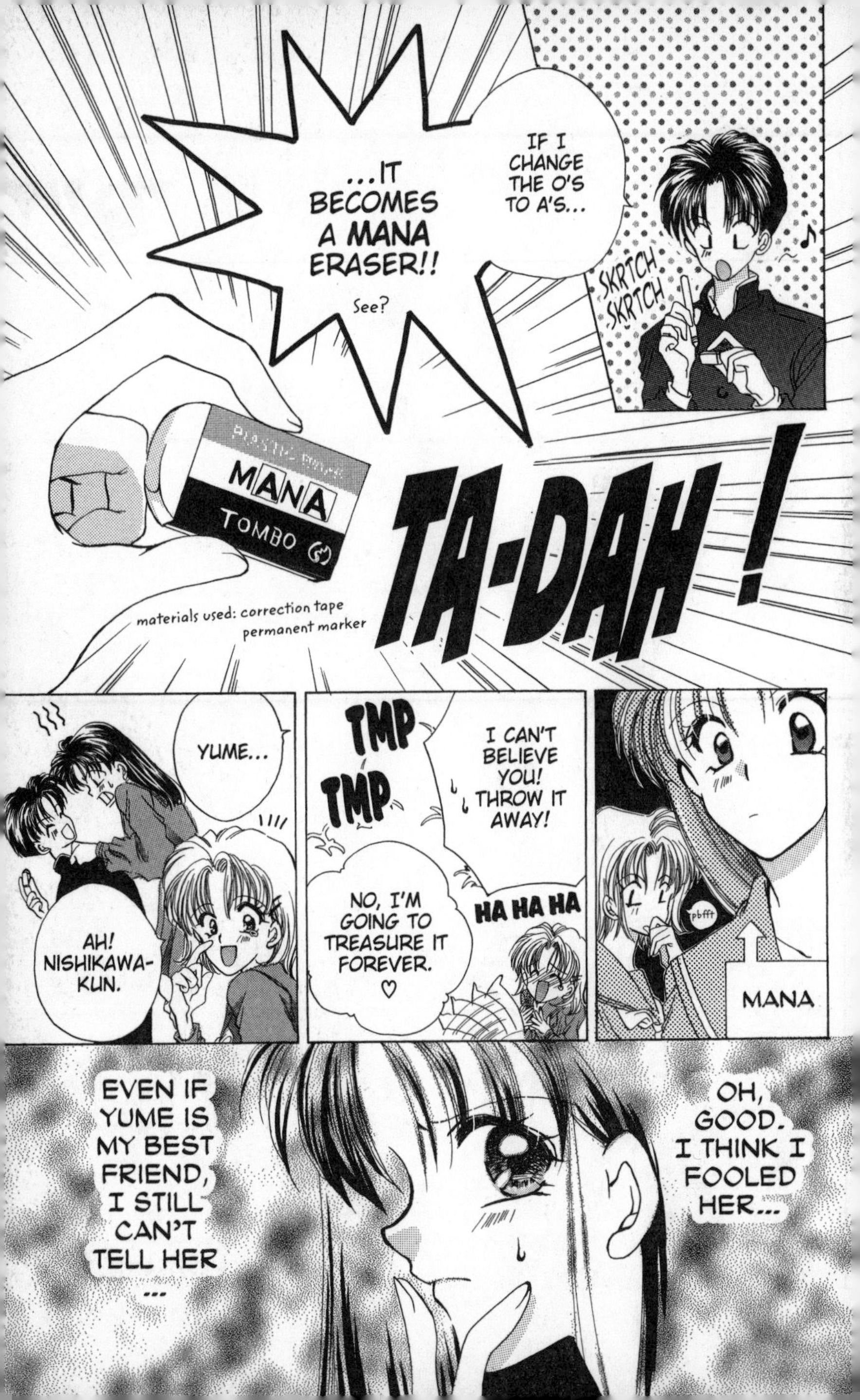
IF I CHANGE THE O'S TO A'S...
SKRTCH SKRTCH
...IT BECOMES A MANA ERASER!!
See?
MANA
TOMBO
TA-DAH!
materials used: correction tape permanent marker
MANA
pbfft
TMP TMP
I CAN'T BELIEVE YOU! THROW IT AWAY!
NO, I'M GOING TO TREASURE IT FOREVER. ♡
HA HA HA
YUME...
AH! NISHIKAWA-KUN.
OH, GOOD. I THINK I FOOLED HER...
EVEN IF YUME IS MY BEST FRIEND, I STILL CAN'T TELL HER ...

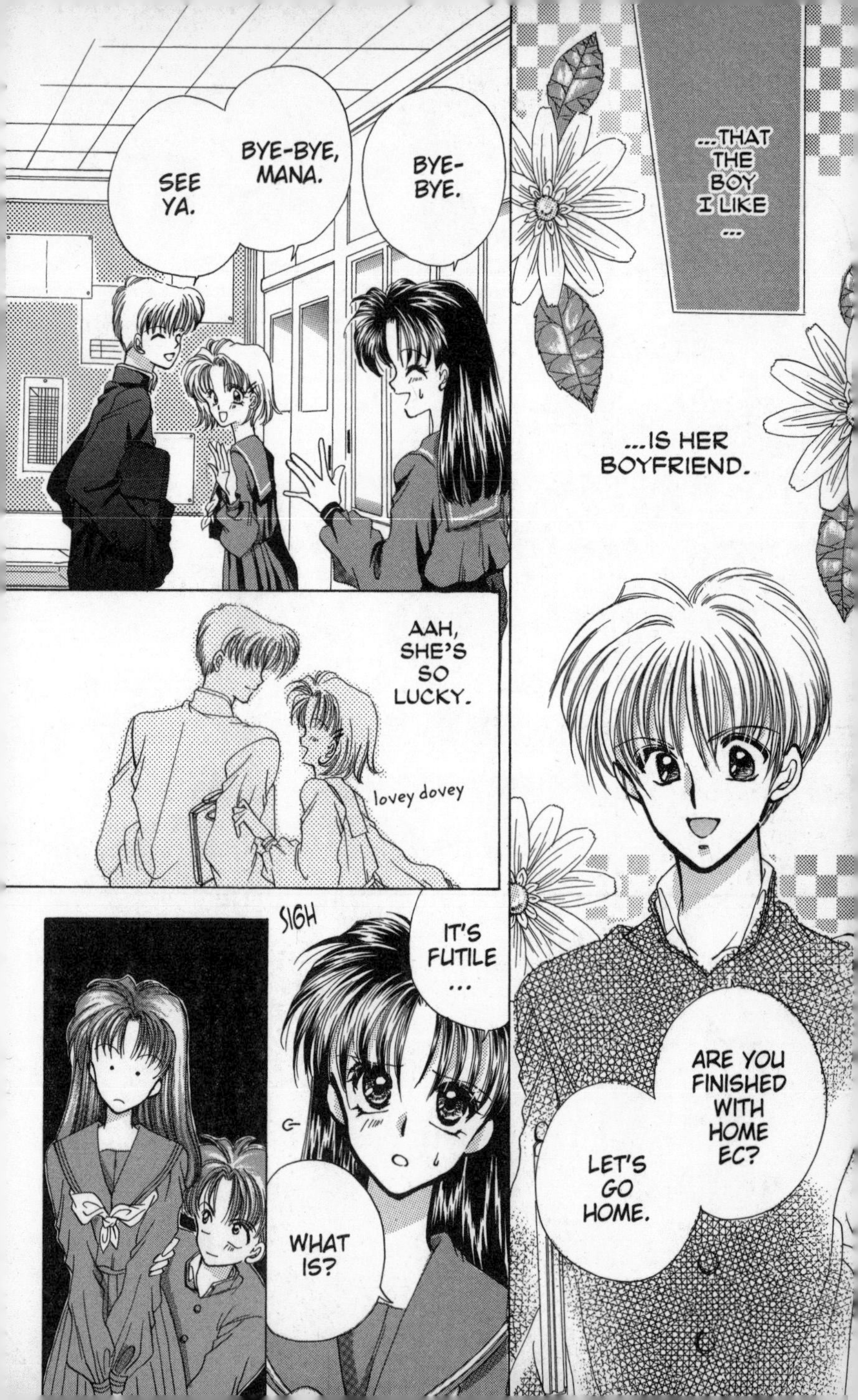
...THAT THE BOY I LIKE ...
...IS HER BOYFRIEND.
ARE YOU FINISHED WITH HOME EC?
LET'S GO HOME.
BYE-BYE.
BYE-BYE, MANA.
SEE YA.
AAH, SHE'S SO LUCKY.
lovey dovey
SIGH
IT'S FUTILE ...
WHAT IS?

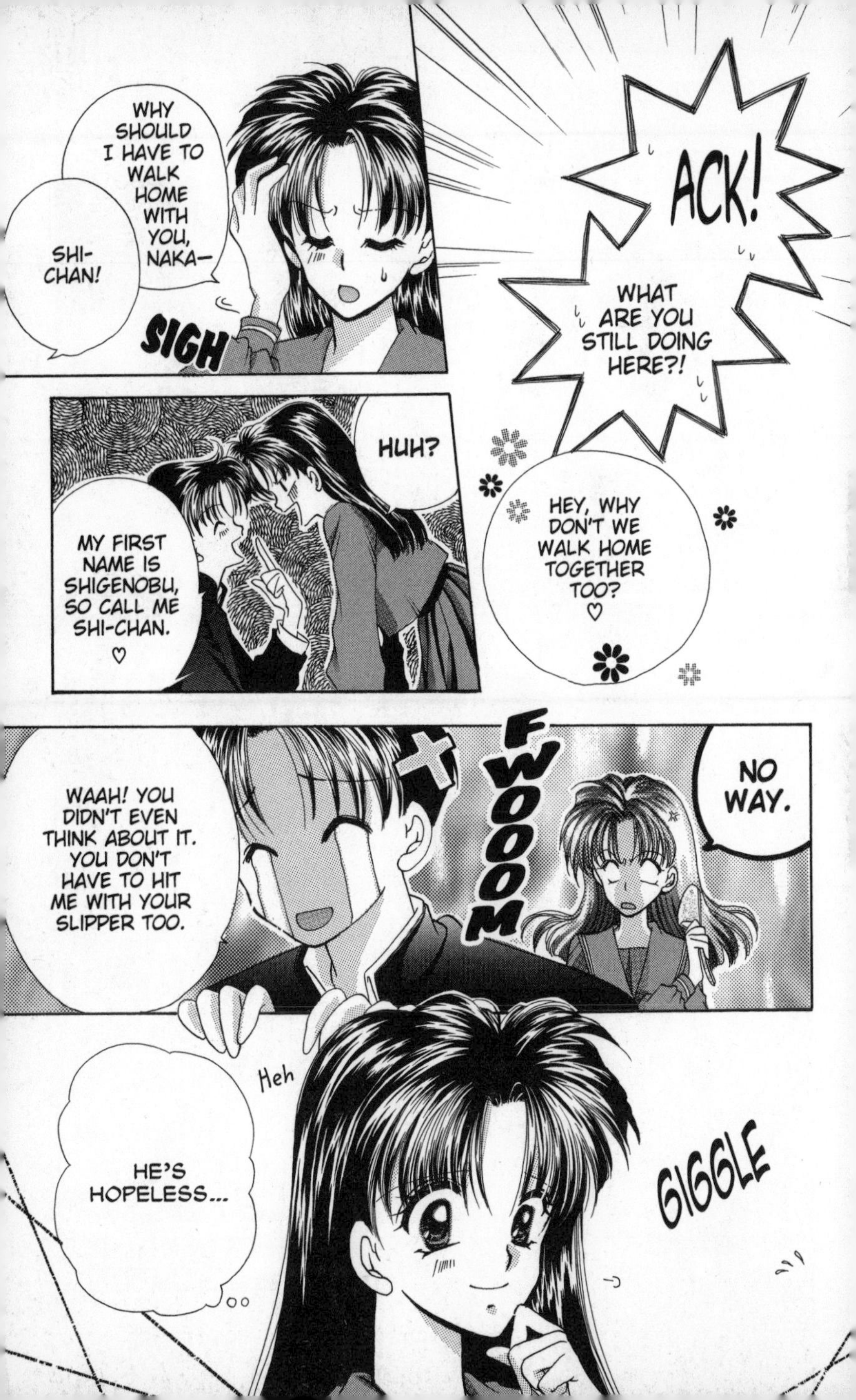
ACK!
WHAT ARE YOU STILL DOING HERE?!
HEY, WHY DON'T WE WALK HOME TOGETHER TOO? ♡
WHY SHOULD I HAVE TO WALK HOME WITH YOU, NAKA—
SIGH
SHI-CHAN!
HUH?
MY FIRST NAME IS SHIGENOBU, SO CALL ME SHI-CHAN. ♡
NO WAY.
FWOOOOM
WAAH! YOU DIDN'T EVEN THINK ABOUT IT. YOU DON'T HAVE TO HIT ME WITH YOUR SLIPPER TOO.
GIGGLE
Heh
HE'S HOPELESS...

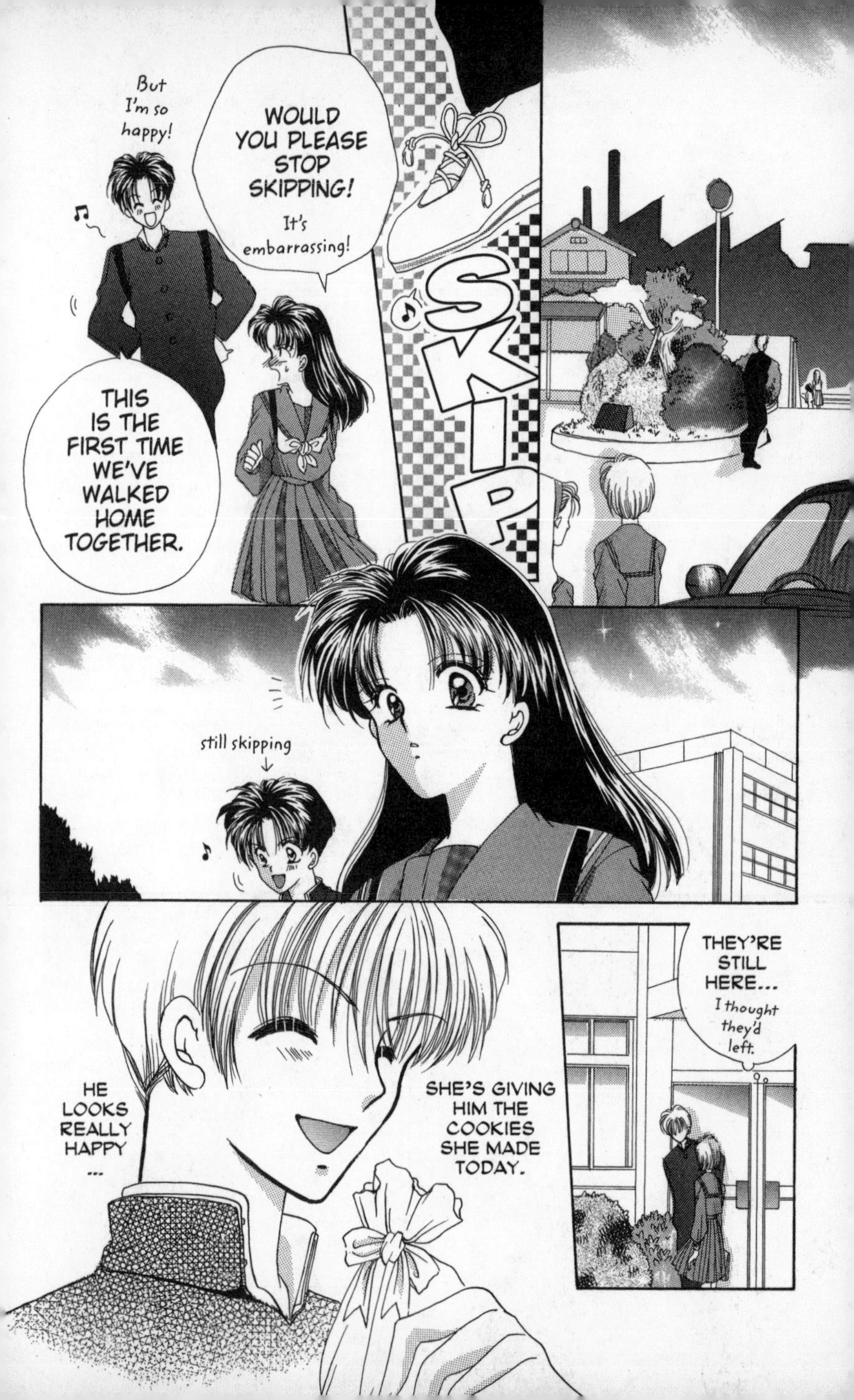
SKIP
WOULD YOU PLEASE STOP SKIPPING! It's embarrassing!
But I'm so happy!
THIS IS THE FIRST TIME WE'VE WALKED HOME TOGETHER.
still skipping
THEY'RE STILL HERE... I thought they'd left.
SHE'S GIVING HIM THE COOKIES SHE MADE TODAY.
HE LOOKS REALLY HAPPY ...

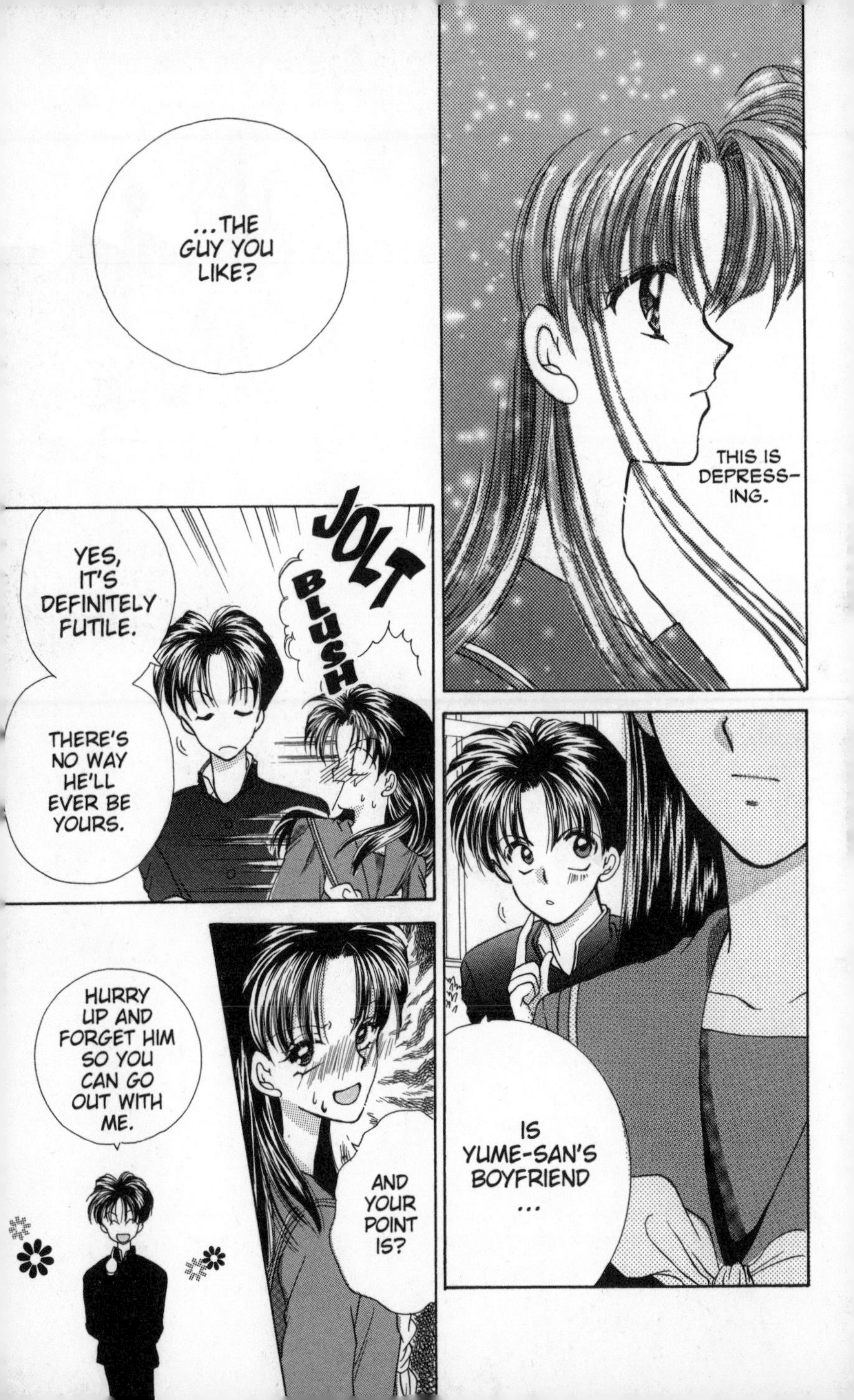
THIS IS DEPRESS-ING.
IS YUME-SAN'S BOYFRIEND ...
...THE GUY YOU LIKE?
JOLT
BLUSH
YES, IT'S DEFINITELY FUTILE.
THERE'S NO WAY HE'LL EVER BE YOURS.
AND YOUR POINT IS?
HURRY UP AND FORGET HIM SO YOU CAN GO OUT WITH ME.

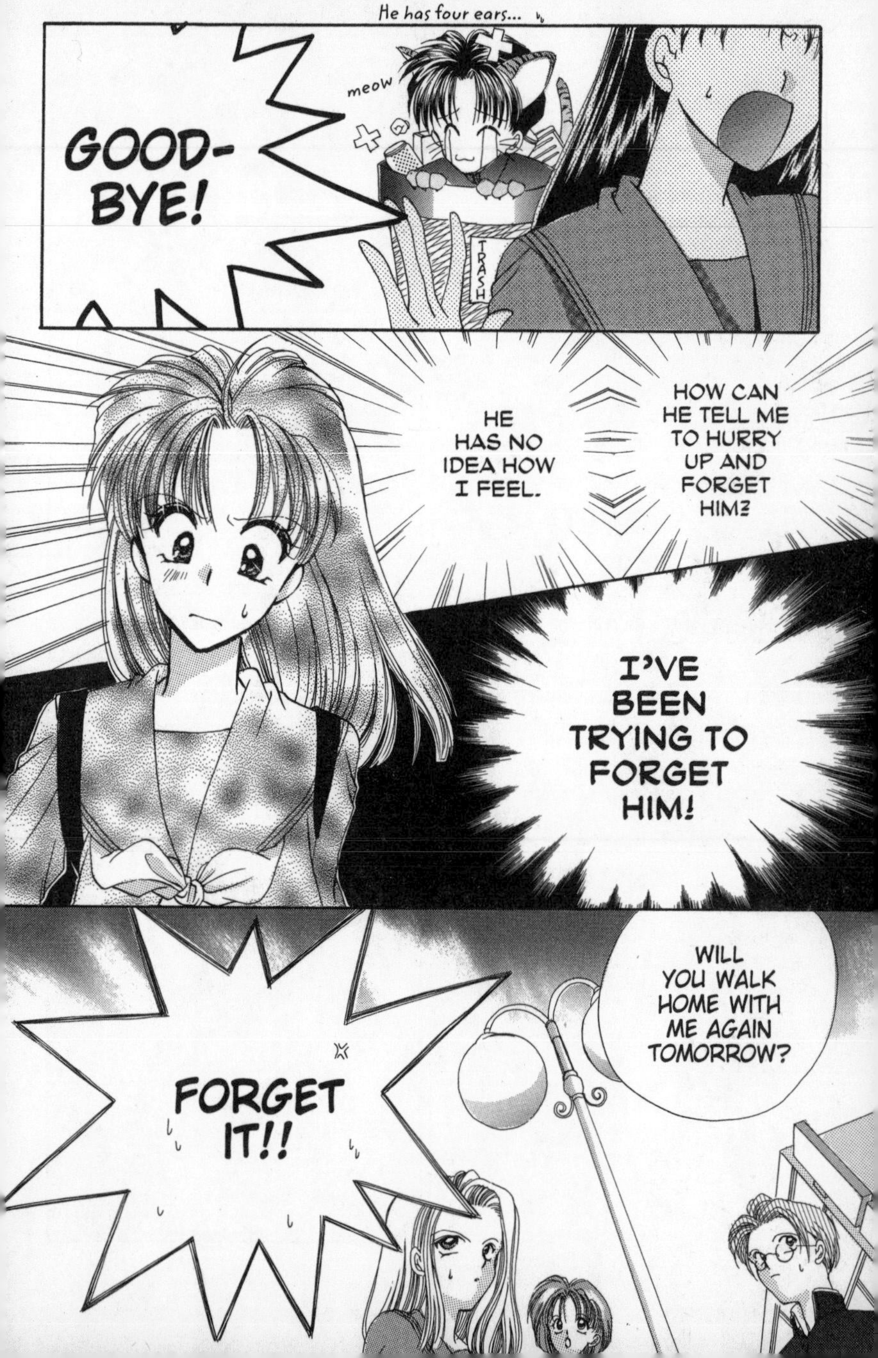
He has four ears...
meow
GOOD-BYE!
TRASH
HOW CAN HE TELL ME TO HURRY UP AND FORGET HIM?
HE HAS NO IDEA HOW I FEEL.
I'VE BEEN TRYING TO FORGET HIM!
WILL YOU WALK HOME WITH ME AGAIN TOMORROW?
FORGET IT!!

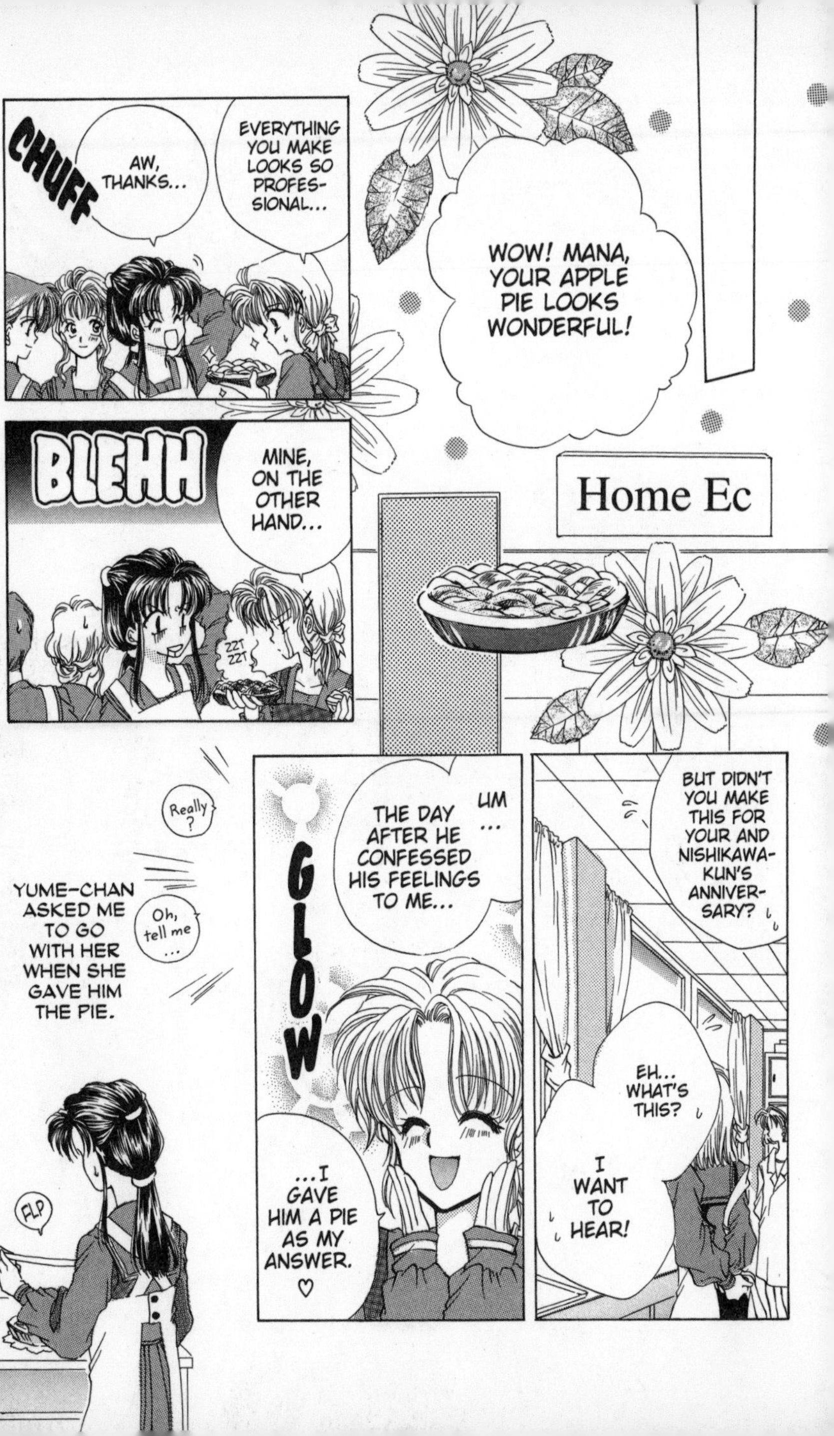
WOW! MANA, YOUR APPLE PIE LOOKS WONDERFUL!
Home Ec
EVERYTHING YOU MAKE LOOKS SO PROFES-SIONAL...
AW, THANKS...
CHUFF
MINE, ON THE OTHER HAND...
BLEHH
ZZT ZZT
BUT DIDN'T YOU MAKE THIS FOR YOUR AND NISHIKAWA-KUN'S ANNIVER-SARY?
EH... WHAT'S THIS?
I WANT TO HEAR!
UM...
THE DAY AFTER HE CONFESSED HIS FEELINGS TO ME...
GLOW
...I GAVE HIM A PIE AS MY ANSWER. ♡
Really?
Oh, tell me...
YUME-CHAN ASKED ME TO GO WITH HER WHEN SHE GAVE HIM THE PIE.
FLP

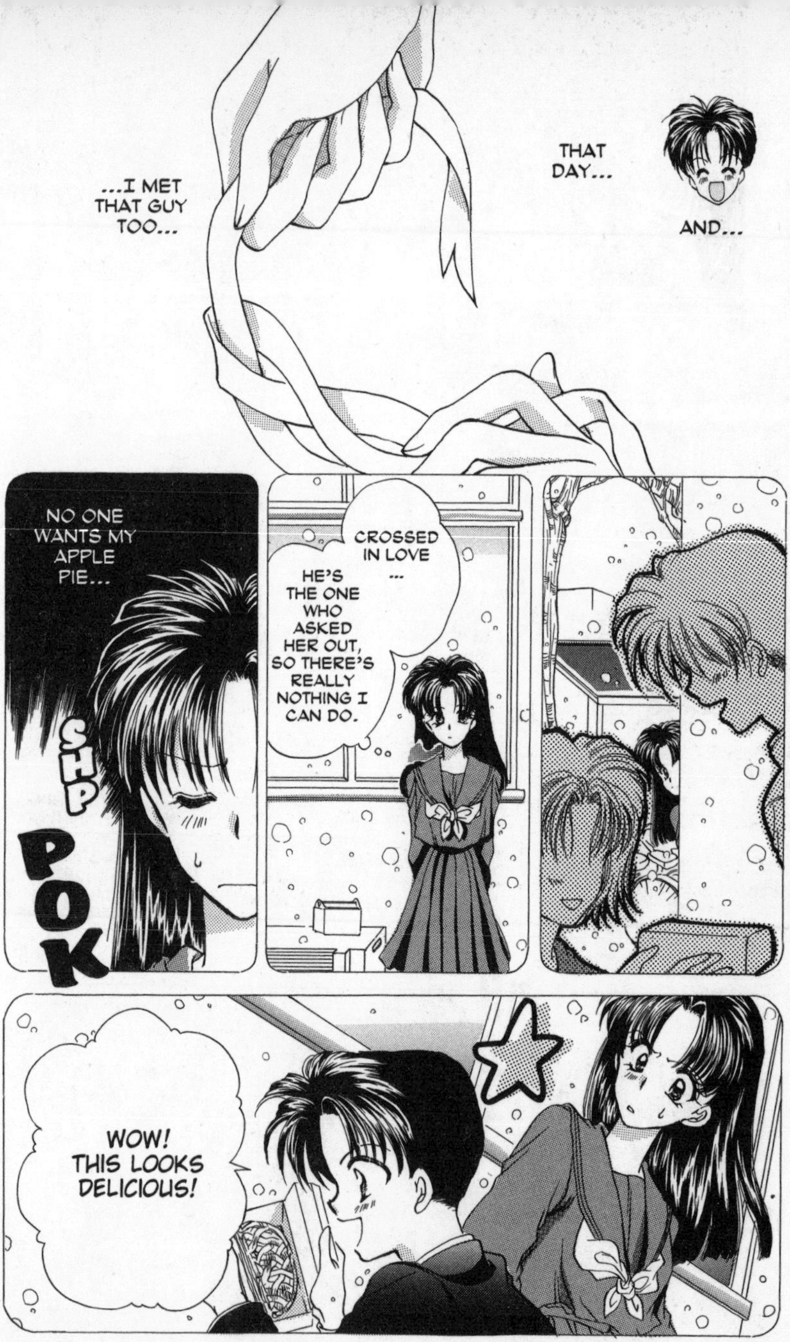
THAT DAY...
AND...
...I MET THAT GUY TOO...
CROSSED IN LOVE ...
HE'S THE ONE WHO ASKED HER OUT, SO THERE'S REALLY NOTHING I CAN DO.
NO ONE WANTS MY APPLE PIE...
SHP
POK
WOW! THIS LOOKS DELICIOUS!

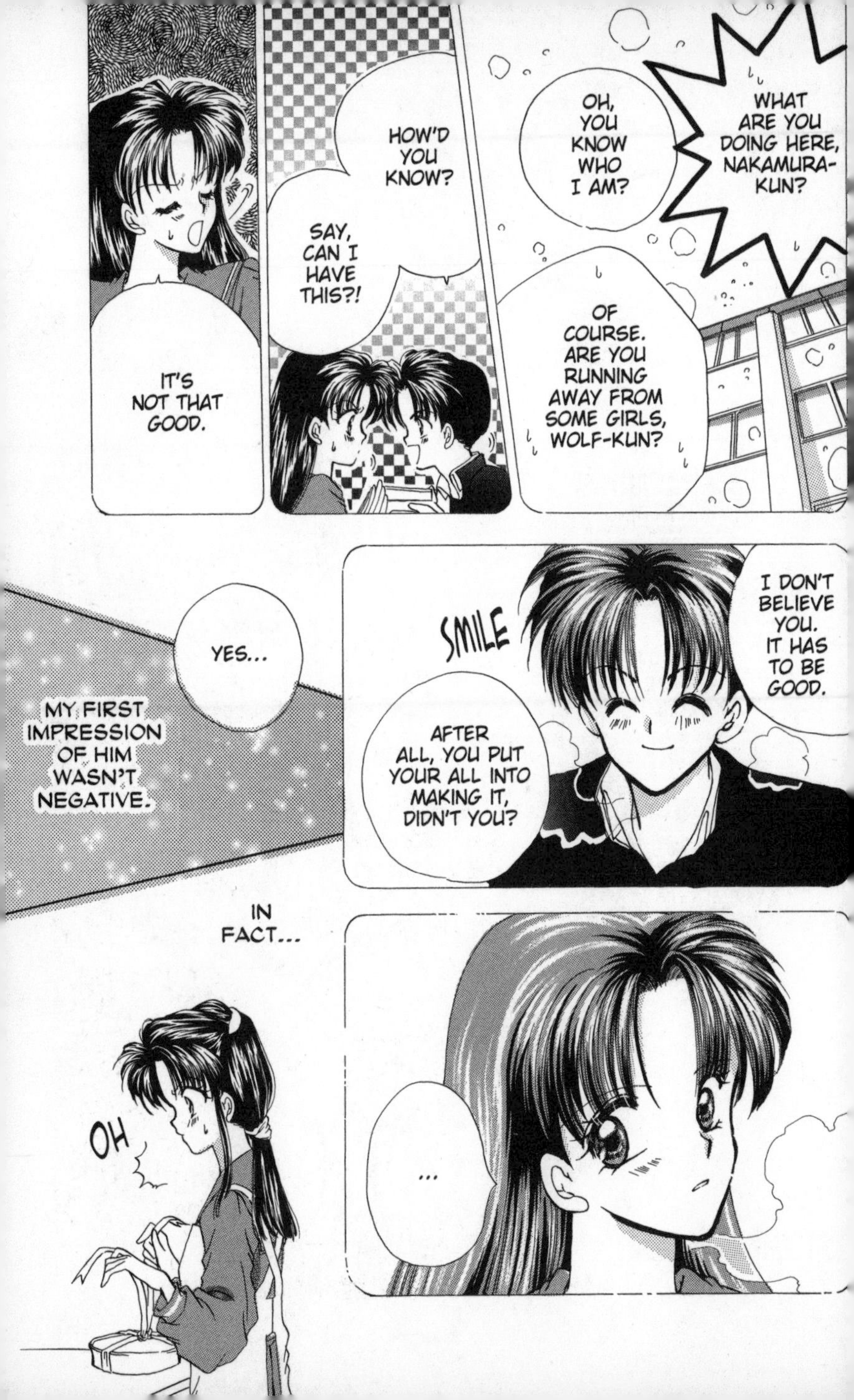
WHAT ARE YOU DOING HERE, NAKAMURA-KUN?
OH, YOU KNOW WHO I AM?
OF COURSE. ARE YOU RUNNING AWAY FROM SOME GIRLS, WOLF-KUN?
HOW'D YOU KNOW?
SAY, CAN I HAVE THIS?!
IT'S NOT THAT GOOD.
I DON'T BELIEVE YOU. IT HAS TO BE GOOD.
SMILE
AFTER ALL, YOU PUT YOUR ALL INTO MAKING IT, DIDN'T YOU?
YES...
MY FIRST IMPRESSION OF HIM WASN'T NEGATIVE.
...
IN FACT...
OH

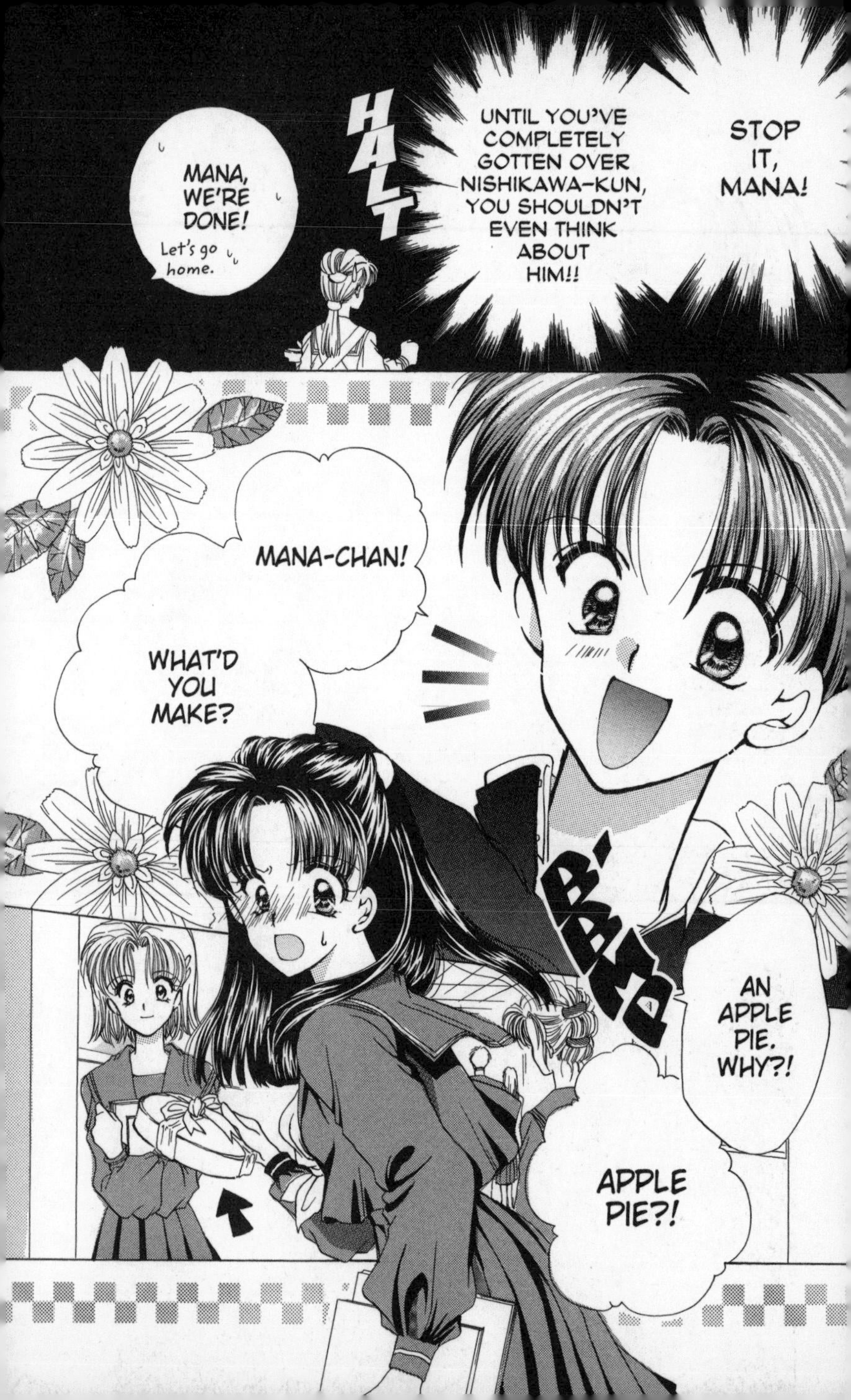
STOP IT, MANA!
UNTIL YOU'VE COMPLETELY GOTTEN OVER NISHIKAWA-KUN, YOU SHOULDN'T EVEN THINK ABOUT HIM!!
HALT
MANA, WE'RE DONE!
Let's go home.
MANA-CHAN!
WHAT'D YOU MAKE?
AN APPLE PIE. WHY?!
APPLE PIE?!

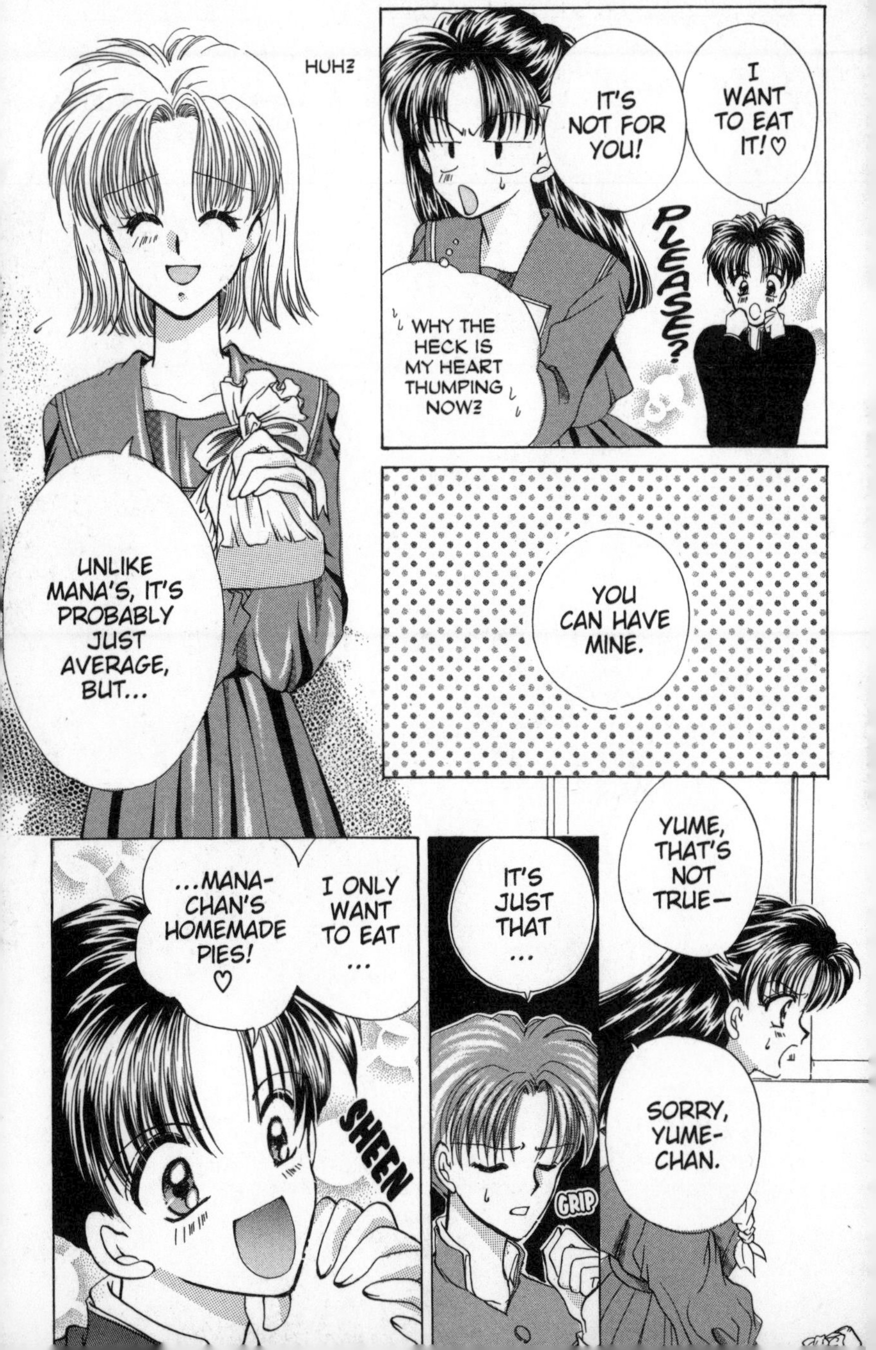
I WANT TO EAT IT! ♡
PLEASE?
IT'S NOT FOR YOU!
WHY THE HECK IS MY HEART THUMPING NOW?
YOU CAN HAVE MINE.
HUH?
UNLIKE MANA'S, IT'S PROBABLY JUST AVERAGE, BUT...
YUME, THAT'S NOT TRUE—
SORRY, YUME-CHAN.
IT'S JUST THAT ...
GRIP
I ONLY WANT TO EAT ...
...MANA-CHAN'S HOMEMADE PIES! ♡
SHEEN

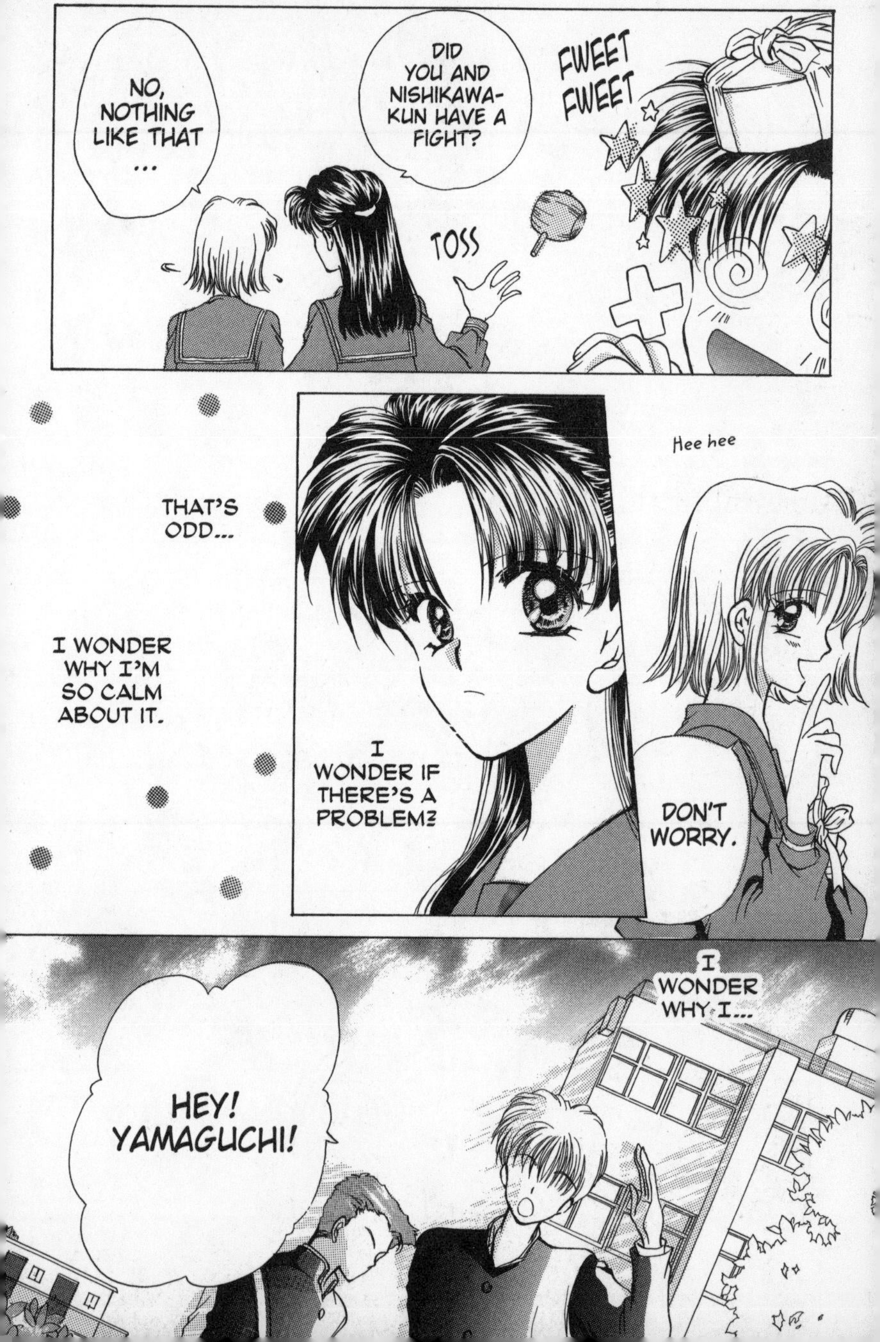
FWEET FWEET
DID YOU AND NISHIKAWA-KUN HAVE A FIGHT?
TOSS
NO, NOTHING LIKE THAT ...
Hee hee
DON'T WORRY.
I WONDER IF THERE'S A PROBLEM?
THAT'S ODD...
I WONDER WHY I'M SO CALM ABOUT IT.
I WONDER WHY I...
HEY! YAMAGUCHI!

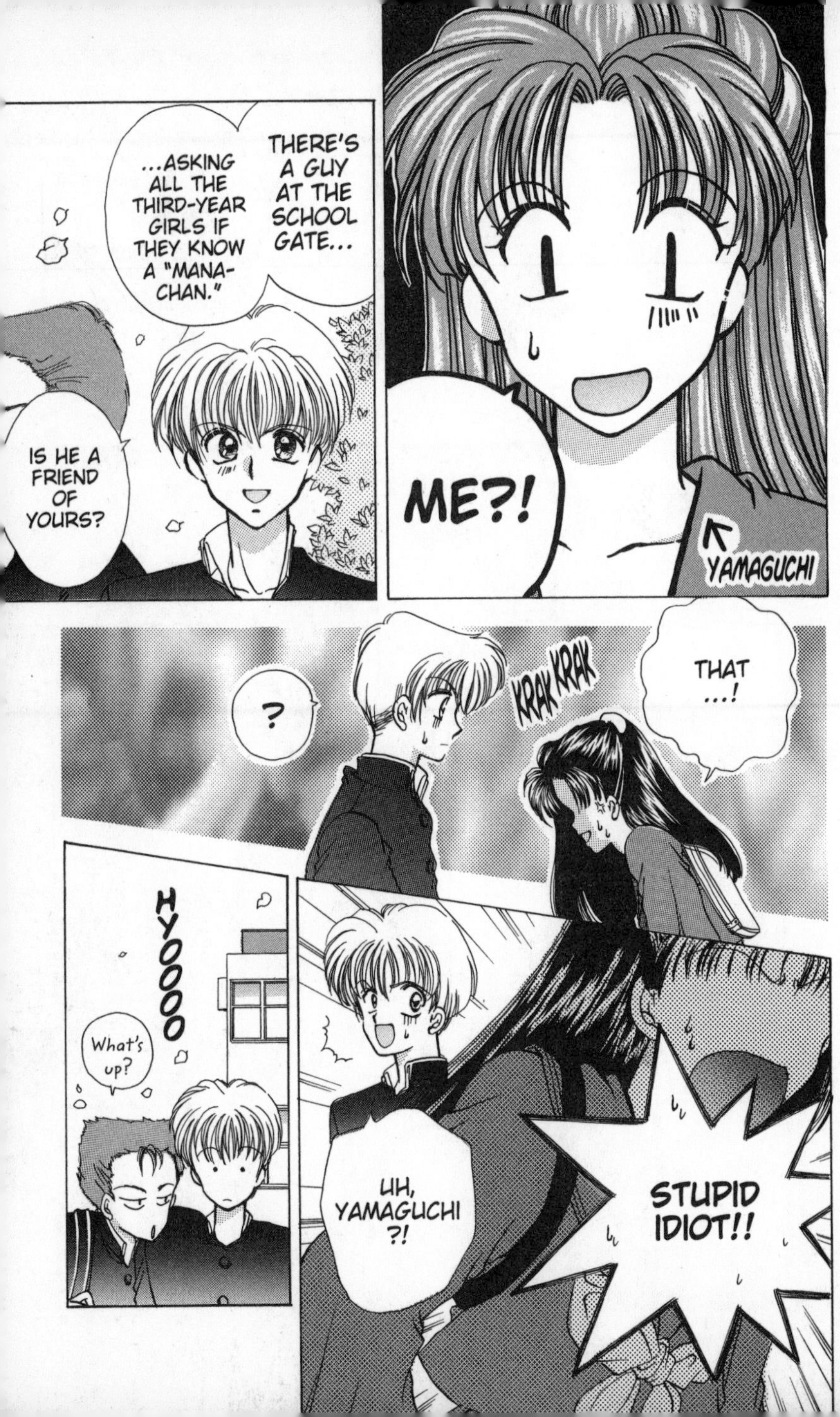
ME?!
YAMAGUCHI
THERE'S A GUY AT THE SCHOOL GATE...
...ASKING ALL THE THIRD-YEAR GIRLS IF THEY KNOW A "MANA-CHAN."
IS HE A FRIEND OF YOURS?
THAT ...!
KRAK KRAK
?
STUPID IDIOT!!
UH, YAMAGUCHI ?!
HYOOOO
What's up?

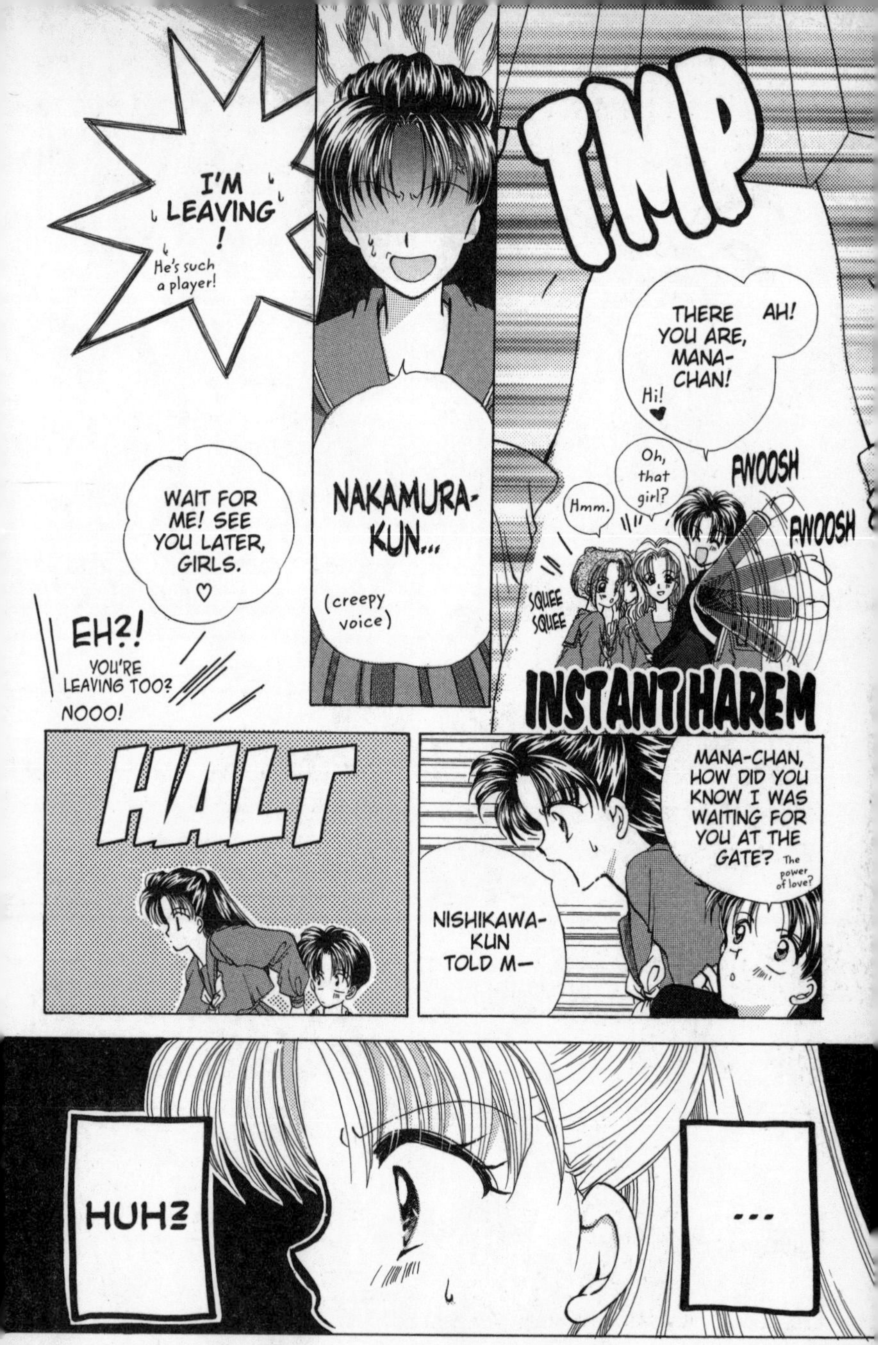
TMP
AH!
THERE YOU ARE, MANA-CHAN!
Hi! ♥
Oh, that girl?
Hmm.
FWOOSH
FWOOSH
SQUEE SQUEE
INSTANT HAREM
NAKAMURA-KUN...
(creepy voice)
I'M LEAVING!
He's such a player!
WAIT FOR ME! SEE YOU LATER, GIRLS. ♡
EH?!
YOU'RE LEAVING TOO?
NOOO!
MANA-CHAN, HOW DID YOU KNOW I WAS WAITING FOR YOU AT THE GATE?
The power of love?
NISHIKAWA-KUN TOLD M—
HALT
...
HUH?

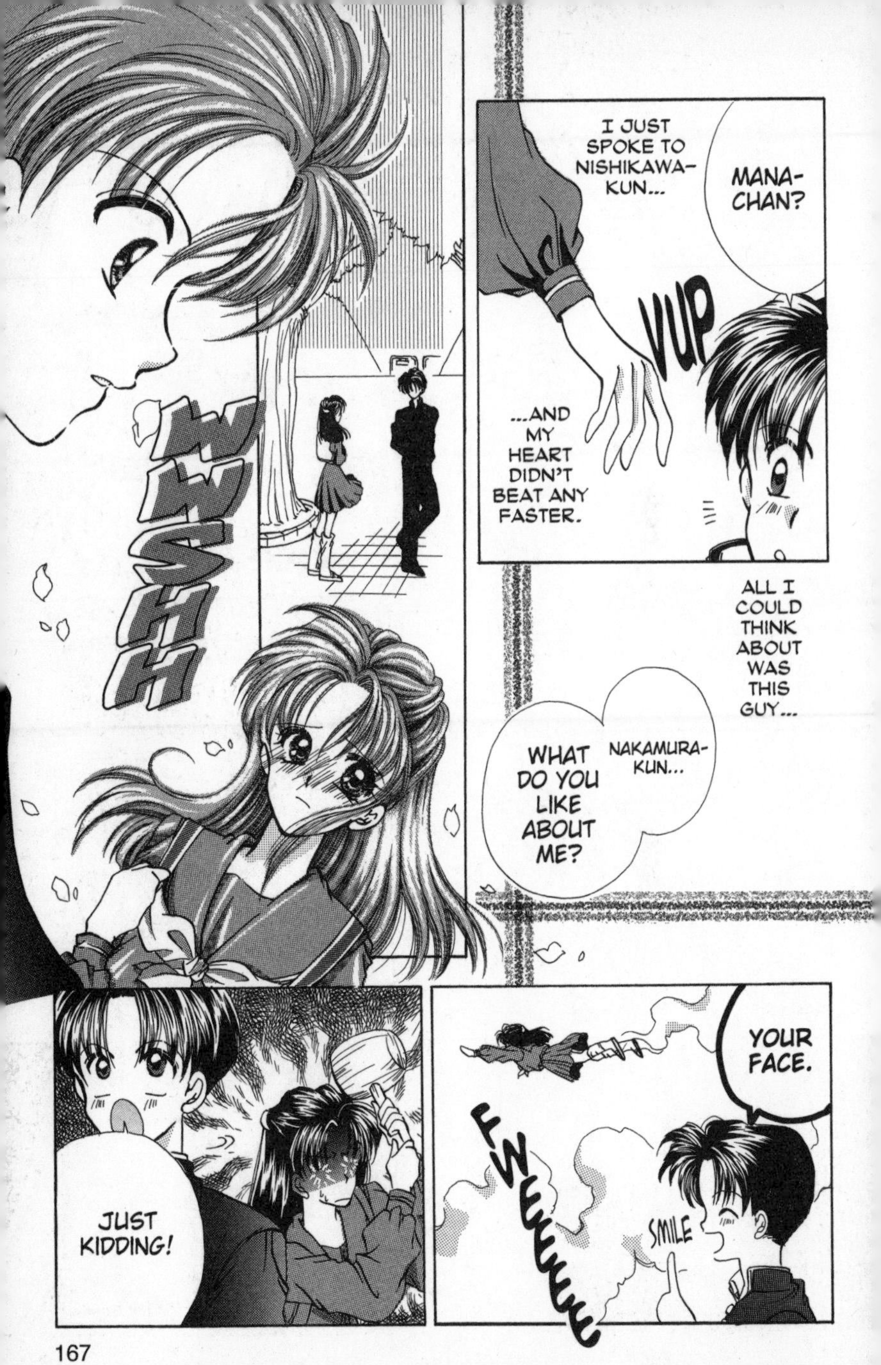
MANA-CHAN?
I JUST SPOKE TO NISHIKAWA-KUN...
VUP
...AND MY HEART DIDN'T BEAT ANY FASTER.
ALL I COULD THINK ABOUT WAS THIS GUY...
NAKAMURA-KUN...
WHAT DO YOU LIKE ABOUT ME?
WWSHH
YOUR FACE.
SMILE
FWUUUUUUU
JUST KIDDING!

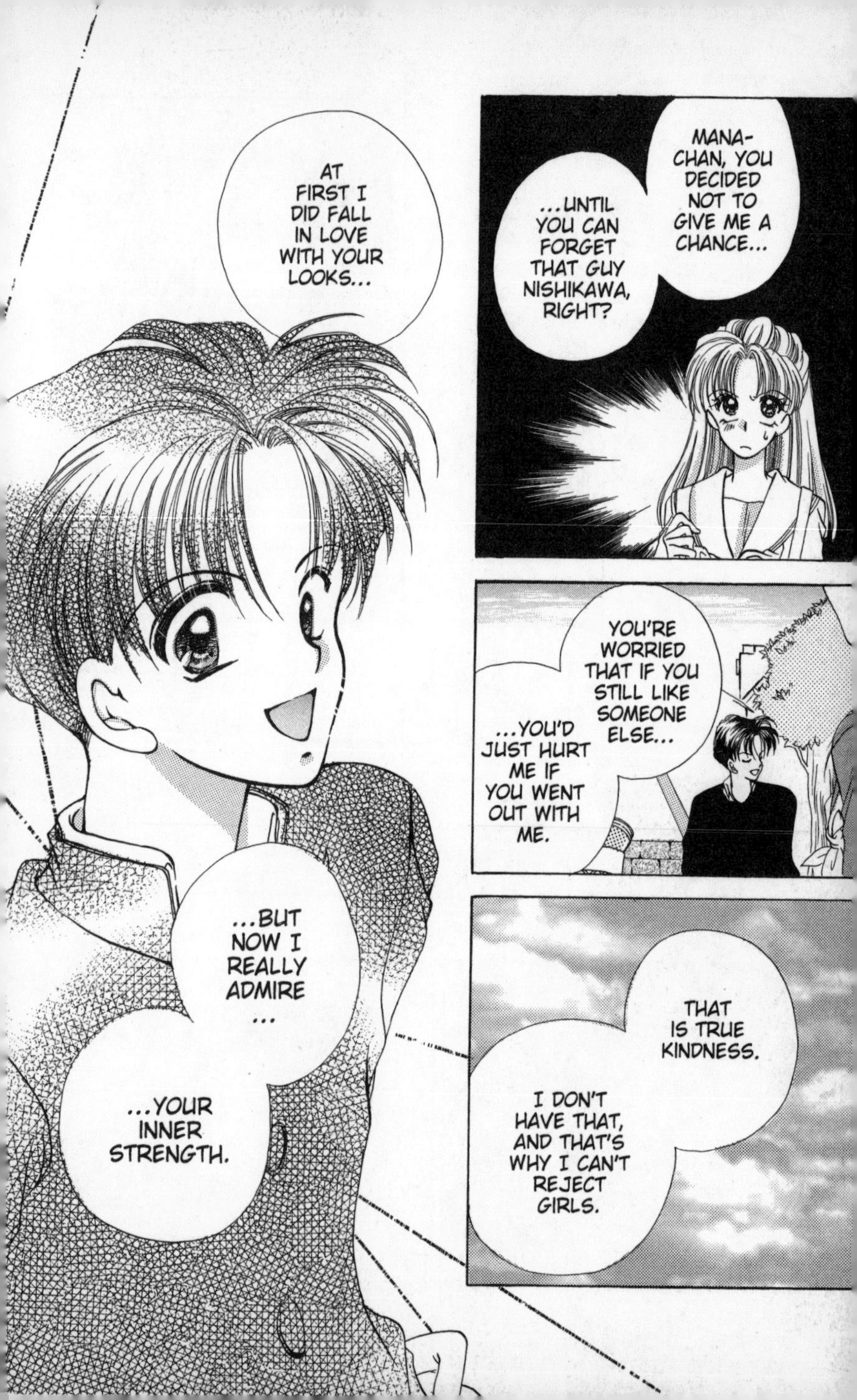
MANA-CHAN, YOU DECIDED NOT TO GIVE ME A CHANCE...
...UNTIL YOU CAN FORGET THAT GUY NISHIKAWA, RIGHT?
YOU'RE WORRIED THAT IF YOU STILL LIKE SOMEONE ELSE...
...YOU'D JUST HURT ME IF YOU WENT OUT WITH ME.
THAT IS TRUE KINDNESS.
I DON'T HAVE THAT, AND THAT'S WHY I CAN'T REJECT GIRLS.
AT FIRST I DID FALL IN LOVE WITH YOUR LOOKS...
...BUT NOW I REALLY ADMIRE ...
...YOUR INNER STRENGTH.

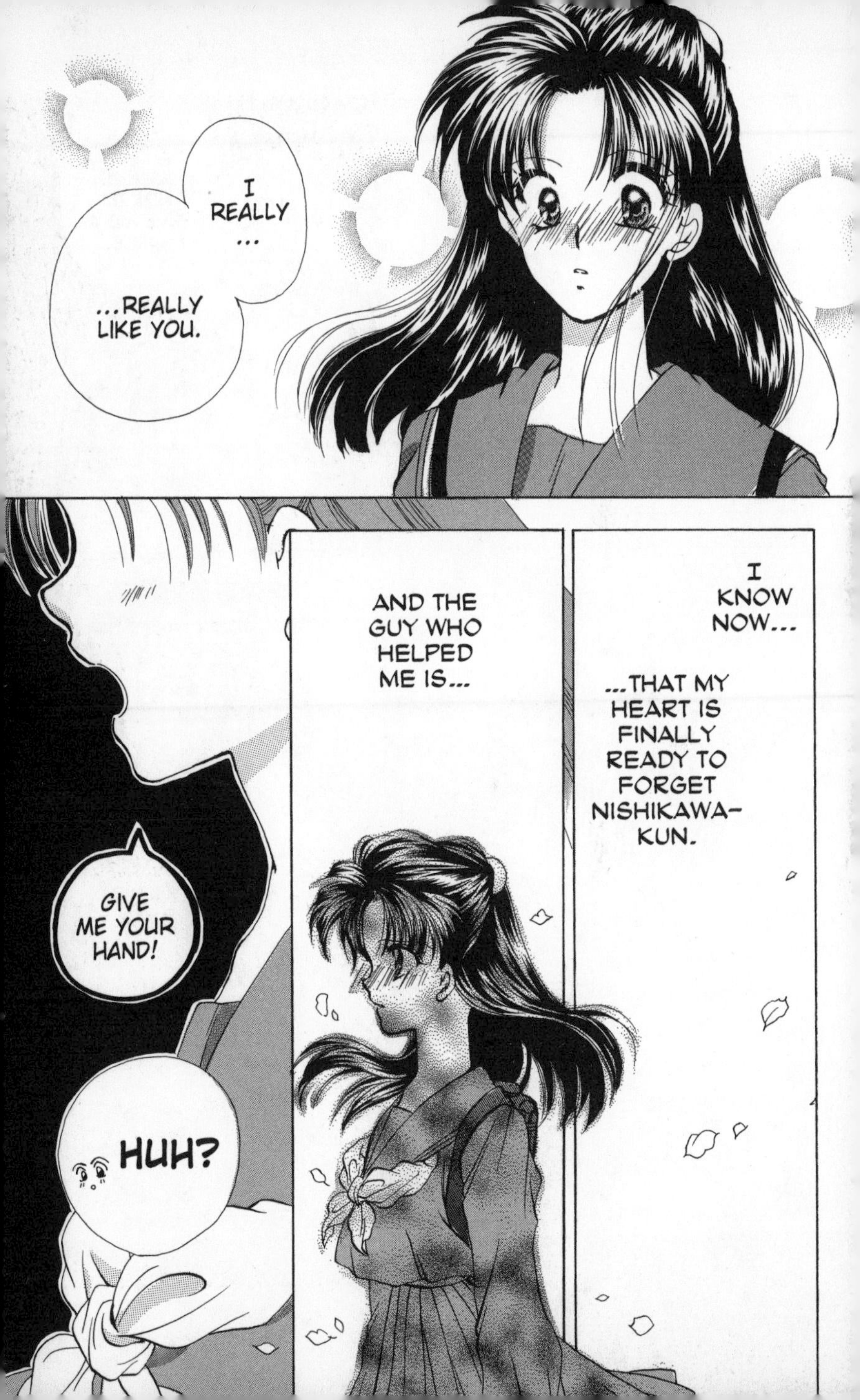
I REALLY...
...REALLY LIKE YOU.
I KNOW NOW...
...THAT MY HEART IS FINALLY READY TO FORGET NISHIKAWA-KUN.
AND THE GUY WHO HELPED ME IS...
GIVE ME YOUR HAND!
HUH?

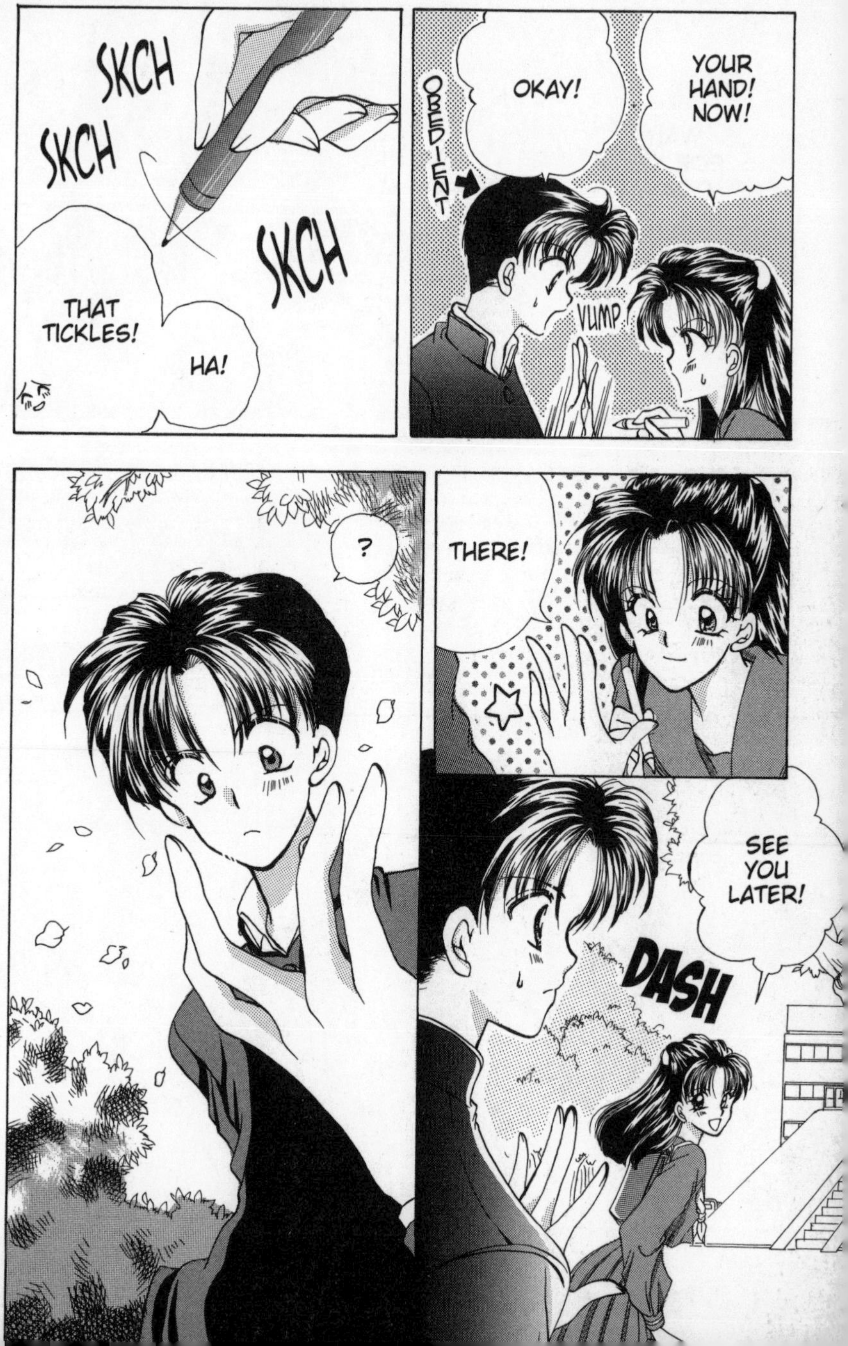
YOUR HAND! NOW!
OKAY!
OBEDIENT
VUMP
SKCH
SKCH
SKCH
THAT TICKLES!
HA!
THERE!
SEE YOU LATER!
DASH
?

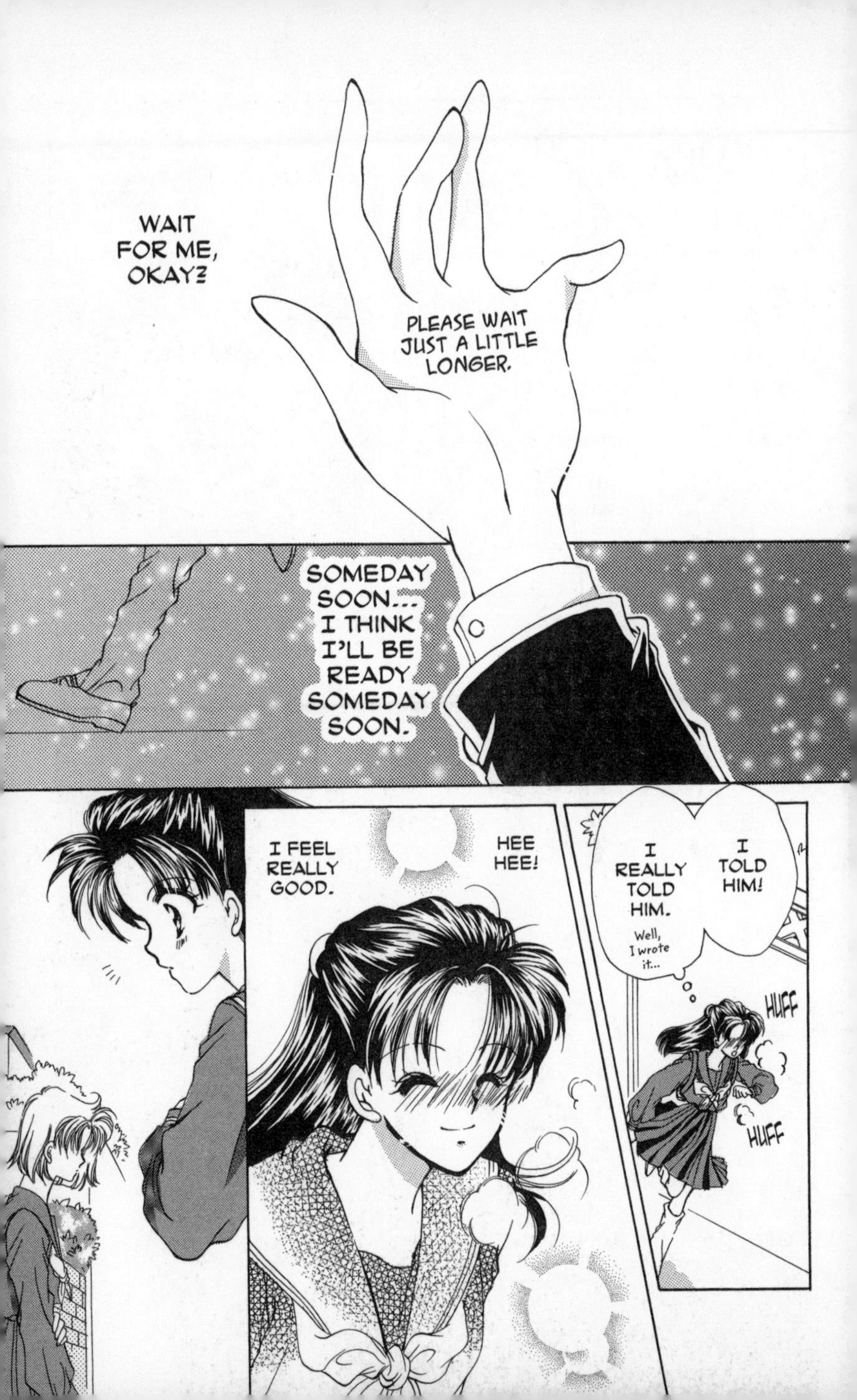
PLEASE WAIT JUST A LITTLE LONGER.
WAIT FOR ME, OKAY?
SOMEDAY SOON... I THINK I'LL BE READY SOMEDAY SOON.
I TOLD HIM!
I REALLY TOLD HIM.
Well, I wrote it...
HUFF
HUFF
HEE HEE!
I FEEL REALLY GOOD.

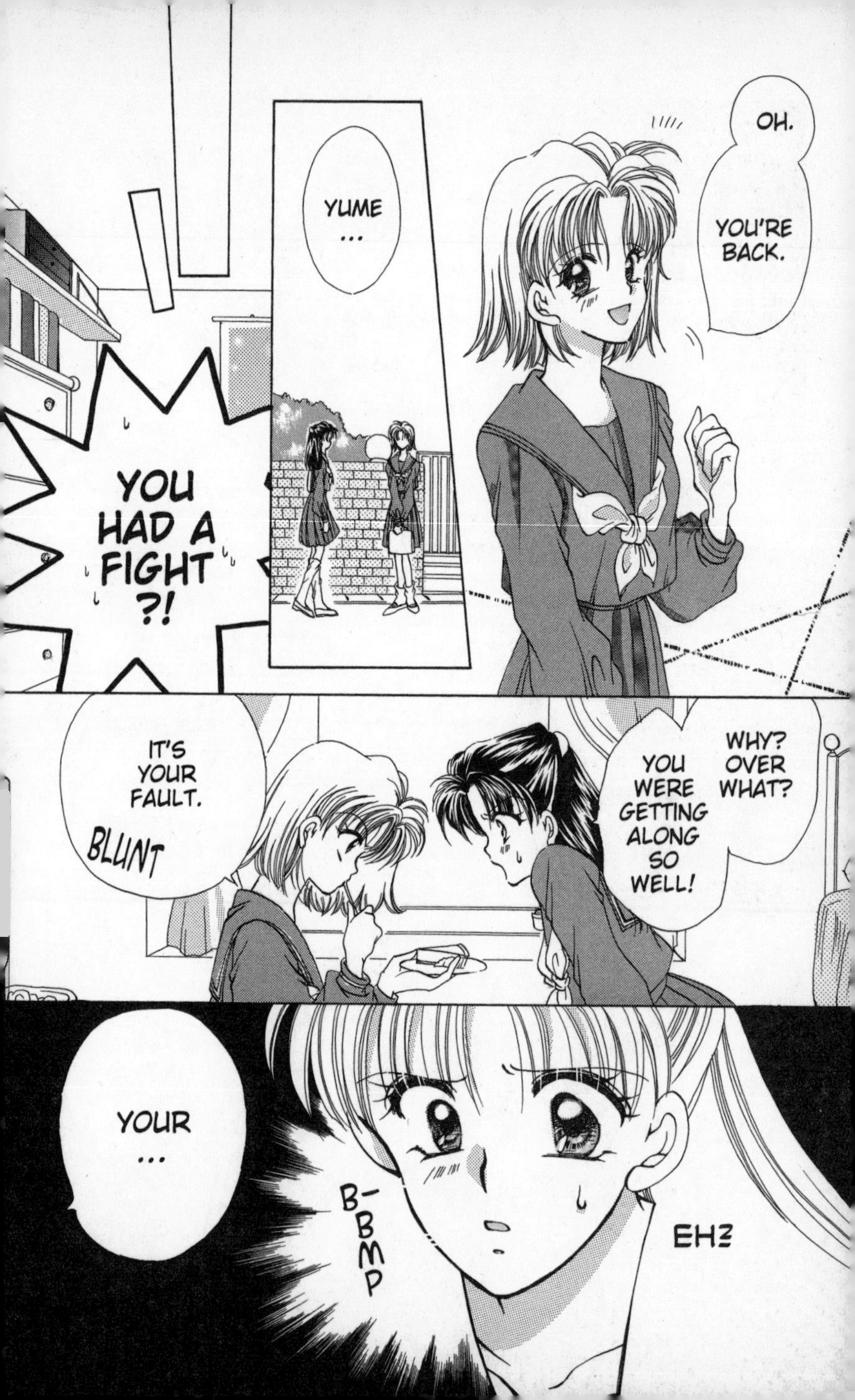
OH.
YOU'RE BACK.
YUME ...
YOU HAD A FIGHT ?!
WHY? OVER WHAT?
YOU WERE GETTING ALONG SO WELL!
IT'S YOUR FAULT.
BLUNT
EH?
B-BMP
YOUR ...

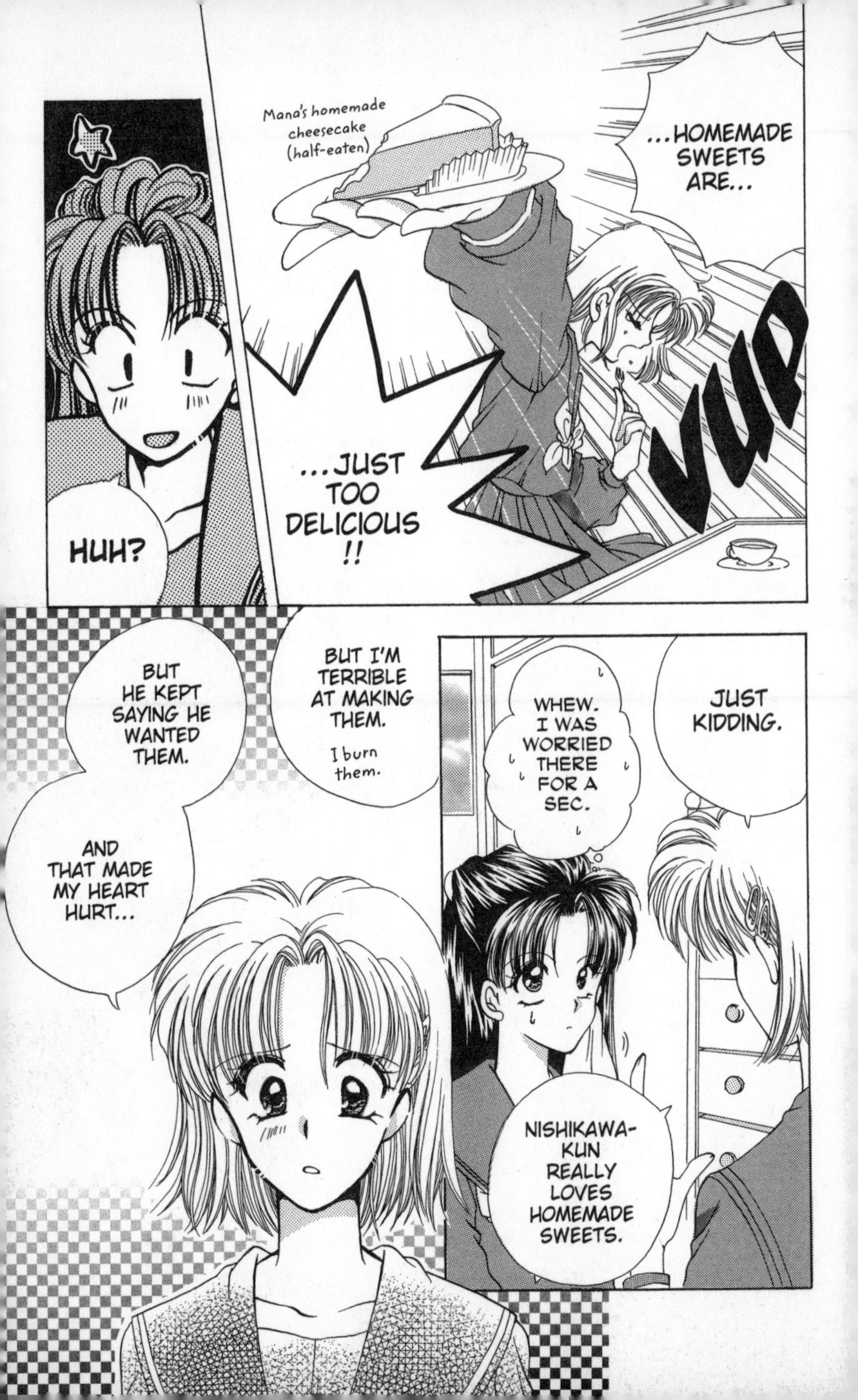
...HOMEMADE SWEETS ARE...
Mana's homemade cheesecake (half-eaten)
VUP
...JUST TOO DELICIOUS !!
HUH?
JUST KIDDING.
WHEW. I WAS WORRIED THERE FOR A SEC.
NISHIKAWA-KUN REALLY LOVES HOMEMADE SWEETS.
BUT I'M TERRIBLE AT MAKING THEM.
I burn them.
BUT HE KEPT SAYING HE WANTED THEM.
AND THAT MADE MY HEART HURT...

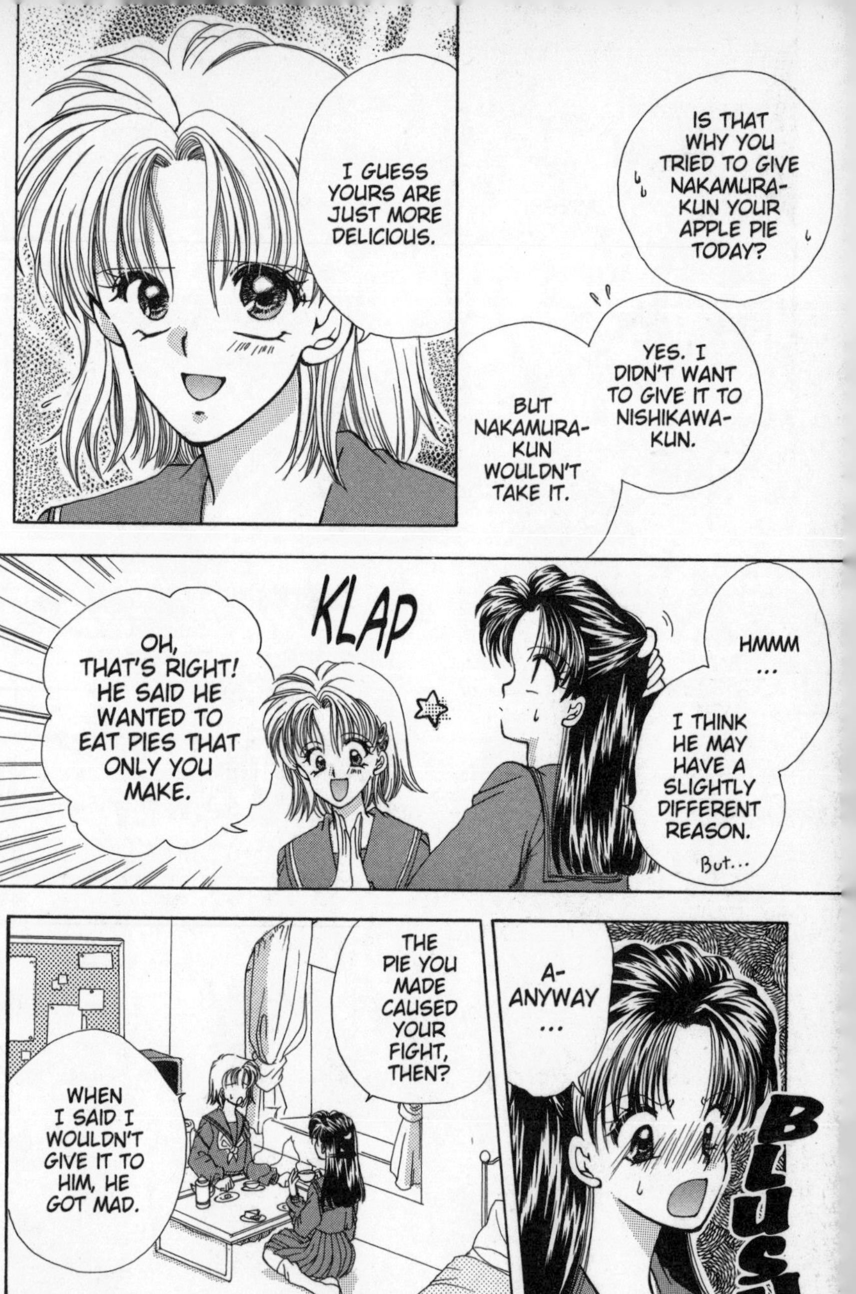
IS THAT WHY YOU TRIED TO GIVE NAKAMURA-KUN YOUR APPLE PIE TODAY?
YES. I DIDN'T WANT TO GIVE IT TO NISHIKAWA-KUN.
BUT NAKAMURA-KUN WOULDN'T TAKE IT.
I GUESS YOURS ARE JUST MORE DELICIOUS.
HMMM ...
I THINK HE MAY HAVE A SLIGHTLY DIFFERENT REASON.
But...
KLAP
OH, THAT'S RIGHT! HE SAID HE WANTED TO EAT PIES THAT ONLY YOU MAKE.
A-ANYWAY ...
BLUSH
THE PIE YOU MADE CAUSED YOUR FIGHT, THEN?
WHEN I SAID I WOULDN'T GIVE IT TO HIM, HE GOT MAD.

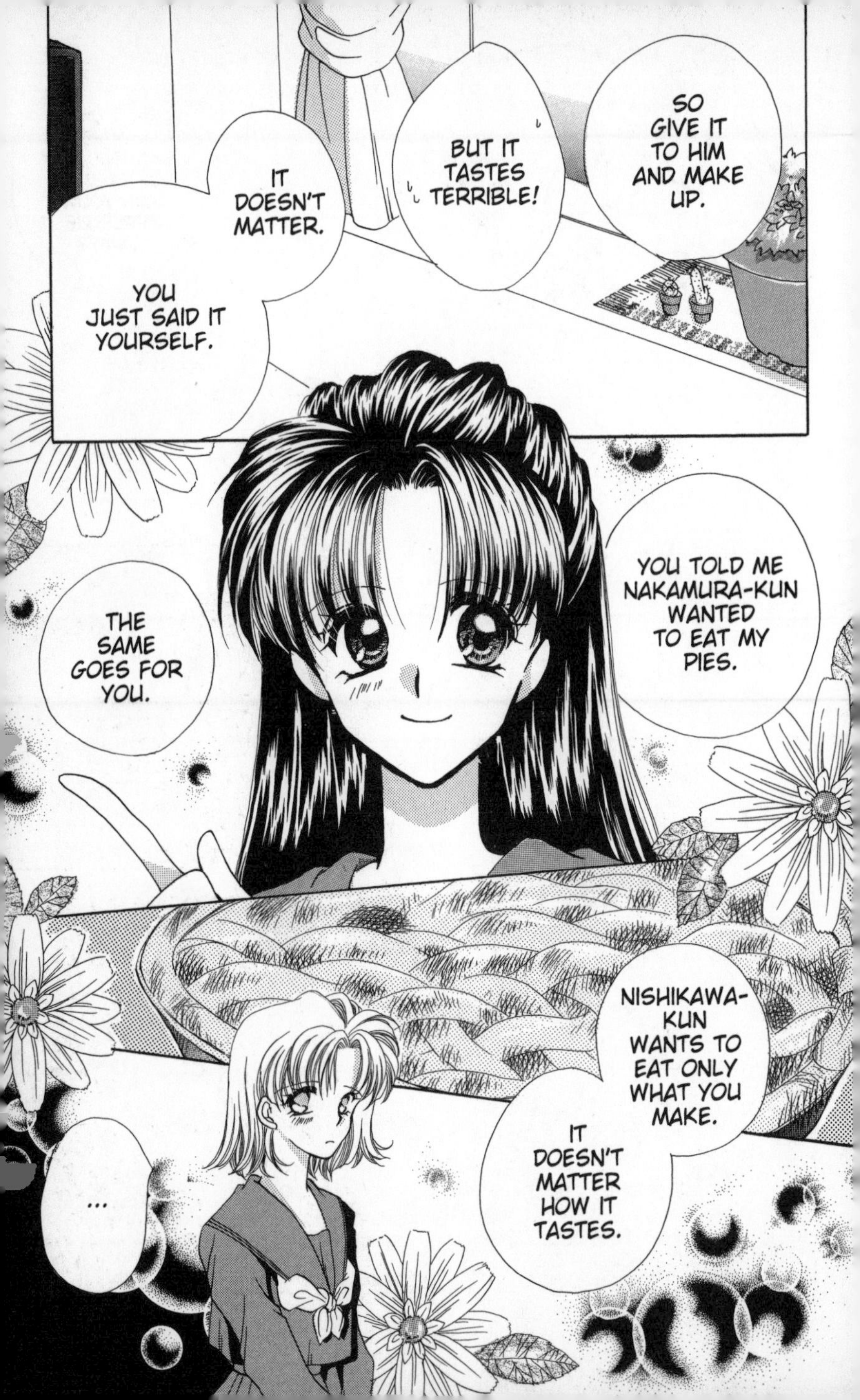
SO GIVE IT TO HIM AND MAKE UP.
BUT IT TASTES TERRIBLE!
IT DOESN'T MATTER.
YOU JUST SAID IT YOURSELF.
YOU TOLD ME NAKAMURA-KUN WANTED TO EAT MY PIES.
THE SAME GOES FOR YOU.
NISHIKAWA-KUN WANTS TO EAT ONLY WHAT YOU MAKE.
IT DOESN'T MATTER HOW IT TASTES.
...

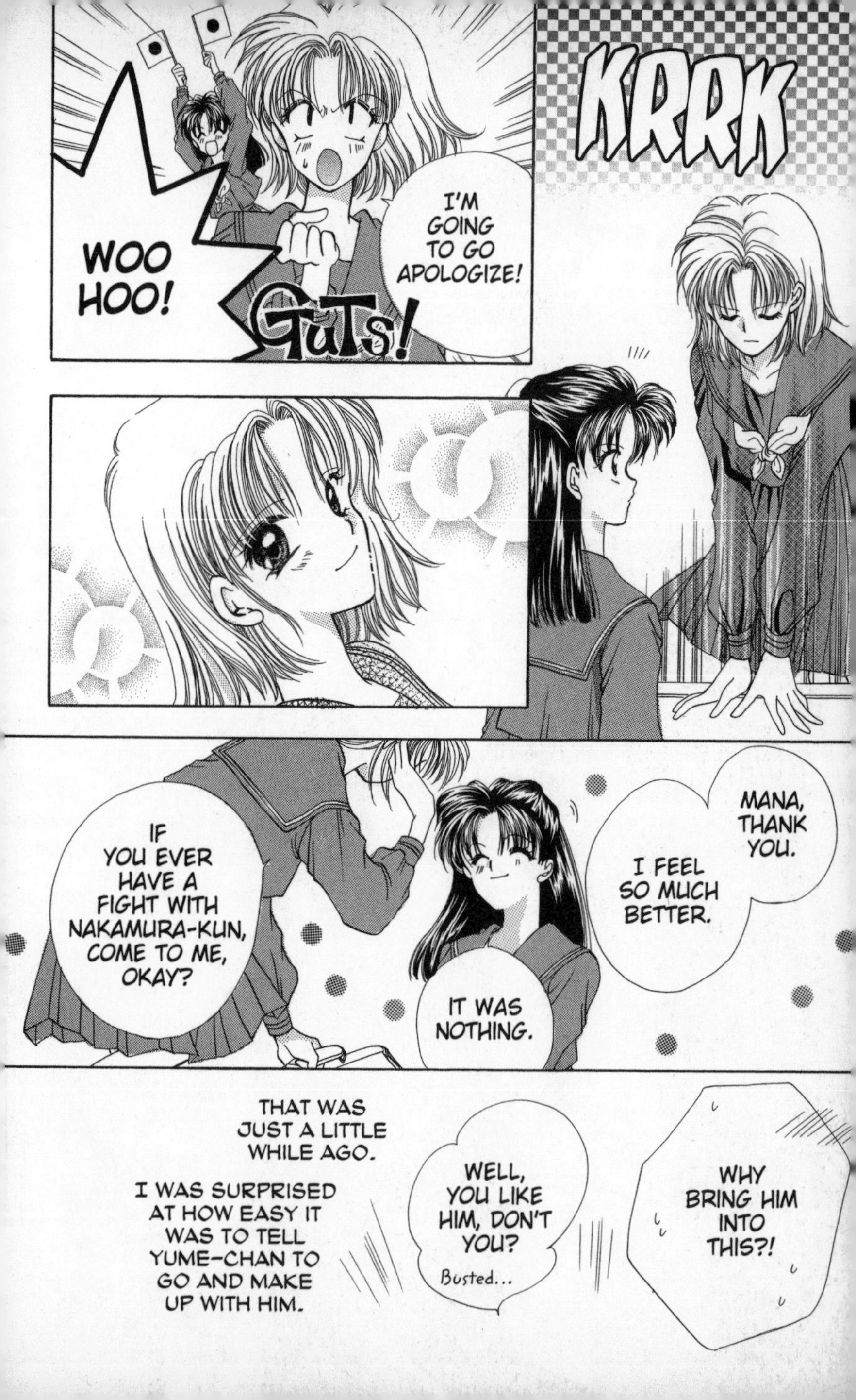
KRRK
I'M GOING TO GO APOLOGIZE!
GUTS!
WOO HOO!
MANA, THANK YOU.
I FEEL SO MUCH BETTER.
IT WAS NOTHING.
IF YOU EVER HAVE A FIGHT WITH NAKAMURA-KUN, COME TO ME, OKAY?
WHY BRING HIM INTO THIS?!
WELL, YOU LIKE HIM, DON'T YOU?
Busted...
THAT WAS JUST A LITTLE WHILE AGO.
I WAS SURPRISED AT HOW EASY IT WAS TO TELL YUME-CHAN TO GO AND MAKE UP WITH HIM.

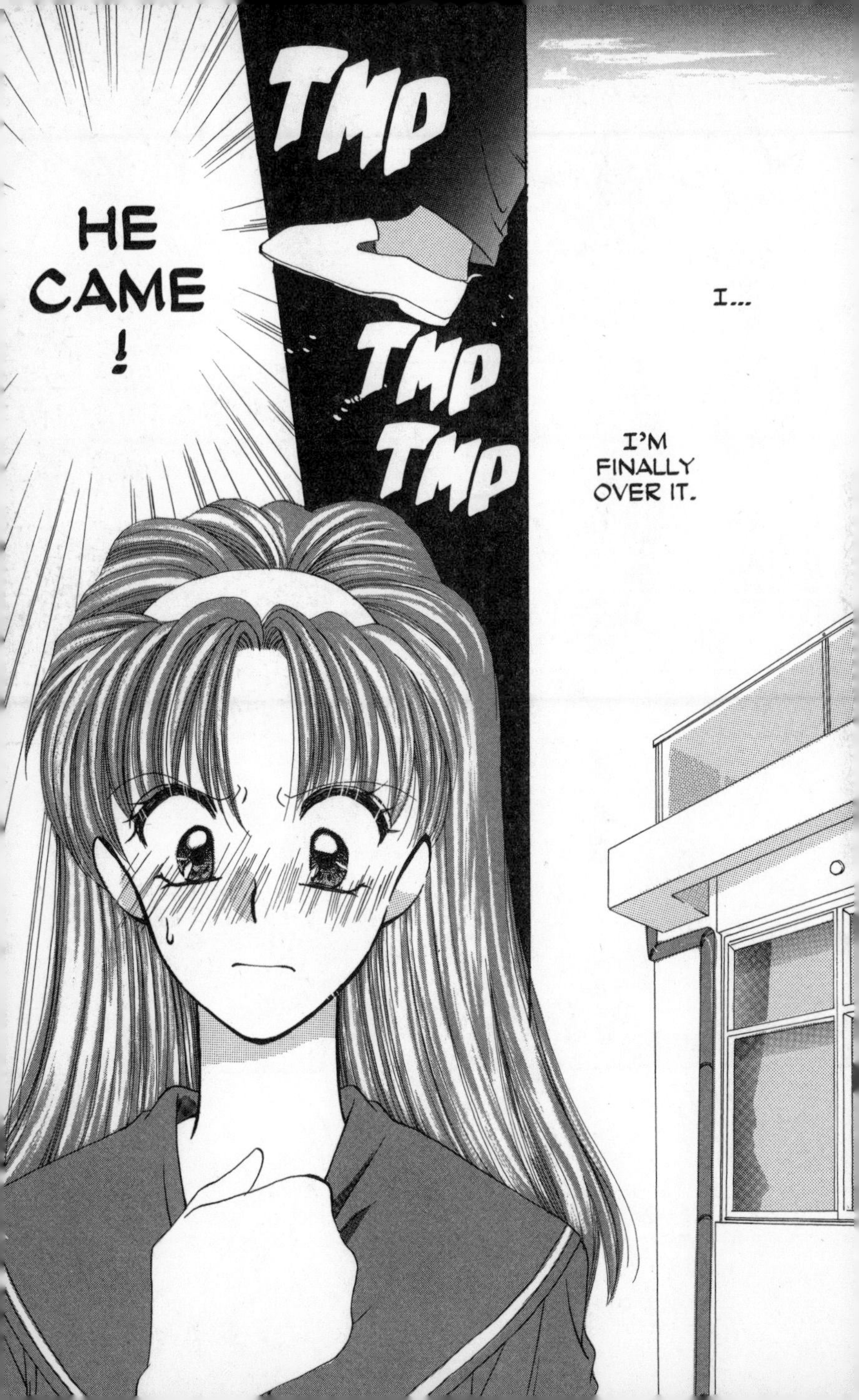
I...
I'M FINALLY OVER IT.
TMP
TMP
TMP
HE CAME!

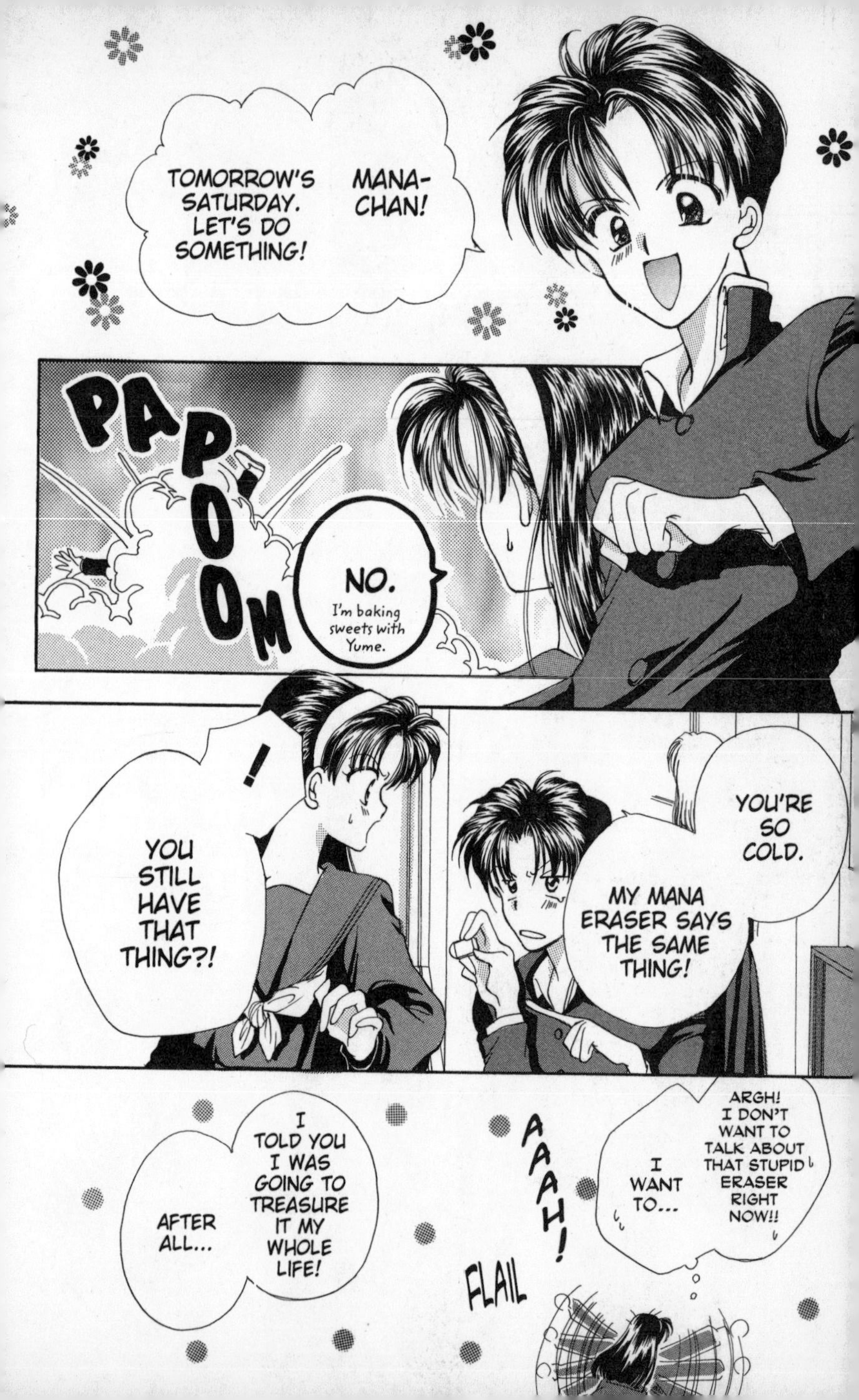
MANA-CHAN!
TOMORROW'S SATURDAY. LET'S DO SOMETHING!
NO.
I'm baking sweets with Yume.
PAPOOM
YOU'RE SO COLD.
MY MANA ERASER SAYS THE SAME THING!
!
YOU STILL HAVE THAT THING?!
ARGH! I DON'T WANT TO TALK ABOUT THAT STUPID ERASER RIGHT NOW!!
I WANT TO...
AAAH!
FLAIL
I TOLD YOU I WAS GOING TO TREASURE IT MY WHOLE LIFE!
AFTER ALL...

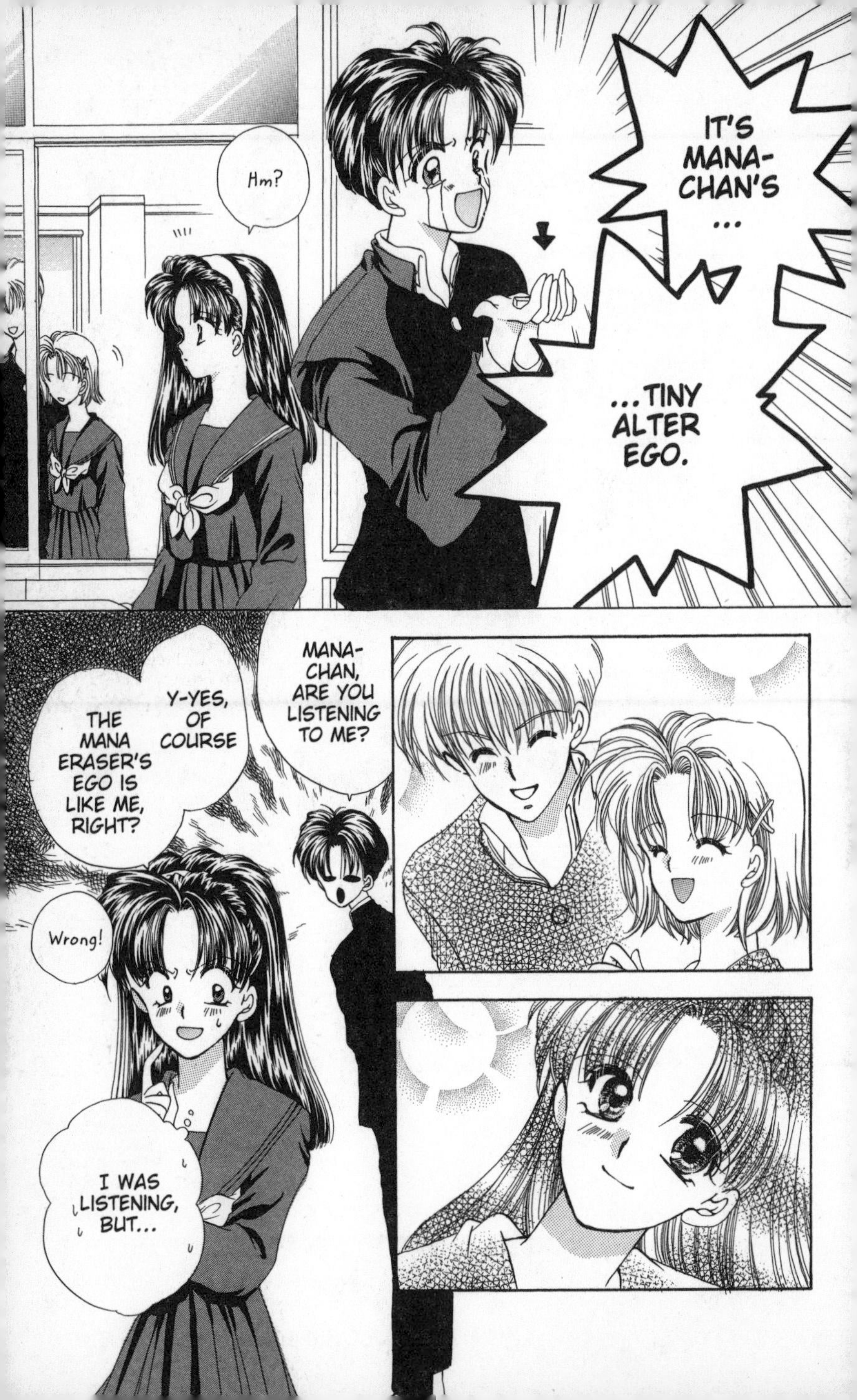
IT'S MANA-CHAN'S ...
...TINY ALTER EGO.
Hm?
MANA-CHAN, ARE YOU LISTENING TO ME?
Y-YES, OF COURSE
THE MANA ERASER'S EGO IS LIKE ME, RIGHT?
Wrong!
I WAS LISTENING, BUT...

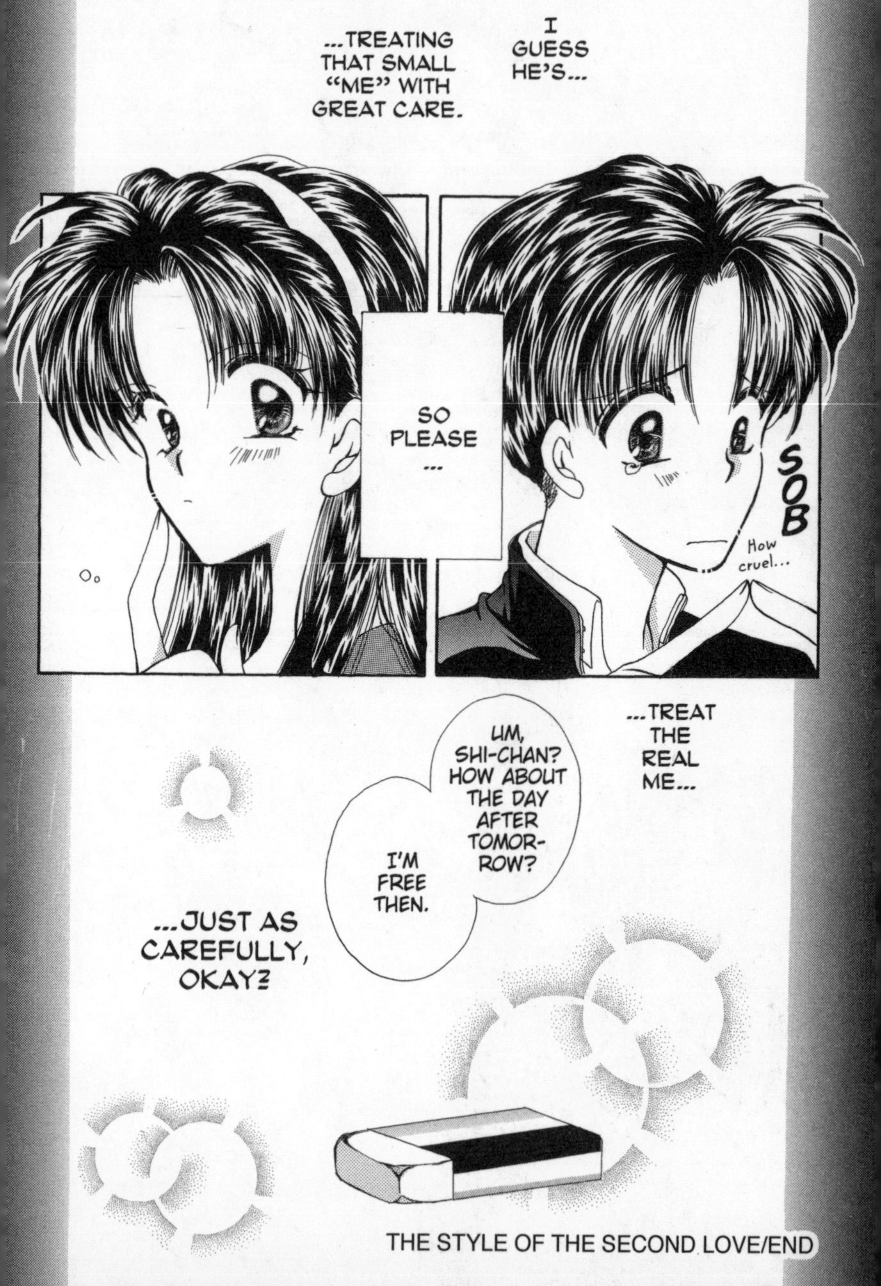
I GUESS HE'S...
...TREATING THAT SMALL "ME" WITH GREAT CARE.
SOB
How cruel...
SO PLEASE ...
Oo
...TREAT THE REAL ME...
UM, SHI-CHAN? HOW ABOUT THE DAY AFTER TOMOR-ROW?
I'M FREE THEN.
...JUST AS CAREFULLY, OKAY?
THE STYLE OF THE SECOND LOVE/END

RAINY AFTERNOONS ARE FOR ROMANTIC HEROINES

THIS WAS MY SECOND MANGA AFTER MY DEBUT. THE TITLE WAS A TAKE-OFF OF A CD MY FRIEND HAD. I THINK IT WAS SHINICHI ISHIHARA'S "NICHIYOU NO GOGO WA MISUTERI NO HIROIN" (SUNDAY AFTERNOONS ARE FOR MYSTERY HEROINES). THE THEME WAS ABOUT WALKING HOME IN THE RAIN... IN OTHER WORDS, IN THE AFTERNOON, YOU CAN BECOME THE MAIN CHARACTER IN A LOVE STORY. ♥ ANYWAY, THAT WAS THE SITUATION MINORI WAS IN. IT WAS A STORY I HAD WANTED TO WRITE EVEN BEFORE MY DEBUT, SO SEEING IT BECOME A REALITY MADE ME REALLY HAPPY. (BUT THE ROUGH LAYOUT TOOK OVER THREE MONTHS TO FINISH. UGH.) THE OPENING ILLUSTRATION WAS ALSO SIGNIFICANT. MINORI-CHAN, WHO PRAYED AT NIGHT FOR RAIN THE NEXT DAY, MADE THE TERUTERU BOZU CRY. ♥ SHE WAS KIND OF SHY, AND I QUITE LIKED HER. ANYWAY, I DECIDED THAT MINORI-CHAN SHOULD BE SUPER-CUTE, AND SO I MADE HER APPEARANCE, HER SPEECH, HER GESTURES—EVERYTHING ABOUT HER—CUTE. (WHEN I LOOK AT IT ALL NOW, I SEE AN OBVIOUS LACK OF FIRE. I'LL APPLY MYSELF MORE.) TAKATO'S NAME CAME FROM THE YOUNGER BROTHER OF A FRIEND (MALE). THAT'S RIGHT, IT'S HIS GIVEN NAME! BUT MY EDITOR TOLD ME THAT "TAKATO" WAS A WEIRD NAME. (I'M STILL SEETHING OVER THIS.) "IT'S GOOD BECAUSE IT'S A REAL NAME!" I COMPLAINED WHILE ANGRILY DRAWING. THE THEME SONG WAS RYOKO HIROSUE'S "MAJI DE KOISURU 5BYOU MAE" (FIVE SECONDS TO TRUE LOVE). SEI-CHAN, A HUGE AMEROMA FAN, SHOWED ME IT WAS THE PERFECT SONG. It really is perfect. ♥
ALSO, JITTERIN' JINN'S "AI AI GASA" (SHARED UMBRELLA) WAS AN INSPIRATION. ♥

THIS LOVE IS NONFICTION

ARTIST'S TALK: THIS WAS MY FOURTH MANGA AFTER MY DEBUT. IT WAS THE FIRST MANGA IN WHICH THE OPENING PAGE WAS DONE IN COLOR. HOWEVER, I WAS EVEN MORE SURPRISED THAT IT BECAME THE OPENING MANGA IN AN EXTRA EDITION. (I WAS REALLY HAPPY, THOUGH! ♥) I REALLY PUT A LOT INTO THE STORY WHEN I DREW IT (SO THE ROUGH LAYOUT WAS LATE), BUT THANKS TO THAT, IT'S ONE OF MY MOST POPULAR WORKS. KARIN-CHAN IS ALSO VERY POPULAR. (SHE'S REALLY POPULAR AMONG MY FRIENDS TOO.) I REMEMBER RECEIVING A LOT OF COMPLIMENTS. (THAT WAS DURING A PERIOD OF TIME WHEN I WAS REALLY WORRIED, SO IT MADE ME QUITE HAPPY. ♥) THE TRUTH IS THAT I LIKE WRITING ROMANTIC STORIES LIKE THIS. I'M STILL VERY TAKEN WITH THIS STORY. AS FAR AS THE MEANING OF THE TITLE GOES—IT'S MEANT TO BE RYO-SAMA'S ANSWER TO KARIN-CHAN'S THOUGHTS AT THE END: "ROMANCE MIRACULOUSLY BLOOMED." IT'S REAL...AT LEAST THAT'S WHAT I MEANT IT TO SAY. YURI-CHAN WAS ALSO POPULAR. (IT ALWAYS SEEMS THAT PEOPLE NEVER HATE THE SUPPORTING CHARACTERS. ♥) I LOVE DOLPHINS—WELL, ALL SEA CREATURES—AND I RECEIVED DOLPHIN PENDANTS FROM SOME FANS. THAT MADE ME HAPPY, AND I DECIDED TO WRITE THIS STORY. I LOVE GETTING PRESENTS FROM MY FANS, BUT PLEASE DON'T GO TO TOO MUCH TROUBLE. A LETTER IS ENOUGH TO MAKE MY DAY. ♥ THERE WASN'T A PARTICULAR THEME SONG, OR MAYBE I JUST FORGOT WHAT IT WAS? (LAUGH)

No time left, so just sketches.

FIRST DRAFTS ARE USUALLY BETTER THAN THIS. (THESE ARE TOO ROUGH.) I'M ACTUALLY NOT VERY GOOD AT DRAWING MALE CHARACTERS.
THIS IS THE MOST POPULAR CHARACTER OF THESE FOUR.
RYO-SAMA WAS VERY POPULAR AS PART OF A COUPLE WITH KARIN.
ABOUT HALF OF MY FANS BECAME FANS BECAUSE OF SHI-CHAN. THE POPULARITY OF MY DEBUT WORK WAS ALSO PROBABLY THANKS TO HIM. ♥
YUGA-KUN IS THE SECOND-MOST POPULAR CHARACTER.

AFTERWORD

OKAY, HOW WAS IT? THANKS FOR STICKING WITH ME WHILE I BABBLED ON. ♥ BUT LOVE STORIES ARE REALLY NICE, AREN'T THEY? ♥ NOWADAYS MANY ADULTS SAY, "SHOJO MANGA ARE BORING," BUT I'M FASCINATED MORE THAN EVER WITH READING MANGA (ESPECIALLY *RIBON*). ♥ I READ MOST OTHER MANGA AS TANKOBON. I DO BUY *JUMP*, THOUGH. BECAUSE I WRITE IN SEVERAL GENRES, I HATE TO BE FORCED INTO ONE CATEGORY BY THOSE KINDS OF PEOPLE. (OKAY, SO I DON'T WRITE IN THAT MANY GENRES...) (LAUGH) BUT IF AN ARTIST DOESN'T HAVE EVEN ONE CHARACTERISTIC OR SPECIALTY, THEN THERE'S NO TRICK. (LAUGH) FOR WHAT IT'S WORTH, WITH MY MANGA, MY OVERALL GOAL IS TO SHOW THAT "TRUE LOVE IS THE ULTIMATE." (IT'S KIND OF DORKY WHEN I LOSE MYSELF IN IT, THOUGH...) IF YOU LIKE, PLEASE CONTINUE TO READ MY "BEST LOVE MANGA FOR GIRLS (OR BOYS) DREAMING ABOUT SOMETHING." ♥ I'LL WORK HARDER TOO, AND TRY TO DRAW MANGA BETTER EVERY DAY.

3.29.1998 ARINA T.

THE STYLE OF THE SECOND LOVE

THIS IS MY DEBUT WORK. I WILL NEVER FORGET IT. (PLEASE DON'T SAY THE ART IS BAD...OKAY?) I SUBMITTED IT WITH THE TITLE AND MARKED IT "TEMPORARY." (ITS ABBREVIATION IS "2(TSU)-KOI.") THE OTHERS HAVE BEEN SHORTENED TO "KANTAMA," "NONFIC," AND "AMEROMA." (SMILE) THE MEANING OF THE TITLE IS APPARENT, BUT IT ALSO RELATES TO THE ITEM THAT SHI-CHAN IS HOLDING IN THE OPENING ILLUSTRATION. WITH THAT ILLUSTRATION, I WANTED TO SHOW MANA-CHAN WINKING AT SHI-CHAN WHILE HE CALMLY PROTECTS HER. ♥ MY IMPETUS FOR WRITING THIS STORY WAS THAT MY FRIEND, SHI-CHAN (MALE), TOLD ME ABOUT MAKING A MANA ERASER FOR HIS GIRLFRIEND, AND IT REALLY MADE ME LAUGH. THEN ONE OF MY GIRLFRIENDS SAID, "YOU HAVE TO USE THAT IN A MANGA." I REDID THE DRAFTS FOR THIS MANGA ABOUT SEVEN TIMES—FOR ALL 32 PAGES. SHEER DETERMINATION GOT ME TO THE END OF THIS MANGA. HOWEVER, THIS STORY WAS THE ONE THAT ALLOWED ME TO CONTINUE DRAWING MANGA. (ALONG WITH MY EDITOR. ♥) THANK YOU VERY MUCH. THE THEME SONG WAS SUGGESTED BY A FAN, AND IT'S TOKYO Q CHANNEL'S "SUNAO NO MAMA DE KOI O SHIYO YO" (LET'S FALL IN LOVE STRAIGHT-FORWARDLY). I CAN IMAGINE MANA-CHAN AND SHI-CHAN LATER ON, AND IT'S A GOOD FEELING.

Short–Tempered Melancholic Notes

The suffixes –*kun* and –*chan* are added to a person's name to show familiarity. The suffix –*sama* is added to show respect for someone who is higher up in the social hierarchy. For an upperclassman, –*senpai* is used to show respect.

Page 4: A *kunoichi* is a female ninja.

Page 6: There's a Japanese saying that hearing the same thing over and over gives you a callus in your ear. *Tako* can mean either "callus" or "octopus."

Page 17: *Nee–san* means "older sister," but the term can also refer to an older woman who is not related to the speaker. *Nee–yan* is a cutesy nickname for nee–san.

Page 28: *Kureha* means "crimson leaf."

Page 38: *Sobakasu* means "freckles."

Page 40: *Oden* is a kind of fish stew made with fish cakes, daikon, and other ingredients cooked in a fish broth.

Page 79: *Anmitsu* is a dessert of jelly and red bean paste with sweet syrup.

Page 86: *Ojou–sama* is comparable to "young miss."

Page 119: The star is a pun on *zuboshi*, which means "bull's–eye."

Page 143: The "ding" and the incense stick are a gag to show Minori has died. Her classmates are paying their respects.

Page 182: *Teruteru bozu* is a handmade doll (they look like the "ghosts" you made in kindergarten) hung outside to prevent rain.

Page 183: *Ribon* and *Jump* are manga magazines in Japan.

Kajika–chan, Karin–chan, Minori–chan, Mana–chan—even now I'm so proud they live in the pages of my manga, laughing and crying. I really love them. I hope they live happily ever after. ♥

Arina Tanemura was born in Aichi, Japan. She got her start in 1996, publishing *Nibanme no Koi no Katachi* (The Style of the Second Love) in *Ribon Original* magazine. Two of her titles, *Kamikaze Kaito Jeanne* and *Full Moon*, were made into popular TV series. Tanemura enjoys karaoke and is a huge *Lord of the Rings* fan.

SHORT-TEMPERED MELANCHOLIC
AND OTHER STORIES

The Shojo Beat Manga Edition

STORY AND ART BY
ARINA TANEMURA

Translation/Mary Kennard
Adaptation/Heidi Vivolo
Touch-up Art & Lettering/Rina Mapa
Design/Yukiko Whitley
Editor/Nancy Thistlethwaite

Editor in Chief, Books/Alvin Lu
Editor in Chief, Magazines/Marc Weidenbaum
VP of Publishing Licensing/Rika Inouye
VP of Sales/Gonzalo Ferreyra
Sr. VP of Marketing/Liza Coppola
Publisher/Hyoe Narita

Printed in Canada

Published by VIZ Media, LLC
P.O. Box 77010
San Francisco, CA 94107

Shojo Beat Manga Edition
10 9 8 7 6 5 4 3 2 1
First printing, August 2008

store.viz.com

Arina Tanemura Series

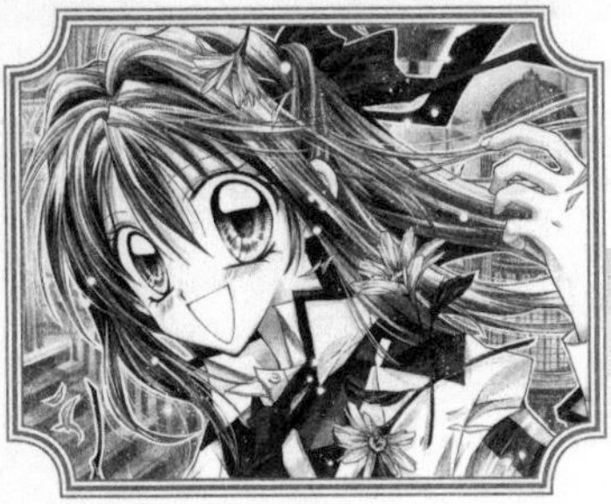

The Gentlemen's Alliance †

Haine Otomiya joins Imperial Academy in pursuit of the boy she's loved since she was a child, unaware that he has many secrets of his own.

I•O•N

Chanting the letters of her first name has always brought Ion Tsuburagi good luck—but her good-luck charm is really the result of psychic powers!

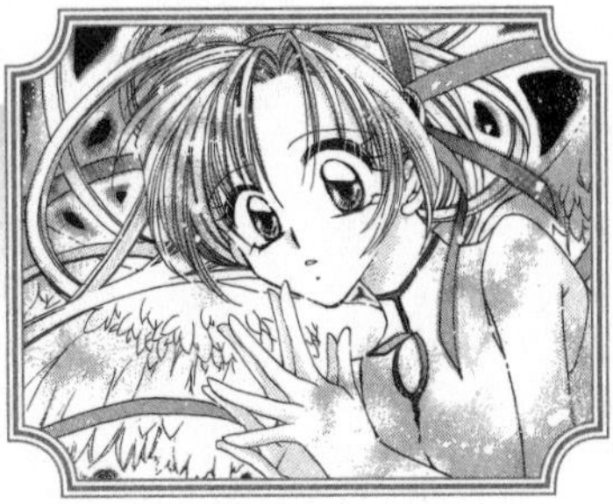

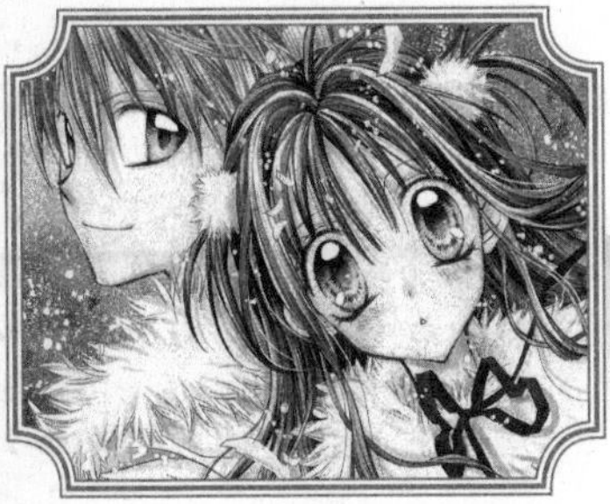

Full Moon

Mitsuki Koyama dreams of becoming a pop star, but she is dying of throat cancer. Can she live out a lifetime of dreams in just one year?

Short-Tempered Melancholic

A collection of short stories including Arina Tanemura's debut manga, "In the Style of the Second Love"!

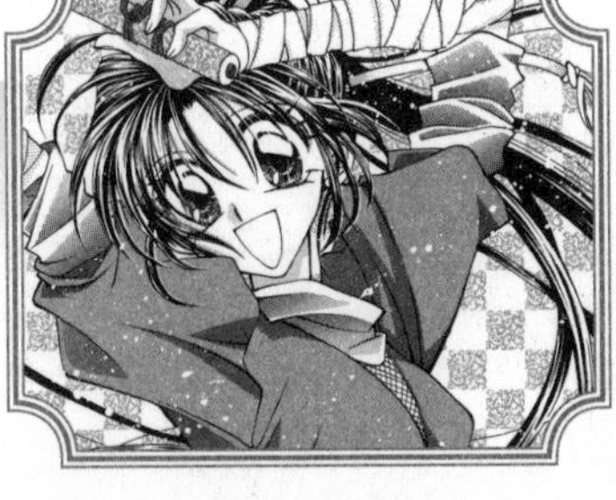

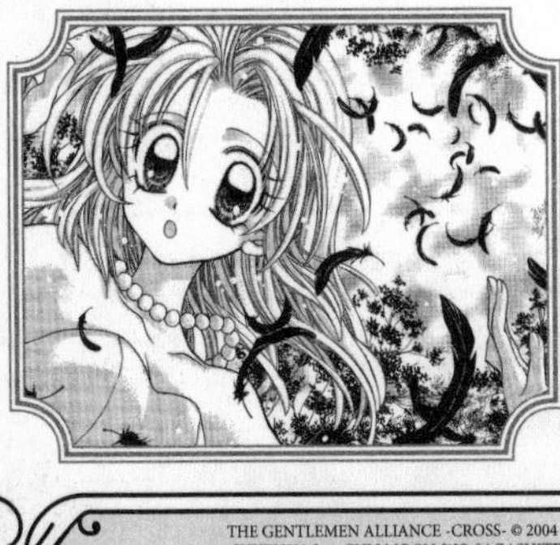

Time Stranger Kyoko

Kyoko Suomi must find 12 holy stones and 12 telepaths to awaken her sister who has been trapped in time since birth.

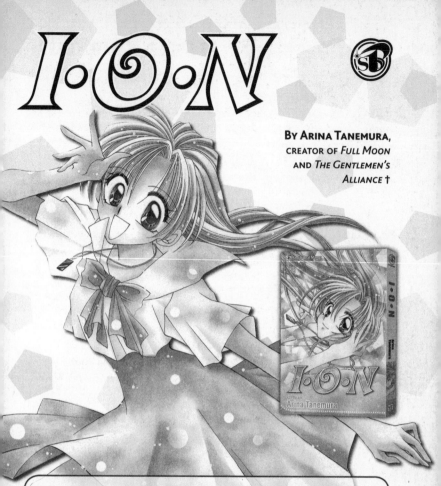

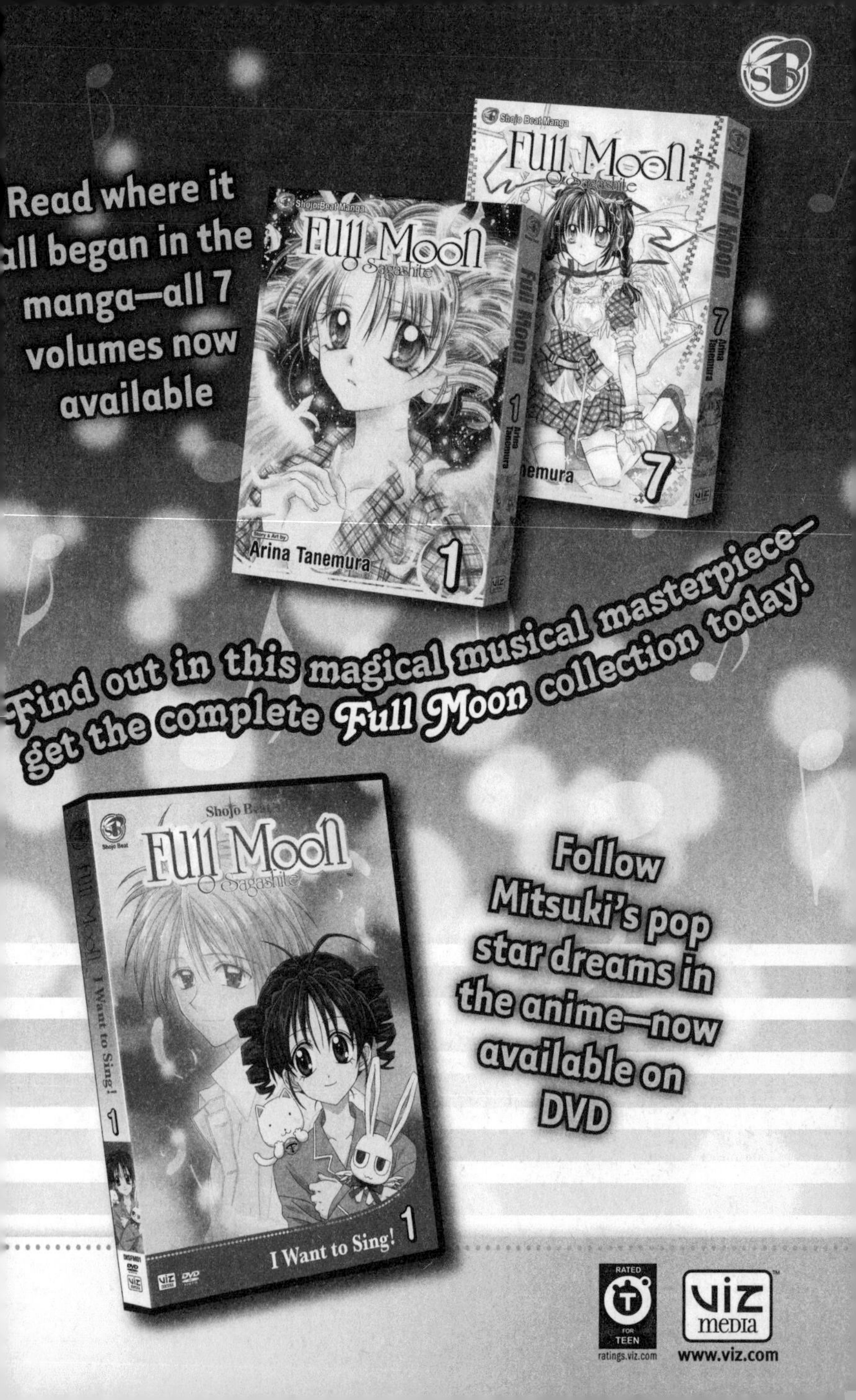

Read where it
ll began in the
manga—all 7
volumes now
available
Shojo Beat Manga
Full Moon
O Sagashite
Arina Tanemura
1
Full Moon
7
Find out in this magical musical masterpiece—
get the complete Full Moon collection today!
Shojo Beat
Full Moon
O Sagashite
I Want to Sing! 1
Follow
Mitsuki's pop
star dreams in
the anime—now
available on
DVD
RATED
T
FOR
TEEN
ratings.viz.com
VIZ
MEDIA
www.viz.com

Full Moon
O Sagashite

By Arina Tanemura
creator of *The Gentlemen's Alliance* †

Mitsuki loves singing, but a malignant throat tumor prevents her from pursuing her passion.

Can two fun-loving Shinigami give her singing career a magical jump-start?

...what you think
...Shojo Beat Manga!

Our survey is now
available online. Go to:

shojobeat.com/mangasurvey

Help us make our
product offerings
better!

Shojo Beat
MANGA from the HEART

THE REAL
DRAMA BEGINS
IN...

VIZ
media